Index to Marriages

OF

Old Rappahannock *and*

Essex Counties, Virginia

1655   1900

by

EVA EUBANK WILKERSON

CLEARFIELD

Originally published
Richmond, Virginia, 1953

Reprinted with permission
Genealogical Publishing Company, Inc.
Baltimore, Maryland
1976, 1983

Reprinted for
Clearfield Company by
Genealogical Publishing Co.
Baltimore, Maryland
2008

Library of Congress Catalogue Card Number 75-34996
ISBN-13: 978-0-8063-0706-0
ISBN-10: 0-8063-0706-4

Made in the United States of America

FOREWORD

Old Rappahannock County embraced lands lying on both sides of the Rappahannock River and was organized in 1656, being formerly a part of Lancaster County which was organized in 1652.

Courts were held alternately on the north and south sides of the river but all records were kept in the Court House on the south side. There are some records, such as, Land Grants, Deeds Etc. of earlier dates than 1656 which were recorded under the name of Lancaster County and remained as records of Rappahannock County after the division was made.

In April, 1692, Old Rappahannock County was divided into two distinct counties, the river dividing the same, the North side became Richmond County and the south side was called Essex County, courts to be held on the tenth of each month.

Records of Deeds, Wills and Court Orders from 1655 to the present time are in the Record Room of the Court House in Tappahannock, Essex County, Virginia. There is no Register of Marriages prior to 1853. Some Marriage Bonds dating back to 1804 have been recently recorded in the Marriage Register which began in 1853 and is known as Book One.

The author in doing much research and in indexing old records found many marriages with record proof and began an Index To Marriages. By reading all Deeds, Wills, Court Orders and Land Trials she has secured a large number of marriages to which have been added marriages from the Marriage Register from 1853 to 1900, also the Marriage Bonds now recorded in this book.

The date of marriages shown in Deeds, Wills and Court Orders is the date of the record in which the marriage is found and not the date of the marriage, these having only the year given and no month nor day.

Terms used in reference, "D" Deeds, "W" Wills, "O" Court Orders, "D&W" both Deeds & Wills, "D&C" both Deeds & Wills, Box 101, "C", "D", Etc. is Steel Box numbered 101, containing original papers, such as, Deeds, Wills, Powers of Attorney Etc. The letter "C", "D", Etc. represent the folder in which the papers are filed according to dates.

E. E. W.

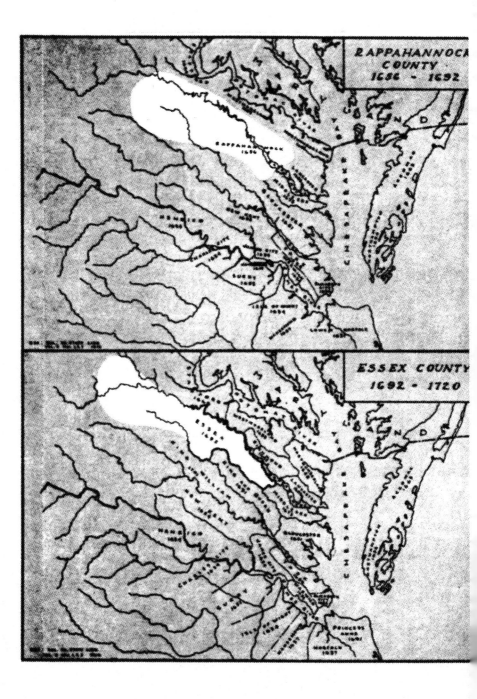

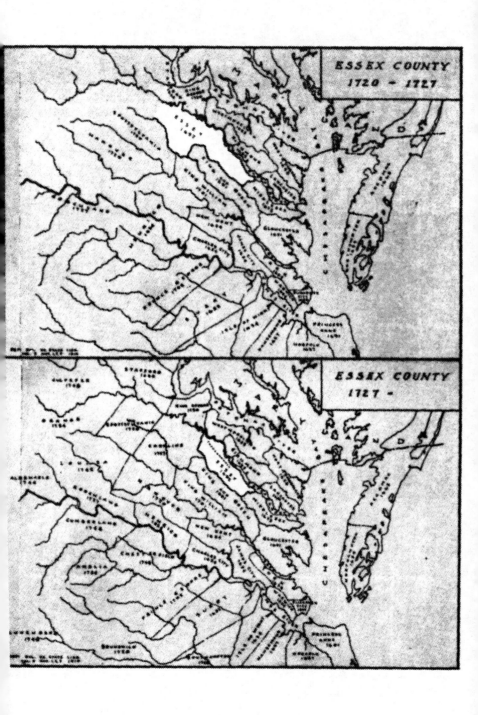

A

1895, Dec. 26	ACIE,	J. H.	Married J. G. Williams	Book 1,	119
1708,	ACRE,	JAMES	Married Mary, dau. of Thomas Coggin	O 4,	92
1883, Oct. 16	ACRES,	CATHERINE	Married Edward F. Brooks	Book 1,	73
1825, Jan. 28	ACRES,	JAMES	Married Nancy Webb	Book 1,	242
1840, Jun. 15	ACRES,	JAMES	Married Mary Ann Davis	Book 1,	254
1863, Mar. 16	ACRES,	JAMES	Married Frances I. Foreacres, widow, formerly Frances Durham	Book 1,	11
1880, Jul. 1	ACRES,	JAMES	Married Mary E. Turner	Book 1,	56
1882, Jan. 16	ACRES,	JAMES	Married Alfred Annetta Shackelford	Book 1,	63
1885, Aug. 4	ACRES,	JAMES	Married Mary Cox	Book 1,	82
1857, Jan. 16	ACRES,	JANE E.	Married Lamarcus Harmons	Book 1,	4
1843, Dec. 23	ACRES,	POLLY	Married Henry Davis	Book 1,	256
1894, Jul. 17	ACRES,	SAMUEL	Married Lavinia Parker	Book 1,	114
1872, Dec. 26	ACRES,	THOMAS	Married Mary E. Clarke	Book 1,	32
1847, Feb. 16	ACREY,	ARTHUR T.	Married Mary Minter	Book 1,	259
1704,	AKERS.	ANN	Married Thomas Dawkins	D&C 12,	6
1861, Jan. 20	ADAMS,	ELIZABETH	Married William E. Chandler	Book 1,	10
1840, Dec. 3	ADAMS,	HENRY	Married Elizabeth Breedlove	Book 1,	254
1677,	ADCOCK,	EDWARD	Married Elizabeth, dau. of Toby &Phebe Smith	D 6,	8,9
1710,	ADCOCK,	JOHN	Married Mary, dau. of Joseph Beland	D&C 13,	317
1677,	ADCOCK,	THOMAS	Married Ann Nichols	W 2,	2
1828, Nov. 4	ALDERSON,	GEO. N.	Married Judith B. Haynes	Book 1,	245
1820, Jun. 10	ALDRIDGE,	ANN	Married Richard Coghill	Book 1,	237
1816, Jan. 16	ALDRIDGE,	FRANCES	Married Israel Glasscock	Book 1,	232
1824,	ALDRIDGE,	MARY	Dau. of Adam, married John Haile	W 20,	298
1839, Oct. 8	ALEXANDER,	GORDON	Married Martha Holderby, widow	Book 1,	254
1863, Dec. 19	ALEXANDER,	JAMES H.	Soldier CSA, married Mary Clarke	Book 1,	12
1827, Apr. 10	ALEXANDER,	JOSEPH	Married Mary Ann Green	Book 1,	254
1816, Dec. 17	ALEXANDER,	MAHALEY	Married Richard L. Haile	Book 1,	232
1824,	ALEXANDER,	MAHALA	Married Richard L. Haile	D 41,	228
1827,	ALEXANDER,	MAHALA	Married Richard L. Haile	D 42,	359

1815, Jan 4	ALEXANDER, MARIA	Married Lewis D. Brooke	Book 1,	231
1851, Apr. 11	ALEXANDER, MARIA	Married Brooking Elliott	Book 1,	262
1809, Jan 16	ALEXANDER, NANCY	Married Joseph Jones	Book 1,	225
1821, Sep 5	ALEXANDER, NANCY	Married James H. Greenwood	Book 1,	238
1827,	ALEXANDER, NANCY	Daughter of Aris, married James H. Greenwood	D 42,	359
1835, Dec. 28	ALEXANDER, OBADIAH	Married Dorothy Jones	Book 1,	251
1851, Jun. 11	ALEXANDER, WILLIAM	Married Matilda Ann Thomas	Book 1,	262
1815, Oct. 12	ALLEN, ADDISON	Married Melesia Dix	Book 1,	231
1885, Nov. 11	ALLEN, ALICE	Married Muscoe R. Dunn	Book 1,	84
1827, Dec. 10	ALLEN, AMELIA	Married Erastus Montague	Book 1,	244
1812,	ALLEN, ANDREW	Married Winney, dau. of Nathaniel Crow	D 38,	293
1875, Aug. 26	ALLEN, ARABELLA	Married Junius E. Tune	Book 1,	39
1849, Nov. 28	ALLEN, AUGUSTUS	Married Lucinda Munday	Book 1,	261
1815, Sep. 12	ALLEN, BARBARA	Married John Bohannon	Book 1,	231
1758,	ALLEN, BENJAMIN	Married Elizabeth, dau. of Thomas Meador	W 11,	129
1817, Dec. 20	ALLEN, BETSEY	Married Biveon Brizendine	Book 1,	232
1819,	ALLEN, CATHARINE	Married William Stevens of Rockbridge County	D 41,	483
1887, Oct. 27	ALLEN, C. B.	Married W. L. Crutchfield	Book 1,	92
1890, Nov. 23	ALLEN, CHARLES	Married Annie B. Martin	Book 1,	105
1693,	ALLEN, CHRISTIAN	Youngest dau. of Valentine Allen married Richard Dison	O 1,	108
1708,	ALLEN, CHRISTIAN	Daughter of Valentine Allen, married Henry Long	D&C 13,	146
1722,	ALLEN, ELINOR	Widow, married Richard Kemp	D 17,	108
1836,	ALLEN, ELIZABETH	Married Jonas Stokes	Book 1,	252
1878, Mar. 13	ALLEN, ELIZABETH	Married Nathan S. Faulconer	Book 1,	48
1869, Jan. 14	ALLEN, ELLEN	Married John M. Collier	Book 1,	22
1807, Jan. 2	ALLEN, FANNIE	Married Spencer Brooke	Book 1,	224
1875, Jan. 14	ALLEN, GEORGE	Married Martha E. Moore	Book 1,	38
1808, Dec. 19	ALLEN, JAMES	Married Frances Boughan	Book 1,	224
1820, Sep. 8	ALLEN, JAMES JR.	Married Amelia Montague	Book 1,	237
1826, Apr. 17	ALLEN, JAMES	Married Clara Fen	Book 1,	242
1851, Dec. 17	ALLEN, JAMES H.	Married Emily Adeline Armstrong	Book 1,	262

					Book	Page
1892, Dec. 22	ALLEN,	J. H.	Married Lela Mundie		Book 1,	110
1834, Jan. 30	ALLEN,	JOHN	Married Lucy Clarke		Book 1,	250
1738,	ALLEN,	JOHN	Married Elizabeth, dau. of Henry Reeves		O 11,	47
1879, Dec. 18	ALLEN,	JOHN	Married James Addie Munday, orphan		Book 1,	53
1852, Nov. 24	ALLEN,	JOSEPH	Married Susan Taylor		Book 1,	263
1722,	ALLEN,	KATHERINE	Daughter of Eleanor Kemp, married James Sames		D 17,	108
1830, Mar. 15	ALLEN,	KATHERINE	Married Lunsford Gouldman		Book 1,	247
1837, Aug. 21	ALLEN,	LEWIS	Married Julia E. Par (Far)		Book 1,	252
1813,	ALLEN,	LILY	Married Robert Harper		O 41,	188
1877, Feb. 27	ALLEN,	LOUELLA	Married Joseph A. Saunders		Book 1,	44
1840, Apr. 11	ALLEN,	LUCINDA	Married Pleasant S. Southall		Book 1,	254
1810, Aug. 20	ALLEN,	LUCY	Married William Banks		Book 1,	226
1838,	ALLEN,	LUCY	Daughter of Thomas, married ? Banks, father of Thomas A. Banks		D 45,	455
1848, Aug. 1	ALLEN,	MARTHA J.	Married John C. Brizendine		Book 1,	260
1693,	ALLEN,	MARY	Sister & co-heir of Samuel, married William Browne		O 1,	108
1722,	ALLEN,	MARY	Daughter of Elinor, now Kemp, married Martin Nalle		D 17,	108
1817, Oct. 24	ALLEN,	MARY	Married James Owen		Book 1,	233
1825,	ALLEN,	MARY	Daughter of Thomas Allen, married James Owen		D 41,	419
1831, Oct. 31	ALLEN,	MARY B.	Married Jonathan Hart		Book 1,	248
1876, Apr. 13	ALLEN,	OLYMPIA	Married William Taylor		Book 1,	42
1825, Apr. 5	ALLEN,	POLLY	Married Thomas Boughton		Book 1,	241
1830, Dec. 21	ALLEN,	POLLY	Married John S. Smither		Book 1,	247
1848, Mar. 10	ALLEN,	ROBERT	Married Martha Schools		Book 1,	260
1854, Dec. 28	ALLEN,	ROBERT	Married Adaline B. Clarke		Book 1,	2
1885, Dec. 26	ALLEN,	ROBERT H.	Married Maud Griffin		Book 1,	85
1896, Dec. 17	ALLEN,	ROBERT N.	Married Lillie B. Clarke		Book 1,	122
1809, Aug. 21	ALLEN,	SALLY	Married Robert Harper		Book 1,	225
1846, Mar. 16	ALLEN,	SARAH	Married Robert Schools		Book 1,	259
1819, Oct. 16	ALLEN,	SUSANNA	Married Henry W. Latane		Book 1,	236
1826,	ALLEN,	SUSANNA	Daughter of James Allen married Henry W. Latane		W 21,	1
1774,	ALLEN,	TAMZINE	Married Richard Gatewood		W 12,	603

					Book	Page
1825, May 3	ALLEN,	THOMAS	Married Rebecca Longest		Book 1,	242
1860, May 2	ALLEN,	THOMAS JR.	Married Angelina Griffin, Widow		Book 1,	9
1884, Jan. 17	ALLEN,	THOMAS	Married Sebina Pitts		Book 1,	75
1676,	ALLEN,	VALENTINE	Married Mary, dau. of Thomas Page		W&D 1,	194
1885, Mar. 11	ALLEN,	WALLER R.	Married Belle M. Tune		Book 1,	81
1886, Dec. 22	ALLEN,	W. D.	Married Nannie C. Mundie		Book 1,	89
1839, Dec. 28	ALLEN,	WILLIAM R.	Married D. M Segar		Book 1,	254
1843,	ALLEN,	WILLIAM R.	Married Drusilla, daughter of James Dunn		W 24,	49
1845, Feb. 4	ALLEN,	WILLIAM R.	Married Martha J. Dunn		Book 1,	258
1874, Dec. 23	ALLEN,	WILLIAM R.	Married Alice Harmon		Book 1,	37
1754,	AMISS,	WILLIAM	Married Hannah, dau. of Daniel Daly		W 10,	23
1882, Aug. 23	ANDERSON,	BENTON P.	Caroline County, married Alberta Brooks		Book 1,	66
1807,	ANDERSON,	CHURCHILL	Married Polly Upshaw		O 39,	138
1742,	ANDERSON,	ELIZABETH	Administratrix of Joseph, Married Nathaniel Pendleton		O 13,	254
1890, Aug 13	ANDERSON,	GEORGIA A.	Married George B. Doggett		Book 1,	104
1829, Jul. 20	ANDERSON,	HANSFORD	Married Sarah Kemp		Book 1,	246
1882, Jan. 11	ANDERSON,	HENRIETTA S.	Married James B. Beazley		Book 1,	63
1897, Feb. 21	ANDERSON,	H. O.	Married S. J. Dishman		Book 1,	124
1870, Apr. 21	ANDERSON,	JOHN A.	Fredericksburg, married Lucie Ella Hundley		Book 1,	25
1890, Sep. 24	ANDERSON,	JOSIE C.	Married Clarence Spindle		Book 1,	104
1899, Nov. 6	ANDERSON,	J. F.	Surgeon of Washington, D. C. married L. T. Hundley		Book 1,	34
1878, Dec. 18	ANDERSON,	MARY L.	Married Charles H. Hagan, Richmond City		Book 1,	49
1819, Dec. 20	ANDERSON,	ROBERT S.	Married Mary B. Hill		Book 1,	235
1864, Dec. 28	ANDERSON,	ROBERT M.	Richmond City, married Harriet S. Lewis		Book 1,	12
1818, Jan. 19	ANDREWS,	ANN	Married James Atkinson		Book 1,	234
1836, Sep. 4	ANDREWS,	ANN C.	Married John S. Fisher		Book 1,	252
1810, Jan. 29	ANDREWS,	COURTNEY	Married Charles T. Southall		Book 1,	226
1827, Dec. 17	ANDREWS,	EDWIN G.	Married Hortensia Sale		Book 1,	243
1815, Dec. 18	ANDREWS,	ELIZABETH	Married James Clark		Book 1,	231
1810, Nov. 15	ANDREWS,	FRANCES	Married Benjamin Fisher		Book 1,	226
1823, Feb. 19	ANDREWS,	HARRIET	Married Achillis Noel		Book 1,	240

				Book	Page
1815, Dec. 20	ANDREWS,	JAMES	Married Catharine Sale	Book 1,	231
1837,	ANDREWS,	JAMES	Married Catharine, dau. of William B. Sale	D 45,	454
1847, Nov. 23	ANDREWS.	JANE G.	Married William G. Garnett	Book 1,	259
1876, Nov. 7	ANDREWS.	JOHN W.	Woodford Co. Kentucky, married Mrs. Martha J. Taylor	Book 1,	43
1890, Jan. 26	ANDREWS.	KATE C.	Married E. J. Bayliss, Caroline County	Book 1,	103
1805, Sep. 16	ANDREWS,	LUCY	Married Philip Pitts	Book 1,	223
1897, Dec. 15	ANDREWS,	L. B.	Married Virginia Tuck	Book 1,	126
1879, Nov. 6	ANDREWS,	MARY SUSAN	Married Francis P. Mundie	Book 1,	52
1896, Nov. 25	ANDREWS,	MEDA M.	Married John R. Kidd	Book 1,	122
1891, Feb. 11	ANDREWS,	PEARL A.	Married C. C. Mundie	Book 1,	106
1806, May 1	ANDREWS,	POLLY	Married Alexander Muse	Book 1,	223
1825, May 27	ANDREWS,	ROBERT P.	Married Mary L O'neale	Book 1,	242
1897, Sep. 22	ANDREWS,	R. L.	Married T. M Collier	Book 1,	126
1898, Dec. 21	ANDREWS,	ROSA	Married W. F. Dunnington	Book 1,	130
1832,	ANDREWS,	SALLY	Daughter of Mark Andrews, married Robert Atkinson	D 44,	3
1825, Dec. 19	ANDREWS,	SARAH	Married Robert Atkinson	Book 1,	242
1845, Aug. 26	ANDREWS,	SARAH F.	Married John W. Harper	Book 1,	258
1864, Oct. 3	ANDREWS,	SARAH F.	Married William S. Muse	Book 1,	12
1856, Oct. 29	ANDREWS,	THOMAS B.	Married Mary Susan Atkinson	Book 1,	4
1860, May 10	ANDREWS,	THOMAS B.	Married Sarah Garnett	Book 1,	9
1869, Mar. 4	ANDREWS,	VIRGINIA M.	Married John S. Rouzie	Book 1,	23
1866, Jan. 11	ANDREWS,	WILLIAM S.	Caroline County, married Alice C. Parker	Book 1,	14
1825,	ANTHONY,	JAMES C.	Married Mary S. Lee, dau. of Philip Lee, Gloucester Co.	D 41,	337
1832, Dec. 12	ANTHONY,	LUCY	Married Milton Vawter	Book 1,	249
1807, May 18	ANTHONY,	MARK	Married Susanna Burk	Book 1,	224
1807, Feb. 5	ANTON,	JAMES	Married Elizabeth B. Layall, daughter of James Layall	Book 1,	224
1836, Jul. 4	ANTON,	POLLY	Married William Edward Vawter	Book 1,	252
1835, Dec. 21	ANTON,	THOMAS	Married Patsy Vawter	Book 1,	252
1689,	ARMISTEAD,	JOHN	Married Mary Brown	O 2,	187
1803,	ARMISTEAD,	MAJ. THOMAS	Married Jane Peachy, sister of William Peachy	W 16,	205
1892, Sep. 6	ARMISTEAD,	M. A.	Married John P. Taylor	Book 1,	110

1758,	ARMSTRONG, AMBROSE	Married Rachel, daughter of Thomas Meador	W	11,	129
1820, Jan. 17	ARMSTRONG, AMBROSE	Married Jane Elliott	Book 1,	237
1853, Dec. 19	ARMSTRONG, BENJAMIN	Married Louisa F. Williamson	Book 1,	264
1845, Jan. 21	ARMSTRONG, CATHARINE	Married John Coleman	Book 1,	258
1813, May 20	ARMSTRONG, ELIZABETH	Married John Munday	Book 1,	229
1811,	ARMSTRONG, ELLIS	Married Fanny, dau. of Caleb Noel	W 18,	145
1851, Dec. 17	ARMSTRONG, EMILY A.	Married James Henry Allen	Book 1,	262
1820,	ARMSTRONG, JOHN	Married Sarah Purkins	D 40,	145
1834, Dec. 15	ARMSTRONG, JOHN I.	Married Melissa Crow	Book 1,	250
1829, May 12	ARMSTRONG, JOSEPH N.	Married Susanna A. Haile	Book 1,	246
1850, Nov. 28	ARMSTRONG, JUDITH F.	Married William I. Beazley	Book 1,	262
1700,	ARMSTRONG, KATHERINE	Married James Jones	D 11,	249
1852, Jan. 6	ARMSTRONG, MARIA ANN	Married Joseph Saunders	Book 1,	263
1860, Nov. 22	ARMSTRONG, MARTHA A.	Married Thomas M. Henley, Jr	Book 1,	10
1865, Jan. 31	ARMSTRONG, MARY S.	Married Algernon B. M. Mickleboro	Book 1,	13
1869, Aug. 1	ARMSTRONG, MARY E.	Married John F. Brooks	Book 1,	23
1812, May 19	ARMSTRONG, MORTON	Married Dolly Williamson	Book 1,	228
1811, Jan. 14	ARMSTRONG, POLLY	Married Richard Beazley	Book 1,	227
1813, Dec. 21	ARMSTRONG, PURKINS	Married Mary Gordon	Book 1,	229
1828,	ARMSTRONG, PURKINS	Married Polly, daughter of Alexander Gordon	D 42,	382
1707,	ARMSTRONG, ROBERT	Married Elizabeth, widow of Joseph Humphreys	O 3,	388
1713,	ARMSTRONG, ROBERT	His grandaughter married James Stodgill	D 17,	266
1851, Dec. 8	ARMSTRONG, ROBERT	Married Frances Stokes	Book 1,	262
1719,	ARMSTRONG, SARAH	Married Samuel Short	O 5,	359
1848, Jun. 19	ARMSTRONG, SUSAN C.	Married James Harper	Book 1,	260
1838, Dec. 3	ARMSTRONG, THOMAS F.	Married Susan Dyke	Book 1,	253
1877, Apr. 12	ARMSTRONG, THOMAS H.	Married Ella T. House	Book 1,	45
1878, Nov. 3	ARMSTRONG, THOMAS H.	Married Jenny L. Faver	Book 1,	49
1848, May 11	ARMSTRONG, VESTILLA	Married Harry H. Lee	Book 1,	260
1691,	ARROWSMITH, THOMAS	Married the Executrix of James Kay	O 2,	313
1704,	ARTHUR, GEORGE	Bristol, Eng. married Rachel, sister of Thomas Gregson	D&C 12,	131

				Book	Page
1848, Jul. 21	ASHBURN,	MARK S.	Married Mary E. Ingram	Book 1,	260
1818, Apr. 10	ATISHIR,	FRANCES	Married William Faver	Book 1,	234
1871, Jun. 4	ATKINS,	ADELAIDE	Married Christopher Lumpkin	Book 1,	28
1844, Jan. 30	ATKINS,	AMANDA	Married Samuel Davis	Book 1,	247
1890, Nov. 23	ATKINS,	B. F.	Married M. E. Parson	Book 1,	104
1895, Dec. 31	ATKINS,	B. A.	Married H. H. Hayes	Book 1,	119
1887, Dec. 4	ATKINS,	CASTEIN	Married Mattie Burch, Middlesex Co.	Book 1,	93
1845, Dec. 4	ATKINS,	ELIZABETH	Married Robert Minter	Book 1,	258
1867, Nov. 5	ATKINS,	EZRA C.	King & Queen Co., married Columbia Brooks	Book 1,	18
1873, Dec. 18	ATKINS,	FRANCES A.	Married Thomas Vickers	Book 1,	35
1876, Mar. 2	ATKINS,	INDIANA	Married John W. Wilson	Book 1,	41
1724,	ADKINS,	JAMES	Married Elizabeth Fisher	D 17,	308
1873,	ATKINS,	JAMES	Married Sarah Munday	Book 1,	32
1879, Nov. 30	ATKINS,	JAMES D.	Married Roberta, daughter of Charles Jones, Caroline Co.	Book 1,	53
1884, Mar. 26	ATKINS,	JAMES T.	King & Queen Co., married Emma S. Parker, dau. of John Parker	Book 1,	76
1859, May 12	ATKINS,	JANE H.	Married Benjamin Lumpkin	Book 1,	7
1841, Mar. 1	ATKINS,	JOHN	Married Mary Wilmore	Book 1,	255
1866, Nov. 22	ATKINS,	JULIA	Married Spencer P. Ball	Book 1,	15
1869, Feb. 24	ATKINS,	LAURA A.C.	Married James E. Fogg	Book 1,	23
1894, Feb. 20	ATKINS,	LAURA B.	Married R. C. Lumpkin	Book 1,	113
1837, Nov. 30	ATKINS,	LUCY ANN	Married Beverley Brooks	Book 1,	252
1837, Mar. 20	ATKINS,	LUNSFORD	Married Lucy Schools	Book 1,	252
1842, Jan. 8	ATKINS,	MARY A.	Married Lowry Norris	Book 1,	256
1845,	ATKINS,	MARY ANN	Daughter of Clayton, married Lowry Norris	W 24,	453
1873, Jul. 2	ATKINS,	MARY E.	Married Peter Revere	Book 1,	34
1889, Jun. 11	ATKINS,	MARY E.	Married Shelby Berch	Book 1,	100
1861, Feb. 7	ATKINS,	RICHARD	Married Martha C. Linn, widow daughter of Josiah Minter	Book 1,	10
1886, Jun. 8	ATKINS,	RICHARD H.	Married Annie F. Lumpkin, King & Queen Co.	Book 1,	87
1873, Feb. 17	ATKINS,	ROBERT H.	Married Catharine Munday	Book 1,	32
1895, May 22	ATKINS,	SALLIE A.	Married W. R. Passagaluppi	Book 1,	118
1813, May 17	ATKINS,	THOMAS	Married Betsey Cox	Book 1,	229

1867, Dec. 26	ATKINS,	VIRGINIA	Married John R. Courtney	Book 1,	19
1703,	ADKINSON,	ANN	Married Thomas Phillips	D&W 11,	94
1836, Jun. 28	ATKINSON,	ALMOND	Married Mary F. Blackburn	Book 1,	252
1701,	ATKINSON,	CHARLES	Married Ann, daughter of Nicholas Copeland	D&W 10,	86
1850, Sep. 22	ATKINSON,	ELIZABETH	Married John Shaddock	Book 1,	262
1822, Feb. 26	ATKINSON,	FANNY	Married John Conoly	Book 1,	239
1818, Jan. 19	ATKINSON,	JAMES	Married Ann Andrews	Book 1,	234
1822, Feb. 25	ATKINSON,	LUCINDA	Married Granville W. Fogg	Book 1,	239
1846, Feb. 4	ATKINSON,	LUCY	Married James B. Radford	Book 1,	259
1856, Oct. 29	ATKINSON,	MARY SUSAN	Married Thomas B. Andrews	Book 1,	4
1825, Dec. 19	ATKINSON,	ROBERT	Married Sarah Andrews	Book 1,	242
1832,	ATKINSON,	ROBERT	Married Sally, daughter of Mark Andrews	D 44,	3
1847, May 5	ATKINSON,	ROGER B.	Married Ann M. Westmore	Book 1,	259
1833, Feb. 6	ATKINSON,	SARAH	Married William Garland	Book 1,	249
1848, Oct. 16	ATKINSON,	SARAH	Married James T. Garnett	Book 1,	260
1740,	ATWOOD,	FRANCIS	Married Ann Reeves, sister of Patience Gatewood	D 22,	219
1684,	AUSTIN,	ANN	Her niece married William Brockenbrough	D 7,	176
1707,	AUSTIN,	DANIEL	Married Susanna, daughter of Thomas Coggin	D&C 13,	59
1684,	AUSTIN,	HENRY	Married Ann, Relict of Thomas Dean	D 7,	176
1697,	AWBREY,	DOROTHY	Relict of Richard, married Thomas Gouldman	D 9,	134
1699,	AWBREY,	DOROTHY	Widow of Richard, married Peter Ransone	D&W 10,	16
1728,	AWBREY,	DOROTHY	Daughter of Richard,married John Billings	D 19,	28
1763,	AYLETT,	ANN	Daughter of William Aylett, Married Augustine Washington	D 29,	186
1763,	AYLETT,	ELIZABETH	Daughter of William Aylett, married William Booth	D 29,	186
1742,	AYRES,	ANN	Daughter of William Ayres, Married Mark Thomas	D 22,	428
1818, Oct. 15	AYRES,	DAVID J.	Married Maria Garnett	Book 1,	234
1820,	AYRES,	DR. DAVID	Married Maria, daughter of Reuben Garnett	W 19,	147
1726,	AYRES,	KATHERINE	Daughter of William, married Thomas Evett	D 18,	241
1810, Mar. 25	AYRES,	POLLY	Married Philip Hudgins	Book 1,	226
1706,	AYRES,	THOMAS	Married Florinda, Executrix of Thomas Thorpe	O 3,	273
1717,	AYRES,	THOMAS	Married Ann, Relict of Thomas Meadoes	O 5,	110

				Book		Page
1750,	AYRES,	THOMAS	Married Mary, daughter of William Scott	D	25,	147
1694,	AYRES,	WILLIAM	Married Ann Smith (License)	O	1,	285
1700	AYRES,	WILLIAM	Married Ann, daughter of Capt. Anthony Smith	D&W	10,	61

1891, Dec. 23	BAGBY,	ALFRED JR.	Columbia, S.C., married Janetta R. Campbell	Book 1,	108
1806, Dec. 1	BAGBY,	GEORGE	Married Lucy Richards	Book 1,	223
1829,	BAGBY,	HENRY	Married Mary Ann Townley, daughter of John Townley	D 43,	37
1822, Mar. 25	BAGBY,	ISHAM	Married Martha Clayton	Book 1,	239
1869, Nov. 20	BAGBY,	LUCY	Married Richmond Banks	Book 1,	23
1889, Sep. 25	BAGBY,	JANY	Married Melville Jeffries	Book 1,	101
1893, Jul. 26	BAGBY,	R. H.	King & Queen Co. married E. B. Cauthorn	Book 1,	112
1829, Feb. 18	BAGBY,	TEMPLE	Married Mary Ann Townley	Book 1,	246
1876, Apr. 25	BAGBY,	THOMAS P.	Fanny E. Scott	Book 1,	41
1714,	BAGGE,	JOHN	Married Mary, widow of Samuel Thacker	D&W 14,	304
1839, Dec. 18	BAIRD,	BENJAMIN F.	Married Sarah F. Rouzie	Book 1,	254
1888, Dec. 26	BAIRD,	J. T.	Columbia County, Florida, Married M. S. Hoskins	Book 1,	97
1832,	BAIRD,	MATTHEW	Married Ophelia, dau. of Reuben Cauthorn	D 43,	561
1831, Sep. 12	BAKER,	ALEXANDER	Married Catharine P. Munday	Book 1,	248
1720,	BAKER,	ANN	Married Richard White, London	W 3,	222
1720,	BAKER,	JOSEPH	Married Amy Gatewood, relict of John Gatewood	W 3,	222
1882, Sep. 7	BALDERSON,	SALATHEL, G. W.	Married Alice V. Moore	Book 1,	66
1889, Dec. 11	BALDWIN,	J. B.	Married Sophronia A. Jordan	Book 1,	93
1805, Jun. 10	BALL,	AARON	Married Lucy Gouldman	Book 1,	222
1798,	BALL,	ABNER	Married Elizabeth, daughter of Henry Cox	W 15,	25
1819, Dec. 20	BALL,	ACHILLAS	Married Judith Edwards	Book 1,	235
1846, Jan. 5	BALL,	ANNAH	Married George Tate	Book 1,	259
1860, Mar. 17	BALL,	BETSEY	Married Upshaw Davis	Book 1,	9
1805, Oct. 5	BALL,	CURTIS	Married Sally Ball	Book 1,	222
1814, Dec. 21	BALL,	CURTIS	Married Patsy Burnett	Book 1,	230
1835, Feb. 6	BALL,	DELILAH	Married Robert D. Longest	Book 1,	252
1828, Dec. 23	BALL,	ELIZA	Married William W. Cox	Book 1,	245
1827,	BALL,	ELIZABETH	Daughter of William, married Richard Burnett	D. 42,	314
1829,	BALL,	ELIZABETH	Married William Cox, Jr.	D. 42,	594

Date	Surname	Given Name	Marriage	Book	Page
1859, May 12	BALL,	ELIZABETH M.	Married Archibald Clarke	Book 1,	7
1848, May 4	BALL,	FENTON F.	Married William W. Frank	Book 1,	260
1814, Dec. 14	BALL,	HARRISON	Married Fanny, daughter of Robert Shearwood	Book 1,	230
1838, Dec. 24	BALL,	HARRISON	Married Catharine Bareford	Book 1,	253
1841, Apr. 16	BALL,	JOHN	Married Jane Lee	Book 1,	255
1866, May 29	BALL,	JOHN H.	Married Mary E. Cauthorn	Book 1,	15
1832,	BALL,	KITTY	Married Henry Wright	D 44,	108
1839, Mar. 18	BALL,	LUCY	Married Lunsford Taylor	Book 1,	254
1847, Nov. 23	BALL,	MARTHA	Married Thomas Carlton	Book 1,	259
1846, Feb. 5	BALL,	MARY ELLEN	Married John A. Haile	Book 1,	259
1876, Dec. 28	BALL,	MOLLIE	Married John L. Hodges	Book 1,	44
1809, Jan. 10	BALL,	MOSES	Married Martha Harmon	Book 1,	225
1809, Mar. 21	BALL,	MOTTA	Married Harriet Faulconer	Book 1,	225
1845, Jul. 7	BALL,	NANCY	Married George Ingram	Book 1,	258
1835, Jan. 27	BALL,	PATSY	Married Robert Clarke, Jr.	Book 1,	251
1868, Jan. 9	BALL,	REUBEN	King & Queen Co., married Sarah J. Harper	Book 1,	20
1805, Oct. 5	BALL,	SALLY	Married Curtis Ball	Book 1,	222
1832, Jan. 16	BALL,	SALLY	Married Edward Barefoot	Book 1,	248
1770,	BALL,	SPENCER M.	Married Elizabeth, daughter of Francis Waring	W 12,	432
1866, Nov. 22	BALL,	SPENCER P.	Married Julia Atkins	Book 1,	15
1848, Jul. 17	BALL,	TAZEWELL	Married Catharine Willmore	Book 1,	260
1673,	BALL,	CAPT. WM.	Lancaster County, married Margaret, dau. of James Williamson	D 5,	289
1805, Apr. 15	BALL,	WILLIAM	Married Lucy Crow	Book 1,	222
1810, Jan. 18	BALL,	WILLIAM, JR.	Married Nancy Gatewood	Book 1,	226
1810, Apr. 15	BALL,	WILLIAM	Married Caty Crow	Book 1,	226
1722,	BALLARD,	RICHARD	Married Joane, daughter of Edward Martin	Box 105, Folder E	
1806,	BALMAIN,	ANDREW	Married James Roy's widow	D 37,	32
1882, Oct. 11	BAMKS,	ADA B.	Married B. H. McDonald, of Missouri	Book 1,	66
1825, Mar. 7	BANKS,	CATHARINE	Married Benjamin Pitts	Book 1,	242
1803,	BANKS,	ELIZABETH	Married William Edmondson	D 36,	180
1819,	BANKS,	ELIZABETH	Married Samuel Muse	W 19,	31

				Book	Page
1821,	BANKS,	ELIZABETH	Daughter of Elizabeth, married Samuel Muse	W 18,	351
1804,	BANKS,	GEORGE W.	Married Catharine, daughter of Griffing Boughan	D 36,	439
1757,	BANKS,	JAMES	Married Lucy, relict of Martin Connor	D 27,	332
1867, Sep. 9	BANKS,	JULIA B.	Married John L. Conoly	Book 1,	18
1845, Aug. 6	BANKS,	LUCY	Married John S. Eubank	Book 1,	258
1880, Dec. 7	BANKS,	LULIE P.	Married William B. Welch of Maryland	Book 1,	57
1814, Nov. 8	BANKS,	MARY	Married William L. Waring	Book 1,	230
1821,	BANKS,	MARY	Daughter of Elizabeth, Married William L. Waring	W 19,	351
1866, Dec. 30	BANKS,	MARY	Married Robert Jones	Book 1,	16
1885, Nov. 20	BANKS,	MARY	Married Harrison Southworth	Book 1,	84
1875, Nov. 20	BANKS,	NESSA	Married Edward Fauntleroy	Book 1,	40
1835, Oct. 9	BANKS,	RICHARD	Married Martha H. Boughan	Book 1,	251
1869, Nov. 20	BANKS,	RICHMOND	Married Lucy Bagby	Book 1,	23
1887, Dec. 15	BANKS,	ROBERT T.	Married Emma F. Welch	Book 1,	93
1876, Nov. 1	BANKS,	SARAH V.	Married William T. Cook	Book 1,	43
1829, May 20	BANKS,	THOMAS A.	Married Frances M. Jones	Book 1,	246
1830,	BANKS,	THOMAS	Married Frances Jones	D 43,	411
1838,	BANKS,	THOMAS A.	His son married Lucy, dau. of Thomas Allen	D 45,	455
1839,	BANKS,	THOMAS A.	Married Frances M Jones	D 46,	227
1805, Aug. 20	BANKS,	WILLIAM	Married Lucy Allen	Book 1,	222
1807, Jun. 4	BANKS,	WILLIAM	Married Polly Boughan	Book 1,	224
1810, Aug. 20	BANKS,	WILLIAM	Married Lucy Allen	Book 1,	226
1819, Jun. 8	BANKS,	WILLIAM	Married Margaret W. Martin	Book 1,	235
1880, Oct. 7	BANLEY,	LOUIS	Married May Hundley	Book 1,	56
1729,	BARBER,	SAMUEL	Married Ann, daughter of John Foster	D 19,	59
1709,	BARBER,	CAPT. WM.	Married Joyce, dau. of Samuel Bayley, Richmond Co.	W 3, Richmond Co.	7
1827, Aug. 21	BARBER,	WILLIAM	Married Elizabeth Toombs	Book 1,	243
1827,	BARBER,	WILLIAM L.	Married Elizabeth Toombs	D 42,	317
1708,	BARBEN,	RICHARD	Former husband of Mary Ward	D&C 13,	258
1835, Oct. 9	BAREFOOT,	ARTHUR	Married Frances Clarke	Book 1,	251
1839,	BAREFOOT,	ARTHUR	Married Frances, widow of Samuel Williamson	D 42,	252

				Book	Page
1851, Sep. 15	BAREFOOT,	ARTHUR	Married Mrs. Jane Tucker	Book 1,	262
1898, Jan. 13	BAREFOOT,	A. B.	Married W. R. Johnson	Book 1,	128
1871, Dec. 24	BAREFOOT,	BETTY	Married John Minter	Book 1,	29
1838, Dec. 24	BAREFOOT,	CATHARINE	Married Harrison Ball	Book 1,	253
1876, Dec. 14	BAREFOOT,	CHARLES E.	Married Martha E. Franklin	Book 1,	43
1869, Dec. 30	BAREFOOT,	CLEMENTINE	Married Thomas H. Wilson	Book 1,	24
1832, Jan. 16	BAREFOOT,	EDWARD	Married Sally Ball	Book 1,	248
1882, Mar. 30	BAREFOOT,	ELLA	Married John H. Brooks	Book 1,	64
1870, Jan. 13	BAREFOOT,	JAMES W.	Married Eliza Cook	Book 1,	25
1869, Feb. 18	BAREFOOT,	LEONARD	Married Rosa A. Saunders	Book 1,	22
1881, Oct. 13	BAREFOOT,	LUCY A.	Married George W. Crow	Book 1,	61
1881, Dec. 27	BAREFOOT,	MARTHA E.	Married William Crow	Book 1,	62
1897, Dec. 28	BAREFOOT,	NANNIE	Married J. S. Jordan	Book 1,	127
1879, Feb. 4	BAREFOOT,	RICHARD H.	Married Ella Haile	Book 1,	50
1844, Dec. 24	BAREFOOT,	ROBERT	Married Martha Elliott	Book 1,	257
1863, Sep. 10	BAREFOOT,	ROBERT	Married Lucy C. Durham	Book 1,	12
1862, Feb. 20	BAREFOOT,	SUSAN	King & Queen Co., married William Henry Greggs, soldier	Book 1,	11
1838, Dec. 24	BAREFOOT,	THOMAS	Married Ann C. McTire	Book 1,	253
1765,	BARKER,	BETTY	Daughter of Thomas & Ann married James Mason	D 30,	13
1689,	BARKER,	LAWRENCE	Married Penelope, Admrx. of Matthew Kelly	O 2,	176
1733,	BARKER,	THOMAS	Married Ann, daughter of Henry Boughan	D 20,	43
1707,	BARKHAM,	MARGERY	Widow of John Barkham, married Hugh Cary	D&C 12,	390
1828, Jun. 16	BARNES,	ARTHUR	Married Mary C. Haile	Book 1,	245
1827, Jan. 10	BARNES,	CHARLOTTE	Married Wm. A. Wright	Book 1,	244
1827,	BARNES,	CHARLOTTE	Daughter of Richard, married William A. Wright	D 42,	361
1818, Oct. 14	BARNES,	MARIA B.B.	Married Claiborne W. Gooch	Book 1,	237
1827,	BARNES,	MARIA B.B.	Daughter of Richard & Rebecca, married Claiborne Gooch	D 42,	348
1838, Nov. 28	BARNES,	MARY C.	Married Byrd C. Leavell	Book 1,	253
1827, Apr. 26	BARNES,	LUCY A.	Married Philip A. Branham	Book 1,	243
1827	BARNES,	LUCY	Sister of Richard, married Philip Branham, Richmond Co.	D 42,	229
1874, Jan. 27	BARNETT,	SUSAN	Married Robert Beazley	Book 1,	36

				Book	Page
1808,	BARROCK,	VINCENT	Married Elizabeth Weeks	O 39,	337
1685,	BARROW,	JOHN	His widow married Dr. Moses Hubbert	O 1,	174
1677,	BARROW,	MARY	Daughter of John, married Peter Foxson (Contract)	D 6,	6
1712,	BARTLETT,	THOMÁS	Married Patience, daughter of Nathaniel Bentley	W 14,	70
1812, May 18	BARTON,	ELIZABETH	Married Edmund Noel	Book 1,	228
1823, Feb. 17	BARTON,	HENRY	Married Polly Terrell	Book 1,	240
1852, Sep. 20	BARTON,	JOHN	Married Sarah Ann Fisher	Book 1,	263
1849, Dec. 20	BARTON,	MARY A.	Married William A. Fidler	Book 1,	261
1808, Dec. 22	BARTON,	NANCY	Married Oswald Noel	Book 1,	224
1832, Mar. 27	BARTON,	POLLY	Widow, married Ephraim Beazley	Book 1,	249
1847, Mar. 31	BARTON,	THOMAS	Married Sydney F. Dyke	Book 1,	259
1869, Dec. 19	BARTON,	WILLIAM M.	Maine, married Mary Dunn	Book 1,	24
1863, Dec. 31	BASKETT,	CATHARINE	Married Lewis W. Carlton	Book 1,	12
1876, Dec. 21	BASKETT,	CHARLES W.	Married Mattie B. Reid, King & Queen Co.	Book 1,	43
1726,	BASKETT,	SARAH	Daughter of Thomas, married Thomas Cooper	O 9,	144
1814, Dec. 12	BASTIN,	JAMES	Married Fanny Longest	Book 1,	230
1837, Apr. 10	BASTIN,	JULIA	Married Zachariah Samuel	Book 1,	258
1688,	BATES,	ELIZABETH	Daughter of John, married Richard Roads	O 2,	115
1688,	BATES,	?	Relict of John, married John Seymour	O 2,	115
1745,	BATES,	PHEBE	Married ? Searles	W 7,	481
1808,	BATES,	WILLIAM	Married Polly Kay	O 29,	350
1827, Feb. 14	BATES,	WILLIAM	Married Alice Lee Smith	Book 1,	243
1708,	BATTAILE,	ELIZABETH	Relict of John, married William Woodford	O 4,	98
1687,	BATTAILE,	JOHN	Married Katherine, daughter of Robert Taliaferro	O 2,	35
1807, Nov. 18	BATTAILE,	JOHN	Married Mary Dangerfield	Book 1,	224
1819, Nov. 24	BAXTER,	MATILDA	Married Collins Clatterbuck	Book 1,	235
1709,	BAYLEY,	JOYCE	Daughter of Samuel, married Capt. William Barber, Richmond Co.	W 3, Richmond Co.	7
1716,	BAYLEY,	SAMUEL	Married Elizabeth, daughter of Jane Dew	W 3, Richmond Co.	310
1850, Jan. 30	BAYLISS,	CHARLES I.	Married M. J. Coghill	Book 1,	262
1890, Jan. 26	BAYLISS,	E. J.	Caroline Co., married Kate C. Andrews	Book 1,	103
1878, Apr. 9	BAYLISS,	MOLLIE P.	Married James E. Moody	Book 1,	48

				Book	Page

1886, Nov. 3 BAYLISS, POLLY S. Married Dovell M. Cammack — Book 1, 88

1851, Dec. 17 BAYLISS, SILAS P. Married Ann Coghill — Book 1, 262

1867, Nov. 5 BAYLOR, ANN B. Married Charles O'. C. Mallory — Book 1, 18

1825, Nov. 15 BAYLOR, ANN E. Married John Capron — Book 1, 241

1810, Dec. 31 BAYLOR, ELIZABETH Married Alexander Tunstall — Book 1, 226

1813, Feb. 6 BAYLOR, LUCY G. Married William Hill, Jr. — Book 1, 229

1863, Feb. 4 BAYLOR, LUCY LATANE Married Samuel Jackson Morrison of Brunswick Co. — Book 1, 11

1807, Jun. 30 BAYLOR, MARIA W. Married Wm. Thornton Brooke — Book 1, 224

1882, Dec. 20 BAYLOR, MARTHA Married Henry Jackson — Book 1, 67

1866, Nov. 23 BAYLOR, MARY G. Married Robert W. Baylor of Norfolk City — Book 1, 15

1834, May 24 BAYLOR, RICHARD Married Lucy Waring, dau. of Robert Payne Waring — Book 1, 250

1844, BAYLOR, RICHARD Married Lucy, dau. of Robert Payne Waring — W. 24, 217

1866, Nov. 23 BAYLOR, ROBERT W. Norfolk City, married Mary G. Baylor — Book 1, 15

1871, May 23 BAYLOR, ROSA Married Cecil Jackson — Book 1, 28

1880, Nov. 30 BAYLOR, WARNER Married Lizzie H. Wright dau. of Wm. Denny Wright — Book 1, 57

1858, Oct. 12 BAYNE, JOHN H. Richmond City, married Margaret Munday — Book 1, 6

1844, Dec. 16 BAYNE, WASHINGTON Married Emily C. Hill — Book 1, 257

1812, Nov. 16 BAYNHAM, JOHN Married Frances Howerton — Book 1, 228

1832, Nov. 5 BAYNHAM, JOHN M. Married Margaret Robb — Book 1, 248

1810, Apr. 26 BAYNHAM, W. M. Married Virginia, dau. of William B. Matthews — Book 1, 226

1689, BEALE, ANN Relict of Thomas, married William Colston — O 2, 161

1893, Jul. 30 BEATTY, F. W. Married B. V. Mitchell — Book 1, 112

1834, Oct. 13 BEAZLEY, ANN Married John C. Dalley — Book 1, 250

1828, Dec. 12 BEAZLEY, CATHARINE Married William Kendall — Book 1, 245

1804, Dec. 19 BEAZLEY, CORNELIUS Married Frances Harper — Book 1, 222

1838, Jan. 2 BEAZLEY, ELIZA ANN Married John W. T. R. Walsh — Book 1, 253

1843, Dec. 18 BEAZLEY, ELIZABETH Married James Verlander — Book 1, 257

1818, Dec. 29 BEAZLEY, EPHRAIM Married Amey Jones — Book 1, 234

1832, Mar. 27 BEAZLEY, EPHRAIM Married Mrs. Polly Barton — Book 1, 248

1843, May 30 BEAZLEY, EPHRAIM Married F. Ann Boughan — Book 1, 256

1857, Sep. 28 BEAZLEY, EPHRAIM Married Amanda J. Miskell — Book 1, 267

				Book	Page
1877, Apr. 12	BEAZLEY,	HARRISON	Married Patsey Lee, dau. of Baldwin Lee	Book 1,	45
1859, Feb. 2	BEAZLEY,	JAMES B.	Married Elizabeth C. Boughan	Book 1,	9
1882, Jan. 11	BEAZLEY,	JAMES B.	Married Henrietta S. Anderson	Book 1,	63
1816, Dec. 26	BEAZLEY,	JOHN	Married Tamzon W. Taylor	Book 1,	232
1819, Dec. 20	BEAZLEY,	JOHN, JR.	Married Laura L Montague	Book 1,	235
1853, Aug. 25	BEAZLEY,	JOHN W.	Married Maria S. Skelton	Book 1,	6
1886, Feb. 10	BEAZLEY,	LIBBENS	Married Laura E. Garrett	Book 1,	86
1881, Dec. 22	BEAZLEY,	LILY H.	Married Henry E. Brooks	Book 1,	62
1893, Nov. 23	BEAZLEY,	L H.	Married Lucy B. Mundie	Book 1,	112
1824, Jun. 7	BEAZLEY,	LUCINDA	Married Henry Latham	Book 1,	241
1848, May 25	BEAZLEY,	LUCINDA C.	Married William R. Johnson	Book 1,	260
1806, Feb. 13	BEAZLEY,	MARTHA	Married John Fogg	Book 1,	223
1856, Aug. 5	BEAZLEY,	MARTHA E.	Married Moses T. Crow	Book 1,	4
1834, Dec. 4	BEAZLEY,	MARY	Married Henry Sale	Book 1,	250
1842, Oct. 21	BEAZLEY,	MARY C.	Married Warner A. Dyke	Book 1,	256
1744,	BEAZLEY,	MARY	Married James Willard	W 7,	274
1820, Aug. 8	BEAZLEY,	MIRANDA	Married Nathaniel Mothershead	Book 1,	237
1813, Jun. 12	BEAZLEY,	NANCY	Married Jeremiah Fox	Book 1,	229
1834,	BEAZLEY,	POLLY	Married Henry T. Sale	D 44,	510
1836,	BEAZLEY,	POLLY	Married Henry T. Sale	D 45,	411
1811, Jan. 14	BEAZLEY,	RICHARD	Married Polly Armstrong	Book 1,	227
1828, Dec. 23	BEAZLEY,	RICHARD H.	Married Lucretia Crittenden	Book 1,	245
1832,	BEAZLEY,	RICHARD H.	Married Creete, dau. of Lemuel Crittenden	D 43,	504
1874, Jan. 27	BEAZLEY,	ROBERT	Married Susan Barnett	Book 1,	36
1837, Sep. 8	BEAZLEY,	THEODRICK	Married Delphia Clayton	Book 1,	252
1864, Dec. 14	BEAZLEY,	VESTILLA	Married Edward B. Blake	Book 1,	12
1894, Aug. 29	BEAZLEY,	V. F.	Married T. C. Doggins	Book 1,	114
1890, Dec. 26	BEAZLEY,	WARNER L.	Married Fanny McTyre	Book 1,	105
1812, Apr. 20	BEAZLEY,	WILLIAM	Married Betsey Burke	Book 1,	228
1850, Nov. 28	BEAZLEY,	WILLIAM I.	Married Judith Frances Armstrong	Book 1,	262
1706,	BEBY,	ELIZABETH	Daughter of John Beby, married Richard Bush	D 7,	479

				Book	Page
1799,	BECKWITH,	PENELOPE	Married Alexander Walker	D 35,	175
1827,	BECKWITH,	PENELOPE	Dau. of Sir Jonathan Beckwith, married Alexander Walker	D 42,	241
1871, Aug. 14	BEEKER,	ELLA M.	Married David L. Billings of Boston, Mass.	Book 1,	29
1720,	BELAND,	MARY	Married John Adcock	D&C 13,	317
1824, Aug. 12	BELFIELD,	DAVID C.	Married Maria B. Smith	Book 1,	241
1827,	BELFIELD,	DAVID C.	Married Maria, dau. of Francis Smith	D 42,	175
1838,	BELFIELD,	DAVID C.	Married Maria B. Smith, dau. of Lettice M. Smith	D 46,	156
1840, Oct. 24	BELFIELD,	DAVID C.	Married Elizabeth Cauthorn	Book 1,	254
1806, Nov. 16	BELFIELD,	JOHN W.	Married Frances T. Jones	Book 1,	224
1806, Dec. 15	BELFIELD,	JOHN	Married Peggy Croxton	Book 1,	223
1762,	BELFIELD,	THO. WRIGHT	Married Mary, dau. of Francis Meriwether	Land Trials,	180
1702,	BELL,	THOMAS	Married Hannah Copnall	O 3,	171
1709,	BELL,	THOMAS	Married Sarah, dau. of Lucretia Burnett	D&C13,	156
1708,	BENDRY,	ELIZABETH	Relict of William, married Job Virgett	O 4,	53
1750,	BENDRY,	ELIZABETH	Daughter of William & Eliz. married William Short	D 25,	129
1686,	BENDRY,	WILLIAM	Married Elizabeth, daughter of Thomas Moss	O 1,	197
1865, Jul. 21	BENNETT,	DARLING A.	Monroe Co. Georgia, married Sarah E. Clarke	Book 1,	13
1893, Nov. 23	BENNETT,	D. A.	South Carolina, married Lucy Turner	Book 1,	112
1891, Jun. 7	BENNETT,	JANE	Married Joe Brooks	Book 1,	107
1890, Jul. 1	BENNETT,	MARY M.	Married William A. Harmon	Book 1,	104
1832, Dec. 17	BENTLEY,	JAMES J.	Married Sarah Parker	Book 1,	248
1843,	BENTLEY,	JOHN G.	Married Sarah, grandaughter of Sally Gouldman	W 24,	175
1861, Jun. 20	BENTLEY,	MARY SUSAN	Married L. R. Holland	Book 1,	11
1712,	BENTLEY,	PATIENCE	Daughter of Nathaniel, married Thomas Bartlett	D&W14,	70
1826, Jan. 16	BENTLEY,	SOPHIA	Married John Saunders	Book 1,	242
1835,	BENTLEY,	WILLIAM	Married Catharine, dau. of William Dickerson	D 45,	56
1889, Jun. 11	BERCH,	SHELBY	Married Mary E. Atkins	Book 1,	100
1688,	BERRY,	SUSANNA	Daughter of Edward, married Charles Brown	D&W10,	5
1712,	BERRY,	WILLIAM	Married Margaret, dau. of Enoch Doughty	D&W14,	107
1796,	BEVERLEY,	ANNA M.	Daughter of Robert Beverley, married Francis Corbin	W 15,	549
1796,	BEVERLEY,	EVELYN B.	Daughter of Robert, married George Lee	W 15,	549

				Book	Page
1790,	BEVERLEY,	LUCY	Daughter of Robert of Bland-field, married Brett Randolph	D 33,	270
1891, Aug. 15	BEVERLEY,	SALLIE M.	Married William G. Kendall	Book 1,	107
1853, Aug. 16	BIGGER,	JOHN B.	Married Anna B. Muse	Book 1,	264
1871, Aug. 14	BILLINGS,	DAVID L.	Boston, Mass, married Ella M. Beeker	Book 1,	29
1729,	BILLINGS,	JOHN	Married Dorothy, dau. of Richard Awbrey	D 19,	27
1672,	BILLINGTON,	ELITIA	Daughter of Luke Billington, married John Russell	W&D 1, 114, 165	
1683,	BILLINGTON,	JOHN	Married Mary, relict of John Day	Box 101	G
1672,	BILLINGTON,	MARY	Daughter of Luke, married Hugh Daniel	W&D 1,	115
1853, Dec. 8	BILLUPS,	HUGH G.	Married Mary Catharine Bray	Book 1,	2
1858,	BILLUPS,	HUGH	Married Mary Bray, dau. of Charles & Mary Susan Bray	D 51,	142
1893, Feb. 22	BILLUPS,	HUGH, JR.	Married C. A. Lumpkin	Book 1,	111
1831, Sep. 24	BILLUPS,	JOHN	Married Mary T. Henley	Book 1,	248
1891, Dec. 22	BILLUPS,	JOHN W.	Married Fannie E. Crow, widow	Book 1,	108
1885, Jan. 20	BILLUPS,	LINDA H.	Married Charles R. Sadler	Book 1,	80
1854, Dec 13	BILLUPS,	SARA M.	Married Jon. F. Sadler	Book 1,	265
1892, Jun. 15	BILLUPS,	SUSIE C.	Married Thomas C. Stewart	Book 1,	109
1857, Jun. 25	BIRCH,	AMANDA F.	Married Downing Harper	Book 1,	5
1852, Aug. 16	BIRCH,	ISAAC	Married Martha P. Dunn	Book 1,	263
1872, Dec. 19	BIRCH,	LEWIS P.	Married Elizabeth Hundley	Book 1,	32
1849, Jan. 2	BIRCH,	STERLING	Married Catharine Broockes	Book 1,	261
1856, May 10	BIRCH,	TALIAFERRO	Married Frances Cauthorn	Book 1,	4
1849, Nov. 4	BIRCH,	WILLIAM S.	Married Nancy A. Williams	Book 1,	261
1714	BIRD,	FRANCES	Relict of Robert Bird, married Robert Ransone	O 4,	586
1801,	BIRD,	FRANCES	Sister of George, married William Eastham, Rockbridge Co.	D 36,	57
1841, Nov. 3	BIRD,	JOHN	Married Sally Jane Ritchie	Book 1,	255
1858, Nov. 9	BIRD,	JOSEPH A.	Baltimore, Md. married Judith E. Eubank	Book 1,	6
1817, Apr. 7	BIRD,	LAWRENCE	Married Elizabeth Bush	Book 1,	233
1840, Jun. 3	BIRD,	MARY	Married Robert Fortune	Book 1,	254
1843,	BIRD,	PHILEMON	Married Elizabeth, daughter of William Oliver	W 24,	152
1703,	BIRD,	RANDALL	Married Arabella, only dau. of Richard White	D 11,	156
1670,	BISHOP	MARY	Widow of Cyprian Bishop, married Evan Davis	D 4,	252

				Book	Page
1743,	BISWELL,	JEREMIAH	Married Elizabeth, daughter of John Butler	D 23,	53
1769,	BISWELL,	JEREMIAH	Married Frances, widow of Thomas Thorpe the elder	D 30,	375
1694,	BLACKBURN,	ABIGAIL	Relict of Christopher, married Thomas Short	O 1,	189
1809, Nov. 4	BLACKBURN,	CHURCHILL	Married Phoeby Parker	Book 1,	225
1806, Jan. 2	BLACKBURN,	ELIZABETH	Married John B. Micou	Book 1,	223
1875, May 5	BLACKBURN,	EUDORA A.	Married James Crouch	Book 1,	39
1846, Jan. 6	BLACKBURN,	JAMES F.	Married Peggy Skelton	Book 1,	258
1889, Jan. 31	BLACKBURN,	J. P.	Norfolk, Va. married Fannie B. Spindle	Book 1,	99
1871, Jan. 26	BLACKBURN,	LETITIA J.	Married Albert S. Parker of King & Queen County	Book 1,	28
1836, Jun. 28	BLACKBURN,	MARY F.	Married Almond Atkinson	Book 1,	252
1880, Apr. 15	BLACKBURN,	MARY S.	Married Washington L. Clarke	Book 1,	55
1849, Jan. 9	BLACKBURN,	ROBERT	Married Eudora A. Skelton	Book 1,	261
1852, Apr. 7	BLACKLEY,	ISABELLA	Married Jon. Mason	Book 1,	263
1685,	BLAGG,	ABRAHAM	Married Margaret, dau. of Honoria Jones	D 6,	64
1694,	BLAISE,	JAMES	Married Millicent, Executrix of John Jones	O 1,	209
1833, Jun. 4	BLAKE,	BENJAMIN	Married Hannah Broocks	Book 1,	249
1849,	BLAKE,	BENJAMIN	Married Hannah, daughter of Mrs. Frances Brooke	W 27,	595
1831, Dec. 3	BLAKE,	CATHARINE	Married Henry Dawson	Book 1,	248
1864, Dec. 14	BLAKE,	EDWARD B.	Married Vestilla Beazley	Book 1,	12
1824, Apr. 29	BLAKE,	FRANCES	Married Austin Brockenbrough	Book 1,	241
1839,	BLAKE,	JAMES	Married Sarah, sister-in-law of Richard Kay	D 46,	243
1817, Dec. 7	BLAKE,	JANE	Married Hubbard T. Minor	Book 1,	233
1843, Dec. 26	BLAKE,	JANE L.	Married Wat. H. Tyler	Book 1,	257
1847,	BLAKE,	JANE LOUISA	Daughter of Benjamin, married Watt Tyler	W 26,	343
1820, Jun. 10	BLAKE,	LOUISA	Married William L. L. Clements	Book 1,	237
1876, Jan. 15	BLAKE,	NANNY	Married Richard Jackson	Book 1,	41
1896, Dec. 17	BLAKEY,	THOMAS E.	Married Martha W. Wright	Book 1,	123
1839, Dec. 28	BLAND,	PASCHAL	Married Eliza Broocke	Book 1,	254
1740,	BLAND,	THEODRICK	Married Frances, dau. of Elizabeth & Drury Bolling	Land Trials,	195
1759,	BLAYSE ,	JAMES	Married Sarah, late Sarah Smith, Relict of Benj. Haile	O 23,	75
1704,	BLOMFIELD,	FRANCES	Only daughter of Samuel, married William Robinson	D&C 12,	59

Date	Surname	Given	Description	Book	Page
1685,	BLOMFIELD,	SAMUEL	Married Relict of Capt. Thomas Hawkins	O 1,	152
1688,	BODINGTON,	JAMES	His widow, married Henry Goring	O 2,	74
1742,	BODDINGTON	JOHN	Married Susanna, dau. of John Williamson	W 7,	257
1754,	BOGG,	GEORGE	Shipmaster of London, married Mary Rodger, sister of Jean	D 27	123
1754,	BOGG,	MARY	Widow, married James Butcher, Greenock Merchant	D 27	121
1821, Nov. 26	BOHANNON,	ANN D.	Married John P. Shackelford	Book 1,	238
1835, Jan. 28	BOHANNON,	A. G.	Married Mary C. Hundley	Book 1,	251
1793,	BOHANNON,	BENOI	Married Mary, daughter of James Boughan	D 34,	50
1756,	BOHANNON,	ELIZABETH	Widow of William Bohannon, married Jonathan Dunn	W 10,	97
1810,	BOHANNON,	HAYNE	Married Robert Gibson	O 40,	354
1815, Sep. 12	BOHANNON,	JOHN	Married Barbara Allen	Book 1,	231
1825,	BOHANNON,	JOHN	Kentucky, married Elizabeth Lafon	D 42,	101
1781,	BOHANNON,	JOSEPH	Married Elizabeth, sister of Major Lafon	D 32,	12
1809, Aug. 26	BOHANNON,	LUCY	Married Basil Brown	Book 1,	225
1807, Aug. 29	BOHANNON,	MARY G.	Married James H. Royster	Book 1,	224
1756,	BOHANNON,	SARAH	Daughter of William, married Isaac Kidd	W 10,	110
1805, Mar. 21	BOHANNON,	SARAH	Married Leroy Hipkins	Book 1,	223
1798,	BOHANNON,	THOMAS	Married Elizabeth Dunn	W 15,	381
1812, Nov. 11	BOOKER,	DOROTHY	Married William A. Garnett	Book 1,	228
1825,	BOOKER,	DOROTHY	Daughter of Lewis, married William A. Garnett	D 41,	469
1838,	BOOKER,	DOROTHY	Married William A. Garnett	W 26,	615
1839, Oct. 22	BOOKER,	ELIZA	Married Henry Boughan	Book 1,	254
1787,	BOOKER,	ELIZABETH	Formerly wife of Ambrose Wright	W 16,	44
1790,	BOOKER,	ELIZABETH	Daughter of James, married Richard Jeffries	W 15,	101
1774,	BOOKER,	JAMES	Marriage Agreement with Elizabeth Wright, widow	D 31,	270
1775,	BOOKER,	JAMES	Married Ann, daughter of John Camm	W 13, / D 31,	30 / 270
1814, Jan. 4	BOOKER,	JAMES	Married Ann Throckmorton	Book 1,	230
1829, Jun. 15	BOOKER,	JUDITH	Married John S. Cox	Book 1,	247
1827, Mar. 24	BOOKER,	SARAH	Married Muscoe Garnett	Book 1,	243
1838,	BOOKER,	SARAH	Married Muscoe Garnett	W 26,	616
1689,	BOOTH,	CATHARINE	Daughter of Humphrey, married Robert Brooke	D 8,	49

				Book	Page
1663,	BOOTH,	HUMPHREY	Married daughter of Mrs. Margaret Lucas	D 2,	327
1763,	BOOTH,	WILLIAM	Married Elizabeth, dau. of William Aylett	D 29,	186
1899, Feb. 28	BOUGHAN,	B. J.	Married A. B. Coleman	Book 1,	132
1812, Dec. 24	BOUGHAN,	CARY CASTON	Married Thomas St. John	Book 1,	228
1804,	BOUGHAN,	CATHARINE	Daughter of Griffing, married George W. Banks	D 36,	439
1804, May 8	BOUGHAN,	CATHARINE	Married Hundley Moody	Book 1,	222
1817, Dec. 24	BOUGHAN,	CATHARINE	Married Josiah Minter	Book 1,	233
1820,	BOUGHAN,	CATHARINE	Married Josiah Minter	D 40,	145
1847, Sep. 6	BOUGHAN,	EDWARD R.	Married Sarah E. Croxton	Book 1,	259
1853,	BOUGHAN,	EDWARD R.	Married Sarah, daughter of James Croxton	W 27,	579
1859, Feb. 2	BOUGHAN,	ELIZABETH C.	Married James B. Beazley	Book 1,	9
1892, Nov. 30	BOUGHAN,	EMMA W.	Married Joseph Davis	Book 1,	110
1711,	BOUGHAN,	FRANCES	Dau. of Major James Boughan, married John Stark	Land Trials,	115
1808, Dec. 19	BOUGHAN,	FRANCES	Married James Allen	Book 1,	224
1843, May 30	BOUGHAN,	F. ANN	Married Ephraim Beazley	Book 1,	256
1808, Oct. 10	BOUGHAN,	HENRY W.	Married Julia Wood	Book 1,	224
1823,	BOUGHAN,	HENRY	Married Julia, daughter of Thomas Wood	D 41,	51
1839, Oct. 22	BOUGHAN,	HENRY	Married Eliza Booker	Book 1,	254
1894, Jan. 4	BOUGHAN,	HENRY	Married Lucy N. Brooks	Book 1,	113
1701,	BOUGHAN,	JAMES JR.	Married Sarah, daughter of Daniel Brown	Land Trials,	140
1724,	BOUGHAN,	JAMES	Married Susanna, dau. of Richard & Susanna Tyler	D 18,	1
1841, Jan. 13	BOUGHAN,	JAMES	Married Martha Ellen Micou	Book 1,	255
1876, Jun. 22	BOUGHAN,	JAMES E.	Married Myrtle Harford	Book 1,	42
1814, May 16	BOUGHAN,	JESSIE	Married Betsey Games	Book 1,	230
1738,	BOUGHAN,	JOHN	Married Cary Caston	W 6,	258
1771,	BOUGHAN,	JOHN	Married Ursula, daughter of James Munday	D 30,	508
1823,	BOUGHAN,	JOHN	His daughter married Hundley Moody	D 41,	49
1824,	BOUGHAN,	JOHN	Married Frances, dau. of Charles Howerton	D 41,	272
1872, Feb. 8	BOUGHAN,	DR. JOHN A.	Married Christian A. Henley	Book 1,	30
1875, Dec. 21	BOUGHAN,	JOHN H.	Married Marian M. Boughan	Book 1,	40
1876, Feb. 15	BOUGHAN,	JOHN G.	Married Georgiana Taylor	Book 1,	44

					Book	Page
1884, Jun. 17	BOUGHAN,	JOHN H.	Married Sarah A. Sadler		Book 1,	77
1897, Mar. 3	BOUGHAN,	LAURA	Married Chastine Griggs		Book 1,	125
1805, Jun. 17	BOUGHAN,	LEWIS	Married Nancy Brooks		Book 1,	222
1834, Dec. 18	BOUGHAN,	LUCY M.	Married Richard Shearwood		Book 1,	250
1873, Jan. 9	BOUGHAN,	MARIAN M.	Married John H. Boughan		Book 1,	32
1835, Oct. 9	BOUGHAN,	MARTHA H.	Married Richard Banks		Book 1,	251
1771,	BOUGHAN,	MARY	Daughter of Augustine, married John Meredith		W 12,	415
1793,	BOUGHAN,	MARY	Daughter of James, married Bennoi Bohannon		D 34,	50
1893, Dec. 20	BOUGHAN,	M. E.	Married R. A. Shearwood		Book 1,	112
1881, Feb. 10	BOUGHAN,	MILLY A.	Married Peter T. Campbell		Book 1,	59
1816, Dec. 26	BOUGHAN,	NANCY	Married James Games		Book 1,	232
1807, Jun. 4	BOUGHAN,	POLLY	Married William Banks		Book 1,	224
1823,	BOUGHAN,	SALLY	Widow of John, married James Games		D 41,	48
1853, Apr. 29	BOUGHAN,	THEODORE P.	Married Margaret A. Croxton		Book 1,	264
1822, Jan. 9	BOUGHAN,	THOMAS	Married Matilda Gordon		Book 1,	239
1843, Mar. 8	BOUGHAN,	THOMAS	Married Mary F. Wood		Book 1,	256
1869, Feb. 18	BOUGHAN,	THOMAS W.	Married Mary E. Taylor		Book 1,	22
1873, Jan. 9	BOUGHAN,	THOMAS	Married Mrs. Mary E. Saunders, widow		Book 1,	32
1869, Feb. 18	BOUGHAN,	WILLIAM F.	Married Betty F. Verlander		Book 1,	22
1835, Dec. 14	BOUGHTON,	ALICE A.	Married Wal. G. Covington		Book 1,	251
1857, Apr. 28	BOUGHTON,	ALICE A.	Married Charles R. Shepherd		Book 1,	5
1808, Aug. 25	BOUGHTON,	ANN	Married Henry Simco		Book 1,	225
1873, Dec. 24	BOUGHTON,	ANN E.	Married Cesla M. Smoot		Book 1,	1
1853, Oct. 27	BOUGHTON,	ALEXANDER	Married Elizabeth Durham		Book 1,	1
1840, Mar. 16	BOUGHTON,	BENJAMIN	Married Sophronia Crow		Book 1,	254
1846, Feb. 11	BOUGHTON,	BENJAMIN	Married Jane Houston		Book 1,	258
1805, Jul.	BOUGHTON,	CATHARINE	Married Thomas Boughton		Book 1,	223
1851, Dec. 15	BOUGHTON,	CATHARINE	Married Walter F. Seward		Book 1,	263
1844, Dec. 21	BOUGHTON,	CHARLES H.	Married Julia C. Broocke		Book 1,	257
1840, Feb. 4	BOUGHTON,	E. A.	Married Silas Conoly		Book 1,	254
1848, Nov. 6	BOUGHTON,	ELIZA	Married Winter B. Lumpkin		Book 1,	260

					Book	Page
1811, Jan. 21	BOUGHTON,	JAMES	Married Frances Shepherd		Book 1,	227
1824	BOUGHTON,	JAMES	Married Frances, daughter of Reuben Shepherd		D 41,	389
1821, Dec. 11	BOUGHTON,	JOHN	Married Ann Howerton		Book 1,	238
1821,	BOUGHTON,	JOHN	Married Ann, daughter of Charles Howerton		D 41,	272
1842, Jan. 17	BOUGHTON,	JOHN S.	Married Lucy S. Seward		Book 1,	256
1808, Dec. 29	BOUGHTON,	JUDITH	Married Stephen Garrett		Book 1,	224
1820, Mar. 15	BOUGHTON,	JUDITH	Married Walter Dix		Book 1,	237
1806, Oct. 20	BOUGHTON,	LUCY	Married Philip Williams		Book 1,	223
1856, Oct. 23	BOUGHTON,	LUCY C.	Married Iverson L. Dunn		Book 1,	4
1808, Jul. 18	BOUGHTON,	MARTHA	Married Vincent Ramsey		Book 1,	224
1838, Jun. 16	BOUGHTON,	MARY E.	Married Robert Scott		Book 1,	253
1849, Sep. 27	BOUGHTON,	MIRA	Married Philip Greenwood		Book 1,	261
1838, Jan. 25	BOUGHTON,	POLLY	Married Austin Brizendine		Book 1,	253
1815, Dec. 20	BOUGHTON,	REUBEN	Married Susanna Broocke		Book 1,	231
1847, Dec. 22	BOUGHTON,	REUBEN B.	Married Ellen Ann Gatewood		Book 1,	259
1863, Nov. 5	BOUGHTON,	REUBEN B.	Married Leah A. Cauthorn, widow	Book 1,	12
1809, Feb. 20	BOUGHTON,	SUSANNA	Married James Crofton		Book 1,	225
1805, Jul.	BOUGHTON,	THOMAS	Married Catharine Boughton		Book 1,	223
1799,	BOUGHTON,	THOMAS	Married Lucy, daughter of Richard Phillips		W 16,	290
1825, Apr. 5	BOUGHTON,	THOMAS	Married Polly Allen		Book 1,	241
1849, Jan. 9	BOUGHTON,	THOMAS A.	Married Matilda C. Cauthorn		Book 1,	261
1849, Dec. 26	BOUGHTON,	THOMAS	Married Prud. Broocke		Book 1,	241
1714,	BOULTER,	WILLIAM	Great Britain, married Margaret, sister of Tho. Robey, Middlesex Co.	D&W 14,	351
1728,	BOULWARE,	ANN	Executrix of Benjamin, married James Murray	O 7,	275a
1758,	BOULWARE,	ANN	Daughter of Mary, married William Pitts	D 28,	106
1804, Nov. 7	BOULWARE,	BETSEY,	Married Lewis Fisher		Book 1,	222
1821, Oct. 2	BOULWARE,	BETSEY	Married Benjamin Vawter		Book 1,	238
1733,	BOULWARE,	ELIZABETH	Relict of John, married Anthony Garnett	D 20,	15
1846, Mar. 28	BOULWARE,	GRAY	Married V. L Wright		Book 1,	258
1678,	BOULWARE,	JAMES	Married daughter of William Gray	W&D 1,	144
1713,	BOULWARE,	JOHN	Married Susanna, daughter of John Williams	D&W 14,	252

				Book		Page
1753,	BOULWARE,	MARGARET	Daughter of Mark, married Caleb Elliott	D	26,	364
1754,	BOULWARE,	MARTHA	Daughter of Mark, married William Harrison	W	10,	2
1732,	BOULWARE,	MARY	Daughter of John, married Edmund Carroll	O	8,	286
1804, Nov. 14	BOULWARE,	SALLY	Married James Parker	Book 1,		222
1802,	BOULWARE,	SARAH	Daughter of William, married Ralph Rouzie	D	36,	92
1739,	BOULWARE,	SUSANNA	Married William Thomas	D	22,	126
1757,	BOULWARE,	THOMAS	Married Elinor, daughter of Daniel Gaines	W	10,	157
1794,	BOULWARE,	THOMAS	Married Susanna, niece of Catharine Jones	D	34,	65
1809,	BOULWARE,	MARGARET	Married Robert Wright	W	16,	139
1756,	BOWCOCK,	?	Married Amy, sister of Philip & Isaac Gatewood	W	10,	127
1814, Oct. 24	BOWIE,	WALTER	Married Juliet Spindle	Book 1,		230
1822,	BOWIE,	WALTER	Married Julia, daughter of Erasmus Jones	O	44,	196
1762,	BOWLING,	DRURY	Married Elizabeth, daughter of Francis Meriwether	Land Trials Page 185		
1807, May 18	BOYCE,	ELIZABETH	Married Thomas Minter	Book 1,		224
1750,	BRADBOURNE,	WILLIAM	Married Sarah, widow of William Crondas	D	25,	180
1883, Apr. 3	BRADLEY,	MAGGIE L.	Married George W. Samuel	Book 1,		26
1880, Mar. 10	BRADLEY,	OSCAR F.	Married Nannie F. Parker	Book 1,		54
1809, Mar. 21	BRADFORD,	SAMUEL	Married Matilda Gatewood	Book 1,		225
1689,	BRAGG,	JOSEPH	Married Mary Tap	O	2,	177
1827, Apr. 26	BRANHAM,	PHILIP	Married Lucy A. Barnes	Book 1,		243
1827,	BRANHAM,	PHILIP	Richmond Co., married Lucy A. Barnes, sister of Richard Barnes	D	42,	229
1896, Dec. 31	BRANHAM,	DAFFAN L.	Married Susan H. Staples	Book 1,		123
1695,	BRASIER,	JOHN	Married Elizabeth, daughter of Richard Holt	O	1,	256
1835, Sep. 19	BRAXTON,	A. M.	Married Dorothea Hoomes	Book 1,		251
1835,	BRAXTON,	AUGUSTINE	Married Dorothy Hoomes	D	45,	34
1819, Nov. 29	BRAXTON,	JUDITH	Married John Daingerfield	Book 1, D	43,	235 16
1811, Sep. 6	BRAXTON,	SARAH F.	Married Temple Elliott	Book 1,		227
1820, Apr. 4	BRAY,	CHARLES	Married Susanna Croxton	Book 1,		237
1871, Dec. 20	BRAY,	CHARLES E.	Married Bettie Faulconer	Book 1,		29
1879, Feb. 26	BRAY,	CHARLES	Married Catharine Jones	Book 1,		51
1806, Feb. 6	BRAY,	ELIZABETH	Married John Collins	Book 1,		223

1812, Jan. 15	BRAY,	ELIZABETH	Married Thomas Pilcher	Book 1,	228
1899, Dec. 27	BRAY,	IDA G.	Daughter of Winter, married J. B. Scott, son of Joseph	Book 1,	135
1691,	BRAY,	?	Relict of Richard, married Richard Willis	O 2,	307
1849, Dec. 24	BRAY,	JAMES	Married Ann E. Cauthorn	Book 1,	261
1817, Jan. 20	BRAY,	MARY ANN	Married Austin Brooks	Book 1,	233
1853, Dec. 8	BRAY,	MARY C.	Married Hugh Gwynn Billups	Book 1,	2
1897, Dec. 2	BRAY,	MARY D.	Married O. D. Hale of Richmond, County	Book 1,	126
1852, Oct. 4	BRAY,	MILDRED C.	Married Dr. Buchanan Richards	Book 1,	263
1821, Jun.	BRAY,	POLLY	Married Evan Rice	Book 1,	238
1804, Feb. 8	BRAY,	SUSANNA	Married Edward Ware	Book 1,	222
1809, Nov. 20	BRAY,	WINTER	Married Mary Ann Croxton	Book 1,	225
1864, Nov. 14	BRAY,	WINTER	Married Fannie Ida Faulconer	Book 1,	18
1774,	BREEDLOVE,	CHARLES	Married Sally Fletcher	W 12,	605
1840, Dec. 3	BREEDLOVE,	ELIZABETH	Married Henry Adams	Book 1,	254
1844, Mar. 21	BREEDLOVE,	LEWIS	Married Matilda Ann Brooks	Book 1,	257
1868, Feb. 19	BREEDLOVE,	MARIA	Married Frederick Jones	Book 1,	20
1815, Dec. 18	BREEDLOVE,	WILLIAM	Married Frances Fisher	Book 1,	231
1858, Dec. 9	BREEDLOVE,	WILLIAM	Married Eliza Ann Davis	Book 1,	7
1852, Feb. 21	BRENT,	MARTHA A.	Married Peter I. Gregg	Book 1,	263
1724,	BRICE,	HENRY	Married Susanna, sister of John Miller	W 6,	74
1718,	BRIDGER,	ELIZABETH	Relict of John Bridger of Surry Co. married John Button, Clerk of Middlesex Co.	D 16,	37
1799,	BRIDGES,	THOMAS	Married Sarah, widow of Robt. Payne Waring	W 15,	502
1764,	BRIDGFORTH,	SARAH	Sister of Thomas, married John Farguson	W 12,	47
1877, Dec. 24	BRIL,	PHILIP	Married Lucy Ellen Davis	Book 1,	46
1815, Jan. 15	BRISTOW,	SALLY	Married Benjamin Tucker	Book 1,	231
1853, Jan. 8	BRISTOW	SCHUYLER	Married Octavia A. Cauthorn	Book 1,	264
1812, Dec. 17	BRIZENDINE,	ABNER	Married Judith Harper	Book 1,	228
1812, Dec. 21	BRIZENDINE,	ABRAHAM	Married Susanna James	Book 1,	228
1895, Apr. 11	BRIZENDINE,	A. B.	Married A. E. Garrett	Book 1,	118
1866, Nov. 15	BRIZENDINE,	ADELINE	Married James A. Shearwood	Book 1,	15
1761,	BRIZENDINE,	ALICE	Married John Williams	D 29,	55

			Book	Page
1883, Jan. 11	BRIZENDINE, ALICE B.	Married Adolphus Norris	Book 1,	69
1761,	BRIZENDINE, ANN	Daughter of William, married William Williamson	D 29,	55
1805, Jun. 10	BRIZENDINE, ANN	Married John Heath	Book 1,	223
1838, Jan. 25	BRIZENDINE, AUSTIN	Married Polly Boughton	Book 1,	253
1869, Aug. 5	BRIZENDINE, AUSTIN	Married Mary J. Fiddler	Book 1,	23
1883, Mar. 22	BRIZENDINE, AUSTIN	Married Catharine Davis	Book 1,	70
1806, Mar. 17	BRIZENDINE, BARTLETT	Married Nancy Minter	Book 1,	223
1888, Dec. 6	BRIZENDINE, BETTIE	Married R. L. Durham	Book 1,	97
1817, Dec. 20	BRIZENDINE, BIVEON	Married Betsey Allen	Book 1,	233
1849, Feb. 23	BRIZENDINE, BURRELL	Married Catharine A. Broocke	Book 1,	261
1809, Sep. 18	BRIZENDINE, CHANEY	Married Polly Davis	Book 1,	225
1812,	BRIZENDINE, CHANEY	Married Polly, daughter of Evan Davis	O 41,	57
1834, Apr. 11	BRIZENDINE, CHURCHILL	Married Catharine Crow	Book 1,	250
1837, May 3	BRIZENDINE, CHURCHILL	Married Ann Shearwood	Book 1,	252
1822, Nov. 19	BRIZENDINE, DELILAH	Married Benjamin Greenwood	Book 1,	239
1878, Dec. 25	BRIZENDINE, EDGAR	Married Mary Susan Lumpkin	Book 1,	50
1834, Jan. 18	BRIZENDINE, ELIZABETH	Married Richard H. Covington	Book 1,	250
1873, Jan. 14	BRIZENDINE, EMILY E.	Married Muscoe R. Dunn	Book 1,	32
1866, Dec. 19	BRIZENDINE, EMMA E.	Married William B. Harmon	Book 1,	16
1879, Dec. 22	BRIZENDINE, EMMA J.	Married Harvey R. Taylor	Book 1,	53
1819, Jul. 20	BRIZENDINE, FANNY	Married John Hodges	Book 1,	235
1890, May 22	BRIZENDINE, F. A.	Married R. B. Gary of King William Co.	Book 1,	104
1898, Jul. 20	BRIZENDINE, F. L.	Married J. H. Taylor	Book 1,	129
1856, Feb. 25	BRIZENDINE, FERIOL	Married Margaret A. Williamson	Book 1,	4
1889, Aug. 1	BRIZENDINE, FLORA	Married Elward F. Croxton	Book 1,	101
1841, Apr. 22	BRIZENDINE, FRANCES	Married Smith T. Shepherd	Book 1,	255
1889, Jun. 13	BRIZENDINE, GEORGE W.	Married Alice Covington	Book 1,	100
1787,	BRIZENDINE, ?	Married Elizabeth, dau. of Thomas Fitzgerald	D 33,	66
1828, Dec. 28	BRIZENDINE, HENRY	Married Jane Greenwood	Book 1,	245
1819, Dec. 23	BRIZENDINE, JAMES	Married Nancy Ursery	Book 1,	235
1807, Dec. 21	BRIZENDINE, JOHN	Married Patsy Dogins	Book 1,	224

				Book	Page
1848, Aug. 1	BRIZENDINE, JOHN C.	Married Martha J. Allen		Book 1,	260
1849, Nov. 12	BRIZENDINE, JOHN C.	Married Elizabeth Owens		Book 1,	261
1850, Jun. 12	BRIZENDINE, JOHN	Married Nancy Brizendine		Book 1,	262
1869, Jan. 14	BRIZENDINE, JOHN R.	Married Betty Durham		Book 1,	22
1827, May 30	BRIZENDINE, JUDITH	Married James Phillips		Book 1,	244
1846, May 5	BRIZENDINE, LARRY	Married John C. Prince		Book 1,	259
1820, Dec. 22	BRIZENDINE, LUCY	Married Henry Greenwood		Book 1,	237
1871, Dec. 5	BRIZENDINE, MAGGIE J.	Married Robert L. Coleman		Book 1,	29
1816, Apr. 10	BRIZENDINE, MARIA	Married Isaac Cauthorn		Book 1,	232
1859, Apr. 28	BRIZENDINE, MARINDA	Married Alexander Crow		Book 1,	7
1846, Dec. 21	BRIZENDINE, M. A.	Married Temple Brizendine		Book 1,	258
1867, Apr. 25	BRIZENDINE, MARGARET	Married John William Clarke		Book 1,	17
1838, Apr. 18	BRIZENDINE, MARTHA	Married Watkins Harper		Book 1,	253
1838,	BRIZENDINE, MARTHA	Daughter of Vincent, married Watkins Harper		D 46,	123
1844, Dec. 23	BRIZENDINE, MARY	Married John G. Garrett		Book 1,	257
1859, Feb. 4	BRIZENDINE, MARY E.	Married Richard H. Sisson		Book 1,	8
1860, Apr. 3	BRIZENDINE, MATILDA C.	Married Jacob Durham		Book 1,	9
1852, Dec. 20	BRIZENDINE, MILDRED C.	Married Robert Brooke		Book 1,	263
1884, Dec. 25	BRIZENDINE, MOLLY K.	Married John R. Shearwood		Book 1,	80
1813, Feb. 10	BRIZENDINE, NANCY	Married Thomas Durham		Book 1,	229
1830, Jul. 22	BRIZENDINE, NANCY	Married Brizendine Williamson		Book 1,	247
1850, Jun. 12	BRIZENDINE, NANCY	Married John Brizendine		Book 1,	262
1870, Mar. 16	BRIZENDINE, NANCY	Married Albert Schools		Book 1,	25
1868, Dec. 24	BRIZENDINE, PHILIP C.	Married Sarah C. Harmon		Book 1,	21
1865, Dec. 21	BRIZENDINE, RICHARD	Married Martha C. Foreacres		Book 1,	14
1873, Feb. 13	BRIZENDINE, RICHARD H.	Married Susan P. Shackelford		Book 1,	32
1874, Dec. 24	BRIZENDINE, ROBERT C.	Married Susan A. Foreacres		Book 1,	38
1860, Mar. 16	BRIZENDINE, SARAH	Married Henry Davis		Book 1,	9
1854, Aug. 22	BRIZENDINE, SUSAN	Married Claiborne Croxton		Book 1,	2
1867, Dec. 31	BRIZENDINE, SUSAN E.	Married Eldred Crow		Book 1,	19
1846, Dec. 21	BRIZENDINE, TEMPLE	Married M. A. Brizendine		Book 1,	258

				Book	Page
1828, Mar. 31	BRIZENDINE, THOMAS	Married Elizabeth Roddin		Book 1,	245
1839, Jan 7	BRIZENDINE, THOMAS	Married Dicey Williamson		Book 1,	254
1848, Sep. 18	BRIZENDINE, THOMAS	Married Elizabeth Tucker		Book 1,	260
1853, May 10	BRIZENDINE, THOMAS H.	Married Martha,W. Williamson		Book 1,	264
1823, Dec. 29	BRIZENDINE, TRAVIS	Married Elizabeth Lambeth		Book 1,	240
1852, Dec. 30	BRIZENDINE, VICTORIA	Married Erastus Dickenson		Book 1,	263
1809, Dec. 18	BRIZENDINE, VINCENT	Married Sally Harris		Book 1,	225
1878, Jul. 18	BRIZENDINE, WILTON	Married Theresa M. Shearwood		Book 1,	49
1834, May 19	BRIZENDINE, ZACHARIAH	Married Letty Williamson		Book 1,	250
1688,	BROAD , KATHERINE	Relict of Thomas, married Thomas Gladman		O 1,	90
1855, Mar. 15	BROADDUS, ALEXANDER W.	Married Fannie E. Croxton		Book 1,	3
1859, Apr. 19	BROADDUS, ALEXANDER W.	Married Sallie M. Haile		Book 1,	7
1838, Oct. 22	BROADDUS, COLUMBIA	Married Howard Montague		Book 1,	253
1837, Jun. 10	BROADDUS, EDWIN	Married Eliza Montague		Book 1,	252
1835, Oct. 19	BROADDUS, FRANKLIN	Married Elizabeth Elliott		Book 1,	251
1873, May 22	BROADDUS, JAMES H.	Married Mary C. Coleman		Book 1,	33
1842, Mar. 19	BROADDUS, JOHN	Married Louisa Gouldman		Book 1,	256
1884, Feb. 26	BROADDUS, JUNIUS M.	Married M. Nettie Hoskins		Book 1,	67
1891, Jan. 1	BROADDUS, LENA M.	Married Hugh Fox, Pine Bluff, Ark.		Book 1,	106
1895, Aug. 29	BROADDUS, L. V.	Married John T. Hoskins		Book 1,	118
1882, Dec. 7	BROADDUS, MANLY	Married Bettie B. Haile		Book 1,	67
1881, Nov. 22	BROADDUS, NANNIE T.	Married Waller J. Parker		Book 1,	61
1806, Apr. 1	BROADDUS, ROBERT L.	Married Sallie Motley		Book 1,	223
1813, Feb. 15	BROADDUS, SALLY	Married Robert Sale		Book 1,	229
1825, Dec. 19	BROACH, BENONI	Married Polly Hill		Book 1,	242
1819, Feb. 4	BROACH, CHANEY	Married Fanny Fletcher		Book 1,	235
1827, Dec. 22	BROACH, CHANEY	Married Dicie Rose		Book 1,	243
1829, Dec. 9	BROACH, CHANEY	Married Sally Griggs		Book 1,	246
1881, Apr. 3	BROACH, CHARLES E.	Married Rosa E. Didlake		Book 1,	59
1841, Dec. 18	BROACH, FRANCES	Married James S. Brook		Book 1,	255
1827, Feb. 19	BROACH, GEORGE	Married Susan T. Simco		Book 1,	243

				Book	Page
1876, Dec. 25	BROACH,	GEORGIA	Married Willie W. Jordan	Book 1,	43
1831, Oct. 10	BROACH,	JOANNA	Married Churchill Fiddler	Book 1,	248
1677,	BROCHE,	JOHN	Married Mary, daughter of Rice Jones	W 2,	74
1692,	BROACHE,	JOHN	Married Mary, sister of John Jones	O 1,	156
1841, Jan. 18	BROACH,	JULIA	Married John Good	Book 1,	255
1866, Dec. 25	BROACH,	MARTHA I.	Married Lewis Taylor	Book 1,	16
1866, Jan. 4	BROACH,	MARY C.	Married Robert L. Dyke	Book 1,	14
1796,	BROACH,	NANCY	Married Thomas Wilson	W 15,	275
1852, Nov. 24	BROACH,	ROBERT	Married Martha Good	Book 1,	263
1850, Jan. 21	BROACH,	SARAH	Married Dabney Brooks	Book 1,	262
1811, Feb. 28	BROCKENBROUGH, ARTHUR	Married Lucy Gray		Book 1,	227
1824, Apr. 29	BROCKENBROUGH, AUSTIN	Married Frances Blake		Book 1,	241
1856, Dec. 10	BROCKENBROUGH, AUSTINA	Married Frances Blake		Book 1,	4
1869, Mar. 16	BROCKENBROUGH, BETTY	Married Samuel F. Harwood		Book 1,	23
1877, Sep. 25	BROCKENBROUGH, BETTIE G.	Married Maxwell Fauntleroy		Book 1,	46
1717,	BROCKENBROUGH, ELIZABETH	Sister of Austin, married Thomas Dickinson		W 3, Richmond Co.	326
1813,	BROCKENBROUGH, ELIZABETH	Daughter of Newman, married John Roane		W 18,	258
1857, Nov. 18	BROCKENBROUGH, FANNIE	Married William W. Gordon		Book 1,	15
1823, Nov. 8	BROCKENBROUGH, FAUNTLEROY	Married Sarah Smith		Book 1,	240
1860, Jun. 13	BROCKENBROUGH, GABRIELLA	Married Joseph W. Chinn		Book 1,	9
1835, May 13	BROCKENBROUGH, HENRIETTA	Married Benjamin Nelson		Book 1,	251
1856, Dec. 10	BROCKENBROUGH, JOHN M.	Married Austina Brockenbrough		Book 1,	4
1684,	BROCKENBROUGH, WILLIAM	Married Mary, niece of Ann Austin		D 7,	176
1832, Apr. 12	BROCKENBROUGH, WILLIAM A.	Married Mary C. Gray		Book 1,	248
1839, May 11	BROOCKE, ALICE	Married Ganon Jackson		Book 1,	254
1841,	BROOCKE, ALICE	Married Gawin Jackson		D 47,	229
1830, Dec. 20	BROOCKE, BENJAMIN	Married Elizabeth Crow		Book 1,	247
1808, Oct. 3	BROOCKE, CATHARINE	Married Philip Griggs		Book 1,	224
1849, Feb. 23	BROOCKE, CATHARINE	Married Burrell Brizendine		Book 1,	261
1873, Jun. 19	BROOCKE, FANNIE B	Married Robert T. Cauthorn		Book 1,	33
1820,	BROOCKE, FRANCES	Daughter of William, married Lewis Seward		W 19,	150

					Book	Page
1836, Dec. 15	BROOCKE,	FRANCES E.	Married James Williams		Book 1,	252
1824,	BROOCKE,	ISAAC	Married Nancy, daughter of Richard St. John		W 20,	32
1867, Jan. 13	BROOCKE,	JAMES R.	Married Laura A. C. Brooke		Book 1,	16
1844, Dec. 21	BROOCKE,	JULIA C.	Married Charles H. Boughton		Book 1,	257
1867, Jan. 13	BROOCKE,	LAURA A. C.	Married James R. Broocke		Book 1,	16
1823, May 3	BROOCKE,	MARINDA	Married Leroy Cauthorn		Book 1,	240
1830, Dec. 21	BROOCKE,	MIRA E.	Married George Rose		Book 1,	247
1830,	BROOCKE,	MIRA	Daughter of Isaac, Married Leroy Cauthorn		D 43,	136
1796,	BROOCKE,	MOLLY	Daughter of Thomas Henry Broock, married Thomas Clarke		W 15,	275
1841,	BROOCKE,	PATSY	Married Joseph Durham		D 47,	229
1849, Dec. 26	BROOCKE,	PRUDENCE	Married Thomas Boughton		Book 1,	241
1845, Jan. 21	BROOCKE,	SARAH	Daughter of Lewis, married Churchill Williams		Book 1,	258
1815, Dec. 20	BROOCKE,	SUSANNA	Married Reuben Boughton		Book 1,	231
1820,	BROOCKE,	SUSANNA	Daughter of William, married Lewis Boughton		W 19,	150
1878, Dec 26	BROOCKE,	VIRGINIA C.	Married William F. Williamson		Book 1,	50
1837, Feb. 20	BROOCKE,	WILLIAM B.	Married Eliza Dyke		Book 1,	252
1790,	BROOKE,	EDMUND	Married Harriet Whiting		D 33,	230
1839, Dec. 28	BROOKE,	ELIZA	Married Paschal Bland		Book 1,	254
1820, Jan. 24	BROOKE,	ELIZABETH G.	Married Richard J. Ludlow		Book 1,	237
1869, Jun. 17	BROOKE,	ELIZA J.	Married Thomas F. Kemp		Book 1,	23
1890, Nov. 12	BROOKE,	ELLEN	Married H. L Fauntleroy		Book 1,	104
1849,	BROOKE,	HANNAH	Daughter of Mrs. Frances Brooke, married Benjamin Blake		W 27,	595
1890, Nov. 12	BROOKE,	HATTIE C.	Married Ro. B. Fauntleroy, King & Queen Co.		Book 1,	104
1829, Jan. 19	BROOKE,	HUMPHREY B.	Married Elizabeth Ferris		Book 1,	246
1839, Nov. 8	BROOKE,	HUMPHREY	Married Sally Coghill		Book 1,	254
1816, Jun. 5	BROOKE,	JAMES	Married Elizabeth Simcoe		Book 1,	232
1853, Apr. 22	BROOKE,	JAMES	Married Elizabeth Harper		Book 1,	264
1872, Dec. 23	BROOKE,	JOHN L.	Married Maria B. Garnett		Book 1,	32
1815, Jan. 4	BROOKE,	LEWIS D.	Married Maria Alexander		Book 1,	231
1825, Dec. 19	BROOKE,	LUCY	Married Giles B. Cooke		Book 1,	241
1826, Dec. 23	BROOKE,	LUCY	Married John Newcomb		Book 1,	242

Date	Surname	Given Name	Marriage	Book	Page
1859, May 12	BROOKE,	MARIA LOUISA	Married Alfred Durham	Book 1,	7
1857, Jun. 4	BROOKE,	MARY A.	Married James A. Croxton	Book 1,	5
1879, Aug. 21	BROOKE,	MARY H.	Married John R. Williams	Book 1,	52
1804, Jan. 9	BROOKE,	NANCY	Married William I. Sale	Book 1,	222
1805,	BROOKE,	PHILIP	Married Jane, daughter of Samuel Mullins	D 36,	466
1827, Dec. 17	BROOKE,	PHILIP	Married Harriet Croxton	Book 1,	243
1853, Dec. 28	BROOKE,	RICHARD	Married Martha Ann Davis	Book 1,	264
1689,	BROOKE,	ROBERT	Married Catharine, daughter of Humphrey Booth	D 8,	49
1758,	BROOKE,	ROBERT	Married Mary, daughter of William Fauntleroy	D 28,	171
1852, Dec. 20	BROOKE,	ROBERT	Married Mildred C. Brizendine	Book 1,	263
1870, Aug. 25	BROOKE,	ROSA L.	Married James K. F. Taylor	Book 1,	26
1803,	BROOKE,	SALLY	Daughter of Mary, married James ? Micou	W 17,	451
1769,	BROOKE,	THOMAS	Married Elizabeth relict of John Wiley & sister of Tho. Clark	D 30,	285
1855, Oct. 29	BROOKE,	THOMAS H.	Married Eliza H. Munday	Book 1,	3
1728,	BROOKE,	WILLIAM	Married sister of Samuel Jones	D 19,	7
1807, Jun. 30	BROOKE,	WM. THORNTON	Married Maria Whitney Baylor	Book 1,	224
1814, Oct. 19	BROOKE,	WILLIAM	Married Jenny Rose	Book 1,	230
1871, Dec. 14	BROOKE,	WILLIAM W.	Married Martha T. Duff	Book 1,	29
1877, Mar. 31	BROOKE,	WILLIAM	Married Nancy Campbell	Book 1,	45
1853, Mar. 28	BROOKE,	WILLIS	Married Mrs. Mary A. Dix	Book 1,	264
1882, Aug. 23	BROOKS,	ALBERTA	Married Benton P. Andrews	Book 1,	66
1880, Apr. 4	BROOKS,	ALEXANDER O.	Married Emma Crow	Book 1,	55
1878, Nov. 10	BROOKS,	ALFRED	Married Sophronia J. Hundley	Book 1,	49
1893, Jan. 12	BROOKS,	ALPHONZO	Married Mary Smith	Book 1,	111
1880, Dec. 23	BROOKS,	AMANDA	Married Edwin E. Brooks	Book 1,	57
1821, Dec. 19	BROOKS,	ANN	Married Sale Davis	Book 1,	238
1844, Aug. 7	BROOKS,	ANN	Married Kemp Davis	Book 1,	257
1855, May 26	BROOKS,	ANN	Married Robert Jeffries	Book 1,	3
1758,	BROOKS,	ANNA	Daughter of Peter, married John Cheyney	W 11,	333
1817, Jan. 20	BROOKS,	AUSTIN	Married Mary Ann Bray	Book 1,	233
1753,	BROOKS,	?	Married Ann, daughter of John Vass	W 10,	49

					Book	Page
1827, Jan. 3	BROOKS,	BARBARA	Married Reuben Taylor		Book 1,	244
1813, Jan. 4	BROOKS,	BETSEY	Married Griffing Chamberlayne		Book 1,	229
1837, Nov. 30	BROOKS,	BEVERLEY	Married Lucy Ann Atkins		Book 1,	252
1816, Dec. 16	BROOKS,	CATHARINE	Married Othneil. Davis		Book 1,	232
1849, Jan. 2	BROOCKES,	CATHARINE	Married Sterling Birch		Book 1,	261
1870, May 10	BROOKS,	CATHARINE	Married John H. Smither		Book 1,	25
1861, Jan. 25	BROOKS,	CHARLES H.	Married Frances A. Taylor		Book 1,	10
1867, Nov. 5	BROOKS,	COLUMBIA	Married Ezra C. Atkins King & Queen Co.		Book 1,	18
1812, Apr. 20	BROOKS,	DABNEY	Married Caty Webb		Book 1,	228
1838, Jan. 15	BROOKS,	DABNEY	Married Louisa Jeffries		Book 1,	253
1850, Jan. 21	BROOKS,	DABNEY	Married Sarah Broach		Book 1,	262
1866, Nov. 18	BROOKS,	DOROTHEA	Married George Verlander		Book 1,	15
1836, Dec. 19	BROOKS,	EDMUND	Married Catharine Dunn		Book 1,	252
1868, Jan. 2	BROOKS,	EDWARD	Married Emeline Crow		Book 1,	20
1883, Oct. 16	BROOKS,	EDWARD F.	Married Catharine Acres		Book 1,	73
1846, Jan. 19	BROOKS,	ELIZA	Married George W. Brooks		Book 1,	258
1804, Apr. 16	BROOKS,	ELIZABETH	Married John Cauthorn		Book 1,	222
1874, Nov. 5	BROOKS,	ELIZABETH F.	Married Ruffin Clarke		Book 1,	37
1879, Mar. 20	BROOKS,	ELLIS	Married Theiza F. Taylor		Book 1,	51
1805, Jan. 17	BROOKS,	FRANCES	Married Lewis Seward		Book 1,	223
1846, Jan. 19	BROOKS,	GEORGE W.	Married Eliza Brooks		Book 1,	258
1872, Jan. 10	BROOKS,	GEORGE T.	Married Frances A. Shearwood		Book 1,	30
1874, Jan. 15	BROOKS,	GEORGE	Married Dorothea A. Dunn		Book 1,	35
1897, Dec. 9	BROOKS,	GEORGE W.	Married O. L. Whitaker		Book 1,	126
1898, Jan. 26	BROOKS,	GEORGE W.	Married Nannie B. Taylor		Book 1,	128
1833, Jun. 4	BROOKS,	HANNAH	Married Benjamin Blake		Book 1,	249
1881, Dec. 22	BROOKS,	HENRY E.	Married Lily H. Beazley		Book 1,	62
1898, Aug. 4	BROOKS,	H. E.	Married L. K. Dyke		Book 1,	129
1891, Feb. 4	BROOKS,	IDA E.	Married Elzer Fogg		Book 1,	106
1755,	BROOKS,	ISAAC	Married Mary, daughter of Richard Williams		W 10,	39
1860, Jan. 8	BROOKS,	ISABELLA	Married Robert Rose		Book 1,	8

				Book	Page
1873, Dec. 11	BROOKS,	IVERSON J.	Married Louisa M. Carter	Book 1,	35
1829, Oct. 20	BROOKS,	JAMES	Married Frances Davis	Book 1,	246
1841, Dec. 18	BROOKS,	JAMES S.	Married Frances Broach	Book 1,	255
1872, Sep. 26	BROOKS,	JAMES A.	Married Maria Elliott	Book 1,	31
1884, Jun. 26	BROOKS,	JAMES W.	Married Rosa L. Taylor	Book 1,	77
1898, May 18	BROOKS,	JAMES A.	Married M. A. Thompson	Book 1,	133
1882, Jan. 24	BROOKS,	JENNIE	Married Theodore Williams, King & Queen Co.	Book 1,	63
1827, Dec. 26	BROOKS,	JOHN	Married Lucy Brooks	Book 1,	243
1865, Dec. 20	BROOKS,	JOHN R.	Married Martha Brooks	Book 1,	14
1869, Aug. 1	BROOKS,	JOHN F.	Married Mary E. Armstrong	Book 1,	23
1874, Aug. 3	BROOKS,	JOHN H.	Married Sarah A. Williams	Book 1,	37
1882, Mar. 30	BROOKS,	JOHN H.	Married Ella Bareford	Book 1,	64
1891, Jun. 7	BROOKS,	JOE	Married Jane Bennett	Book 1,	107
1874, Dec. 28	BROOKS,	JOSEPH	Married Winny Kidd	Book 1,	38
1891, Dec. 31	BROOKS,	JOSEPH A.	Married Lucy A. Shackleford	Book 1,	108
1827, Apr. 12	BROOKS,	KEZIAH	Married William Broocks	Book 1,	243
1894, Dec. 27	BROOKS,	LALLY	Married M. E. Longest	Book 1,	116
1828, Apr. 24	BROOKS,	LARKIN	Married Manerva Brooks	Book 1,	245
1821, Dec. 12	BROOKS,	LEWIS D.	Married Fanny Griggs	Book 1,	238
1827, Nov. 5	BROOKS,	LEWIS D.	Married Sally Rose	Book 1,	243
1892, Jun. 29	BROOKS,	LEWIS L.	Married Mattie A. Davis	Book 1,	109
1826, Nov. 28	BROOKS,	LIDDY	Married Henry W. Langford	Book 1,	242
1883, Jan. 10	BROOKS,	LISTON	Married Sarah F. Brooks	Book 1,	69
1877, Dec. 20	BROOKS,	LOUISA	Married Thomas R. Taylor	Book 1,	46
1842, Jan. 5	BROOKS,	LOWRY	Married Susan Hodges	Book 1,	256
1870, Dec. 22	BROOKS,	LUCINDA P.	Married Lewis E. Dix	Book 1,	27
1827, Dec. 26	BROOKS,	LUCY	Married John Brooks	Book 1,	243
1876, Jun. 7	BROOKS,	LUCY G.	Married George William Catlett	Book 1,	42
1894, Jan. 4	BROOKS,	LUCY N.	Married H. E. Boughan	Book 1,	113
1841, Jan. 18	BROOKS,	MAJOR	Married Ann A. Greenwood	Book 1,	255
1828, Apr. 24	BROOKS,	MANERVA	Married Larkin Brooks	Book 1,	245

				Book	Page
1842, Feb. 7	BROOKS,	MARTHA	Married Joseph Durham.	Book 1,	256
1865, Dec. 20	BROOKS,	MARTHA	Married John R. Brooks	Book 1,	14
1848, Dec. 21	BROOKS,	MARY	Married Robert Williamson	Book 1,	260
1880, Dec. 30	BROOKS,	MARY	Married Charles Patterson	Book 1,	58
1844, Mar. 21	BROOKS,	MATILDA A.	Married Lewis Breedlove	Book 1,	257
1866, Dec. 9	BROOKS,	MILDRED	Married Henry C. Tune	Book 1,	15
1805, Jun. 17	BROOKS,	NANCY	Married Lewis Boughan	Book 1,	222
1816, Apr. 7	BROOKS,	NANCY	Married William Davis	Book 1,	233
1860, Jan. 4	BROOKS,	PEGGY	Married John Goode	Book 1,	8
1721,	BROOKS,	PETER	Married Ann Stephens, widow, mother of Samuel	D 17,	14
1808, Apr. 18	BROOKS,	PETER	Married Patsy Cauthorn	Book 1,	224
1794,	BROOKS,	PHILIP	Married Jane, daughter of Samuel Mullins	D 34,	48
1889, Nov. 7	BROOKS,	PHILIP H.	Married Sarah Alice Jones	Book 1,	101
1859, Dec. 20	BROOKS,	POLLY	Married Charles H. Schools	Book 1,	8
1806, Jan. 1	BROOKS,	REUBEN	Married Elizabeth Croxton	Book 1,	222
1838, Jan. 2	BROOKS,	REUBEN	Married Catharine Howe	Book 1,	253
1893, Mar. 23	BROOKS,	RICHARD	Married Virginia Dix	Book 1,	111
1845, Dec. 29	BROOKS,	ROBERTA	Married Richard Grimes	Book 1,	258
1845, Jul. 8	BROOKES,	ROBERT	Married Mary E. Delano	Book 1,	258
1877, Jun. 20	BROOKS,	ROBERT P.	Married Henrietta Foreacres	Book 1,	45
1876, Aug. 16	BROOKS,	ROSA	Married James W. Davis	Book 1,	42
1888, Oct. 14	BROOKS,	ROSSER	Married Evelyn Q. Nunn	Book 1,	96
1867, Feb. 14	BROOKS,	SARAH E.	Married Robert Henry Dunn	Book 1,	17
1883, Jan 10	BROOKS,	SARAH F.	Married Liston Brooks	Book 1,	69
1840, Sep. 21	BROOKS,	S. M.	Married Rosa Hayes	Book 1,	254
1844, Mar. 25	BROOKS,	SHEARWOOD	Married Lucy Clarke	Book 1,	257
1807, Jan. 2	BROOKS,	SPENCER	Married Fannie Allen	Book 1,	224
1894, Jul. 5	BROOKS,	STAPLETON	Married F. E. Harmon	Book 1,	114
1870, Dec. 22	BROOKS,	SUSAN M.	Married Travis Prince	Book 1,	27
1846, Feb. 4	BROOKS,	THOMAS	Married Rachel Newbill	Book 1,	258
1849, Mar. 27	BROOKS,	WASHINGTON	Married Bertha C. Fisher	Book 1,	261

				Book	Page
1851, Apr. 15	BROOKS,	WASHINGTON	Married Nancy Jeffries	Book 1,	262
1827, Apr. 12	BROOKS,	WILLIAM	Married Keziah Broocks	Bo>k 1,	243
1848, Mar. 8	BROOKS,	WILLIAM	Married Mary Goode	Book 1,	260
1865, Dec. 30	BROOKS,	WILLIAM E.	Married Emily F. Dunn	Book 1,	14
1828, Feb. 11	BROOKS,	WILLIS	Married Elizabeth Jones	Book 1,	245
1835,	BROOKS,	WILLIS	Married Elizabeth, daughter of Joseph & Nancy Jones	D 44,	441
1871, Dec. 26	BROOKS,	WILLIS, JR.	Married Brinda Troy Carter	Book 1,	30
1899, Mar. 16	BROOKS,	W. A.	Married Rosie A. Davis	Book 1,	132
1741,	BROOKING,	ROBERT	King & Queen Co. married Frances, daughter of Thomas Vivion of King George Co.	D 22,	235
1804, May 21	BROOKING,	ROBERT	Married Lucy Throckmorton	Book 1,	222
1805, Jan. 20	BROOKING,	ROBERT E.	Married Judith Throckmorton	Book 1,	222
1722,	BROWN,	ANN	Daughter of Daniel, married Samuel Farguson	D 13,	153
1832, May 1	BROWN,	BARNETT	Married Martha Jeffries	Book 1,	248
1809, Aug. 26	BROWN,	BASIL	Married Lucy Bohannon	Book 1,	225
1788,	BROWN,	BENNETT	King William Co. married Mary, daughter of Mrs. Sarah Campbell	W 14,	171
1798,	BROWN,	?	Married Mary, daughter of Leonard & Sarah Hill	W 15,	467
1857, Mar. 21	BROWN,	BETTY	Married Oswald Hardy Dyke	Book 1,	4
1894, Apr. 4	BROWN,	BETTIE F.	Married William B. Kay	Book 1,	114
1750,	BROWN,	CATHARINE	Daughter of Charles, married William Tiller	D 25,	270
1857, Dec. 23	BROWN,	CATHARINE K.	Married George Washington Coleman	Book 1,	6
1807, Dec. 31	BROWN,	CATY	Married Richard Jones	Book 1,	224
1688,	BROWN,	CHARLES	Married Susanna Berry	O 1,	63
1868, Oct. 8	BROWN,	CHARLES E.	Married Mary F. Gouldman	Book 1,	21
1802,	BROWN,	DANIEL	Married Betsey Faver, daughter of Thomas Faver	W 16,	121
1841, Jan. 12	BROWN,	EDWARD B.	Married Catharine Coghill	Book 1,	255
1867, Jan. 27	BROWN,	ELIJAH	Married Judith Lewis	Book 1,	16
1834, Jul. 7	BROWN,	ELIZA	Married Daniel Fisher	Book 1,	250
1835,	BROWN,	ELIZA	Married David Fisher	D 45,	20
1684,	BROWN,	ELIZABETH	Relict of William, married Evan Morgan	O 1,	53
1686,	BROWN,	ELIZABETH	Mother of William, married James Tayler	D 7,	323

				Book	Page
1747,	BROWN,	ELIZABETH	Daughter of Joseph, married James Fisher of Amelia Co.	D 24,	165
1819, Oct. 23	BROWN,	ELIZABETH	Married Thomas Haynes	Book 1,	235
1844, Mar. 18	BROWN,	FRANCES	Married Henry Watts	Book 1,	257
1821, Dec. 27	BROWN,	HARRIET	Married Billington Dunn	Book 1,	238
1804, Dec. 17	BROWN,	HENRY	Married Mary Brown	Book 1,	222
1865, Apr. 19	BROWN,	JAMES M.	Married Annie M. Eubank, widow	Book 1,	13
1867, Dec. 19	BROWN,	JAMES L.	Married Ann E. Ingram	Book 1,	19
1848, Mar. 29	BROWN,	JANE	Married Robert C. Watts	Book 1,	260
1785,	BROWN,	JOHN	Married Mary, daughter of Henry Kidd	W 15,	23
1875, Dec. 28	BROWN,	JOHN	Married Rachel Ann Covington	Book 1,	40
1886, Nov. 11	BROWN,	JOHN H.	Married Mary E. L. Hayes	Book 1,	89
1891, Jun. 11	BROWN,	J. P.	Married T. A. Coghill	Book 1,	107
1820, Dec. 19	BROWN,	JOSEPH B.	Married Elizabeth S. Munday	Book 1,	237
1834, Dec. 15	BROWN,	JULIA C.	Married Alexander Mitchell	Book 1,	250
1835,	BROWN,	JULIA	Daughter of Daniel, married Alexander Mitchell	D 45,	19
1812, May 12	BROWN,	LEWIS	Married Catharine Pitts	Book 1,	228
1898, Dec. 15	BROWN,	L. K.	Married John R. Elliott	Book 1,	130
1833, Nov. 29	BROWN,	LORENZO D.	Married Agnes W. Southall	Book 1,	249
1820, Mar. 19	BROWN,	MARIA J.	Married Larkin Noel	Book 1,	237
1835,	BROWN,	MARIA	Married Larkin Noel	D 45,	19
1885, Feb. 12	BROWN,	MARTHA E.	Married James A. Garrett	Book 1,	81
1689,	BROWN,	MARY	Married John Armistead	O 2,	187
1696,	BROWN,	MARY	Daughter of William & Elizabeth married James Landrum	D 9,	52
1722,	BROWN,	MARY	Daughter of Buckingham, married John Clements	W 5,	350
1729,	BROWN,	MARY	Widow of Charles, married James Crosby	D 17, / D 19,	49 / 27
1804, Nov. 19	BROWN,	MARY H.	Married William Todd	Book 1,	222
1804, Dec. 17	BROWN,	MARY	Married Henry Brown	Book 1,	222
1862, Feb. 28	BROWN,	MARY SUSAN	Married George D. Coates	Book 1,	11
1825, May 21	BROWN,	MATILDA	Married James Powers	Book 1,	242
1817, Sep. 7	BROWN,	MERRIDAY	Married Frances Gouldman Davis	Book 1,	233
1899, Oct. 23	BROWN,	M. W.	Married H. B. Williams	Book 1,	134

				Book	Page
1813, Nov. 12	BROWN,	NANCY	Married Edmund Munday	Book 1,	229
1898, Oct. 19	BROWN,	PAUL	Married Sarah Jackson	Book 1,	130
1809, May 22	BROWN,	POLLY	Married Peter Dishman	Book 1,	225
1842, May 12	BROWN,	PRISCILLA	Married Dr. John M. Garnett	Book 1,	256
1806,	BROWN,	SARAH	Daughter of Bennett, married William Fleet	O 38,	481
1807,	BROWN,	SARAH	Daughter of Mary Brown, married William Fleet	W 17,	99
1829, Jul. 23	BROWN,	SARAH	Married Robert T. Gwathmey	Book 1,	246
1832,	BROWN,	SARAH	Daughter of Charles, married Robert T. Gwathmey	D 43,	504
1832, Apr. 18	BROWN,	SARAH	Married Thomas F. Dunn	Book 1,	248
1867, Mar. 5	BROWN,	SARAH	Married Ryburn A. Shackelford	Book 1,	17
1868, Feb. 18	BROWN,	SARAH	Married Sally E. Munday	Book 1,	20
1834, Dec. 15	BROWN,	SUSAN M.	Married Edward Powers	Book 1,	250
1835,	BROWN,	SUSAN	Married Edward Powers	D 45,	19
1659,	BROWN,	URSULA	Accomac Co. widow of John Brown, married Alexander Fleming	D 2,	174
1867,	BROWN,	VERNANGUS	Married Edward D. Munday	Book 1,	18
1688,	BROWN,	WILLIAM	Married Frances, daughter of William Moss	O 2,	115
1693,	BROWN,	WILLIAM	Married Mary, Daughter of Valentine Allen	O 1,	108
1693,	BROWN,	WILLIAM	Married Mary, sister & coheir of Samuel Allen	O 1,	108
1708,	BROWN,	WILLIAM	Married Jane, sister of Thomas Meriwether	D & C 13,	185
1722,	BROWN,	WILLIAM	Married Margaret, daughter of Thomas Clouson	D 17,	36
1888, Oct. 9	BROWN,	WILLIAM A.	Married Wirginia B. Pilkington	Book 1,	96
1898, Feb. 16	BROWN,	JAMES	Married E. A. Saunders	Book 1,	128
1720,	BRYANT,	THOMAS	Married Susanna, relict of John Boughan	W 4,	194
1678,	BRYCE	BRIDGETT	Daughter of Capt. George Bryce, married Christopher Pridum	D 6,	70
1807,	BUCKNER,	FRANCIS	Married Martha, daughter of James Upshaw Jr.,	O 39,	138
1718,	BUNBERRY,	MARY	Daughter of Robert, married Richard Day	D&W 15,	261
1870, Dec. 15	BUNDAY,	ELIZA H.	Married James H. Clarke	Book 1,	26
1830, Dec. 20	BUNDAY,	MARTHA	Married William Davis	Book 1,	247
1825,	BUNDAY,	RYBURN	Married daughter of Sarah Chandler	D 41,	338
1873, Sep. 15	BURCH,	ELLA	Married Thomas H. Parson	Book 1,	34
1869, Jun. 10	BURCH,	LELIA	Married Judson Davis	Book 1,	23

Date	Surname	Given Name	Description	Book	Page
1855, Jul. 7	BURCH,	LUCINDA	Married J. J Holland	Book 1,	266
1887, Dec. 4	BURCH,	MATTIE C.	Married Castein Atkins	Book 1,	93
1894, Dec. 6	BURCH,	M. E.	Married A. S. Harper	Book 1,	115
1798,	BURKE,	BARBARA	Daughter of Richard, married John Chenault	W 16,	88
1812, Apr. 20	BURKE,	BETSEY	Married William Beazley	Book 1,	228
1868, Jul. 15	BURKE,	BETTY W.	Married James M. Jesse	Book 1,	20
1807,	BURKE,	MARY	Daughter of Richard, married Richard Meador	D 37,	264
1856, Jun. 12	BURKE,	MARY SUSAN	Married Robert G. Haile	Book 1,	4
1822, Jun. 11	BURKE,	NANCY	Married Tandy Dix	Book 1,	239
1824, Aug. 16	BURKE,	POLLY	Married Vernon Eskridge	Book 1,	241
1825,	BURKE,	POLLY	Daughter of Martin Burke, married Vernon Eskridge	D 41,	464
1815, Dec. 20	BURK,	SUSANNA	Married Mark Anthony	Book 1,	231
1699,	BURKETT,	THOMAS	Married Jane, Executrix of John Powell	D&W 10,	14
1874, Apr. 10	BURNETT,	BETTY	Married John W. Clarke	Book 1,	36
1810, Jul. 12	BURNETT,	DELPHIA	Married John Gibson	Book 1,	226
1806, Jul. 20	BURNETT,	JOSEPH	Married Winifred Croxton	Book 1,	223
1823, Aug. 13	BURNETT,	JULIA	Married Thomas Jones	Book 1,	240
1871, Feb. 9	BURNETT,	MARTHA	Married Spencer Clarke	Book 1,	28
1814, Dec. 21	BURNETT,	PATSEY	Married Curtis Ball	Book 1,	230
1827,	BURNETT,	RICHARD	Married Elizabeth, daughter of William Ball	D 42,	314
1709,	BURNETT,	SARAH	Daughter of Lucretia, married Thomas Bell	D&C 13,	156, 255
1843, Sep. 18	BURT,	CORNELIA E.	Married Edward W. West	Book 1,	257
1833,	BURTON,	JAMES	Married Elizabeth Yarrington	D 44,	216
1816, Dec. 17	BURWELL,	ANN ELIZABETH	Married William C. Latane	Book 1,	232
1811, Nov. 18	BUSH,	ALICE	Married Thomas Williams	Book 1,	227
1829,	BUSH,	ALICE	Daughter of John Bush, married Thomas Williams	D 43,	36
1758,	BUSH,	BIBBY	His widow married Stephen Neale	O 22,	255
1829, Jun. 19	BUSH,	CORDELIA	Married Richard Stone	Book 1,	246
1829,	BUSH,	CORDELIA	Daughter of John Bush, married Richard Stone	D 43,	36
1830,	BUSH,	ELIZA	Married Larkin Hundley	D 43,	308
1817, Apr. 7	BUSH,	ELIZABETH	Married Lawrence P. Bird	Book 1,	233

				Book		Page
1829,	BUSH,	FANNY	Married John Johnson	D	43,	37
1828, Nov. 8	BUSH,	FRANCES	Married John Johnson	Book 1,		245
1836,	BUSH,	IZARD B.	Married Mary B. Sullivan dau. of Obadiah Sullivan	D	45,	128
1816, Mar. 23	BUSH,	JANE	Married Charles Clondas	Book 1,		232
1830,	BUSH,	JANE	Married Charles Clondas	D	43,	306
1832,	BUSH,	JANE	Married Charles Clondas	D	47,	367
1721,	BUSH,	JOHN	Married Sarah, daughter of John Smith	D	17,	3
1741,	BUSH,	JOHN	Married Susannah, daughter of John Cheyney	O	12,	219
1799,	BUSH,	MARGARET	Married John Davis	O	35,	156
1852, Dec. 30	BUSH,	MARY	Married Edward Tate	Book 1,		263
1809, Mar. 20	BUSH,	MOLLY	Married Philip Clarke	Book 1,		225
1811, Aug. 19	BUSH,	PATSY	Married John Clark	Book 1,		227
1810, Nov. 20	BUSH,	POLLY	Married Larkin Clarke	Book 1,		226
1848, Dec. 21	BUSH,	POLLY	Married Samuel Williamson	Book 1,		260
1706,	BUSH,	RICHARD	Married Elizabeth, daughter of John Beby	D&C 12,		234
1835,	BUSH,	SANDY	Married Peggy, daughter of Elizabeth Hawes	D	44,	449
1807, Sep. 1	BUSH,	SUSANNA	Married Jesse Fearn Clarke	Book 1,		224
1765,	BUSHROD,	ANN	Daughter of William Dangerfield, married William Meredith	D	30,	35
1724,	BUTCHER,	ELIZABETH	Married Andrew Scrimshaw	D	17,	365
1744,	BUTCHER,	JOANNA	Sister of Christopher, married Edward Cason, Spottsylvania Co.	D	23,	190
1691,	BUTCHER,	JOHN	Married Mary Tap	O	2,	307
1691,	BUTCHER,	JOHN	Married Mary, relict of Walter Lowick	O	2,	321
1744,	BUTCHER,	SARAH	Sister of Christopher, married George Gibson, Caroline Co.	D	23,	244
1823, Dec. 2	BUTLER,	CATHARINE	Married Warner Lewis	Book 1,		240
1700,	BUTLER,	JOHN	Married Jane Jackson, daughter of Robert Gullocke	D&W 11,		72
1843,	BUTLER,	LUCY	Daughter of Ann S. Butler, married William O. Harris	W	24,	219
1674,	BUTTON,	JANE	Widow of Thomas, married Thomas Gordon	D	5,	363
1718,	BUTTON	JOHN	Clerk of Middlesex Co. married Elizabeth, relict of Joseph Bridger Mariner of Surry Co.	D	16,	37
1666,	BUTTON,	THOMAS	Married Jane, Executrix of John Gillet	D	3,	59
1835, Jan. 20	BYRD,	JOHN	Married Elizabeth Pruitt	Book 1,		251
1893, Jul. 23	BYRD,	M. B.	Married Effie Peterson	Book 1,		111

				Book	Page
1823, Dec. 19	BYRD,	LOUISA	Married Brooking Carter	Book 1,	240
1771,	BYROM,	ANN	Daughter of James, married Archer West of Chesterfield Co.	D 30,	461
1728,	BYROM,	ELINOR	Married John Wimpee	W 8,	240
1717,	BYROM,	FRANCES	Relict of Henry,.married Alexander Somerville	W 3,	38
1702,	BYROM,	HENRY	Married Frances, daughter of Mary Mills	D&W 11,	42
1709,	BYROM,	HENRY	Married Frances, daughter of Robert Mills	D&C 13,	290

C

				Book	Page
1820, Jul. 13	CALLIS,	CATHARINE	Married Theodrick Garrett	Book 1,	237
1832, Jul. 26	CALLIS,	HANNAH	Married James M. Smither	Book 1,	249
1835,	CALLIS	HANNAH	Married James Smither	D 45,	122
1832, Mar. 19	CALLIS,	ROBERT H.	Married Elizabeth Faver	Book 1,	248
1835, Oct. 14	CALLIS,	ROBERT H.	Married Margaret Tombs	Book 1,	251
1857,	CALLIS,	ROBERT	Married Margaret, daughter of Gabriel Toombs	W 27,	723
1825,	CALLIS,	RICHARD	Married Sally, daughter of Lemuel & Susanna Crittenden	D 41,	413
1775,	CAMM,	ANN	Daughter of John, married James Booker	W 13,	30
1886, Nov. 3	CAMMACK,	DOVELL M.	Married Polly S. Bayliss	Book 1,	88
1893, Jan. 28	CAMMACK,	H. L.	Married W. A. Gresham	Book 1,	111
1854, Mar. 3	CAMMACK,	JOSEPH J.	Married Frances Ann Jones	Book 1,	2
1710,	CAMMACK,	MARGARET	Daughter of Margaret, married Paul Micou	W 3, Richmond Co.	234
1886, Jun. 15	CAMMACK,	SARAH B.	Married Reginald Potts, Minister of Lancaster Co.	Book 1,	87
1696,	CAMMILL,	JOHN	Married Sarah, daughter of John Killman	D 9,	74
1691,	CAMMILL,	PATRICK	Married Sarah, orphan of John Kilman	O 2,	289
1886, Dec. 13	CAMPBELL,	EMMA	Married W. E. Wright	Book 1,	89
1812, Dec. 21	CAMPBELL,	GEORGE	Married Priscilla Doggins	Book 1,	228
1873, Dec. 25	CAMPBELL,	HARRIET	Married Manhen Jackson	Book 1,	35
1891, Dec. 23	CAMPBELL,	JANETTA R.	Married Alfred Bagby, Jr. Columbia, S. C.	Book 1,	108
1805, Mar. 18	CAMPBELL,	LUCY	Married James Davis	Book 1,	222
1897, Dec. 9	CAMPBELL,	MAGGIE	Married James Kendall	Book 1,	126
1788,	CAMPBELL,	MARY	Daughter of Sarah, married Bennett Brown	W 14,	71
1806, Dec. 21	CAMPBELL,	MARY ANN	Married James Roy	Book 1,	223
1882, Jan. 5	CAMPBELL,	MARY E.	Married Justin L. Derieux	Book 1,	63
1877, Mar. 31	CAMPBELL,	NANCY	Married William Brooke	Book 1,	45
1816, Dec. 7	CAMPBELL,	PETER	Married Mary Hundley	Book 1,	232
1881, Feb. 10	CAMPBELL,	PETER T.	Married Milly A. Boughan	Book 1,	59
1819, Dec. 27	CAMPBELL,	PRISCILLA	Married George Davis	Book 1,	235
1828,	CAMPBELL,	PRISCILLA	Widow of George Campbell, married George Davis	D 42,	382
1897, Jun. 17	CAMPBELL,	P. C.	Married R. G. Neale	Book 1,	25

				Book	Page
1818, Dec. 24	CAMPBELL,	REUBEN	Married Fanny Gibson	Book 1,	234
1798,	CAMPBELL,	SARAH	Formerly wife of Leonard Hill	W 15,	465
1867, Dec. 3	CAMPBELL,	WILLIAM	Married Jannett R. Latane	Book 1,	18
1870, Oct. 26	CANNON,	JAMES G.	Married Virgie Haile	Book 1,	26
1884, Jun. 25	CANNON,	JAMES G.	Married Lucy E. Haile	Book 1,	77
1825, Nov. 15	CAPRON,	JOHN	Married Ann E. Baylor	Book 1,	241
1693,	CARDEN,	JOHN	Married Ann Parker	O 1,	235
1889, Jun. 6	CARLTON,	ANNIE M.	Married Silas Ewell	Book 1,	100
1827, Dec. 26	CARLTON,	ELIZABETH	Married John Ursery	Book 1,	244
1897, Jun. 9	CARLTON,	ELLA M.	Married Robert H. Stubbs Gloucester Co.	Book 1,	125
1899, Nov. 9	CARLTON,	E. M.	Married R. E. Lumpkin	Book 1,	134
1881, Dec. 27	CARLTON,	ETTA	Married James W. Evans	Book 1,	62
1884, Sep. 25	CARLTON,	GARRETT	Married Mrs. Mary T. Cauthorn	Book 1,	78
1872, Mar. 21	CARLTON,	HENRY L.	Married Virginia A. Williams	Book 1,	30
1893, Sep. 12	CARLTON,	H. L.	Married S. C. Parron	Book 1,	112
1866, Dec. 25	CARLTON,	JOHN A.	Married Eliza Taff	Book 1,	16
1846, Mar. 11	CARLTON,	LEWIS	Married Jane Longest, widow	Book 1,	258
1863, Dec. 31	CARLTON,	LEWIS J.	Married Catharine W. Baskitt	Book 1,	12
1837, Nov. 17	CARLTON,	SARAH A.	Married William D. Clarke	Book 1,	252
1866, Sep. 20	CARLTON,	THEODORE	Married Virginia Ann Dunn	Book 1,	15
1847, Nov. 23	CARLTON,	THOMAS	Married Martha Ball	Book 1,	259
1883, Aug. 30	CARLTON,	VIRGINIA C.	Married James M. Woodlin Gloucester Co	Book 1,	72
1892, Dec. 15	CARLTON,	WILLIAM G.	Married Laura A. Greenwood	Book 1,	110
1771,	CARNAL,	JOHN	Married Sarah, daughter of Thomas Hipkins	W 12,	421
1726,	CARNELL,	WILLIAM	Married Mary Gresham	O 9,	196
1881, Mar. 22	CARNEALE,	ADALINE	Married Julius F. Thomas	Book 1,	59
1876, Oct. 22	CARNEALE,	AMANDA	Married John L. Stevens	Book 1,	43
1891, Jul. 29	CARNEALE,	A. R.	Married Ella G. Taylor	Book 1,	107
1888, Mar. 29	CARNEALE,	C. A.	Married A. J. Griffin	Book 1,	95
1836, Dec. 5	CARNEALE,	ELIZABETH	Married Joel Halbert	Book 1,	252
1874, Mar. 12	CARNEALE,	FANNY	Married Delaware Stokes	Book 1,	36

				Book	Page
1877, Jan. 25	CARNEALE,	HOWARD B.	Married Ann E. Munday	Book 1,	44
1832, Dec. 19	CARNEALE,	JAMES	Married Mary Noel	Book 1,	248
1888, Oct. 4	CARNEALE,	JOHN	Married Hausie Munday	Book 1,	96
1894, Dec. 27	CARNEALE,	J. R.	Married L. T. Schools	Book 1,	116
1861, Mar. 7	CARNEALE,	LELAND T.	Married Virginia Ann Faulconer	Book 1,	10
1881, Jan. 13	CARNEALE,	MARY S.	Married Lewis E. Schools	Book 1,	58
1836, Dec. 28	CARNEALE,	THOMAS	Married Elizabeth Dunn	Book 1,	252
1874, Feb. 27	CARNEALE,	THOMAS	Married Annie Schools	Book 1,	36
1887, Jul. 5	CARNEALE,	VIRGIE C.	Married Albert R. Munday	Book 1,	92
1836, Nov. 23	CARR,	CHARLES	Married Alice Jasper	Book 1,	252
1810, Oct. 16	CARROLL,	BEVERLEY	Married Sally Hundley	Book 1,	226
1732,	CARROLL,	EDMUND	Married Mary, daughter of John Boulware	O. 8,	286
1711,	CARROLL,	WILLIAM	Married Rosamond, relict of William Covington	Land Trials	173
1732,	CARROLL,	WILLIAM	Married Rosamond, Executrix of William Covington	O 8,	310
1853, Nov. 7	CARTER,	ADALINE	Married Charles H. Greer	Book 1,	3
1847, Dec. 18	CARTER,	ARENA	Married Arthur I. Sale	Book 1,	259
1875, Dec. 28	CARTER,	BENJAMIN F.	Married Elizabeth Carter	Book 1,	38
1881, Feb. 3	CARTER,	BETTIE	Married Emund Lane	Book 1,	58
1871, Dec. 19	CARTER,	BROOKING	Married Louisa Byrd	Book 1,	240
1823, May. 19	CARTER,	CATHARINE	Married Louisa Byrd	Book 1,	240
1870, May 26	CARTER,	CATHARINE	Married James W. Carter	Book 1,	26
1833, Dec. 13	CARTER,	CHARLES	Married Nancy Miller	Book 1,	249
1874, Dec. 24	CARTER,	CHARLES M.	Married Alice J. Crow	Book 1,	38
1877, Apr. 3	CARTER,	CHARLES H.	Married Edna R. Taylor	Book 1,	45
1848, Feb. 28	CARTER,	CURTIS	Married Fanny A. Taliaferro	Book 1,	260
1874, Dec. 30	CARTER,	DAVID	Married Mrs. Martha Collins	Book 1,	38
1831, Dec. 17	CARTER,	DELIA	Widow, married Landon Carter	Book 1,	248
1852, Jul. 23	CARTER,	ELIZA M.	Married Jonathan Hart	Book 1,	263
1853, Sep. 13	CARTER,	ELIZA A.	Married George W. Price	Book 1,	264
1875, Dec. 28	CARTER,	ELIZABETH	Married Benjamin F. Carter	Book 1,	40
1869, Apr. 29	CARTER,	EMELINE V.	Married Sthreshley Dunn	Book 1,	23

				Book	Page
1806, Jul. 21	CARTER,	JAMES	Married Elizabeth Clarke	Book 1,	223
1815, Apr. 17	CARTER,	JAMES	Married Nancy Tucker	Book 1,	231
1852, Feb. 11	CARTER,	JAMES H.	Married Elizabeth D. Tucker	Book 1,	263
1870, May 26	CARTER,	JAMES W.	Married Catharine Carter	Book 1,	26
1883, Dec. 27	CARTER,	JAMES W.	Married Sarah A. Halbert	Book 1,	74
1870, Dec. 22	CARTER,	JANE	Married Samuel Parker	Book 1,	27
1889, Dec. 7	CARTER,	J. C.	Married E. B. Samuel	Book 1,	130
1898, Jan. 6	CARTER,	J. H.	Married Myrtle Williams	Book 1,	128
1805, Jul. 9	CARTER,	JOHN	Married Lucy Jones	Book 1,	222
1897, Feb. 17	CARTER,	JOHN	Married Virginia Long	Book 1,	124
1831, Dec. 17	CARTER,	LANDON	Married Delia Carter, widow	Book 1,	248
1873, Dec. 11	CARTER,	LOUISA M.	Married Iverson J. Brooks	Book 1,	35
1889, Jan. 3	CARTER,	LUCY	Married William Landrum	Book 1,	99
1817, Jan. 21	CARTER,	MARGARET	Married William Cokeley	Book 1,	233
1850, Dec. 27	CARTER,	MARTHA J.	Married Watkins Harper	Book 1,	262
1701,	CARTER,	MARY	Relict of Richard, married Henry Smith	D&W 10,	95
1898, Dec. 29	CARTER,	J	Married E. M. Hodges	Book 1,	131
1762,	CARTER,	OWEN	Married Sarah, daughter of Bernard Noell	O 24,	96
1848, Feb. 29	CARTER,	RALEIGH D.	Married Sarah P. Sale	Book 1,	260
1858, Aug. 6	CARTER,	RALEIGH D.	Lancaster Co. married Eliza A. Currier	Book 1,	6
1688,	CARTER,	RICHARD	Married Relict of George Coltclough	O 2,	66
1896, Jun. 3	CARTER,	S. J.	Married Lucy Davis	Book 1,	121
1877, Oct. 13	CARTER,	THOMAS	Married Mary Moody	Book 1,	46
1828, Nov. 26	CARTER,	TOWNSEND	Married Martha Southworth	Book 1,	245
1890, Sep. 25	CARTER,	WILLIAM	Married Emma Greenwood	Book 1,	104
1812, Jul. 23	CARTER,	ZACHARIAH	Married Elizabeth Jones	Book 1,	228
1841, Dec. 24	CARTER,	ZACHARIAH	Married Catharine Johnson	Book 1,	255
1843, Dec. 18	CARTER,	ZACHARIAH	Married Martha Jane Tucker	Book 1,	256
1898, Jan. 6	CARTER,	ZACK	Married B. L. Williams	Book 1,	128
1833, Oct. 30	CARTER,	ZEBULON	Married Frances Lumpkin, widow	Book 1,	253
1752,	CARY	HUGH	His grandaughter Ester, married Simon Golding	W 9,	212

Date	Surname	Given Name	Description	Book	Page
				Book	Page
1854, Sep. 14	CASH,	JAMES W.	Married Sarah I. Dishman	Book 1,	3
1894, Nov. 29	CASHELL,	F. H.	Married E. V. Ferry	Book 1,	115
1744,	CASON,	EDWARD	Spottsylvania Co. married Joanna Butcher, sister of Christopher	D 23,	190
1838, Jun. 18	CASON,	MALVINA	Married Otway Rennolds	Book 1,	253
1720,	CASTON,	CARY	Relict of Class Caston, married Henry Purkins	W 3,	208
1715,	CASTON,	CLASS	Married Cary, daughter of John Farguson	W 3,	8
1709,	CATLETT,	ELIZABETH	Married Benjamin Moseley	D&C 13,	261
1876, Jun. 7	CATLETT,	GEORGE W.	Married Lucy G. Brooke	Book 1,	42
1663,	CATLETT,	JOHN	Married Elizabeth, widow of Capt. Francis Slaughter	D 2,	326
1724,	CATLETT,	LAWRENCE	Married Alice, daughter of Francis Thornton	Box 105,	H
1687,	CATLETT,	SARAH	Daughter of John & Elizabeth, married Robert Taliaferro	O 2,	25
1819, Apr. 10	CATLETT,	THOMAS	Married Nancy Toombs	Book 1,	236
1828,	CAUTHORN,	ALICE	Daughter of John, married John T. Purkins	D 43,	255
1832, Feb. 20	CAUTHORN,	ALLEN	Married Elizabeth Harmon	Book 1,	248
1852, Dec. 23	CAUTHORN,	AMANDA F.	Married Jon. A. Sadler	Book 1,	263
1811, Nov. 5	CAUTHORN,	AMOS	Married Fanny Richards	Book 1,	227
1817, Jan. 7	CAUTHORN,	AMOS	Married Polly Fisher	Book 1,	233
1793,	CAUTHORN,	ANN	Sister of Vincent, dau. of Richard, married Thomas Jessie, Middlesex County	D 33,	498
1823, Jan. 11	CAUTHORN,	ANN E.	Married George W. Didlake	Book 1,	240
1840, Jun. 25	CAUTHORN,	ANN	Married Isaac Greenwood	Book 1,	254
1849, Dec. 24	CAUHTORN,	ANNA E.	Married James Bray	Book 1,	261
1831, Apr. 19	CAUHTORN,	CATHARINE	Married Ythel Parry	Book 1,	248
1814, Sep. 19	CAUHTORN,	ELIZABETH	Married William Dillard	Book 1,	230
1840, Oct. 24	CAUHTORN,	ELIZABETH	Married David C. Belfield	Book 1,	254
1841, Mar. 16	CAUHTORN,	ELIZABETH F.	Married Henry B. Scott	Book 1,	255
1845, Apr. 21	CAUTHORN,	E. A.	Married Henry Goode	Book 1,	258
1876, Jan. 6	CAUTHORN,	EMELINE E.	Married Joseph B. Gentry	Book 1,	16
1893, Jul. 26	CAUTHORN,	E. B.	Married R. H. Bagby, King & Queen Co.	Book 1,	112
1847, Jun. 14	CAUTHORN,	ETHELBERT	Married Leah A. Oliver	Book 1,	259
1809, May 19	CAUTHORN,	FRANCES	Married James Cooper	Book 1,	225
1841, Nov. 30	CAUHTORN,	FRANCES	Married William P. Garrett	Book 1,	255

· 49 ·

				Book	Page
1842, Aug. 15	CAUTHORN,	FRANCES C.	Married Robert W. Ferneyhough	Book 1,	256
1856, May 10	CAUTHORN,	FRANCES	Married Taliaferro Birch	Book 1,	4
1804, Dec. 17	CAUTHORN,	GODFREY	Married Harriet Stark	Book 1,	222
1863, Nov. 3	CAUTHORN,	HENRIETTA I.	Married Temple R. Gwathmey	Book 1,	12
1816, Apr. 10	CAUTHORN,	ISAAC	Married Maria Brizendine	Book 1,	232
1860, Dec. 11	CAUTHORN,	ISAAC	Married Eliza Goode	Book 1,	10
1804, Apr. 16	CAUTHORN,	JOHN	Married Elizabeth Brooks	Book 1,	222
1816, Nov. 18	CAUTHORN,	JOHN	Married Ruthy Greenwood	Book 1,	232
1848, Jan. 4	CAUTHORN,	JOHN R.	Married Frances Taylor	Book 1,	260
1851, May 2	CAUTHORN,	JON. I.	Married Dorinda M. Dunn	Book 1,	262
1870, Oct. 26	CAUTHORN,	JOSEPH	Married Susan E. Smith	Book 1,	26
1877, Apr. 10	CAUTHORN,	JULIA	Married Henry C. Jones	Book 1,	45
1833, Sep. 30	CAUTHORN,	KETURAH	Married Kaufmann Gresham	Book 1,	249
1834, Dec. 9	CAUTHORN,	LEAH	Married William Dunn	Book 1,	250
1863, Nov. 5	CAUTHORN,	LEAH A.	Married Reuben B. Boughton	Book 1,	12
1823, May 3	CAUTHORN,	LEROY	Married Marinda Broocke	Book 1,	240
1829,	CAUTHORN,	LEROY	Married Mira, daughter of Isaac Broocks	D 43,	136
1832, Feb. 2	CAUTHORN,	LORENZO D.	Married Polly Dunn	Book 1,	248
1848, Jan. 24	CAUTHORN,	LOUISA C.	Married Enas Healy	Book 1,	260
1855, Oct. 29	CAUTHORN,	LUCINDA E.	Married Lewis Jones	Book 1,	4
1844, Jun. 7	CAUTHORN,	LUCY	Married Thomas Harper	Book 1,	257
1850, Aug. 26	CAUTHORN,	LUCY	Married Dunbar Edwards	Book 1,	262
1824, Aug. 30	CAUTHORN,	MARIA	Married Henry Davis	Book 1,	241
1842, Dec. 19	CAUTHORN,	MARTHA A.	Married Thomas P. Fox	Book 1,	256
1843, Feb. 13	CAUTHORN,	MARTHA	Married William Dansey	Book 1,	256
1826,	CAUTHORN,	MARY	Daughter of Reuben, married Meredith Edmonds	D 42,	74
1866, May 29	CAUTHORN,	MARY E.	Married John H. Ball	Book 1,	15
1868, Dec. 24	CAUTHORN,	MARY F.	Married Wallace R. McGeorge	Book 1,	21
1884, Sep. 25	CAUTHORN,	MARY T.	Widow, married Garrett Carlton	Book 1,	78
1849, Jan. 9	CAUTHORN,	MATILDA C.	Married Thomas A. Boughton	Book 1,	261
1845, Feb. 26	CAUTHORN,	NANCY	Married Thomas Corr	Book 1,	258

				Book	Page
1853, Jan. 8	CAUTHORN,	OCTAVIA A.	Married Schuyler Bristow	Book 1,	264
1832,	CAUTHORN,	OPHELIA	Daughter of Reuben, married Matthew Baird, Alexandria, Va.	D 43,	561
1808, Apr. 18	CAUTHORN,	PATSY	Married Peter Brooks	Book 1,	224
1791,	CAUTHORN,	PEGGY	Daughter of Vincent, married Richard Holt	W 14,	282
1804, Feb. 21	CAUTHORN,	REUBEN	Married Ruthy Fisher	Book 1,	222
1823, Jan. 8	CAUTHORN,	RICE	Married Lucy Harper	Book 1,	240
1847, Apr. 14	CAUTHORN,	RICE	Married Agnes Rouse	Book 1,	259
1885, Mar. 11	CAUTHORN,	RICHARD G.	Married Mollie L. Durham	Book 1,	81
1873, Jun. 19	CAUTHORN,	ROBERT T.	Married Fannie Bell Broock	Book 1,	33
1845, Dec. 31	CAUTHORN,	R. F. T.	Married Frances Greenwood	Book I,	258
1830, Dec. 20	CAUTHORN,	ROSS A.	Married Sarah Harmon	Book 1,	247
1860, Jul. 10	CAUTHORN,	ROSS A.	Married Mildred H. Frank	Book 1,	9
1811, Jul. 3	CAUTHORN,	RUTHEY	Married Vincent Edmunds	Book 1,	235
1845, Dec. 22	CAUTHORN,	SUSAN E.	Married Sylvanus Gresham	Book 1,	258
1808, May 16	CAUTHORN,	THOMAS	Married Nancy Patterson	Book 1,	224
1835, Sep. 29	CAUTHORN,	THOMAS	Married Mildred Dunn	Book 1,	251
1801,	CAUTHORN,	VINCENT	Married Jane, daughter of Heritage Howerton	D 35,	465
1835, Jul. 30	CAUTHORN,	VIRGINIA V.	Married John H. Parry	Book 1,	251
1834,	CAUTHORN,	WILLIAM	Married Sally, daughter of John Games	D 45,	321
1808,	CAVANAUGH,	PHEBE	Daughter of James, married John Glanton	D 37,	7
1808,	CAVANAUGH,	POLLY	Daughter of James, married Burwell Glanton	D 37,	7
1808,	CAVANAUGH,	ROADIE	Daughter of James, married Daniel Gaines	D 37,	7
1688,	CAWARD,	JAMES	Married Relict of Zechia Collig	O 2,	65
1821, Dec. 24	CHAMBERLAYNE, CURTIS		Married Catharine Harper	Book 1,	238
1813, Jan. 4	CHAMBERLAYNE, GRIFFING		Married Betsey Brooks	Book 1,	229
1726,	CHAMBERLAIN, GRIZELL		Relict of John, married Thomas Hardee (Hardy)	O 9,	101
1715,	CHAMBERLAIN, JOHN		Married Grizell Coleman, Daughter of Robert & Ann	D&W 15,	93
1821, Jun. 11	CHAMBERLAYNE, JOHN		Married Lucy Dalley	Book 1,	238
1887, Dec. 25	CHAMBERLAINE, PETER		Married Martha Holmes	Book 1.	93
1861, Jan. 20	CHANDLER,	WILLIAM H.	Married Elizabeth Ann Adams	Book 1,	10
1805, Nov. 12	CHANEY,	ANN	Married James Greenwood	Book 1,	223

Date	Surname	Given Name	Description	Book	Page
1780,	CHAPMAN,	REUBEN	Married Ann, daughter of Robert Rennolds	W 13,	338
1842, Dec. 21	CHARLES,	IVERSON	Married Elizabeth Williams	Book 1,	256
1716,	CHARLESWORTH, ROBERT		Married Elizabeth Foster	O 5,	17
1865, Dec. 14	CHARTTERS,	XANTHUS	Spottsylvania Co. married Evelyn Montague	Book 1,	14
1800,	CHEYNEY,	ANN	Widow, married Ben Johnson	W 16,	77
1782,	CHEANEY,	ELIZABETH	Daughter of John, married John Hoskins, King & Queen Co.	D 33,	1
1758,	CHEANEY,	JOHN	Married Anna, daughter of Peter Brooks	W 11,	333
1741,	CHEYNEY,	SUSANNA	Daughter of John, married John Bush	O 12,	219
1798,	CHEANEY,	THOMAS	Charlotte, Co. married Rachel daughter of Heritage Howerton	D 35,	205
1778,	CHEANEY,	WILLIAM	Married Susannah, daughter of Henry Crutcher	W 13,	300
1779,	CHEEK,	WILLIAM	Married Mary Ryland	O 29,	452
1798,	CHENAULT,	JOHN	Married Barbara Burke	W 16,	88
1889, Dec. 31	CHENAULT,	MILTON F.	Married Betty J. Martin	Book 1,	102
1751,	CHENAULT,	STEPHEN	Orange, Co. married Mary, dau. of Benjamin Rouzie	D 25,	212
1887, Dec. 14	CHENAULT,	W. T.	Married Annie Davis	Book 1,	93
1812, Mar. 9	CHILTON,	PATSY	Married James Jones	Book 1,	228
1860, Jun. 13	CHINN,	JOSEPH W.	Married Gabriella Brockenbrough	Book 1,	9
1863, Feb. 16	CHINN,	SALLIE S.	Married Robert H. Tyler, Prince William Co.	Book 1,	11
1885, Nov. 3	CHRISTIAN,	EDWARD	Married Agnes Roy Pendleton	Book 1,	84
1848, Aug. 11	CLAIBORNE,	BURCH	Married Lucinda C. Williams	Book 1,	260
1666,	CLAPHAM,	ELIZABETH	Widow of William, formerly wife of Epaphroditus Lawson	D 3,	63
1708,	CLAPHAM,	MARY	Widow of William, married Thomas Richardson	O 3,	378, 408
1899, Sep. 7	CLARKE,	ADA P.	Married R. R. Collier	Book 1,	134
1854, Dec. 28	CLARKE,	ADALINE B.	Married Robert Allen	Book 1,	2
1682,	CLARKE,	ANN	Daughter of Henry, married Francis Gower	D 7,	542
1859, May 12	CLARKE,	ARCHIBALD	Married Elizabeth M. Ball	Book 1,	7
1832, Dec. 22	CLARKE,	AUSTIN	Married Lucy Hodges	Book 1,	248
1840, Feb. 26	CLARKE,	BENEDICT	Married Mary M. Gatewood	Book 1,	254
1841,	CLARKE,	BENEDICT	Married Mary, daughter of Travis Gatewood	D 47,	97
1868, Dec. 30	CLARKE,	BENJAMIN F.	Married Mildred A. Taylor	Book 1,	21

				Book	Page
1812, Nov. 16	CLARKE,	BETSEY	Married Andrew Noel	Book 1,	228
1816, Dec. 30	CLARKE,	BURKETT	Married Phoebe Gouldman	Book 1,	232
1868, Dec. 29	CLARKE,	BURTON	Married Joanna Crouch	Book 1,	21
1823, Dec. 24	CLARKE,	CATHARINE	Married Bartholomew Vawter	Book 1,	240
1888, Dec. 27	CLARKE,	CATHARINE	Married Robert S. Davis	Book 1,	97
1745,	CLARKE,	CHARLES	(Saddler) married Mary only dau. of James and Esther Johnson	D 23,	325
1896, Dec. 23	CLARKE,	COLUMBIA F.	Married Charles J. Whitaker	Book 1,	123
1846, Jan. 15	CLARKE,	DAVID	Married Clemenzie Lee	Book 1,	258
1853,	CLARKE,	DAVID	Married Clemenzie Lee, daughter of Fielding Lee	W 27,	409
1860, Jan. 17	CLARKE,	ELIZA E.	Married James R. Dishman	Book 1,	8
1688,	CLARKE,	ELIZABETH	Daughter of Henry, married Angell Jacobus	D 6,	5
1804, Dec. 18	CLARKE,	ELIZABETH	Married William D. Thruston	Book 1,	222
1806, Jul. 21	CLARKE,	ELIZABETH	Married James Carter	Book 1,	223
1813, Sep. 20	CLARKE,	ELIZABETH	Married John Williamson	Book 1,	229
1829, Dec. 21	CLARKE,	ELIZABETH	Married William D. Goode	Book 1,	246
1831,	CLARKE,	ELIZABETH	Daughter of Robin, married William Goode	D 43,	415
1860, Feb. 28	CLARKE,	ELIZABETH J.	Married William Tinsbloom, Jr.	Book 1,	8
1868, Jul. 23	CLARKE,	ELIZABETH	Married Robert W. Taylor	Book 1,	20
1870, Mar. 22	CLARKE,	ELTHA ANN	Married Charles H. Schools	Book 1,	25
1868, Jan. 8	CLARKE,	EMILY	Married Churchill A. Greenwood	Book 1,	20
1813, Dec. 27	CLARKE,	FANNY	Married Davis Longest	Book 1,	229
1826,	CLARKE,	FRANCES	Married Carter Lumpkin	Book 1,	242
1835, Oct. 9	CLARKE,	FRANCES	Married Arthur Barefoot	Book 1,	251
1856, Jan. 23	CLARKE,	FRANCES	Married Robert G. Richardson	Book 1,	3
1874, Nov. 5	CLARKE,	GEORGE M.	Married Bettie McGeorge	Book 1,	42
1818, Feb. 16	CLARKE,	HAPPY	Married Jesse Gouldman	Book 1,	234
1847, Feb. 15	CLARKE,	HENRY	Married Catharine Davis	Book 1,	259
1854, Dec. 15	CLARKE,	HENRY	Married Julia Catharine Tune	Book 1,	2
1865, Oct. 19	CLARKE,	HENRY	Married Mary Dillard	Book 1,	13
1871, Mar. 21	CLARKE,	IRA E.	Married Sarah W. Moore	Book 1,	28
1815, Dec. 18	CLARKE,	JAMES	Married Elizabeth Andrews	Book 1,	231

				Book	Page
1843, Mar. 8	CLARKE,	JAMES	Married Martha Prince	Book 1,	256
1853, Mar. 16	CLARKE,	JAMES	Married Julia Tucker	Book 1,	264
1870, Dec. 15	CLARKE,	JAMES H.	Married Eliza H. Bunday	Book 1,	26
1872, Sep. 26	CLARKE,	JAMES P.	Married Emily Haile	Book 1,	31
1897, Mar. 31	CLARKE,	JAMES R.	Married Nannie Rouse	Book 1,	125
1815, Sep. 5	CLARKE,	JANE	Married Robert Ellet	Book 1,	231
1873, Nov. 26	CLARKE,	JANNETTA	Married John Wilson	Book 1,	35
1807, Sep. 1	CLARKE,	JESSE FEARN	Married Susanna Bush	Book 1,	224
1791,	CLARKE,	JOHN	Married Mary, daughter of John Yarrington	W 14,	291
1807, Jan. 19	CLARKE,	JOHN	Married Ann Dobyns	Book 1,	224
1809,	CLARKE,	JOHN	Married Ann, daughter of William Dobbins	W 16,	291
1811, Aug. 19	CLARKE,	JOHN	Married Patsy Bush	Book 1,	227
1829, Dec. 21	CLARK,	JOHN	Married Julia Dunn	Book 1,	246
1854, Dec. 28	CLARKE,	JOHN THOMAS Married Fanny Elizabeth Goode		Book 1,	2
1857, May 2	CLARKE,	JOHN	Married Emily Taylor	Book 1,	6
1861, Jan. 20	CLARKE,	JOHN T.	Married Lucy A. Gatewood	Book 1,	10
1867, Apr. 25	CLARKE,	JOHN WILLIAM Married Margaret Brizendine		Book 1,	17
1874, Apr. 10	CLARKE,	JOHN W.	Married Mrs. Betty Burnett	Book 1,	36
1893, Aug. 3	CLARKE,	J. R.	Married Kate Wilson	Book 1,	112
1858, Apr. 27	CLARKE	JON.	Married Mary Taylor	Book 1,	268
1874, Jan. 29	CLARKE,	JOSEPH	Married Azarilla Martin	Book 1,	35
1807, May 5	CLARKE,	JUDITH	Married William Rouse	Book 1,	224
1858, Nov. 19	CLARKE,	JULIA	Widow, married Albert Gresham King & Queen Co.	Book 1,	6
1836, Jan. 19	CLARKE,	KITTY	Married Upshaw Ferrell	Book 1,	252
1810, Nov. 20	CLARKE,	LARKIN	Married Polly Bush	Book 1,	226
1832, Nov. 24	CLARKE,	LEONARD	Married Frances Williamson	Book 1,	248
1840, Feb. 17	CLARKE,	LEONARD	Married Sophia Southword	Book 1,	254
1843, Jan. 4	CLARKE,	LEONARD	Married Margaret Halbert	Book 1,	256
1896, Dec. 12	CLARKE,	LILLIE B.	Married Robert N. Allen	Book 1,	122
1825, Mar. 1	CLARKE,	LUCY	Married Thomas Vaughan	Book 1,	242
1834, Jan. 30	CLARKE,	LUCY	Married John Allen	Book 1,	250

				Book	Page
1844, Mar. 25	CLARKE,	LUCY	Married Shearwood Brooks	Book 1,	257
1860, Feb. 3	CLARKE,	LUCY	Married John Williamson, Jr.	Book 1,	8
1865, Aug. 17	CLARKE,	MARGARET	Married Dennis Gristol, New York	Book 1,	13
1832, Feb.29	CLARK,	MARIA	Married Robinson Davis	Book 1,	248
1892, Oct. 2	CLARKE,	MARIA	Married R. H. Holbert, King George Co.	Book 1,	110
1811, Dec. 23	CLARKE,	MARTHA	Married Beverley Elliott	Book 1,	227
1846, Oct. 9	CLARKE,	MARTHA	Married John Lee	Book 1,	259
1847, May 3	CLARK,	MARTHA A.	Married Richard W. Franklin	Book 1,	259
1858, Aug. 7	CLARKE,	MARTHA ANN	Married Henry Cox	Book 1,	6
1860, Dec. 24	CLARKE,	MARTHA J.	Married Richard Turner	Book 1,	10
1813, Nov. 15	CLARKE,	MARY	Married Henry Duerson	Book 1,	229
1833, May 30	CLARK,	MARY	Married Woodford Southworth	Book 1,	249
1863, Dec. 19	CLARKE,	MARY ANN	Married James Henry Allen, Soldier, C. S. A.	Book 1,	12
1872, Dec. 26	CLARKE,	MARY E.	Married Thomas Acres	Book 1,	32
1877, Sep. 20	CLARKE,	MARY ANNA	Married Richard Johnson	Book 1,	46
1806, Apr. 21	CLARKE,	NANCY	Married Richard Jones	Book 1,	223
1822, Feb. 5	CLARKE,	NANCY	Married Washington Davis	Book 1,	239
1844, Apr. 12	CLARKE,	NANCY	Married Richard Mason	Book 1,	257
1877, Feb. 28	CLARKE,	NANCY	Married John N. Gowin, King William Co.	Book 1,	44
1899, Nov. 2	CLARKE,	OSIE E.	Married J. L. Covington	Book 1,	134
1844, Mar. 4	CLARKE,	PATTY A.	Married Walker Schools	Book 1,	257
1845, Jan. 4	CLARKE,	PAT H.	Married V. A. Gouldman	Book 1,	258
1809, Mar. 20	CLARKE,	PHILIP	Married Molly Bush	Book 1,	225
1828, Jan. 30	CLARKE,	POLLY	Married Upshaw Davis	Book 1,	245
1809, Jun. 29	CLARKE,	RITCHIE	Married Nancy Martin	Book 1,	225
1806, Apr. 22	CLARKE,	ROBERT	Married Rachel Elliott	Book 1,	223
1807, Aug. 1	CLARK,	ROBERT	Married Marann Dunn	Book 1,	224
1835, Jan. 27	CLARKE,	ROBERT JR.	Married Patsey Ball	Book 1,	251
1863, Oct. 1	CLARKE,	RUFFIN	Married Nancy E. Hays	Book 1,	12
1874, Nov. 5	CLARKE,	RUFFIN	Married Elizabeth F. Brooks	Book 1,	37
1898, Feb. 12	CLARKE,	RUFFIN	Married Harriet Dunn	Book 1,	128

· 55 ·

				Book	Page
1805, Jul. 28	CLARKE,	SALLY	Married Walker Clarke	Book 1,	222
1898, Jul. 7	CLARKE,	SANDY	Married Alice Shackelford	Book 1,	129
1846, Dec. 29	CLARKE,	SARAH A.	Married Edward Kay	Book 1,	259
1865, Jul. 21	CLARKE,	SARAH E.	Married Darling A. Bennett, Monroe County, Ga.	Book 1,	13
1834, May 1	CLARK,	SUSAN	Married George Wyatt	Book 1,	250
1840,	CLARKE,	SUSAN	Daughter of Robert, married George Wyatt	D 47,	81
1864, Dec. 29	CLARKE,	SUSAN C. E.	Married William I. Duff	Book 1,	13
1807, Jul. 22	CLARK,	SUSANNA	Married Alexander Noel	Book 1,	224
1833, Jul. 8	CLARK,	SUSANNA	Married John G. Edwards	Book 1,	249
1832, Mar. 22	CLARKE,	SPENCER	Married Nancy Williamson	Book 1,	248
1871, Feb. 9	CLARKE,	SPENCER	Married Martha Burnett	Book 1,	28
1796,	CLARKE,	THOMAS	Married Molly, daughter of Thomas Henry Broock	W 15,	275
1805, Aug. 13	CLARKE,	THOMAS	Married Oney Walden	Book 1,	222
1827, Dec. 17	CLARKE,	THOMAS	Married Ann Gatewood	Book 1,	243
1847,	CLARKE,	THOMAS N.	Married Ann, daughter of Sally Gatewood	W 26,	202
1820, Apr. 28	CLARKE,	THORNTON T.	Married Lucy B. Montague	Book 1,	237
1805, Jul. 28	CLARKE,	WALKER	Married Sally Clarke	Book 1,	222
1848, Jan. 13	CLARK,	WASHINGTON L.	Married Lucinda B. Crow	Book 1,	260
1880, Apr. 15	CLARKE,	WASHINGTON L.	Married Mary S. Blackburn	Book 1,	55
1807, Dec. 21	CLARK,	WILLIAM	Married Jane Owen	Book 1,	224
1810, Aug. 17	CLARK,	WILLIAM	Married Fanny Thomas	Book 1,	226
1816, Nov. 30	CLARK,	WILLIAM	Married Jane Fisher	Book 1,	232
1825, Apr. 28	CLARK,	WILLIAM	Married Lilly Davis	Book 1,	241
1828, Nov. 22	CLARK,	WILLIAM D.	Married Eliza Greenwood	Book 1,	245
1837, Nov. 17	CLARKE,	WILLIAM D.	Married Sarah A. Carlton	Book 1,	252
1870, Dec. 22	CLARK,	WILLIAM	Married Martha E. Davis	Book 1,	27
1820, Dec. 28	CLARKSON,	BENJAMIN	Married Fanny Games	Book 1,	237
1834,	CLARKSON,	BENJAMIN	Married Fanny, daughter of John Games	D 45,	321
1881, Nov. 3	CLARKSON,	J. A.	Married Kate A. Derieux	Book 1,	61
1886, Sep. 6	CLARKSON,	JAMES L.	Married Evelyn G. Derieux	Book 1,	88
1811, Jan. 23	CLARKSON,	JOHN	Married Mary Gatewood	Book 1,	227

					Book	Page
1830, Dec. 22	CLARKSON,	MARY	Married Carter Croxton, Jr.		Book 1,	247
1835,	CLARKSON,	MARY	Daughter of Susan L. Clarkson, married Carter Croxton		D 45,	124
1876, Dec. 14	CLARKSON,	MARY E.	Married Robert Hutchinson		Book 1,	43
1822, Dec. 7	CLARKSON,	JOSEPH	Married Susanna Games		Book 1,	239
1834,	CLARKSON,	JOSEPH	Married Susan, daughter of John Games		D 45,	321
1866, Dec. 18	CLARKSON,	JOSEPH J.	Married Ann E. Covington		Book 1,	16
1844, Dec. 2	CLARKSON,	LUCY E.	Married W. G. Covington		Book 1,	257
1878, Feb. 19	CLARKSON,	LUCIE D.	Married Collin P. Garrett, Middlesex Co.		Book 1,	48
1813, Nov. 18	CLARKSON,	RICHARD	Married Susan L. Crittenden		Book 1,	229
1835,	CLARKSON,	SUSAN	Daughter of Susan L. Clarkson, married Francis Munday		D 45,	124
1835, Dec. 9	CLARKSON,	SUSAN	Married Francis Munday		Book 1,	252
1836, Mar. 9	CLARKSON,	SUSAN L.	married Lowry Elliott		Book 1,	252
1836,	CLARKSON	SUSAN L.	Widow of Richard, married Lowry Elliott		D 45,	124
1842, Jan. 17	CLARKSON,	SUSAN E.	Married George W. Phillips		Book 1,	256
1849, Sep. 17	CLARKSON,	VIRGINIA	Married Arthur J. Derieux		Book 1,	261
1844, Mar. 14	CLARKSON,	WILLIAM J.	Married Lucy Ann Cox		Book 1,	257
1847,	CLARKSON,	WILLIAM	Married Mary, daughter of Sally Gatewood		W 26,	202
1819, Nov. 24	CLATTERBUCK, COLLINS		Married Matilda Baxter		Book 1,	235
1854, Aug. 23	CLAVOE,	GEORGE W.	Married Sara J. Trimyer		Book 1,	265
1837, Sep. 8	CLAYTON,	DELPHIA	Married Theodrick Beazley		Book 1,	252
1689,	CLAYTON,	JAMES	Married Joan, widow of Dennis Sullivant		D 8,	116
1822, Mar. 25	CLAYTON,	MARTHA	Married Isham Bagby		Book 1,	239
1822, Oct. 17	CLEMENTS,	ANN L.	Married William J. Fisher		Book 1,	239
1832,	CLEMENTS,	ANN	Daughter of Ewen Clements, married William Fisher		D 44,	15
1834,	CLEMENTS,	ANN	Only child of Ewen, married William Fisher		D 45,	346
1839,	CLEMENTS,	ANN L.	Daughter of Ewen, married Charles B. Moss		D 46,	192
1812, Oct. 20	CLEMENTS.	ELIZABETH	Married William S. Foster		Book 1,	228
1805, Feb. 8	CLEMENTS,	EWIN	Married Susan Purkins		Book 1,	222
1707,	CLEMENTS,	JOHN	Physitian, married Mary, dau. of Mary Latane		D 23,	281
1722,	CLEMENTS,	?	Married Mary, daughter of Buckenham Brown		D 17,	49
1734,	CLEMENTS,	JOHN	Married Mary Brown		W 5,	343

1804, May	CLEMENTS,	MACE	Married Elizabeth Purkins	Book 1,	222
1821, May 30	CLEMENTS,	MARY S.	Married Richard Croxton	Book 1,	238
1820, Jun. 10	CLEMENTS,	WILLIAM L.	Married Louisa Blake	Book 1,	237
1806, Jan. 16	CLONDAS,	ALICE	Married Major Wyatt	Book 1,	223
1816, Mar. 23	CLONDAS,	CHARLES	Married Jane Bush	Book 1,	232
1832,	CLONDAS,	CHARLES	Married Jane Bush	D 47,	367
1860, Jun. 17	CLONDAS,	JOHN P.	Married Mary E. Dunn	Book 1,	9
1804,	CLONDAS,	LUCY	Married Edward Read, Middlesex, Co.	D 36,	407
1848, Nov. 20	CLONDAT,	ANN	Married Ellett Gardner	Book 1,	260
1848, Jun. 7	CLOPTON,	EDWARD A. J.	Married Ann W. Latane	Book 1,	260
1827, May 23	CLOPTON,	JONES C.	Married Mary Juliet Ritchie	Book 1,	243
1833,	CLOPTON,	JONES C.	Married Mary Juliet Ritchie, daughter of Archibald Ritchie	W 23,	245
1854, Jul. 20	CLOPTON,	MARY JULIET	Married Beverley Dickie Roy	Book 1,	2
1725,	CLOUTSON,	ANN	Sister of Cornelius, married Philip Stockdale	D 18,	167
1722,	CLOUSON,	MARGARET	Daughter of Thomas, married William Brown	D 17,	36
1809, Sep. 18	COATES,	ELIZABETH	Married Gilbe Tureman	Book 1,	225
1843, Nov. 20	COATES,	FRANCES	Married James Durham	Book 1,	256
1862, Feb. 28	COATES,	GEORGE D.	Married Mary Susan Brown	Book 1,	11
1707,	COATES,	SAMUEL	Married Margaret Watkins	D&C 13,	31
1855, Dec. 25	COATES,	SARAH F.	Married Samuel W. Y Muse	Book 1,	3
1872, May 9	COATES,	SARAH	Married Robert A. Jenkins	Book 1,	30
1838, Mar. 24	COATES,	THOMAS	Married Frances Jane Taylor	Book 1,	253
1843,	COATES,	THOMAS	Married Frances, daughter of Nancy Taylor	W 24,	149
1891, Mar. 19	COATES,	WILLIAM H.	Married Mary Johnson	Book 1,	107
1866, Aug. 11	COBB,	LEWIS	Married Mary Ann Shepperd	Book 1,	15
1818, Dec. 21	COCKBURN,	JAMES	Married Alice T. Smith	Book 1,	234
1700,	COFFEY,	EDWARD	Married Anne, daughter of Thomas Powell	D&W 10,	75
1715,	COFTON,	JASPER	Married Mary, daughter of Ealse Shipley	D&W 14,	475
1716,	COFTON,	JASPER	Married Mary, sister of Sarah Shipley, heir of George Boyce	D&W 15,	1,2
1721,	COFTON,	JASPER	Married Mary, admrx. of John Hupley	O 5,	611

				Book	Page
1715,	COFTON,	WILLIAM	Married Mary, daughter of Francis Meriwether	O 4,	550
1708,	COGGIN,	ELIZABETH	Married Robert Leverett, Richmond Co.	O 4,	92
1708,	COGGIN,	MARY	Married James Acres	O 4,	92
1707,	COGGIN,	SUSANNA	Daughter of Thomas, married Daniel Austin	D&C 13,	59
1860, Jun. 24	COGHILL,	ALEXANDER	Married Susan Thomas	Book 1,	9
1868, Dec. 24	COGHILL,	ARCHIBALD	Married Ann Eliza Thomas	Book 1,	21
1825,	COGHILL,	BENJAMIN	Married Susanna, daughter of William Noel	D 41,	369
1876, Aug. 13	COGHILL,	BENJAMIN F.	Married Harriet P. Parker	Book 1,	42
1851, Dec. 17	COGHILL,	BETTIE ANN	Married Silas P. Bayliss	Book 1,	262
1841, Jan. 12	COGHILL,	CATHARINE	Married Edward P. Brown	Book 1,	255
1860, May 10	COGHILL,	ELI	Married Elizabeth Vawter	Book 1,	9
1866, Jan. 13	COGHILL,	ELI	Married Roberta Parker	Book 1,	14
1705,	COGHILL,	FREDERICK	Married Sarah, sister of John Goss	D&C 12,	95
1877, Feb. 1	COGHILL,	IDA E.	Married Norborne Pitts, Jr.	Book 1,	44
1783,	COGHILL,	JOHN	Married Nancy, daughter of Thomas & Sarah Wise	D 32,	193
1816, Oct. 23	COGHILL,	JOHN	Married Polly Pitts	Book 1,	233
1853, Oct. 6	COGHILL,	JOHN JR.	Married Virginia Parker	Book 1,	1
1860, May 10	COGHILL,	LUCY	Married John Tinsbloom	Book 1,	9
1691,	COGHILL,	MARGARET	Daughter of James, married John Powell	O 1,	242
1865, Oct. 15	COGHILL,	MARTHA S.	Married George W. Anderson	Book 1,	13
1687,	COGHILL,	MARY	Executrix of James, married Henry Duxbery	O 2,	52
1844, Oct. 1	COGHILL,	MARY C.	Married Robert S. Haile	Book 1,	257
1850, Aug.	COGHILL,	MARY	Married Godfrey Ingram	Book 1,	262
1850, Jan. 30	COGHILL,	M. J.	Married Charles I. Bayliss	Book 1,	262
1841, Jun. 7	COGHILL,	NANCY	Married William Taylor	Book 1,	255
1820, Jun. 10	COGHILL,	RICHARD	Married Ann Aldridge	Book 1,	237
1839, Nov. 8	COGHILL,	SALLY	Married Humphrey Brooke	Book 1,	254
1815, Feb. 8	COGHILL,	SMALLWOOD	Married Elizabeth Garrett	Book 1,	231
1806,	COGHILL,	THOMAS	Married Rose, daughter of Thomas Pitts.	W 16,	436
1814, Oct. 19	COGHILL,	THOMAS	Married Elizabeth Noel	Book 1,	230
1824, Mar. 15	COGHILL,	THOMAS	Married Mary F. Micou	Book 1,	241

				Book	Page
1875, Mar. 11	COGHILL,	THOMAS A.	Married Ella J. Munday	Book 1,	38
1891, Jun. 11	COGHILL,	T. A.	Married J. P. Brown	Book 1,	107
1817, Jan. 21	COKELEY,	WILLIAM	Married Margaret Carter	Book 1,	233
1867, May 11	COLES,	ADDISON	Married Susan Ann Quarles	Book 1,	17
1680,	COLE,	ELIZABETH	Widow of John, married John Taverner	D 6,	63
1857, Dec. 23	COLE,	GEORGE W.	Married Catharine Kidd Brown	Book 1,	6
1821, Dec. 24	COLE,	JAMES C.	Married Rebecca Shepherd	Book 1,	238
1699,	COLE,	JOHN	Married Ann, daughter of William Gauntlet	D&W 10,	4
1761,	COLE,	ROBERT	Married Franky, widow of Richard Gatewood	D 29,	81
1827, Nov. 26	COLE,	THOMAS	Married Charlotte Howerton	Book 1,	243
1832,	COLE,	THOMAS	Married Charlotte, daughter of William Howerton	D 43,	595
1707,	COLE,	WILLIAM	Married Elizabeth, daughter of Thomas Watkins	D&C 13,	30
1899, Feb. 28	COLEMAN,	A. B.	Married B. G. Boughan	Book 1,	132
1715,	COLEMAN,	ANN	Relict of Robert, married John Hunter	D&W 14,	358
1885, Sep. 15	COLEMAN,	CAROLINE	Married Adolphus McTyre, Middlesex, Co.	Book 1,	83
1827, Aug. 17	COLEMAN,	CATHARINE	Married Jackson Dyke	Book 1,	243
1848, Jul. 15	COLEMAN,	COURTNEY	Married Julia A. Dyke	Book 1,	260
1711,	COLEMAN,	EDWARD	Married Ann Reeves	O 4, D&W 15,	427 32
1733,	COLEMAN,	EDWARD	Married Elizabeth, widow of George Gwynne	D 20,	246
1749,	COLEMAN,	ELIZABETH	Widow of Thomas, married Thomas Hastie	D 25,	1
1856, Dec. 15	COLEMAN,	ELIZABETH	Married John Cox	Book 1,	5
1868, Dec. 17	COLEMAN,	EMILY	Married Thomas Greenstreet, Caroline, Co.	Book 1,	21
1820, Aug. 16	COLEMAN,	FRANCIS	Married Elizabeth Griffin	Book 1,	237
1715,	COLEMAN,	GRIZELL	Daughter of Robert, married John Chamberlain	D&W 15,	93
1812, Feb. 5	COLEMAN,	JAMES	Married Nancy Satterwhite	Book 1,	228
1845, Jan. 21	COLEMAN,	JOHN	Married Catharine Armstrong	Book 1,	258
1859, Dec. 26	COLEMAN,	JOHN	Married Susan E. Griggs	Book 1,	8
1874, Feb. 26	COLEMAN,	JOHN	Married Caroline Vawter	Book 1,	36
1885, Apr. 20	COLEMAN,	JOHN WILLIAM	Married Lettie C. Durham	Book 1,	82
1894, Nov. 29	COLEMAN,	JOSEPH	Married Harriet Robinson	Book 1,	115
1813, Dec. 20	COLEMAN,	LEWIS	Married Nancy Walker	Book 1,	229

					Book	Page
1830, Mar. 16	COLEMAN,	LOTTSEY	Married Edwin Stokes		Book 1,	247
1865, Feb. 12	COLEMAN,	LUCY C.	Married Robert L. Morris, Louisa, Co.		Book 1,	13
1723,	COLEMAN,	MARTHA	Relict of George, married John Hoskins		D 17,	180
1830, Jan. 18	COLEMAN,	MARTHA	Married William Stokes		Book 1,	247
1806, Jan. 7	COLEMAN,	MARTIN	Married Patsy Hoskins		Book 1,	223
1812, Mar. 3	COLEMAN,	MARY	Married James Muse		Book 1,	228
1841, Jun. 21	COLEMAN,	MARY ANN	Married Nicholas Faulconer		Book 1,	255
1873, May 22	COLEMAN,	MARY C.	Married James H. Broaddus		Book 1,	33
1805, Mar. 18	COLEMAN,	PHILIP	Married Dolly Miles		Book 1,	222
1819, Jun. 16	COLEMAN,	REUBEN	Married Catharine Dunn		Book 1,	235
1871, Dec. 5	COLEMAN,	ROBERT L.	Married Maggie Jane Brizendine		Book 1,	29
1824, Jun. 3	COLEMAN,	SAMUEL	Married Sarah A. Rennolds		Book 1,	241
1715,	COLEMAN,	SPILSBY	Married Mary, daughter of John Crow		D&W 15, W 3,	93 28
1808, Aug. 30	COLEMAN,	SUSANNA	Married John Showard		Book 1,	225
1824, Apr. 16	COLEMAN,	THOMAS	Married Ann Stokes		Book 1,	241
1829, Jan. 14	COLEMAN,	THOMAS	Married Felicia L. Faulconer		Book 1,	246
1876, Feb. 3	COLEMAN,	THOMAS	Married Levinia Johnson		Book 1,	41
1808, Jan. 5	COLEMAN,	WILLIAM	Married Polly Rouse		Book 1,	224
1822, Oct. 15	COLEMAN,	WILLIAM	Married Catharine L. Hill		Book 1,	239
1838, May 25	COLEMAN,	WILSON	Married Catharine Ann Shearwood		Book 1,	253
1799,	COLGEN,	GRACE	Married William Jones		O 35,	164
1884, Dec. 18	COLLAWN,	FRANK P.	Married Mary E. Collawn		Book 1,	79
1884, Dec. 18	COLLAWN,	MARY E.	Married Frank P. Collawn		Book 1,	79
1881, Dec. 15	COLLAWN,	ROBERT S.	Married Mollie F. Spindle		Book 1,	62
1871, Sep. 6	COLLIER,	ELIZABETH	Widow, dau. of Uriah Schools, married Philip Thomas		Book 1,	29
1869, Jan. 14	COLLIER,	HENRY	Married Amy Muse		Book 1,	22
1857, Dec. 17	COLLIER,	JAMES HENRY	Married Mary Susan Collier		Book 1,	5
1852, Jan. 21	COLLIER,	JAMES	Married Polly Mahon		Book 1,	263
1867, Oct. 17	COLLIER,	JAMES	Married Elizabeth Schools		Book 1,	18
1720,	COLLIER,	JANE	Married John Jones		O 5,	551
1869, Jan. 14	COLLIER,	JOHN M.	Married Ellen Allen		Book 1,	22

				Book	Page
1899, Dec. 21	COLLIER,	JUDY	Married William Marshall	Book 1,	135
1899, Jan. 19	COLLIER,	L. B.	Married Wortley Hayes	Book 1,	132
1857, Dec. 17	COLLIER,	MARY SUSAN	Married James Henry Collier	Book 1,	5
1881, May 5	COLLIER,	MARY A.	Married Thomas W. Griffin	Book 1,	60
1814, Jan. 25	COLLIER,	POLLY	Married Sthreshley Elliott	Book 1,	230
1899, Sep. 7	COLLIER,	R. R.	Married Ada P. Clarke	Book 1,	134
1886, Sep. 6	COLLIER,	SARAH M.	Married John Hayes, Jr.	Book 1,	88
1897, Sep. 22	COLLIER,	T. M.	Married R. L. Andrews	Book 1,	126
1842, Dec. 23	COLLINS,	ANN D.	Married James H. Shepard	Book 1,	256
1828, Dec. 24	COLLINS,	CATHARINE	Married John A. Crewdson	Book 1,	245
1884, Apr. 24	COLLINS,	CATHARINE A.	Married William T. Griffin	Book 1,	77
1841, Feb. 12	COLLINS,	CHRISTOPHER	Married Lucy Torrent	Book 1,	255
1686,	COLLINS,	JOHN	Married daughter of Abraham Weeks, Middlesex, Co.	O 1,	232
1806, Feb. 6	COLLINS,	JOHN	Married Elizabeth Bray	Book 1,	223
1827, Dec. 15	COLLINS,	JOHN H.	Married Sarah Purkins	Book 1,	243
1854, Nov. 18	COLLINS,	JOHN H.	Married Mary E. Crow	Book 1,	2
1712,	COLLINS,	KATHERINE	Married Thomas Montague	O 4,	442
1828, Jul. 21	COLLINS,	LEONARD	Married Mildred Howerton	Book 1,	245
1874, Dec. 30	COLLINS,	MARTHA	Widow, married David Carter	Book 1,	38
1844, Feb. 3	COLLINS,	MARY E.	Married William Hall	Book 1,	257
1707,	COLLINS,	MATTHEW	Married Mary, daughter of Henry Peters	D&C 13,	82
1709,	COLLINS,	MATTHEW	Married daughter of William Gannocke	D&C 13,	289
1870, Sep. 29	COLLINS,	RICHARD R.	Married Martha E. Crispin	Book 1,	26
1819, May 25	COLLINS,	THOMAS	Married Virginia Garland	Book 1,	235
1823, Apr. 21	COLLINS,	THOMAS	Married Nancy Gowan	Book 1,	240
1833, Mar. 2	COLLINS,	VIRGINIA	Married George T. Lorimer	Book 1,	249
1806, Jul. 20	COLLINS,	WILLIAM	Married Nancy Greenwood	Book 1,	223
1689,	COLSTON,	WILLIAM	Married Mrs. Ann Hull	O 2,	87
1689,	COLSTON,	WILLIAM	Married Ann Beale, relict of Thomas Beale	O 2,	161
1720,	COMBER,	THOMAS	Married Keziah Henshaw, widow	D 16,	277
1674,	COMBES,	ARCHDALL	Married Elizabeth, widow of Col. William Underwood	D 5,	412

				Book	Page
1876, Dec. 28	COMMODORE, ANDERSON		Married Rosalie Roane	Book 1,	43
1866, Mar. 6	CONDAS,	MARY E.	Married James H. Good	Book 1,	14
1757,	CONNER,	LUCY	Relict of Martin Conner, married James Banks	D 27,	332
1757,	CONNER,	MARGARET	Daughter of Martin, married Joseph Hawkins	D 27,	332
1698,	CONNALIE,	EDMUND ?	Married Margaret, daughter of Cornelius Noell	D 9,	327
1808,	CONNOLY,	ELIZABETH	Married William Fisher	O 39,	377
1827, Nov. 20	CONOLY,	ELIZABETH	Married Riley Gouldman	Book 1,	243
1870, Dec. 7	CONOLY,	EMMA J.	Married Muscoe R. Dunn	Book 1,	26
1822, Feb. 26	CONOLY,	JOHN	Married Fanny Atkinson	Book 1,	239
1867, Sep. 19	CONOLY,	JOHN L.	Married Julia B. Banks	Book 1,	18
1834, Feb. 17	CONOLY,	MARY	Married Benjamin Williams	Book 1,	250
1849,	CONOLY,	MARY	Daughter of Catharine, married Benjamin Williams	W 27,	187
1812, Aug. 17	CONOLY,	SALLY	Married William Thomas	Book 1,	228
1840, Feb. 4	CONOLY,	SILAS	Married E. A. Boughton	Book 1,	254
1831, Apr. 7	CONOLY,	SUSAN	Married Mordecai Oliver	Book 1,	248
1808,	CONNOLY,	TABITHA	Married Henry Ramsey	O 39,	377
1713,	CONNALY,	THOMAS	Married Ann, daughter of Robert Mayfield	D&W 14,	385
1697,	CONTANCEAU, PETER		Married Mary, daughter of William Young	D 9,	140
1849, Mar. 22	COOKE,	ALEXANDER	Married Susan Tucker	Book 1,	261
1810, Dec. 29	COOK,	AMBROSE H.	Married Jane Taylor	Book 1,	226
1782,	COOK,	ANNA	Gloucester, Co. married William Roane	D 32,	144
1856, Mar. 27	COOK,	DINAH	Married William A. Davis	Book 1,	4
1870, Jan. 13	COOK,	ELIZA	Married James W. Barefoot	Book 1,	25
1853, May 9	COOK,	EMELINE	Married William A. Davis	Book 1,	264
1825, Dec. 19	COOK,	GILES B.	Married Lucy Brooke	Book 1,	241
1726,	COOK,	HANNAH	Married William Motley	W 4,	205
1733,	COOK,	JOHN	Married Mary, daughter of Cornelius Sale	W 5,	159
1856, Sep. 10	COOK,	LUCY	Widow, married John C. Prince, King & Queen Co.	Book 1,	4
1750,	COOK,	MARY	Married Joel Halbert	D 27,	71
1855, Apr. 18	COOK,	MARY E.	Married Richard W. Franklin	Book 1,	3
1820, Nov. 6	COOK,	PASCAL	Married Catharine Hill	Book 1,	237

				Book	Page
1816, Aug. 30	COOK,	RHODA	Married Gabriel Gatewood	Book 1,	233
1818, Dec. 14	COOK,	SALLY	Married Carter Taylor	Book 1,	234
1824, Mar. 3	COOK,	WILLIAM B.	Married Emily Foushee Tebbs	Book 1,	241
1833,	COOK,	WILLIAM B.	Married Emily, daughter of Foushee Tebbs	D 44,	192
1876, Nov. 1	COOK,	WILLIAM T.	Married Sarah Virginia Banks	Book 1,	43
1877, Dec. 6	COOK,	WILLIAM H.	Married Nettie B. Mitchell	Book 1,	46
1733,	COOPER,	ANN	Daughter of Thomas Cooper of Bristol, Eng. married Thomas Gregson, Attorney in Virginia	D 20,	246
1823, Oct. 21	COOPER,	DICEY	Married Solomon Ryan	Book 1,	240
1733,	COOPER,	ELIZABETH	Daughter of Thomas Cooper of Bristol, Eng. married James New, Bristol Shipwright	D 20,	246
1809, May 19	COOPER,	JAMES	Married Frances Cauthorn	Book 1,	225
1822, Jan. 10	COOPER,	JAMES	Married Ann Heath	Book 1,	239
1821, Jul. 18	COOPER,	JOHN	Married Nancy Hardy	Book 1,	238
1822, Nov. 13	COOPER,	JOHN	Married Conna Davis	Book 1,	239
1881, Mar. 17	COOPER,	REBECCA	Married William H. Martin	Book 1,	59
1845, Nov. 17	COOPER,	RICHARD	Married W. E. Montague	Book 1,	258
1852, Dec. 28	COOPER,	RICHARD	Married Susan Dennett	Book 1,	263
1866, Sep. 15	COOPER,	RICHARD	Married Catharine Smith	Book 1,	15
1726,	COOPER,	THOMAS	Married Sarah, daughter of Thomas Baskett	O 9,	144
1690,	COOPER,	WILLIAM	Married Elizabeth, daughter of Thomas St. John	D 9,	225
1701,	COPELAND,	ANN	Married Charles Atkinson	D&W 10,	86
1712,	COPELAND,	ANN	Daughter of Nicholas, married Thomas Phillips	W 3,	139
1764,	CORBIN,	ALICE	Married Meriwether Smith	D 29,	330
1796,	CORBIN,	FRANCIS	Married Anna Munford Beverley, Daughter of Robert Beverley	W 15,	549
1704,	CORBIN,	COL. GAWIN	Married Jane, Exec. of Capt. Willis Wilson, King & Queen Co.	O 3,	111
1696,	CORBIN,	JOHN	Richmond Co. married Elizabeth daughter of Wm. Smith	D 9,	55
1696,	CORPE,	JOHN	Married Elinor, daughter of William Covington	D 9,	105
1844, Oct. 17	CORR,	JOHN	Married Elizabeth Johnson	Book 1,	257
1845, Feb. 26	CORR,	THOMAS	Married Nancy Cauthorn	Book 1,	258
1785,	CORRIE,	CATHARINE	Daughter of John, married Thaddeus Williams	W 14,	76
1896, Nov. 4	COSBY,	LELAND	Married Nellie B. Eubank	Book 1,	122

					Book	Page
1891, Apr. 21	COSBY,	MARY E.	Married J. M. Spencer		Book 1,	107
1721,	COUGHLAND, ANN		Married John Rose		O 5,	636
1763,	COUGHLAND, JAMES		Married Mary, widow of William St. John		W 12,	187
1885, Dec. 21	COURTNEY, ALICE W.		Married Gregory Davis		Book 1,	85
1875, Dec. 23	COURTNEY, AUGUSTUS G.		Married Florence L. Seal		Book 1,	40
1876, Jan. 20	COURTNEY, CONSTANTINE		Married Ariadne Smith		Book 1,	41
1867, Dec. 26	COURTNEY, JOHN R.		Married Virginia E. Atkins		Book 1,	19
1837, Dec. 18	COURTNEY, JOSEPH C.		Married Dorothy I. Jones		Book 1,	252
1829, Feb. 20	COURTNEY, OLIVIA		Married Warner Lewis		Book 1,	246
1899, Jun. 7	COURTNEY, P. C.		Married Ida S. Powers		Book 1,	133
1879, Jan. 30	COURTNEY, THOMAS L.		Married Jane Alice Fogg		Book 1,	50
1848, Sep. 16	COUSINS, HENRY		Married Hyacinth Lomax		Book 1,	260
1889, Jun. 13	COVINGTON ALICE		Married George W. Brizendine		Book 1,	100
1817, Jan. 4	COVINGTON, AMEY		Married Evan Davis		Book 1,	233
1739,	COVINGTON, ANN		Sister of Richard, married Thomas Hawkins		W 6,	250
1816, Oct. 29	COVINGTON, ANN		Married William Howerton		Book 1,	232
1866, Dec. 18	COVINGTON, ANN E.		Married Joseph E. Clarkson		Book 1,	16
1820, Dec. 19	COVINGTON, CATHARINE		Married Jacob Durham		Book 1,	237
1823,	COVINGTON, EDMOND		Married Ann, daughter of Charles Saunders		D 41,	42
1808, Dec. 19	COVINGTON, EDWARD		Married Nancy Saunders		Book 1,	224
1881, Dec. 13	COVINGTON, IDA E.		Widow, married John Durham		Book 1,	62
1811, Dec. 5	COVINGTON, JOHN		Married Caty Greenwood		Book 1,	227
1877, Mar. 18	COVINGTON, JOHN A.		Married Rheida Mertine Durham		Book 1,	45
1889, May 23	COVINGTON, JOHN		Married Jessey C. Greenwood		Book 1,	100
1899, Nov. 2	COVINGTON, J. L.		Married Osie E. Clarke		Book 1,	134
1833, Dec. 10	COVINGTON, JULIA		Married M. H. Taylor		Book 1,	249
1837,	COVINGTON, JULIA		Daughter of John, married Horace Taylor		D 45,	275
1837, Dec. 18	COVINGTON, LOUISA		Married James Foreacres		Book 1,	252
1809, Nov. 20	COVINGTON, MARY		Married Henry Saunders		Book 1,	225
1865, Jan. 24	COVINGTON, MARY G.		Married George W. Dillard		Book 1,	13
1875, Dec. 28	COVINGTON, RACHEL ANN		Married John Brown		Book 1,	40

1697,	COVINGTON,	RICHARD	Married Ann, daughter of William Young	D	9,	141
1811, Jul. 29	COVINGTON,	RICHARD	Married Ann Kercheval	Book 1,		227
1834, Jan. 18	COVINGTON,	RICHARD H.	Married Elizabeth Brizendine	Book 1,		250
1847, Jan. 2	COVINGTON,	RICHARD L.	Married Emily C. Trible	Book 1,		243
1861, Dec. 26	COVINGTON,	RICHARD T.	Married Adeline Williams	Book 1,		11
1732,	COVINGTON,	ROSAMOND	Executrix of William, married William Carroll	O	8,	310
1740,	COVINGTON,	ROSAMOND	Relict of William, married William Carroll	O	12,	95
1727,	COVINGTON,	SARAH	Sister of Richard, married John Smith	D	18,	282
1818, Jan. 21	COVINGTON,	SARAH	Married Samuel Doggins	Book 1,		234
1837, Sep. 18	COVINGTON,	SARAH	Married Silas McKendrie	Book 1,		252
1846, Dec. 1	COVINGTON,	SARAH C.	Married James H. Noel	Book 1,		259
1832, Feb. 20	COVINGTON,	SOPHRONIA D.	Married Thomas Howerton	Book 1,		249
1834,	COVINGTON,	SOPHRONIA	Daughter of Richard, married Thomas Howerton, Halifax, Co.	D	45,	343
1884, Apr. 17	COVINGTON,	SUSAN A.	Married Richard S. Shepherd	Book 1,		77
1701,	COVINGTON,	THOMAS	Married Mary, daughter of Neale & Elinor Peterson	D&W 10,		94
1701,	COVINGTON,	THOMAS	Married Mary Peterson	D&W 10,		103
1835, Dec. 14	COVINGTON,	WAL. G.	Married Alice A. Boughton	Book 1,		251
1844, Dec. 2	COVINGTON,	W. G.	Married Lucy E. Clarkson	Book 1,		257
1733,	COVINGTON,	WILLIAM	Married Ann, daughter of Robert Coleman	D	20,	77
1741,	COVINGTON,	WILLIAM JR.	Married Amy, widow of Richard St. John	O	12,	304
1778,	COVINGTON,	WILLIAM	Married Sarah, daughter of Henry Crutcher	W	13,	300
1835, Dec. 23	COVINGTON,	WILLIAM	Married Lucy Greenwood	Book 1,		251
1834, Aug. 26	COWLES,	JOHN	Married Drusilla Trible	Book 1,		250
1884, Dec. 30	COX,	ALEXANDER C.	Married Susan Cox	Book 1,		80
1850, Sep. 16	COX,	ANN A.	Married Bevin Tucker	Book 1,		262
1876, Dec. 28	COX,	BETTIE	Married Charles L. Hodges	Book 1,		44
1877, May 1	COX,	BETTY B.	Married Richard Mahon	Book 1,		45
1695,	COX,	ELIZABETH	Daughter of Henry Cox, married John Smith	D	9,	62
1782,	COX,	ELIZABETH	Daughter of Henry, married William Ball	W	15,	25
1808,	COX,	ELIZABETH	Daughter of Thomas, married Gabriel Gordon	W	17,	118
1819, Jul. 29	COX,	ELIZABETH	Married George King	Book 1,		236

					Book	Page
1875, Oct. 28	COX,	ELTON	Married Mace Dunn		Book 1,	39
1853, Nov. 29	COX,	FLEET W.	Married Sarah E. Muse		Book 1,	1
1859, Jan. 18	COX,	FRANCES E.	Married Benjamin Tucker		Book 1,	7
1834, Feb. 17	COX,	GEORGE	Married Alice Gordon		Book 1,	250
1858, Aug. 7	COX,	HENRY	Married Martha Ann Clarke		Book 1,	6
1857, Oct. 1	COX,	JAMES R.	Married Susan E. Watkins		Book 1,	5
1822, Dec. 14	COX,	JOHN JR.	Married Joannah Croxton		Book 1,	239
1829, Jun. 15	COX,	JOHN S.	Married Judith Booker		Book 1,	247
1837,	COX,	JOHN	Married Judith, daughter of Lewis Booker Sr.		D 45,	382
1856, Dec. 15	COX,	JOHN	Married Elizabeth Coleman		Book 1,	5
1873, Feb. 27	COX,	JOHN L.	Married Mrs. Mary A. Fogg		Book 1,	32
1882, Apr. 5	COX,	JOHN L.	Married Elizabeth Dickerson		Book 1,	64
1886, Jan. 31	COX,	JOHN L.	Married Susan E. Crow		Book 1,	86
1844, Mar. 14	COX,	LUCY ANN	Married William J. Clarkson		Book 1,	257
1889, Mar. 20	COX,	MARTHA W.	Married J M. Hayes		Book 1,	99
1885, Aug. 4	COX,	MARY	Married James Acres		Book 1,	82
1810, Dec. 15	COX,	NANCY	Married Charles Minter		Book 1,	226
1834, Dec. 8	COX,	STHRESHLEY	Married Kitty Dunn		Book 1,	250
1869, Dec. 23	COX,	STHRESHLEY A.	Married Julia E. Taylor		Book 1,	24
1884, Dec. 30	COX,	SUSAN	Married Alexander C. Cox		Book 1,	80
1705,	COX,	THOMAS	Married Ann Haile		O 3,	198
1715,	COX,	THOMAS	Married only surviving daughter of John Haile dec'd		D&W 14,	497
1699,	COX,	WILLIAM	Married Frances, widow of John Wood		D&W 10,	13
1825, Dec. 20	COX,	WILLIAM	Married Sally Newbill		Book 1,	241
1828, Dec. 23	COX,	WILLIAM W.	Married Eliza Ball		Book 1,	245
1829,	COX,	WILLIAM JR.	Married Elizabeth Ball		D 42,	594
1832, Nov. 21	COX,	WILLIAM C.	Married Mary W. Dunn		Book 1,	248
1865, Dec. 28	COX,	WILLIAM A.	Married Frances E. Tuck		Book 1,	14
1870, Dec. 29	CRAFTON,	LUCY C.	Married John H. Prince		Book 1,	27
1883, Dec. 27	CRAFTON,	MARY	Married Thomas F. Hudgins, Gloucester Co.		Book 1,	74
1818, Jul. 4	CRAFTON,	SUSANNA	Married William DeShazo		Book 1,	234

					Book	Page

Date	Surname	Name	Description	Book	Page
1838, Jan. 15	CRAFTON,	WILLIAM	Married Jane B. DeShazo	Book 1,	253
1868, Feb. 27	CRAFTON,	WILLIAM	Married Margaret Garrett	Book 1,	20
1802,	CRAINE,	JAMES	Married Elizabeth, daughter of Thaddeus McCarty	D 35,	522
1816, Dec. 20	CRAINE,	PRISCILLA	Married Fielding Croxton	Book 1,	233
1685,	CRASKE,	EDMUND	Married Elizabeth, relict of Thomas Moss	O 1,	197
1710,	CRASKE,	ELIZABETH	Married James Lockhart, Richmond Co.	W 3, Richmond Co.	34
1676,	CREIGHTON,	HENRY	Married Jane, Exec. of Rice Jones	W 2,	42, 74
1828, Dec. 24	CREWDSON,	JOHN G.	Married Catharine Collins	Book 1,	245
1808, Jan. 21	CRIDLAND,	ANN	Married Richard Waters	Book 1,	225
1870, Dec. 29	CRIDLIN,	JAMES A.	Married Sarah Temple Reid	Book 1,	27
1860, Oct. 30	CRIDLIN,	WILLIAM W.	Married Lucy Ann Gary	Book 1,	9
1869, Dec. 28	CRISPIN,	AMERICA	Middlesex Co. married William L. Foreacres	Book 1,	24
1832, Mar. 13	CHRISPIN,	JOHN C.	Married Sarah Eubank	Book 1,	248
1870, Sep. 29	CRISPIN,	MARTHA E.	Married Richard R. Collins	Book 1,	26
1832,	CRITTENDEN,	CREETE	Daughter of Lemuel, married Richard H. Beazley	D 43,	504
1816, Sep. 18	CRITTENDEN,	E. S.	Married Richard Smith	Book 1,	232
1825,	CRITTENDEN,	ELIZA	Daughter of Lemuel & Susanna, married Richard Smith	D 41,	413
1743,	CRITTENDEN,	HENRY	Married Margaret, daughter of John Butler	D 23,	53
1809, Oct. 27	CRITTENDEN,	JOHN	Married Rachel Thomas	Book 1,	225
1825,	CRITTENDEN,	LEMUEL	Married Susanna, daughter of Benjamin Fisher	D 41,	413
1825,	CRITTENDEN,	LORINDA	Daughter of Lemuel & Susanna, married Richard Clarkson	D 41,	413
1828, Dec. 23	CRITTENDEN,	LUCRETIA	Married Richard H. Beazley	Book 1,	245
1825,	CRITTENDEN,	SALLY	Daughter of Lemuel & Susanna, married Richard Callis	D 41,	413
1813, Nov. 18	CRITTENDEN,	SUSAN L.	Married Richard Clarkson	Book 1,	229
1846, Jan. 28	CRITTENDEN,	SUSANNA	Married John Longest	Book 1,	259
1847, Dec. 2	CRITTENDEN,	SUSAN F.	Married Thomas Walker	Book 1,	260
1809, Nov. 21	CRITTENDEN,	WILLIAM	Married Mary Thomas	Book 1,	225
1869, Jan. 28	CRITTENDEN,	WILLIAM H.	H. Married Sally Ann Jones	Book 1,	22
1809, Feb. 20	CROFTON,	JAMES	Married Susanna Boughton	Book 1,	225
1750,	CRONDAS,	SARAH	Widow of William, married William Bradbourne	D 25,	180
1842, Apr. 25	CROPFIELD,	JAMES	Married Sophronia Jordan	Book 1,	256

				Book	Page
1729,	CROSBY,	JAMES	Married Mary, widow of Charles Brown	D 19,	27
1773,	CROSS,	JOHN	Married Rosey, daughter of William Thomas	W 12,	539
1831, Apr. 18	CROSS,	LUCY	Married Dawson Schools	Book 1,	248
1815, Feb. 27	CROSS,	THOMAS	Married Polly Fiddler	Book 1,	231
1828, Aug. 14	CROUCH,	ELIZABETH	Married George Harper	Book 1,	245
1838,	CROUCH,	?	Married Harriet Garrett, daughter of Banks Garrett	D 45,	458
1874, Apr. 15	CROUCH,	FONTAINE W.	Married Emma F. Reid	Book 1,	36
1836, Sep. 19	CROUCH,	JAMES	Married Harriet Garrett	Book 1,	252
1875, May 5	CROUCH,	JAMES	Married Eudora A. Blackburn	Book 1,	39
1897, Feb. 3	CROUCH,	JAMES L.	Married E. A. Parker	Book 1,	124
1868, Dec. 29	CROUCH,	JOANNA	Married Burton Clarke	Book 1,	21
1887, Sep. 18	CROUCH,	MARY J.	Married Willie Jackson Dyke	Book 1,	92
1885, Sep. 21	CROUCH,	SOPHRONIA	Married John Munday	Book 1,	83
1834, Jun. 5	CROUCH,	WILLIS	Married Mary E. Shelton	Book 1,	250
1863, Jul. 17	CROW,	ADELINE	Married Robert I. Greenwood	Book 1,	12
1859, Apr. 28	CROW,	ALEXANDER	Married Marinda Brizendine	Book 1,	7
1874, Dec. 24	CROW,	ALICE J.	Married Charles M. Carter	Book 1,	38
1821, Dec. 11	CROW,	ANN	Married John Gordon	Book 1,	238
1837, Dec. 18	CROW,	ANN	Married James Harper	Book 1,	252
1865, Feb. 21	CROW,	ANN	Married Joan Passagaluppi	Book 1,	13
1843, Feb. 20	CROW,	ANNA H.	Married John Jesse	Book 1,	256
1804, Dec. 17	CROW,	BARBARY	Married John Renno	Book 1,	222
1858, Apr. 30	CROW,	BAYLOR F.	Married Emeline Williamson	Book 1,	6
1834, Apr. 11	CROW,	CATHARINE	Married Churchill Brizendine	Book 1,	250
1810, Apr. 15	CROW,	CATY	Married William Ball	Book 1,	226
1883, Jun. 20	CROW,	DONNIA	Married Charles Shelton, Spottsylvania Co.	Book 1,	72
1867, Dec. 31	CROW,	ELDRED	Married Susanna E. Brizendine	Book 1,	19
1810, Jul. 16	CROW,	ELIZABETH	Married Robert Houston	Book 1,	226
1830, Dec. 20	CROW,	ELIZABETH	Married Benjamin Broocke	Book 1,	247
1868, Jan. 2	CROW,	EMELINE	Married Edward Brooks	Book 1,	20
1880, Apr. 14	CROW,	EMMA	Married Alexander O. Brooks	Book 1,	55

				Book	Page
1885, Apr. 8	CROW,	EUGENE L.	Married Fannie E. Lumpkin	Book 1,	81
1888, Sep. 6	CROW,	EVAN R.	Married Clara B. Durham	Book 1,	96
1891, Dec. 22	CROW,	FANNIE E.	Married John W. Billups	Book 1,	108
1808, Dec. 19	CROW,	FIELDING	Married Polly Lumpkin	Book 1,	224
1826,	CROW,	FIELDING S.	Married Polly, daughter of John Lumpkin	D 22,	305
1852, Oct. 4	CROW,	FRANCES C.	Married William Shackelford	Book 1,	263
1881, Oct. 13	CROW,	GEORGE W.	Married Lucy A. Bareford	Book 1,	61
1826, Jun. 20	CROW,	INNIS	Married Missouri Dobbins	Book 1,	242
1852, Dec. 18	CROW,	JAMES T.	Married Mary Elliott	Book 1,	263
1818, Feb. 28	CROW,	JOHN	Married Fanny Terrell	Book 1,	234
1831, Aug. 15	CROW,	JOHN	Married Mary Jane Dennett	Book 1,	248
1832, Apr. 6	CROW,	JOHN SR.	Married Martha Shackelford	Book 1,	248
1850, Dec. 23	CROW,	JOHN N.	Married Eliza Skelton	Book 1,	262
1899, Jan. 19	CROW,	JOHN T.	Married L. E. Shearwood	Book 1,	132
1852, Dec. 10	CROW,	LOUISA	Married Anthony Tune	Book 1,	263
1848, Jan. 13	CROW,	LUCINDA L.	Married Washington L. Clarke	Book 1,	260
1874, Apr. 14	CROW,	LUCINDA C.	Married Robert G. Elliott	Book 1,	36
1805, Apr. 15	CROW,	LUCY	Married William Ball	Book 1,	222
1866, Oct. 30	CROW,	MARINDA A.	Married Muscoe R. Dunn	Book 1,	15
1854, Jan. 16	CROW,	MARTHA A. F.	Married Arthur P. Davis	Book 1,	265
1819, Dec. 20	CROW,	MARY M.	Married Nathaniel Crow	Book 1,	235
1820,	CROW,	MARY	Daughter of John, married Robert Houston	W 19,	155
1854, Nov. 18	CROW,	MARY E.	Married John H. Collins	Book 1,	2
1834, Dec. 15	CROW,	MELISSA	Married John I. Armstrong	Book 1,	250
1856, Aug. 5	CROW,	MOSES T.	Married Martha Ellen Beazley	Book 1,	4
1819, Dec. 20	CROW,	NATHANIEL	Married Mary M. Crow	Book 1,	235
1807, Jul. 21	CROW,	POLLY E.	Married Lewis Gatewood	Book 1,	224
1816, Jan. 9	CROW,	POLLY	Married Alexander Houston	Book 1,	232
1820, Jan. 3	CROW,	ROBERT	Married Elizabeth Turner	Book 1,	237
1888, May 11	CROW,	ROBERT	Married M. E. Turner	Book 1,	95
1821, Jun. 5	CROW,	SARAH	Married James Croxton	Book 1,	238

				Book	Page
1840, Mar. 16	CROW,	SOPHRONIA	Married Benjamin Boughton	Book 1,	254
1886, Jan. 31	CROW,	SUSAN E.	Married John L. Cox	Book 1,	86
1841, Jan. 19	CROW,	SUSANNA S.	Married John M. Power	Book 1,	255
1853, Oct. 20	CROW,	THORNTON A.	Married Susan A. Lumpkin	Book 1,	2
1881, Dec. 27	CROW,	WILLIAM	Married Martha E. Barefoot	Book 1,	62
1812,	CROW,	WINNEY	Daughter of Nathaniel, married Andrew Allen	D 38,	293
1857, Dec. 18	CROXTON,	AMANDA M.	Married Alfred Derieux	Book 1,	5
1857,	CROXTON,	AMANDA	Married Alfred Derieux	D 51,	120
1856, Mar. 26	CROXTON,	ANN E.	Married Peter Toombs	Book 1,	4
1795,	CROXTON,	CARTER	Married Nancy, daughter of William Dunn	W 15,	506
1825,	CROXTON,	CARTER	Married Frances Faulconer	D 41,	452
1830, Dec. 22	CROXTON,	CARTER JR.	Married Mary Clarkson	Book 1,	247
1834,	CROXTON,	CARTER	Married Frances, sister of J. W. Faulconer	D 44,	489
1818, Jan. 2	CROXTON,	CATHARINE	Married Thomas Shearwood	Book 1,	234
1821, Jan. 10	CROXTON,	CATHARINE	Married Peter J. Derieux	Book 1,	238
1804, May 21	CROXTON,	CATY	Married Isaac Croxton	Book 1,	222
1819, May 20	CROXTON,	CATY	Married John Dunn	Book 1,	235
1854, Aug. 22	CROXTON,	CLAIBORNE	Married Susan Brizendine	Book 1,	2
1859, Dec. 21	CROXTON,	CORNELIA B.	Married William G. Purkins, Stafford, Co.	Book 1,	8
1889, Aug. 1	CROXTON,	EDWARD F.	Married Flora Brizendine	Book 1,	101
1827, Dec. 4	CROXTON,	ELIZA	Married Jonah Pruett	Book 1,	244
1806, Jan. 1	CROXTON,	ELIZABETH	Married Reuben Broocks	Book 1,	223
1831, Oct. 3	CROXTON,	ELIZABETH	Married Johnson Gaines	Book 1,	248
1873, Nov. 19	CROXTON,	EVELYN C.	Married James R. Gordon	Book 1,	35
1855, Mar. 15	CROXTON,	FANNIE E.	Married Alexander W. Broaddus	Book 1,	3
1867, Dec. 26	CROXTON,	FANNIE R.	Married John E. Shepperd	Book 1,	19
1816, Dec. 20	CROXTON,	FIELDING	Married Priscilla Craine	Book 1,	223
1824, Mar. 27	CROXTON,	FIELDING	Married Juliett Dobbins	Book 1,	241
1827, Dec. 17	CROXTON,	HARRIET	Married Philip Broocke	Book 1,	243
1804, May 21	CROXTON,	ISAAC	Married Caty Croxton	Book 1,	222
1771,	CROXTON,	JAMES	Married Mary, daughter of James Munday	D 30,	508

				Book	Page
1808, Dec. 19	CROXTON,	JAMES	Married Nancy Croxton	Book 1,	224
1821, Jun. 5	CROXTON,	JAMES	Married Sarah Crow	Book 1,	238
1845, Dec. 18	CROXTON,	JAMES	Married Mary Williamson	Book 1,	258
1857, Jun. 4	CROXTON,	JAMES A.	Married Mary A. Brooke	Book 1,	5
1859, Dec. 22	CROXTON,	JAMES M.	Married Sarah Y. Henley	Book 1,	8
1822, Dec. 14	CROXTON,	JOANNAH	Married John Cox, Jr.	Book 1,	239
1846, Apr. 20	CROXTON,	JOHN	Married Susan A. Taylor	Book 1,	258
1855, Sep. 11	CROXTON,	LOUISA C.	Married Philip A. Sandy	Book 1,	4
1868, Dec. 22	CROXTON,	LUCY A.	Married Walter H. Stewart, Westmoreland, Co.	Book 1,	21
1853, Mar. 29	CROXTON,	MARGARET A.	Married Theodore P. Boughan	Book 1,	264
1844, Oct. 21	CROXTON,	MARTHA	Married Leonard Henley	Book 1,	257
1853,	CROXTON,	MARTHA	Daughter of James, married Leonard Henley	W 27,	579
1809, Nov. 20	CROXTON,	MARY ANN	Married Winter Bray	Book 1,	225
1823,	CROXTON,	MARY	Daughter of Thomas Crutcher, mother of Fielding Croxton	W 20,	21
1845, Nov. 10	CROXTON,	MARY	Married Zebulon S. Farland	Book 1,	258
1847, Sep. 11	CROXTON,	MARY ANN	Married Edward Sandy	Book 1,	259
1849,	CROXTON,	MARY ANN	Daughter of Frances, married E. M. Sandy	W 26,	489
1849, Dec. 24	CROXTON,	MARY C.	Married Richard M. McKennon	Book 1,	261
1867, Dec. 17	CROXTON,	MARY L.	Married John W. McDaniel	Book 1,	19
1808, Dec. 19	CROXTON,	NANCY	Married James Croxton	Book 1,	224
1821, Apr. 26	CROXTON,	NANCY	Married William H. Hill	Book 1,	238
1806, Dec. 15	CROXTON,	PEGGY	Married John Belfield	Book 1,	223
1821, May 30	CROXTON,	RICHARD	Married Mary S. Clements	Book 1,	238
1826, Mar. 15	CROXTON,	RICHARD	Married Frances G. Ware	Book 1,	242
1822, Dec. 10	CROXTON,	ROBERT	Married Cynthia Ann Garnett	Book 1,	239
1804, Jul. 16	CROXTON,	SALLIE	Married Barker Minter	Book 1,	222
1847, Sep. 6	CROXTON,	SARAH E.	Married Edward Boughan	Book 1,	259
1869, Jul. 29	CROXTON,	SARAH Y.	Married James H. Muse	Book 1,	23
1852, Aug. 10	CROXTON,	SUSAN F.	Married Wm. George Jeffrey	Book 1,	263
1877, May 23	CROXTON,	SUSAN C.	Married Edward Macon Ware	Book 1,	45
1820, Apr. 4	CROXTON,	SUSANNA	Married Charles Bray	Book 1,	237

				Book	Page
1843, Jul. 4	CROXTON,	THOMAS	Married Louisiana Gatewood	Book 1,	256
1847,	CROXTON,	THOMAS	Married Louisiana Gatewood daughter of Sally Gatewood	W 26,	202
1753,	CROXTON,	THOMAS	Married Susanna, daughter of James Boughan	D 26,	286
1886, Aug. 26	CROXTON,	THOMAS B.	Married Julia A. Mitchell	Book 1,	88
1829, Jan. 12	CROXTON,	WILLIAM S.	Married Sophronia Ann Smith	Book 1,	246
1832,	CROXTON,	WILLIAM	Married Caty Crutcher, daughter of Thomas Crutcher	D 43,	579
1806, Jul. 20	CROXTON,	WINIFRED	Married Joseph Burnett	Book 1,	223
1873, Feb. 20	CRUTCHFIELD, ANN ELIZABETH		Married Henry Munday	Book 1,	32
1833, Oct. 14	CRUTCHFIELD, OSCAR		Married Susan E. M. Gatewood	Book 1,	249
1836,	CRUTCHFIELD, OSCAR		Spottsylvania Co. married Susan, dau. of Kemp Gatewood	D 45,	297
1778,	CRUTCHER,	CATY	Daughter of Henry, married Heritage Howerton	W 13,	300
1832,	CRUTCHER,	CATY	Daughter of Thomas, married William Croxton	D 43,	579
1781,	CRUTCHER,	HENRY	Married Jane, sister of John Howerton	W 13,	344
1778,	CRUTCHER,	MARGARET	Daughter of Henry, married William Harper	W 13,	300
1778,	CRUTCHER,	SARAH	Daughter of Henry, married William Covington	W 13,	300
1778,	CRUTCHER,	SUSANNA	Daughter of Henry, married William Cheyney	W 13,	300
1885, Nov. 3	CULPEPPER, DR. J. F.		Married Jennie Payne Fauntleroy	Book 1,	84
1867, Dec. 26	CURRIE,	MARTHA ANN	Married Benjamin Jackson	Book 1,	19
1834, Jan. 1	CURRIE,	POLLY	Married James West	Book 1,	250
1858, Aug. 6	CURRIER,	ELIZA D.	New Hampshire, married Raleigh D. Carter, Lancaster Co.	Book 1,	6
1790,	CURRIN,	ROBERT	Married Jenny, daughter of Charles Weeks	W 14,	230
1759,	CURTIS,	CHARLES	Married Anna, relict of Robert Edmondson	D 28,	282
1783,	CURTIS,	JOHN	Married Sarah, dau. of James Griffing	D 32,	170
1727,	CUTTS,	WILLIAM	Married Martha, Executrix of Richard Goode	O 7,	207
1802,	CUTHBERT,	WILLIAM	Married Nancy, dau. of Thaddeus McCarty, Lancaster Co.	D 35,	523

D

				Book	Page
1810,	DABNEY,	GEORGE	Married Susanna, daughter of Henry Quarles	W 17,	243
1824, Mar. 30	DABNEY,	GEORGE H.	Married Martha E. Tebbs	Book 1,	241
1690,	DABNEY,	JAMES	Married Ann, daughter of Philip Sherwood	D 8,	278
1857, Nov. 21	DABNEY,	MARY LUNSFORD	Married William G. Wright King & Queen Co.	Book 1,	5
1853, Aug. 30	DABNEY,	THOMAS J.	Married Mary Lunsford Wright	Book 1,	1
1690,	DACRES,	ANN	Relict of Charles, married William Tomlin	O 2,	295
1806, Nov. 17	DAILY,	ELIZABETH	Married Solomon Rian	Book 1,	223
1765,	DAILY,	JOHN	Married Ann, daughter of Frances Jones	W 12,	257
1754,	DALY,	HANNAH	Daughter of Daniel, married William Amiss	W 10,	23
1837, Sep. 18	DALLEY,	ANN	Married George Taylor	Book 1,	253
1834, Oct. 13	DALLEY,	JOHN C.	Married Ann Beazley	Book 1,	250
1821, Jun. 11	DALLEY,	LUCY	Married John Chamberlayne	Book 1,	238
1694,	DANGERFIELD,	FRANCES	Widow, married Edwin Thacker	O 1,	306
1860, Oct. 2	DAINGERFIELD,	HENRY W.	Married Eliza Courtney Upshaw	Book 1,	10
1686,	DANGERFIELD,	JOHN	Married Margaret, widow of Daniel Gaines	O 1,	184
1819, Nov. 29	DAINGERFIELD,	JOHN	Married Judith S. Braxton	Book 1,	235
1829,	DAINGERFIELD,	JOHN JR.	Married Judith, daughter of Carter Braxton	D 43,	16
1807, Nov. 18	DAINGERFIELD,	MARY	Married John Battaile	Book 1,	224
1672,	DANIEL,	HUGH	Married Mary, daughter of Luke Billington	W&D 1,	115
1672,	DANIEL,	MARY	Relict of Hugh, married Richard Hinds	D 4,	502
1819, Jan. 29	DANIEL,	PAMELIA ANN	Married John T. Evans	Book 1,	235
1796,	DANIEL,	ROBERT	Married Feaby, daughter of John Sadler	W 16,	42
1824, Dec. 28	DANIEL,	ROBERT	Married Lucinda Jessee	Book 1,	241
1874, Jun. 4	DANIEL,	ROBERT	Married Louisa W. Hoskins	Book 1,	36
1898, Nov. 23	DANIEL,	ROBERT JR.	Married Mary S. Waring	Book 1,	130
1843, Feb. 13	DANSEY,	WILLIAM	Married Martha Cauthorne	Book 1,	256
1877, Mar. 29	DAVIS,	ANNA A.	Married Charles L. Dunn	Book 1,	45
1887, Dec. 14	DAVIS,	ANNIE	Married W. T. Chenault	Book 1,	93
1887, Dec. 26	DAVIS,	A. C.	Married Nettie S. Mitchell	Book 1,	93
1854, Jan. 16	DAVIS,	ARTHUR P.	Married Martha A. F. Crow	Book 1,	265

					Book	Page
1806, May 10	DAVIS,	BETSEY	Married Ephraim Shepard		Book 1,	223
1847, Feb.15	DAVIS,	CATHARINE	Married Henry Clarke		Book 1,	259
1876, Aug. 1	DAVIS,	CATHARINE	Married Charles H. Tilton		Book 1,	42
1883, Mar. 22	DAVIS,	CATHARINE A.	Married Austin Brizendine		Book 1,	70
1814, Feb. 21	DAVIS,	CATY	Married Edmund Terrell		Book 1,	230
1825, Oct. 17	DAVIS,	CATY,	Married Anderton Griggs		Book 1,	241
1897, Feb. 10	DAVIS,	CELIA	Married J. R. Mitchell		Book 1,	124
1898, Dec. 29	DAVIS,	C. W.	Married C. E. Saunders		Book 1,	131
1798,	DAVIS,	CLARA	Heir of Oswald, married William Hill		W 16,	267
1820, Dec. 18	DAVIS,	CLARY	Married Gustave Fer		Book 1,	237
1878, Jan. 17	DAVIS	COLUMBIA	Married John Davis		Book 1,	47
1822, Nov. 13	DAVIS,	CONNA	Married John Cooper		Book 1,	239
1891, Jan. 8	DAVIS,	CORA E.	Married J. R. Southard		Book 1,	106
1897, Mar. 11	DAVIS,	CORA	Married C. F. Durham		Book 1,	125
1895, Aug. 17	DAVIS,	D. E.	Married James M. Davis		Book 1,	118
1872, Dec. 24	DAVIS,	DRUCILLA E.	Married N. B. Taylor		Book 1,	32
1822, Feb. 13	DAVIS,	DUNSTON	Married Margaret Tucker		Book 1,	239
1793,	DAVIS,	EDWARD G.	Married Betsey, daughter of Thomas Gouldin		W 15,	313
1808,	DAVIS,	EDWARD	Married Margaret Weeks		O 39,	337
1833, Nov. 11	DAVIS,	EDWARD G.	Married Mary Kay		Book 1,	249
1828, Dec. 15	DAVIS,	ELIZA	Married Joseph Newcomb		Book 1,	245
1858, Dec. 9	DAVIS,	ELIZA ANN	Married William Breedlove		Book 1,	7
1865, Dec. 28	DAVIS,	ELIZA A.	Married John L. Hodges		Book 1,	14
1817, Mar. 17	DAVIS,	ELIZABETH	Married Lewis H. Thomas		Book 1,	233
1823, Dec. 23	DAVIS,	ELIZABETH C.	Married John Tune		Book 1,	240
1826,	DAVIS,	ELIZABETH	Daughter of Edward Davis, married Lewis Thomas		D 41,	529
1829, Dec. 24	DAVIS,	ELIZABETH	Married Richard Vawter		Book 1,	246
1861, Mar. 6	DAVIS,	ELIZABETH	Married Henry Trimble, Hanover, Germany		Book 1,	10
1827, Jan. 20	DAVIS,	ELITHA	Married James Davis		Book 1,	243
1880, Nov. 20	DAVIS,	EMMA E.	Married Ranny S. Taylor		Book 1,	57
1670,	DAVIS,	EVAN	Married Mary, widow of Cyprian Bishop		D 4,	252

				Book	Page
1817, Jan. 4	DAVIS,	EVAN	Married Amey Covington	Book 1,	233
1806, Jan. 25	DAVIS,	FANNY	Married Samuel Williamson	Book 1,	223
1812,	DAVIS	FANNY	Daughter of Evan, married Samuel Williamson	O 41,	57
1827, Apr. 16	DAVIS,	FANNY	Married John Foreacres	Book 1,	243
1889, Mar. 26	DAVIS,	FANNIE C.	Married William L. Reeves	Book 1,	100
1817, Sep. 7	DAVIS,	FRANCES G.	Married Merriday Brown	Book 1,	233
1819, Dec. 27	DAVIS,	GEORGE	Married Priscilla Campbell	Book 1,	235
1828,	DAVIS,	GEORGE	Married Priscilla, widow of George Campbell	D 42,	382
1857, May 29	DAVIS,	GEORGE H.	Married Judith A. Davis	Book 1,	267
1806, Mar. 18	DAVIS,	GODFREY	Married Nancy Davis	Book 1,	223
1827, Nov. 20	DAVIS,	GREGORY	Married Lucy Griggs	Book 1,	243
1885, Dec. 21	DAVIS,	GREGORY	Married Alice W. Courtney	Book 1,	85
1824, Aug. 30	DAVIS,	HENRY	Married Maria Cauthorn	Book 1,	241
1843, Dec. 23	DAVIS,	HENRY	Married Polly Acres	Book 1,	256
1860, Mar. 18	DAVIS,	HENRY	Married Sarah Brizendine	Book 1,	9
1860, Feb. 1	DAVIS,	HORACE	Married Dorinda Webb	Book 1,	8
1859, Mar. 30	DAVIS,	ISAAC	Married Martha E. Dunn	Book 1,	7
1863, Jun. 19	DAVIS,	ISAAC	Married Martha Jane Greenwood	Book 1,	12
1752,	DAVIS,	JAMES	Married Catharine, Exec. of Henry Samuel	O 18,	275
1805, Mar. 18	DAVIS,	JAMES	Married Lucy Campbell	Book 1,	222
1810, Feb. 5	DAVIS,	JAMES	Married Sally I. James	Book 1,	226
1827, Jan. 20	DAVIS,	JAMES	Married Elitha Davis	Book 1,	243
1844, Dec. 23	DAVIS,	JAMES H.	Married Jane Prince	Book 1,	257
1876, Aug. 16	DAVIS,	JAMES W.	Married Rosa Ann Brooks	Book 1,	42
1883, Apr. 18	DAVIS,	JAMES R.	Married Fanny C. Prince	Book 1,	71
1889, Dec. 31	DAVIS,	JAMES H.	Married Maria Prince	Book 1,	102
1895, Aug. 17	DAVIS,	JAMES M.	Married D. E. Davis	Book 1,	118
1799,	DAVIS,	JOHN	Married Margaret Bush	O 35,	156
1878, Jan. 17	DAVIS,	JOHN	Married Columbia Davis	Book 1,	47
1893, Mar. 22	DAVIS,	J. R.	Married I. M. Williams	Book 1,	111
1858, Dec. 24	DAVIS,	JOSEPH E.	Married Louisa Goudy	Book 1,	9

					Book	Page
1892, Nov. 30	DAVIS,	JOSEPH	Married Emma W. Boughan		Book 1,	110
1857, May 29	DAVIS,	JUDITH A.	Married George H. Davis		Book 1,	267
1852, Dec. 23	DAVIS,	JUDSON	Married Maria Johnson		Book 1,	263
1869, Jun. 10	DAVIS,	JUDSON	Married Lelia Burch		Book 1,	23
1844, Aug. 7	DAVIS,	KEMP	Married Ann Brooks		Book 1,	257
1830, May 18	DAVIS,	KITTY C.	Married Bowler C. Gordon		Book 1,	247
1799,	DAVIS,	LEROY	Married Rosy Fuller		D 35,	173
1805, Dec. 10	DAVIS,	LEROY	Married Elizabeth Fisher		Book 1,	222
1806, Mar. 8	DAVIS,	LETTY	Married Thomas Gatewood		Book 1,	222
1825, Apr. 28	DAVIS,	LILLY	Married William Clarke		Book 1,	241
1810, Mar. 2	DAVIS,	LINDSAY	Married Amey Marlow		Book 1,	226
1877, Dec. 24	DAVIS,	LUCY ELLEN	Married Philip Bril		Book 1,	46
1892, May 18	DAVIS,	LUCY B.	Married William B. Moody		Book 1,	109
1896, Jun. 3	DAVIS,	LUCY	Married S. J. Carter		Book 1,	121
1806, Mar. 7	DAVIS,	MAJOR	Married Pheba Terrell		Book 1,	223
1878, Dec. 26	DAVIS,	MARGARET A.	Married Leland Dyke		Book 1,	49
1853, Dec. 28	DAVIS,	MARTHA ANN	Married Richard Brook		Book 1,	264
1866, Mar. 8	DAVIS,	MARTHA JANE	Married Alfred C. Greenwood		Book 1,	14
1870, Dec. 22	DAVIS,	MARTHA E.	Married William Clark		Book 1,	27
1875, Jun. 9	DAVIS,	MARTHA E.	Married James Parker		Book 1,	39
1670,	DAVIES,	MARY	Widow of Evan, married Arthur Hodges		D 1,	254
1840, Jun. 15	DAVIS,	MARY ANN	Married James Acres		Book 1,	254
1850, Oct. 8	DAVIS,	MARY	Married George Taylor, Jr.		Book 1,	262
1849, Sep. 27	DAVIS,	MATILDA N.	Married Howard Guess		Book 1,	261
1871, Aug. 18	DAVIS,	MATILDA	Married Major Marlow		Book 1,	29.
1892, Jun. 29	DAVIS,	MATTIE A.	Married Lewis L. Brooks		Book 1,	109
1875, Mar. 18	DAVIS,	MILDRED A.	Married William E. Wyatt		Book 1,	38
1882, Feb. 23	DAVIS,	MILDRED	Married James P. Ennis		Book 1,	63
1809, Aug. 21	DAVIS,	MOLLY	Married Edmund Ferrell		Book 1,	225
1798,	DAVIS,	NANCY	Heir of Oswald, married Brooking Sale		W 16,	267
1806, Mar. 18	DAVIS,	NANCY	Married Godfrey Davis		Book 1,	223

Date	Surname	Given	Description	Book	Page
1812,	DAVIS,	NANCY	Daughter of Evan, married Daniel Schelling	O 41,	57
1863, Feb. 4	DAVIS,	NARCISSA I.	Married John Johnston	Book 1,	11
1888, Mar. 15	DAVIS,	NEWTON	Married Mary J. Sirles	Book 1,	95
1816, Dec. 16	DAVIS,	OTHNEIL	Married Catharine Broocks	Book 1,	232
1804, Dec. 17	DAVIS,	PATSY	Married Griffin Harper	Book 1,	222
1812,	DAVIS,	PATSEY	Daughter of Evan, married Griffin Harper	O 41,	57
1805, Feb. 26	DAVIS,	PETER	Married Peggy Mann	Book 1,	222
1746,	DAVIS,	PHILIP	Married Hannah Virgett, dau. of Elizabeth Virgett, formerly Elizabeth Bendry	D 24,	138
1816, Nov. 7	DAVIS,	PHILIP	Married Lucy Taylor	Book 1,	233
1809, Sep. 18	DAVIS,	POLLY	Married Chaney Brizendine	Book 1,	225
1860, Dec. 6	DAVIS,	POLLY	Married Churchill A. Greenwood	Book 1,	10
1849, Dec. 26	DAVIS,	PRISCILLA	Married Thomas Harper	Book 1,	261
1850, Sep. 28	DAVIS,	RICHARD	Married Margaret Dunn	Book 1,	262
1887, Mar. 3	DAVIS,	RICHARD	Married Alice Gray	Book 1,	91
1885, Dec. 16	DAVIS,	ROBERT H.	Married Nina M. Winder	Book 1,	84
1888, Dec. 27	DAVIS,	ROBERT S.	Married Catharine Clarke	Book 1,	97
1899, Dec. 7	DAVIS,	ROBERT L.	Married L. M. Greenwood	Book 1,	135
1832, Feb. 29	DAVIS,	ROBINSON	Married Maria Clarke	Book 1,	248
1899, Mar. 16	DAVIS,	ROSIE A.	Married W. A. Brooks	Book 1,	132
1821, Dec. 19	DAVIS,	SALE	Married Ann Brooks	Book 1,	238
1840, Jan. 20	DAVIS,	SALE	Married Tamzin Taylor	Book 1,	254
1806, Oct. 20	DAVIS,	SALLY	Married Joseph Dennison	Book 1,	223
1812, Apr. 27	DAVIS,	SALLY	Married Bow ler Vawter	Book 1,	228
1844, Jan. 30	DAVIS,	SAMUEL	Married Amanda Atkins	Book 1,	247
1798,	DAVIS,	SARAH	Heir of Oswald, married William Salvator Jones	W 16,	267
1883, Apr. 19	DAVIS,	SOPHRONIA	Married Robert Guess	Book 1,	71
1821, Feb. 13.	DAVIS,	SUSAN	Married Brizendine Williams	Book 1,	238
1886, Jan. 12	DAVIS,	THOMAS W.	Married Lillie R. Tilton	Book 1,	85
1828, Jan. 30	DAVIS,	UPSHAW	Married Polly Clark	Book 1,	245
1860, Mar. 17	DAVIS,	UPSHAW	Married Betsey Ball	Book 1,	9

1861, Jan. 5	DAVIS,	VIRGINIA	Married Kemp Evans	Book 1,	10
1830, Nov. 30	DAVIS,	WALKER	Married Catharine Taylor	Book 1,	247
1843,	DAVIS,	WALKER	Married Catharine, daughter of Nancy Taylor	W 24,	149
1822, Feb. 5	DAVIS,	WASHINGTON	Married Nancy Clarke	Book 1,	239
1804, Dec. 17	DAVIS,	WILLIAM	Married Daisy Williamson	Book 1,	222
1809, May 16	DAVIS,	WILLIAM	Married Lucy Doggins	Book 1,	225
1816, Apr. 7	DAVIS,	WILLIAM	Married Nancy Broocks	Book 1,	233
1825, Jan. 17	DAVIS,	WILLIAM	Married Mary Toon	Book 1,	241
1830, Dec. 20	DAVIS,	WILLIAM	Married Martha Bunday	Book 1,	247
1845, Sep. 2	DAVIS,	WILLIAM B.	Married Julia Mann	Book 1,	258
1853, May 9	DAVIS,	WILLIAM A.	Married Emeline Cook	Book 1,	264
1856, Mar. 27	DAVIS,	WILLIAM A.	Married Dinah Cook	Book 1,	4
1887, Nov. 23	DAVIS,	WILLIAM G.	Married Addie L. Parr	Book 1,	92
1831, Dec. 3	DAWSON,	HENRY	Married Catharine Blake	Book 1,	248
1830, Feb. 18	DAWSON,	SAMUEL I.	Married Catharine Haile	Book 1,	247
1711,	DAWSON,	WILLIAM	Married Elizabeth, daughter of Sarah Stone	W 3, Richmond Co.	324
1819, May 21	DAY,	ANN	Married Benjamin Perry	Book 1,	236
1822, May 20	DAY,	HENRIETTA	Married Samuel Kendall	Book 1,	239
1683, Apr. 12	DAY,	MARY	Relict of John, "This day married John Billington"	Box 101,	G
1718,	DAY,	RICHARD	Married Mary, daughter of Robert Bunberry	D&W 15,	261
1676,	DAY,	THOMAS	Married Dorothy, daughter of Thomas Hudson	D 5,	514
1738,	DEANE,	THOMAS	Married Jane, daughter of John Smith	W 7,	189
1758,	DEGRAFFENREIDT, ISCHARNER		Married Sarah, daughter of John Lowry	W 12,	49
1799,	DE JARNETTE, JOHN		Married Fanny Faver, orphan of Theophilus Faver	O 35,	416
1845, Jul. 8	DELANO,	MARY E.	Married Robert Broocks	Book 1,	258
1710,	DEMING,	ANN	Late wife of Adam, married John Watkins	O 4,	299
1684,	DENBY,	MARY	Daughter of William, married John Walker	D 7,	136
1819, Nov. 9	DENNETT,	GREGORY	Married Rebecca Gordon	Book 1,	235
1812, Dec. 14	DENNETT,	LUCY	Married Thomas Griggs	Book 1,	228
1831, Aug. 15	DENNETT,	MARY JANE	Married John Crow	Book 1,	248
1852, Dec. 28	DENNETT,	SUSAN	Married Richard Cooper	Book 1,	263

				Book	Page
1814, Feb. 14	DENNETT,	THOMAS	Married Ann Doggins	Book 1,	230
1806, Oct. 20	DENNISON,	JOSEPH	Married Sally Davis	Book 1,	223
1831,	DENNISON,	SARAH	Widow of Joseph, married ? Drinkwater	D 43,	438
1883, Mar. 8	DENISTON,	ABBY	Croton Falls, N. Y. married Dr. William Fisher	Book 1,	70
1881, Feb. 25	DENNISTON,	CATHARINE A.	Married John W. Ennis	Book 1,	59
1741,	DENNY,	GEORGE	Married Elizabeth, widow of Benjamin Rouzie	D 22,	250
1866, Jan. 11	DENNY,	GEORGE H.	Married Charlotte Matilda Wright	Book 1,	14
1703,	DEPUTY,	ROBERT	Middlesex, Co. married Elizabeth, dau. of Hugh Meade, Piscataway	D 11,	48
1857, Dec. 17	DERIEUX,	ALFRED	Married Amanda M. Croxton	Book 1,	5
1849, Sep. 17	DERIEUX,	ARTHUR J.	Married Virginia Clarkson	Book 1,	261
1886, Sep. 6	DERIEUX,	EVELYN G.	Married James L. Clarkson	Book 1,	88
1881, Nov. 3	DERIEUX,	KATE A.	Married J. A. Clarkson	Book 1,	61
1882, Jan. 5	DERIEUX,	JUSTIN L.	Married Mary E. Campbell	Book 1,	63
1842, Jun. 20	DERIEUX,	M. M. M.	Married W. L. Waring	Book 1,	256
1844, Oct. 15	DERIEUX,	MARY A.	Married Thomas Waring	Book 1,	257
1869, May 13	DERIEUX,	MARY C.	Married Joseph W. Hart	Book 1,	23
1881, Nov. 3	DERIEUX,	M. E.	Married William E. Rouzie	Book 1,	61
1821, Jan. 10	DERIEUX,	PETER J.	Married Catharine Croxton	Book 1,	238
1866, Dec. 13	DERIEUX,	PETER P.	Married Mary E. Wright	Book 1,	15
1883, Sep. 26	DERIEUX,	SUSIE S.	Married Alfred H. Ryland	Book 1,	73
1838, Jan. 15	DESHAZO,	JANE B.	Married William Crafton	Book 1,	253
1854, Jan. 10	DESHAZO,	THOMAS L.	Married Joanna S. Powers	Book 1,	1
1818, Jul. 4	DESHAZO,	WILLIAM	Married Susanna Crafton	Book 1,	234
1885, Sep. 5	DEVERISEY,	ADDERENA	Married James T. Ellett	Book 1,	83
1804, Mar. 10	DEW,	ELIZABETH	Married Robert Kay	Book 1,	222
1716,	DEW,	ELIZABETH	Daughter of Jane, married Samuel Bayley	W 3,	310
1875, Dec. 29	DICKINSON,	ALEXANDER	Married Ella Wheeler	Book 1,	40
1835,	DICKERSON,	CATHARINE	Daughter of William, married William Bentley	D 45,	56
1882, Apr. 5	DICKERSON,	ELIZABETH	Married John L. Cox	Book 1,	64
1852, Dec. 30	DICKENSON,	ERASTUS	Married Victoria Brizendine	Book 1,	263
1827, Oct. 24	DICKENSON,	FRANCES	Married William Gravatt	Book 1,	243

				Book	Page
1835, Nov. 30	DICKENSON,	FRANCES M.	Married Mordecai Spindle	Book 1,	251
1822, Apr. 17	DICKERSON,	JOHN	Married Mahaly Dogging	Book 1,	239
1848, Jun. 17	DICKENSON,	JOHN F.	Married Virginia G. Saunders	Book 1,	260
1868, Dec. 25	DICKENSON,	LARKIN	Married Lucy E. Jordan	Book 1,	21
1833, Mar. 14	DICKENSON,	LUCY ANN	Married John S. Quesenberry	Book 1,	249
1835,	DICKENSON,	LUCY ANN	Daughter of William, married John Qusenberry	D 45,	130
1871, May 17	DICKINSON,	WILLIAM F.	Married Nancy Rose	Book 1,	28
1874, Jul. 16	DICKINSON,	WILLIAM F.	Married Eliza Greenwood	Book 1,	37
1857, Apr. 29	DIDLAKE,	AMANDA	Married Wilson Rowe	Book 1,	5
1823, Jan. 11	DIDLAKE,	GEORGE W.	Married Ann E. Cauthorn	Book 1,	240
1859, Jan. 15	DIDLAKE,	JOHN H.	Married Maria L. Edwards	Book 1,	7
1889, Jan. 23	DIDLAKE,	J. M.	Married Nina L. Goode	Book 1,	99
1830, Dec. 30	DIDLAKE,	NANCY	Widow, married William Oliver	Book 1,	247
1881, Apr. 3	DIDLAKE,	ROSA E.	Married Charles E. Broach	Book 1,	59
1691,	DIKE,	JOHN	Married Mary, sister of John Sharpe	D 8,	281
1896, Nov. 11	DILLARD,	ALICE E.	Married Robert H. Dillard	Book 1,	122
1873, Feb. 5	DILLARD,	ANNIE E.	Married Robert W. Smith	Book 1,	32
1837, May 10	DILLARD,	D. A. E.	Married Joseph B. Smith	Book 1,	253
1854, Mar. 3	DILLARD,	FLORA M.	Married Moore G. Fauntleroy	Book 1,	265
1865, Jan. 24	DILLARD,	GEORGE W.	Married Mary G. Covington	Book 1,	13
1880, Jun. 1	DILLARD,	J. W.	Married Martha C. Smith	Book 1,	56
1898, Jun. 8	DILLARD,	J. H.	Married M. K. Parr	Book 1,	129
1865, Oct. 19	DILLARD,	MARY	Married Henry Clarke	Book 1,	13
1879, Apr. 15	DILLARD,	ROBERT P.	Married Fanny Gray Waring	Book 1,	52
1896, Nov. 11	DILLARD,	ROBERT H.	Married Alice E. Dillard,	Book 1,	122
1878, May 9	DILLARD,	SARAH T.	Married Bailey Van Wagner	Book 1,	48
1734,	DILLARD,	THOMAS	Married Winifred, daughter of Martin & Mary Nalle	W 5,	272
1829, Apr. 6	DILLARD,	THOMAS	Married Mira Oliver	Book 1,	246
1814, Sep. 19	DILLARD,	WILLIAM	Married Elizabeth Cauthorn	Book 1,	230
1888, Oct. 18	DILLARD,	W. E.	Married Zora S. Owen	Book 1,	96
1721,	DIMACK,	THOMAS	Married Rachel Pettit	O 5,	634
				O 6,	67

				Book	Page
1835, Mar. 7	DISHMAN,	ANN	Married John W. Fisher	Book 1,	251
1826, May 20	DISHMAN,	ARABELLA	Married Edmund Pilkington	Book 1,	242
1898, Sep. 27	DISHMAN,	C. M.	Married N. J. Watts	Book 1,	129
1806, Mar. 25	DISHMAN,	DAVID	Married Margaret Rennolds	Book 1,	223
1832, Jan. 24	DISHMAN,	EMILY	Married Asa Gouldman	Book 1,	249
1841, Sep. 20	DISHMAN,	F. SIDNEY	Married Absalom Gouldman	Book 1,	255
1847, Jan. 6	DISHMAN,	FAUNTLEROY	Married Annie E. Smith	Book 1,	259
1860, Jan. 17	DISHMAN,	JAMES R.	Married Eliza E. Clarke	Book 1,	8
1847, Nov. 20	DISHMAN,	JOHN W.	Married Selina Gray	Book 1,	259
1834, May 3	DISHMAN,	MARY	Married William W. Dishman	Book 1,	250
1809, May 22	DISHMAN,	PETER	Married Polly Brown	Book 1,	225
1811, Dec. 7	DISHMAN,	SAMUEL	Married Sarah Gray	Book 1,	227
1854, Sep. 14	DISHMAN,	SARAH I.	Married James W. Cash	Book 1,	3
1834, Jan. 7	DISHMAN,	SELINA	Married Hiram Gouldman	Book 1,	250
1806, Dec. 24	DISHMAN,	SUSANNAH	Married Thomas Minter	Book 1,	223
1897, Feb. 21	DISHMAN,	S. J.	Married H. O. Anderson, Caroline, Co.	Book 1,	124
1834, May 3	DISHMAN,	WILLIAM W.	Married Mary Dishman	Book 1,	250
1868, Feb. 12	DISHMAN,	WILLIAM L.	Married Mary E. Watts	Book 1,	20
1693,	DISKIN,	JOHN	Married Relict of Caleb Lyon	O 1,	115
1689,	DISKIN,	MARY	Relict of John, married Edward Jeffries	O 2,	199
1693,	DISON,	RICHARD	Married Christian, youngest daughter of Valentine Allen	O 1,	108
1828, Jun. 16	DIX,	ANN	Married Achilles Lumpkin	Book 1,	245
1846, May 18	DIX,	CATHARINE	Married.Edward Smith	Book 1,	259
1751,	DIX,	JOHN	Caroline Co. married Keren Happuck, widow of Peter Jett	D 25,	281
1814, Dec. 19	DIX,	JOHN	Married Martha M. Edmondson	Book 1,	230
1870, Dec. 22	DIX,	LEWIS E.	Married Lucinda P. Brooks	Book 1,	27
1899, Feb. 2	DIX,	MAGRUDER	Married Addie B. Jeffries	Book 1,	132
1784,	DIX,	MARY	Daughter of Thomas, married John Haile	W 14,	138
1853, Mar. 28	DIX,	MARY A.	Widow, married Willis Brooke	Book 1,	264
1815, Oct. 12	DIX,	MELESIA	Married Addison Allen	Book 1,	231
1822, Jun. 11	DIX,	TANDY	Married Nancy Burk	Book 1,	239

				Book	Page
1805, Oct. 21	DIX,	THOMAS	Married Elizabeth Wood	Book 1,	222
1893, Mar. 28	DIX,	VIRGINIA	Married Richard Brooks	Book 1,	111
1820, Mar. 15	DIX,	WALTER	Married Judith Boughton	Book 1,	237
1842, Jan. 12	DIX,	WILLIAM	Married Julia Taylor	Book 1,	256
1851, Sep. 30	DIX,	WILLIAM	Married Mary T. Fisher	Book 1,	262
1699,	DIXON,	ELIZABETH	Relict of John, married Peter Sullenger	D&W 10,	12
1810,	DOBBINS,	ANN	Daughter of William, married John Clarke	W 17,	294
1834, Jul. 7	DOBBINS,	ANN	Married Gideon P. Dunn	Book 1,	250
1810,	DOBBINS,	BOB	Married Victoria, daughter of John Montague (Ran away)	W 17,	170
1692,	DOBBINS,	DURA	Married Catharine, daughter of Thomas St. John	O 1,	32
1824,	DOBBINS,	DURA	Married Catharine, daughter of Richard St. John	W 20,	32
1824, Mar. 27	DOBBINS,	JULIETT	Married Fielding Croxton	Book 1,	241
1836, Jan. 28	DOBBINS,	LEROY W.	Married Vannangus A. Samuel	Book 1,	252
1826, Jun. 20	DOBBINS,	MISSOURI	Married Innis Crow	Book 1,	242
1819, Feb. 27	DOBBINS,	VICTORIA	Married William Sadler	Book 1,	236
1807, Jan. 19	DOBYNS,	ANN	Married John Clarke	Book 1,	224
1855, Dec. 22	DOBYNS,	ANN E. R.	Married William D. Wright	Book 1,	3
1881, Oct. 12	DOBYNS,	ANNIE B.	Married John S. Exall	Book 1,	61
1688,	DOBYNS,	DANIEL	Married Elizabeth Smith	O 2,	111
1849, May 31	DOBYNS,	H. M.	Married Sarah I. Jones, widow	Book 1,	261
1870, Dec. 22	DOBYNS,	JENNIE E.	Married Joshua W. Williams	Book 1,	26
1870, Dec. 22	DOBYNS,	VANNANGUS A.	Married Muscoe Garnett, Jr.	Book 1,	26
1890, Aug. 13	DOGGETT,	GEORGE B.	Married Georgie A. Anderson	Book 1,	104
1814, Feb. 14	DOGGINS,	ANN	Married Thomas Dennett	Book 1,	230
1841, Jan. 21	DOGGINS,	ANN	Married Obadiah Greenwood	Book 1,	258
1806, Apr. 20	DOGGINS,	HAPPY	Married Jackson Dunn	Book 1,	223
1824,	DOGGINS,	HAPPY	Daughter of Samuel, married Jackson Dunn	D 41,	107
1863, Dec. 30	DOGGINS,	JAMES S.	Married Sarah E. Pruett	Book 1,	12
1809, May 16	DOGGINS,	LUCY	Married William Davis	Book 1,	225
1822, Apr. 17	DOGGINS,	MAHALY	Married John Dickerson	Book 1,	239
1807, Dec. 21	DOGGINS,	PATSY	Married John Brizendine	Book 1,	224

				Book	Page
1812, Dec. 21	DOGGINS,	PERCILLA	Married George Campbell	Book 1,	228
1818, Jan. 21	DOGGINS,	SAMUEL	Married Sarah Covington	Book 1,	234
1894, Aug. 29	DOGGINS,	T. C.	Married V. F. Beazley	Book 1,	114
1889, Jan. 18	DOGGINS	WILLIAM M.	Married Nannie B. Parr	Book 1,	99
1692,	DOHODY,	JANE	Married John Smith	O 1,	32
1824, Mar. 30	DOLLINS,	RILEY	Married Nancy Sullivan	Book 1,	241
1747,	DONOHOE,	ELINOR	Daughter of Patrick, married Cornelius Noell	W 8,	49
1814, May 25	DONNAHOE,	GEORGE	Married Lucy May	Book 1,	230
1748,	DONOHOE,	MILDRED	Daughter of Patrick, married Daniel Farguson	W 8,	49, 61
1694,	DONOLANE,	EDWARD	Married Jane Smith (License)	O 1,	325
1722,	DONAPHAN,	ALEXANDER	Married Sarah Sallis	O 5, O 6,	756 9
1811, Jan. 22	DONNELSON,	SALLIE	Widow, married Daniel Drinkwater	Book 1,	227
1854, Nov. 11	DORSEY,	JOSEPH S.	Married Amanda F. Mitchell	Book 1,	265
1859, Jan. 27	DOUGLASS,	RICHARD T.	Married Elton Longest	Book 1,	7
1858, Oct. 24	DOUGLASS,	RUSSELL A.	Married Lucinda Newbill	Book 1,	6
1712,	DOUGHTY,	MARGARET	Daughter of Enoch, married William Berry	D&W 14,	107
1677,	DOWNER,	FRANCIS	Married Katherine, relict of Robert Hoskins (Hopkins)	D 6,	31
1803,	DOWNEY,	JOHN	Married Rachel, daughter of John Sadler	W 16,	221
1811, May 22	DOWNEY,	JOHN	Married Diana Evans	Book 1,	227
1849, Dec. 28	DOWNEY,	N. J. M.	Married Obed Mann	Book 1,	261
1824, Jan. 19	DOWNEY,	POLLY	Married James Dunn	Book 1,	241
1810, Nov. 12	DOWNEY,	SALLY	Married John Turner	Book 1,	226
1823,	DOWNMAN,	RALEIGH	Lancaster, Co. married Sarah, daughter of Foushee Tebbs	D 41,	93
1809, May 15	DOZER,	NELSON	Married Ann B. Marshall	Book 1,	225
1811, Jan. 22	DRINKWATER,	DANIEL	Married Mrs. Sallie Donnelson	Book 1,	227
1831,	DRINKWATER,	?	Married Sarah, widow of Joseph Denison	D 43,	448
1849, May 26	DRINKWATER,	S. D.	Married John H Williams	Book 1,	261
1715,	DUCKBARY,	MARY	Married Jôhn Willis	D&W 14,	428
1716,	DUDLEY,	DOROTHY	Married Richard Gatewood	D&W 15,	79
1828, Sep. 22	DUDLEY,	RICHARD	Married Mira W. Whiting	Book 1,	245
1813, Nov. 15	DUERSON,	HENRY	Married Mary Clark	Book 1,	229

1871, Dec. 14	DUFF,	MARTHA F.	Married William W. Brooke	Book 1,	29
1883, Oct. 10	DUFF,	OLIVIA A.	Married Samuel Williams	Book 1,	73
1838, Jun. 19	DUFF,	PETER	Married Olivia D. Dunn	Book 1,	253
1843,	DUFF,	PETER	Married Olivia, daughter of James Dunn	W 24,	49
1871, Sep. 19	DUFF,	RICHARD H.	Married Margaret Dunn	Book 1,	29
1864, Dec. 29	DUFF,	WILLIAM I.	Married Susan C. E. Clarke	Book 1,	13
1888, May 23	DUKE,	R. J.	Married Annie B. Stone	Book 1,	95
1804, Dec. 11	DULING,	WILLIAM	Married Philadelphia Garnett	Book 1,	222
1807,	DULING,	WILLIAM	Married Philadelphia Green	O 39,	1
1850, Aug. 26	DUNBAR,	EDWARD	Married Lucy Cauthorn	Book 1,	262
1783,	DUNLOP,	JAMES	Married Elizabeth, daughter of Leonard Hill	Chancery Suits Box 1774-1787	
1798,	DUNLOP,	JAMES	Married Elizabeth, daughter of Leonard Hill	W 15,	467
1825, Jan. 17	DUNN,	ALEXANDER	Married Catharine Meadows	Book 1,	241
1869, Jun. 10	DUNN,	BENJAMIN F.	Married Amanda J. Taylor	Book 1,	23
1821, Dec. 27	DUNN,	BILLINGTON	Married Harriet Brown	Book 1,	238
1848, Dec. 26	DUNN,	CAROLINE V.	Married Arthur Taylor	Book 1,	260
1804, Jul. 13	DUNN,	CATHARINE	Married John H. Gatewood	Book 1,	222
1808, Sep. 24	DUNN,	CATHARINE	Married Thomas Hart	Book 1,	224
1819, Jun. 16	DUNN,	CATHARINE	Married Reuben Coleman	Book 1,	235
1829,	DUNN,	CATHARINE	Married Samuel Johnson	D 43,	37
1836, Dec. 19	DUNN,	CATHARINE	Married Edmund Broockes	Book 1,	252
1877, Mar. 29	DUNN,	CHARLES L.	Married Anna A. Davis	Book 1,	45
1824, Dec. 24	DUNN,	COLUMBIA	Married George Wyatt	Book 1,	241
1841, May 17	DUNN,	DELILA F.	Married Daniel I. Moody	Book 1,	255
1802,	DUNN,	DIANA	Formerly wife of Philip Cheyney	D 36,	136
1851, May 2	DUNN,	DORINDA M.	Married Jon. I. Cauthorn	Book 1,	262
1874, Jan. 15	DUNN,	DOROTHEA A.	Married George Brooks	Book 1,	35
1829, Mar. 20	DUNN,	DRUSILLA	Married Richard C. Segar	Book 1,	246
1843,	DUNN,	DRUSILLA	Daughter of James, married William R. Allen	W 24,	49
1826, Mar. 25	DUNN,	EDMOND	Married Lucy Ursery	Book 1,	242
1832,	DUNN,	EDMUND	Married Daughter of Thomas Ursery	D 44,	13

				Book	Page
1841, Sep. 27	DUNN,	EDMUND	Married Mary Ursery	Book 1,	250
1834, Mar. 17	DUNN,	EDMONIA C.	Married William Webb	Book 1,	250
1841, Aug. 13	DUNN,	EMILY C.	Married Charles C. Smith	Book 1,	255
1865, Dec. 30	DUNN,	EMILY F.	Married William E. Brooks	Book 1,	14
1798,	DUNN,	ELIZABETH	Married Thomas Bohannon	W 15,	387
1810, Oct. 30	DUNN,	ELIZABETH	Married Joshua Dunn	Book 1,	226
1820, Dec. 22	DUNN,	ELIZABETH	Married Thomas Harper	Book 1,	237
1836, Dec. 28	DUNN,	ELIZABETH	Married Thomas Carneal	Book 1,	252
1837, Sep. 18	DUNN,	ELIZABETH	Married Carter Shackelford	Book 1,	253
1894, May 2	DUNN,	ELMORE	Married E. J. Hayes	Book 1,	114
1850, Dec. 24	DUNN,	FRANCES A.	Married James H. Taylor	Book 1,	262
1863, Aug. 14	DUNN,	GEORGE W.	Married Maria A. Stevens	Book 1,	12
1876, Feb. 3	DUNN,	GEORGE W.	Married Bettie Johnson	Book 1,	41
1880, Nov. 11	DUNN,	GEORGE W. JR.	Married Lucy Williams	Book 1,	57
1885, Apr. 4	DUNN,	GEORGE JR.	Married Sarah Gresham	Book 1,	81
1834, Jul. 7	DUNN,	GIDEON P.	Married Ann Dobbins	Book 1,	250
1854, Mar. 15	DUNN,	HANNAH L.	Married James B. Hundley	Book 1,	265
1890, May 22	DUNN,	H. W.	Married Waller Robinson	Book 1,	104
1898, Feb. 12	DUNN,	HARRIET	Married Ruffin Clarke	Book 1,	128
1867, Dec. 19	DUNN,	INDIA A.	Married John Hay, King William Co.	Book 1,	19
1856, Oct. 23	DUNN,	IVERSON L.	Married Lucy C. Boughton	Book 1,	4
1806, Apr. 20	DUNN,	JACKSON	Married Happy Doggins	Book 1,	223
1824,	DUNN,	JACKSON	Married Happy, daughter of Samuel Doggins	D 41,	107
1821, Jul. 14	DUNN,	JAMES	Married Caty Gibson	Book 1,	238
1824, Jan. 19	DUNN,	JAMES	Married Polly Downey	Book 1,	241
1842, May 9	DUNN,	JAMES	Married Virginia Hundley	Book 1,	256
1842, Nov. 21	DUNN,	JAMES	Married Susan Mullins	Book 1,	256
1846,	DUNN,	JAMES	Married Susan Mullins	W 26,	442
1851, Sep. 18	DUNN,	JAMES A.	Married Eliza Pitts	Book 1,	262
1838, Dec. 12	DUNN,	JANE	Married James McFarlaine	Book 1,	253
1829,	DUNN,	JOANNA	Married George Martin	D 43,	53

				Book	Page
1808, Nov. 21	DUNN,	JOHN	Married Mary Hayes	Book 1,	224
1819, May 20	DUNN,	JOHN	Married Caty Croxton	Book 1,	235
1831, Dec. 21	DUNN,	JOHN	Married Patsy Stewart	Book 1,	248
1833, Jan. 21	DUNN,	JOHN	Married Sarah Foreacres	Book 1,	249
1872, Nov. 7	DUNN,	JOHN L.	Married Lucy A. McKendrie	Book 1,	31
1756,	DUNN,	JONATHAN	Married Elizabeth, widow of William Bohannon	W 10,	97
1822, May 20	DUNN,	JONATHAN	Married Harriet Shipp	Book 1,	239
1810, Oct. 30	DUNN,	JOSHUA	Married Elizabeth Dunn	Book 1,	226
1829, Dec. 21	DUNN,	JULIA	Married John Clarke	Book 1,	246
1835, Dec. 8	DUNN,	JULIA D.	Married Thomas Parron	Book 1,	251
1843,	DUNN,	JULIA	Daughter of James, married Thomas Parron	W 24,	49
1854, Dec. 13	DUNN,	JULIA A.	Married Alfred Goudy	Book 1,	3
1834, Dec. 8	DUNN,	KITTY	Married Sthreshley Cox	Book 1,	250
1832, Jan. 16	DUNN,	LEWIS	Married Polly Johnson	Book 1,	248
1835, Dec. 21	DUNN,	LEWIS	Married E. F. Mahon	Book 1,	251
1837, Dec. 20	DUNN,	LOUISA	Married John Sale	Book 1,	252
1844, Dec. 11	DUNN,	LUCY ANN	Married James E. Fogg	Book 1,	257
1860, Jan. 4	DUNN,	LUCY A.	Married William F. McKendrie	Book 1,	8
1875, Oct. 28	DUNN,	MACE	Married Elton Cox	Book 1,	23
1807, Aug. 1	DUNN,	MARANN	Married Robert Clark	Book 1,	224
1820, Dec. 18	DUNN,	MARGARET D.	Married George Taylor	Book 1,	237
1850, Sep. 28	DUNN,	MARGARET	Married Richard Davis	Book 1,	262
1871, Sep. 19	DUNN,	MARGARET	Married Richard H. Duff	Book 1,	29
1813, Jul. 30	DUNN,	MARIA	Married Lewis Rouse	Book 1,	229
1826,	DUNN,	MARIA	Daughter of Thomas married Lewis Rouse	D 42,	15
1876, Jul. 5	DUNN,	MARIA E.	Widow, married John Trice, King & Queen Co.	Book 1,	42
1895, Apr. 24	DUNN,	M. L.	Married W. H. Tune	Book 1,	118
1821, Dec. 27	DUNN,	MARTHA	Married Turner Holderby	Book 1,	238
1845, Feb. 4	DUNN,	MARTHA J.	Married William R. Allen	Book 1,	258
1852, Aug. 16	DUNN,	MARTHA P.	Married Isaac Birch	Book 1,	263
1859, Mar. 30	DUNN,	MARTHA E.	Married Isaac Davis	Book 1,	7

				Book	Page
1802,	DUNN,	MARY	Daughter of John & Judith, married John Smith	D 36,	134
1809, Feb. 20	DUNN.	MARY	Married Jesse Griggs	Book 1,	225
1811, Dec. 16	DUNN,	MARY	Married Charles Saunders	Book 1,	227
1828, Dec. 15	DUNN,	MARY	Married Curtis Johnson	Book 1,	245
1832, Nov. 21	DUNN,	MARY W.	Married William C. Cox	Book 1,	248
1857, Jan. 7	DUNN,	MARY ELIZABETH Married Thomas H. Dunn		Book 1,	4
1860, Jun. 17	DUNN,	MARY E.	Married John P. Clondas	Book 1,	9
1861, Dec. 26	DUNN,	MARY E.	Married John T. Harmon	Book 1,	11
1869, Dec. 19	DUNN,	MARY	Married William M. Barton, Maine	Book 1,	24
1874, Dec. 31	DUNN,	MARY ELLEN Married Robert Lumpkin		Book 1,	38
1835, Sep. 29	DUNN,	MILDRED	Married Thomas Cauthorn	Book 1,	251
1859, Jan. 31	DUNN,	MILDRED	Married Arthur Taylor	Book 1,	7
1844, Jan. 18	DUNN,	MILSEY ANN Married Tazwell Dunn		Book 1,	257
1899, Apr. 4	DUNN,	M. L.	Married James T. Elliott	Book 1,	133
1809, Sep. 18	DUNN,	MOLLY	Married John B. Turner	Book 1,	225
1866, Oct. 30	DUNN,	MUSCOE R.	Married Marinda A. Crow	Book 1,	15
1870, Dec. 7	DUNN,	MUSCOE R.	Married Emma J. Conoly	Book 1,	26
1873, Jan. 14	DUNN,	MUSCOE R.	Married Emily E. Brizendine	Book 1,	32
1885, Nov. 11	DUNN,	MUSCOE R.	Married Alice Allen	Book 1,	84
1812, Apr. 15	DUNN,	NANCY	Married Habern Moore	Book 1,	228
1850, Dec. 26	DUNN,	NANCY	Married John C. Kay	Book 1,	262
1795,	DUNN,	NANCY	Daughter of William, married Carter Croxton	W 15,	506
1837, Feb. 4	DUNN,	OLIVIA D.	Married Peter Duff	Book 1,	253
1843,	DUNN,	OLIVIA	Daughter of James, married Peter Duff	W 24,	49
1828, Dec. 9	DUNN,	OPHELIA	Married Pitman Mitchell	Book 1,	245
1804,	DUNN,	PEACHEY	Married Catharine, daughter of James Leaker, Charlotte, Co.	D 36,	386
1821, Nov. 29	DUNN,	POLLY	Married Thomas Williamson	Book 1	238
1825, Dec. 28	DUNN,	POLLY	Married Pitman Johnson	Book 1,	241
1832, Feb. 2	DUNN,	POLLY	Married Lorenzo D. Cauthorn	Book 1,	248
1832,	DUNN,	POLLY	Daughter of Caty, married John Smith	D 43,	580
1866, Jan. 25	DUNN,	PRISCILLA	Married John Owen	Book 1,	14

					Book	Page
1822, Aug. 19	DUNN,	RICHARD	Married Peggy Jones		Book 1,	239
1859, Feb. 17	DUNN,	RICHARD H.	Married Priscilla Courtney		Book 1,	9
1805, Dec. 16	DUNN,	ROBERT L.	Married Polly Gordon		Book 1,	222
1867, Feb. 14	DUNN,	ROBERT HENRY	Married Sarah E. Brooks		Book 1,	17
1830, Oct. 19	DUNN,	SAMUEL	Married Elizabeth McTyre		Book 1,	247
1822, Apr. 17	DUNN,	SARAH	Married George Wyatt		Book 1,	239
1860, Jul. 4	DUNN,	SARAH	Married Joseph B. Griffith		Book 1,	9
1837, Nov. 21	DUNN,	STHRESHLEY	Married Ann Moody		Book 1,	252
1869, Apr. 29	DUNN,	STHRESHLEY	Married Emeline V. Carter		Book 1,	23
1882, Jun. 27	DUNN,	SUSAN	Married Edgar R. Saunders		Book 1,	66
1809, Sep. 18	DUNN,	SUSANNA	Married Vincent Dyke		Book 1,	225
1844, Jan. 18	DUNN,	TAZWELL	Married Milsey Ann Dunn		Book 1,	257
1806, Apr. 8	DUNN,	THOMAS L.	Married Cary Purkins		Book 1,	223
1829,	DUNN,	THOMAS L.	Married Cary, daughter of Thomas Purkins		D 42,	594
1816, Dec. 13	DUNN,	THOMAS	Married Elizabeth Jeffries		Book 1,	232
1832, Apr. 18	DUNN,	THOMAS F.	Married Sarah Brown		Book 1,	248
1857, Jan. 7	DUNN,	THOMAS H.	Married Mary Elizabeth Dunn		Book 1,	4
1840, May 27	DUNN,	VIRGINIA ANN	Married John E. Seward		Book 1,	254
1862, Sep. 16	DUNN,	VIRGINIA A.	Married Richard M. McKan		Book 1,	11
1866, Sep. 20	DUNN,	VIRGINIA ANN	Married Theodore Carlton		Book 1,	15
1812, May 21	DUNN,	WILLIAM	Married Lucy Harper		Book 1,	228
1820, Apr. 17	DUNN,	WILLIAM	Married Patsey Shepherd		Book 1,	237
1830, Dec. 20	DUNN,	WILLIAM	Married Milly Harper		Book 1,	247
1834, Dec. 9	DUNN,	WILLIAM	Married Leah Cauthorn		Book 1,	250
1844, Jan. 4	DUNN,	WILLIAM	Married Laura Thomas		Book 1,	257
1898, Dec. 21	DUNNINGTON,	W. F.	Married Rosa Andrews		Book 1,	130
1859, May 12	DURHAM,	ALFRED	Married Maria Louisa Brooke		Book 1,	7
1885, Sep. 4	DURHAM,	ATLEE	Married R. B. Mitchell		Book 1,	83
1869, Jan. 14	DURHAM,	BETTY	Married John R. Brizendine		Book 1,	22
1888, Sep. 6	DURHAM,	CLARA B.	Married Evan R. Crow		Book 1,	96
1897, Mar. 11	DURHAM,	C. F.	Married Cora E. Davis		Book 1,	125

Date	Surname	Given	Marriage	Book	Page
1853, Oct. 27	DURHAM,	ELIZABETH	Married Alexander S. Boughton	Book 1,	1
1811, Jan. 21	DURHAM,	FANNY	Married William Taylor	Book 1,	227
1858, Feb. 27	DURHAM,	FRANCES	Married Absalom Foreacres	Book 1,	6
1828, Sep. 29	DURHAM,	GEORGE	Married Polly Jones	Book 1,	245
1861, Mar. 28	DURHAM,	GEORGE W.	Married Annie E. Taylor	Book 1,	10
1820, Dec 19	DURHAM,	JACOB	Married Catharine Covington	Book 1,	237
1860, Apr. 3	DURHAM,	JACOB	Married Matilda C. Brizendine	Book 1,	9
1889, Jan. 6	DURHAM,	JACOB S.	Married Eliza E. Jones	Book 1,	100
1810, Jan. 15	DURHAM,	JAMES	Married Elizabeth Minter	Book 1,	226
1830, Dec. 20	DURHAM,	JAMES	Married Harriet Minter	Book 1,	247
1843, Nov. 20	DURHAM,	JAMES	Married Frances Coates	Book 1,	256
1854, Dec. 25	DURHAM,	JAMES A.	Married Ann E. Harper	Book 1,	3
1866, Dec. 18	DURHAM,	JAMES	Married Lucy E. Read	Book 1,	16
1866, Feb. 13	DURHAM,	JANET	Married William P. Richardson	Book 1,	14
1881, Dec. 13	DURHAM,	JOHN E.	Married Ida M. Covington, widow	Book 1,	62
1899, Dec. 13	DURHAM,	JOHN E.	Married L. E. Sheppard	Book 1,	135
1842, Feb. 7	DURHAM,	JOSEPH	Married Martha Brooks	Book 1,	56
1885, Apr. 20	DURHAM,	LETTIE C.	Married John William Coleman	Book 1,	82
1857, Oct. 8	DURHAM,	LOUISA C.	Married Thomas Durham, Jr.	Book 1,	5
1886, Apr. 12	DURHAM,	LOUISA	Married Charles W. Guthrie	Book 1,	87
1838, Feb. 28	DURHAM,	LUCY ANN	Married Robert Harmon	Book 1,	253
1863, Sep. 10	DURHAM,	LUCY C.	Married Robert Farefoot	Book 1,	12
1887, Mar. 30	DURHAM,	LUCY A.	Married W. S. Harper	Book 1,	91
1865, Dec. 12	DURHAM,	MARY A.	Married William F. Durham	Book 1,	13
1898, Jan. 13	DURHAM,	MINNIE	Married Eugene Garrett	Book 1,	128
1858, Dec. 21	DURHAM,	MOLLY M.	Married Thomas J. Saunders	Book 1,	6
1885, Mar. 11	DURHAM,	MOLLIE L.	Married Richard G. Cauthorn	Book 1,	81
1871, Mar. 1	DURHAM,	OLIVIA	Married Dawson Schools	Book 1,	28
1825, Nov. 28	DURHAM,	POLLY	Married Leroy Taylor	Book 1,	242
1877, Mar. 18	DURHAM,	RHEIDA MERTINE	Married John A. Covington	Book 1,	45
1888, Dec. 6	DURHAM,	R. L.	Married Bettie Brizendine	Book 1,	97

1850, Feb. 18	DURHAM,	SARAH E.	Married Robert McFarland	Book 1,	262
1890, Feb. 6	DURHAM,	SARAH E.	Married William F. Garrett, King & Queen Co.	Book 1,	103
1862, Jan. 1	DURHAM,	SUSAN A.	Married William A. Jordan	Book 1,	11
1813, Feb. 10	DURHAM,	THOMAS	Married Nancy Brizendine	Book 1,	229
1846, May 26	DURHAM,	THOMAS	Married Rachel Garrett	Book 1,	258
1857, Oct. 8	DURHAM,	THOMAS JR.	Married Louisa C. Durham	Book 1,	5
1869, Nov. 7	DURHAM,	THOMAS H.	Married Mary H. Smith	Book 1,	23
1893, Feb. 1	DURHAM,	THOMAS L.	Married L. E. Southworth	Book 1,	111
1865, Dec. 12	DURHAM,	WILLIAM F.	Married Mary A. Durham	Book 1,	13
1687,	DUXBERY,	HENRY	Married Mary, Exec. of James Coghill	O 2,	52
1824, Jan. 14	DYKE,	ALICE	Married John Hundley	Book 1,	241
1832,	DYKE,	ALICE	Daughter of Bowler, married John Hundley	D 43,	501
1872, Feb. 15	DYKE,	AMANDA J.	Married John R. Shearwood	Book 1,	30
1877, Feb. 1	DYKE,	BETTIE	Married James L. Phillips	Book 1,	46
1806,	DYKE,	CATHARINE	Daughter of Jackson, married Reuben Sale	D 37,	165
1880, Dec. 2	DYKE,	CATHARINE E.	Married George W. Saunders	Book 1,	57
1854, Jan. 11	DYKE,	DOROTHY	Married Peter A. Seward	Book 1,	265
1837, Feb. 20	DYKE,	ELIZA	Married William B. Brooke	Book 1,	252
1878, Dec. 26	DYKE,	ETTA F.	Married Robert B. Gray	Book 1,	50
1848, Mar. 21	DYKE,	HENRY JACKSON,	Married Catharine R. Pyne	Book 1,	260
1882, Aug. 1	DYKE,	HENRY N.	Married Bettie A. Taff	Book 1,	66
1818, Mar. 16	DYKE,	JACK	Married Mary Taylor	Book 1,	234
1818,	DYKE,	JACKSON	Married Polly Taylor	D 41,	116
1827, Aug. 17	DYKE,	JACKSON	Married Catharine Coleman	Book 1,	243
1813; Nov. 29	DYKE,	JAMES	Married Betsey Hundley	Book 1,	229
1831, Dec. 3	DYKE,	JOHN	Married Ann C. Roy	Book 1,	248
1866, Dec. 20	DYKE,	JOHN L.	Married Margaret C. Dyke	Book 1,	16
1848, Jul. 15	DYKE,	JULIA A.	Married Courtney Coleman	Book 1,	260
1878, Dec. 26	DYKE,	LELAND	Married Margaret A. Davis	Book 1,	49
1831, Nov. 11	DYKE,	LUCY W.	Married Elijah Hundley	Book 1,	248
1898, Aug. 4	DYKE,	L. K.	Married H. E. Brooks	Book 1,	129

					Book	Page
1859, Apr. 4	DYKE,	MARGARET M.	Married William C. Gardner, Middlesex Co.		Book 1,	7
1866, Dec. 20	DYKE,	MARGARET C.	Married John L. Dyke		Book 1,	16
1804, Apr.	DYKE,	MARY	Married Lewis Hill		Book 1,	222
1833, Dec. 16	DYKE,	MARY A.	Married Philip T. Hodges		Book 1,	249
1835, Dec. 19	DYKE,	MARY	Married Richard H. Hill		Book 1,	251
1853, Jun. 16	DYKE,	MARY A.	Married George H. Taylor		Book 1,	264
1816, Nov. 25	DYKE,	MISKEL	Married Maria Hundley		Book 1,	232
1806,	DYKE,	NANCY	Daughter of Jackson, married Philip Dunn		D 37,	165
1857, Mar. 21	DYKE,	OSWALD H.	Married Betty Brown		Book 1,	4
1866, Jan. 4	DYKE,	ROBERT L.	Married Mary C. Broach		Book 1,	14
1881, Apr. 15	DYKE,	SARAH	Married Edward D. Valentine, Lancaster, Co.		Book 1,	59
1853, Jan. 8	DYKE,	SOPHRONIA J.	Married James H. Hundley		Book 1,	264
1838, Dec. 3	DYKE,	SUSAN	Married Thomas F. Armstrong		Book 1,	253
1858, Dec. 30	DYKE,	SUSAN M.	Married Lawrence Harper		Book 1,	9
1847, Mar. 31	DYKE,	SYDNEY F.	Married Thomas Bareford		Book 1,	259
1811, Feb. 18	DYKE,	THOMAS	Married Polly Edmondson		Book 1,	227
1809, Sep. 18	DYKE,	VINCENT	Married Susanna Dunn		Book 1,	225
1842, Oct. 21	DYKE,	WARNER A.	Married Mary C. Beazley		Book 1,	256
1811, Dec. 16	DYKE,	WILLIAM	Married Nancy Hundley		Book 1,	227
1851, May 31	DYKE,	WILLIAM B.	Married Margaret A. Smithers		Book 1,	262
1877, Jun. 21	DYKE,	WILLIAM T.	Married Catharine Small		Book 1,	45
1887, Sep. 18	DYKE,	WILLIE J.	Married Mary C. Crouch		Book 1,	92
1898, Dec. 25	DYOTT,	J. C.	Married C. B. Stevens		Book 1,	130
1693,	DYSON,	CHRISTIAN	Married Robert Johnson		O 1,	260

1750,	EASTHAM,	EDWARD	Married Ann, daughter of James Taylor, King & Queen Co.	D	25,	180
1801,	EASTHAM,	WILLIAM	Rockbridge Co. married Frances, sister of George Byrd	D	36,	57
1826,	EDMONDS,	MEREDITH	Married Mary, daughter of Reuben Cauthorn	D	42,	74
1819, Jul. 3	EDMONDS,	VINCENT	Married Ruthey Cauthorn	Book 1,		235
1758,	EDMONDSON, ANNA		Relict of Robert, married Charles Curtis	D	28,	282
1828,	EDMONDSON, CARTER		Married Susan, daughter of Anna Vessels	D	42,	347
1803,	EDMONDSON, EDMUND		Married Jane, daughter of Thomas Howerton	D	36,	326
1741,	EDMONDSON, ELIZABETH		Daughter of James, married ? Hay	Box 109,		H
1865, Oct. 15	EDMONDSON, GEORGE W.		Married Martha S. Coghill	Book 1,		13
1700,	EDMONDSON, JAMES		Married Judith, relict of Philip Parr	D&W 10,		70
1761,	EDMONDSON, JUDITH		Daughter of Thomas, married Gabriel Throckmorton	O	23,	406
1814, Dec. 19	EDMONDSON, MARTHA M.		Married John Dix	Book 1,		230
1738,	EDMONDSON, MARY		Widow of John, married Gabriel Jones, Orange, Co.	D O	24, 11,	247 45
1811, Feb. 18	EDMONDSON, POLLY		Married Thomas Dyke	Book 1,		227
1759,	EDMONDSON, ROBERT		Married Anna Elliott	D	28,	282
1741,	EDMONDSON, SARAH		Daughter of James, married ? Townley	Box 109,		H
1753,	EDMONDSON, SUCKEY		Daughter of John, married Thomas Wiatt, Spottsylvania, Co.	D	26,	384
1794,	EDMONDSON, SUSANNA		Daughter of John, married Lawrence Lewis	D	34,	64
1799,	EDMONDSON, WILLIAM		Married Diana, relict of Charles Evans	O	35,	455
1803,	EDMONDSON, WILLIAM		Married Elizabeth Banks	D	36,	180
1868, Sep. 2	EDWARDS,	CORNELIUS A.	Married Lucy E. Tate	Book 1,		21
1850, Aug. 26	EDWARDS,	DUNBAR	Married Lucy Cauthorn	Book 1,		262
1799,	EDWARDS,	EDWARD	Married Ann Gordon	O	35,	327
1833, July 8	EDWARDS,	JOHN G.	Married Susanna Clarke	Book 1,		249
1819, Dec. 20	EDWARDS,	JUDITH	Married Achillas Ball	Book 1,		235
1835, Jul. 13	EDWARDS,	JUDITH	Married Thomas McNorton	Book 1,		251
1859, Jan. 15	EDWARDS,	MARIA L.	Married John H. Didlake	Book 1,		7
1857, Oct. 15	EDWARDS,	LAWRENCE B.	Married Martha E. Mitchell	Book 1,		5
1848, Nov. 13	EDWARDS,	ROBERT D.	Married Mary C. Owens	Book 1,		260
1687,	ELDER,	ELIZABETH	Relict of Peter, married Edward Morris	O	2,	101

				Book	Page
1872, Jul. 4	ELLETT,	JAMES T.	Married Julia A. Stokes	Book 1,	31
1880, Feb. 15	ELLETT,	JAMES H.	Married Patsey Gatewood	Book 1,	54
1880, Feb. 15	ELLETT,	JAMES H.	Married Patsey Gatewood	Book 1,	54
1885, Sep. 5	ELLETT,	JAMES T.	Married Adderena Deverisey	Book 1,	83
1872, Sep. 26	ELLETT,	MARIA	Married James A. Brooks	Book 1,	51
1815, Sep. 5	ELLETT,	ROBERT	Married Jane Clarke	Book 1,	231
1819, Feb. 10	ELLIOTT,	ALEXANDER	Married Dorothy Harper	Book 1,	235
1758,	ELLIOTT,	ANNA	Married Robert Edmondson	D 28,	282
1811, Dec. 23	ELLIOTT,	BEVERLEY	Married Martha Clark	Book 1,	227
1851, Apr. 11	ELLIOTT,	BROOKING	Married Maria Alexander	Book 1,	262
1753,	ELLIOTT,	CALEB	Married Margaret, daughter of Mark Boulware	D 26,	364
1804, Mar. 14	ELLIOTT,	CALEB	Married Nancy Noel	Book 1,	222
1819, Jan. 18	ELLIOTT,	CALEB	Married Sarah Phillips	Book 1,	235
1805,	ELLIOTT,	CATHARINE	Widow of Caleb, married Enoch Horton	W 16,	438
1835, Sep. 19	ELLIOTT,	ELIZABETH	Married Franklin Broaddus	Book 1,	251
1898, Jan. 12	ELLIOTT,	E. J.	Married J. R. Gatewood	Book 1,	128
1871, Dec. 26	ELLIOTT,	JAMES T.	Married Dicey T. Stokes	Book 1,	30
1899, Apr. 4	ELLIOTT,	JAMES T.	Married M. L. Dunn	Book 1,	133
1820, Jan. 17	ELLIOTT,	JANE	Married Ambrose Armstrong	Book 1,	237
1742,	ELLIOTT,	JOHN	Westmoreland, Co. married Sarah, Daughter of Robert Jones	D 22,	419
1898, Dec. 15	ELLIOTT,	JOHN R.	Married L. R. Brown	Book 1,	130
1824, Oct. 13	ELLIOTT,	LOWRY	Married Mary Younger	Book 1,	241
1836, Mar. 9	ELLIOTT,	LOWRY	Married Susan L. Clarkson	Book 1,	252
1844, Dec. 24	ELLIOTT,	MARTHA	Married Robert Barefoot	Book 1,	257
1852, Dec. 18	ELLIOTT,	MARY	Married James Thornton Crow	Book 1,	263
1805, Jan. 12	ELLIOTT,	MOURTEN	Married Phoebe Taylor	Book 1,	223
1806, Apr. 22	ELLIOTT,	RACHEL	Married Robert Clarke	Book 1,	223
1874, Apr. 14	ELLIOTT,	ROBERT G.	Married Lucinda C. Crow	Book 1,	36
1814, Jan. 25	ELLIOTT,	STHRESHLEY	Married Polly Collier	Book 1,	230
1844, Jun. 17	ELLIOTT,	SUSAN	Married John Noell	Book 1,	257
1835, Dec. 23	ELLIOTT,	TAZWELL	Married Susan Sullivan	Book 1,	251

				Book	Page
1837,	ELLIOTT,	TAZWELL	Married Susan Sullivan	D 45,	391
1811, Sep. 6	ELLIOTT,	TEMPLE	Married Sarah F. Braxton	Book 1,	227
1838, Feb. 19	ELLIOTT,	WASHINGTON	Married Lucy Parker	Book 1,	253
1867, Mar. 21	ELLIS,	BETTY	Married Thornton Ellis	Book 1,	17
1814, Dec. 20	ELLIS,	GEORGE	Married Sarah I. Pitts	Book 1,	230
1888, Dec. 6	ELLIS,	JOHN R.	Married Fannie B. Marshall	Book 1,	97
1853, Dec. 1	ELLIS,	LELIA O.	Married James William Smith, King & Queen, Co.	Book 1,	1
1891, Dec. 9	ELLIS,	R. L.	Married Alice J. Gresham	Book 1,	108
1849, Feb. 21	ELLIS,	SARAH A.	Married John H. Pitts	Book 1,	261
1816, Aug. 17	EMMERSON,	WILLIAM	Married Elizabeth Purkins	Book 1,	232
1723,	END,	JOSEPH	Married Rachel, sister of Arthur Jackson, Stafford, Co.	D 17,	146
1679,	ENGLISH,	ELIZABETH	Widow of John, married Robert Henley	D 6,	86
1882, Feb. 23	ENNIS,	JAMES P.	Married Mildred Davis	Book 1,	63
1881, Feb. 25	ENNIS,	JOHN W.	Married Catharine A. Denniston	Book 1,	59
1678,	ERWIN,	ANN	Widow of Charles, married Giles Matthews	D 6,	56
1824, Aug. 16	ESKRIDGE,	VERNON	Married Polly Burke	Book 1,	241
1825,	ESKRIDGE,	VERNON	Married Polly, daughter of Martin Burke	D 41,	464
1675,	ESSEX,	JOHN	Married Bridget, mother of Thomas Pickett	D 5,	402
1865, Apr. 19	EUBANK,	ANNIE M.	Married James M. Brown	Book 1,	13
1855, Sep. 25	EUBANK,	BERNARD	Married Mary Susan Munday	Book 1,	3
1811,	EUBANK,	EASTHER	Now living in Georgia, daughter of Caleb Noel	W 18,	145
1888, Apr. 22	EUBANK,	HILA	Married Peter Tabb	Book 1,	95
1845, Aug. 6	EUBANK,	JOHN S.	Married Lucy C. Banks	Book 1,	258
1835, Jan. 15	EUBANK,	JOSEPH C.	Married Edmonia E. Layton	Book 1,	251
1856,	EUBANK,	JOSEPH	Married Edmonia, daughter of Charles Layton	W 27,	659
1865, Dec. 25	EUBANK,	JOSEPH C.	Married Lucy I. Street	Book 1,	14
1852, Dec. 10	EUBANK,	JOSEPH	Married Betty B. Mann	Book 1,	263
1858, Nov. 9	EUBANK,	JUDITH E.	Married Joseph A. Bird, Baltimore, Md.	Book 1,	6
1854, Dec. 11	EUBANK,	JULIET B.	Married Edwin C. Jordan	Book 1,	2
1848, Dec. 18	EUBANK,	MARIA A.	Married Richard F. Rouzie	Book 1,	260
1850, Sep. 16	EUBANK,	MARTHA	Married Jefferson Hughes	Book 1,	262

· 95 ·

Date	Surname	Given Name	Event	Book	Page
1837, Dec. 12	EUBANK,	MARY E.	Married William B. B. Seward	Book 1,	253
1896, Nov. 4	EUBANK,	NELLIE B.	Married A. Leland Cosby	Book 1,	122
1892, Feb. 17	EUBANK,	M. J.	Married W. J. Taylor, Maryland	Book 1,	109
1832, Mar. 13	EUBANK,	SARAH	Married John C. Crispenn	Book 1,	248
1878, Apr. 24	EUBANK,	WILLIAM	Married Nannie Buckner Hoskins	Book 1,	46
1799,	EVANS,	CHARLES	His relict, married Thomas Edmondson	O 35,	455
1811, May 22	EVANS,	DIANA	Married John Downey	Book 1,	227
1723,	EVANS,	EDWARD	Married Ann, eldest daughter of Richard Kemp	D 17,	95
1721,	EVANS,	ELIZABETH	Relict of Rees Evans, married William Hunter	O 5,	617
1723,	EVANS,	ELIZABETH	Married James Noel	W 4,	136
1749,	EVANS,	ESTHER	Sister of Micajah & Greensbee Evans, married Edward Lewis	W 8,	312
1814, Dec. 30	EVANS,	HETTY	Married Edmond Mecklebrough	Book 1,	230
1813, Dec. 11	EVANS,	JAMES	Married Sarah Hipkins	Book 1,	229
1820, Mar. 11	EVANS,	JAMES E.	Married Nancy K. Jesse	Book 1,	237
1871, Oct. 17	EVANS,	JAMES	Married Eveline Johnson	Book 1,	29
1881, Dec. 27	EVANS,	JAMES W.	Married Etta Carlton	Book 1,	62
1743,	EVANS,	JOHN	Married Mary, daughter of Herbert Waggoner	W 7,	36
1749,	EVANS,	JOHN	Married Ursula Patten	D 24,	403
1819, Jan. 29	EVANS,	JOHN T.	Married Pamelia Ann Daniel	Book 1,	235
1867, Feb. 17	EVANS,	JULIA	Married Jeremiah Jackson	Book 1,	17
1861, Jan. 5	EVANS,	KEMP	Married Virginia Davis	Book 1,	10
1799,	EVANS,	MARY	Married Peter Taff	O 35,	213
1888, May 16	EVANS,	MCDONALD	Married Copeland F. Taff	Book 1,	95
1854, Nov. 23	EVANS,	MORTIMER	Married Jane Ritchie McDonald	Book 1,	2
1878, May 2	EVANS,	MORTON B.	Married Lucy R. Jesse	Book 1,	48
1834, Nov. 22	EVANS,	NANCY	Married Robert Harmon	Book 1,	250
1845, Jun. 19	EVANS,	SARAH	Married Samuel McCawley	Book 1,	258
1819, Feb. 27	EVANS,	SOPHRONIA	Married Larkin Hundley	Book 1,	235
1895, Nov. 20	EVANS,	T. B.	Middlesex, Co. married Lucy W. Smith	Book 1,	119
1812, May 18	EVANS,	WILLIAM B.	Married Sophronia Montague	Book 1,	228
1877, Dec. 25	EVANS,	WILLIAM T.	Married Mary E. Jesse	Book 1,	46

				Book	Page
1717,	EVARS,	ALICE	Only daughter of Garrett, married Ralph Huse	D 15,	134
1726,	EVETT,	THOMAS	Married Katherine, daughter of William Ayres	D 18,	241
1889, Jun. 6	EWELL,	SILAS	Matthews, Co. married Annie M. Carlton, dau. of Theodore	Book 1,	100
1881, Oct. 12	EXALL,	JOHN S.	Married Annie B. Dobyns	Book 1,	61

1710,	FAGEN,	EDWARD	Married Margaret, daughter of John Smith	D&C 13,	348
1837, Aug. 21	FAR,	JULIA E.	Married Lewis Allen	Book 1,	252
1715,	FARGUSON,	CARY	Daughter of John, married Class Caston	D&C 12, W 3,	208 8
1748,	FARGUSON,	DANIEL	Married Mildred, daughter of Patrick Donohoe	W 8,	61
1769,	FARGUSON,	ELIZABETH	Daughter of John, married Joseph Ryland	W 12,	382
1769,	FARGUSON,	JAEL	Daughter of John, married Thomas Ryland	W 12,	382
1683,	FARGUSON,	JOHN	Married Ann, daughter of Stubble Stubbleson	D 7,	129
1769,	FARGUSON,	KATHERINE	Daughter of John, married Benjamin Haile	W 12,	382
1764,	FARGUSON,	?	Married Sarah, sister of Thomas Bridgforth	W 12,	147
1722,	FARGUSON,	SAMUEL	Married Ann, daughter of Daniel Brown	Box 105,	E
1735,	FARGUSON,	SARAH·	Married Thomas Redd	W 5,	386
1876, Apr. 20	FARINHOLT,	WILLIAM H.	Married Elizabeth Booth Hundley	Book 1,	40
1886, Jan. 5	FARINHOLT,	WILLIAM G.	King & Queen Co. married Bettie F. Newbill, widow, James City, Co.	Book 1,	87
1889, Apr. 30	FARLAND,	M. F.	Daughter of Zebulon, married John Leslie Hall	Book 1,	100
1845, Nov. 10	FARLAND,	ZEBULON S.	Married Mary Croxton	Book 1,	258
1852, Nov. 29	FARLAND,	ZEBULON S.	Married Ella Garnett	Book 1,	263
1854, Sep. 16	FARLAND,	ZEBULON S.	Married Jane P. Gordon	Book 1,	2
1864, Aug. 4	FARLAND,	ZEBULON S.	Married Ellen Douglas Gordon	Book 1,	12
1817, Mar. 11	FARMER,	MARGARET	Married James Harrison	Book 1,	233
1824,	FARMER,	MARGARET	Married James Harrison	D 41,	357
1831, May 19	FARMER,	THOMAS	Married Frances Noel	Book 1,	248
1842,	FARRAR,	WILLIAM M.	Married Mary E. Micou	D 47,	416
1889, Sep. 7	FAULKNER,	A. L.	Married Valvin Martin	Book 1,	134
1860, Sep. 12	FAULCONER,	BETTIE	Married John S. Trible	Book 1,	10
1871, Dec. 20	FAULCONER,	BETTIE	Married Charles R. Bray	Book 1,	29
1842, Jan. 30	FAULCONER,	CATHARINE	Married Christian Peters	Book 1,	252
1721,	FAULKNER,	EDWARD	Married Ann Wheeler	O 5,	634
1855, Nov. 8	FAULCONER,	ELIZABETH F.	Married Festus Dickinson Seal	Book 1,	3
1864, Nov. 14	FAULCONER,	FANNIE IDA	Married Winter Bray	Book 1,	18
1829, Jan. 14	FAULCONER,	FELECIA L.	Married Thomas Coleman	Book 1,	246

			Book	Page
1825,	FAULCONER, FRANCES	Married Carter Croxton	D 41,	452
1834,	FAULCONER, FRANCES	Married Carter Croxton	D 44,	489
1809, Mar. 21	FAULCONER, HARRIET	Married Motta Ball	Book 1,	225
1881, Dec. 13	FAULCONER, JAMES	Caroline, Co. married Dolly Lee Greenwood	Book 1,	62
1888, Dec. 5	FAULCONER, J. W.	Married Carrie C. Jones, King William, Co.	Book 1,	97
1849, Aug. 4	FALKNER, JANE S.	Married John S. Rennolds	Book 1,	261
1787,	FAULCONER, MARY	Daughter of Nicholas, married William Halbert	W 14,	49
1861,	FAULCONER, MILDRED S.	Married Joseph E. Taylor	Book 1,	11
1878, Mar. 13	FAULCONER, NATHAN S.	Married Elizabeth Allen	Book 1,	48
1898, Dec. 28	FALKNER, N. L.	Married Etta Lee Schools	Book 1,	131
1756,	FAULCONER, ?	Married Mary Phitsimmons	W 10,	95
1790,	FAULCONER, NICHOLAS	Married Martha Greenhill, sister of Ambrose Greenhill	W 15,	188
1841, Jun. 21	FAULCONER, NICHOLAS	Married Mary Ann Coleman	Book 1,	255
1858, Mar. 29	FAULCONER, PHELECIA C.	Married William Taylor, Richmond, Co.	Book 1,	6
1861, Mar. 7	FAULCONER, VIRGINIA A.	Married Leland Thomas Carneale	Book 1,	10
1828, Jan. 1	FAULCONER, WILLIAM F.	Married Catharine Thomas	Book 1,	245
1867, Mar. 7	FAULCONER, WILLIAM H.	Married Mary A. Morrison	Book 1,	17
1875, Nov. 20	FAUNTLEROY, EDWARD	Married Nessa Banks	Book 1,	40
1890, Nov. 12	FAUNTLEROY, H. L	Married Ellen Brooke	Book 1,	104
1885, Nov. 3	FAUNTLEROY, JENNIE PAYNE	Married Dr. J. F. Culpepper	Book 1,	84
1761,	FANTLEROY, JOHN	Married Elizabeth, Daughter of Thomas Waring	W 11,	302
1867, Dec. 28	FAUNTLEROY, JUDITH	Married Philip Johnson	Book 1,	19
1884, Apr. 17	FAUNTLEROY, KATE G.	Married George W. Rice	Book 1,	77
1883, Dec. 27	FAUNTLEROY, LUCY	Married Landrum Thomas	Book 1,	74
1758,	FANTLEROY, MARY	Daughter of William, married Robert Brooke	D 28,	171
1877, Sep. 25	FAUNTLEROY, MAXWELL	Married Bettie G. Brockenbrough, Richmond, Co.	Book 1,	46
1814, Dec. 20	FAUNTLEROY, MOORE G.	Married Ann C. R. Latane	Book 1,	230
1854, Mar. 3	FAUNTLEROY, MOORE G.	Married Flora M. Dillard	Book 1,	265
1889, Apr. 11	FAUNTLEROY, NANNIE	Married Clarence Motley	Book 1,	100
1655,	FANTLEROY, PHEBE	Sister of Moore Fantleroy, married Toby Smith	D 2,	35
1890, Nov. 12	FAUNTLEROY, ROBERT B.	Married Hattie C. Brooke	Book 1,	104

				Book	Page
1684,	FANTLEROY,	WILL	Married Katherine, sister of Col. Leroy Griffin	D 7,	144
1802,	FAVER,	BETSEY	Daughter of Thomas, married Daniel Brown	W 16,	121
1810,	FAVER,	CLARA	Daughter of Thomas & Susanna, married William Garrett	D 38,	14
1810,	FAVER,	CLARA	Daughter of Thomas, married William Garrett	D 38,	14
1832, Mar. 19	FAVER,	ELIZABETH	Married Robert H. Callis	Book 1,	248
1799,	FAVER,	FANNY	Married John DeJarnette	O 35,	416
1838, Aug. 28	FAVER,	FRANCES ANN	Married Seylor F. House	Book 1,	253
1878, Nov. 3	FAVER,	JENNY L.	Married Thomas H. Armstrong	Book 1,	49
1795,	FAVER,	SUSANNA	Married Lewis Sale	W 16,	120
1839, Jan. 16	FAVER,	THEOPHILUS	Married Susan A. Jones	Book 1,	254
1844, Dec. 9	FAVER,	THOMAS	Married Lucy Ann Taylor	Book 1,	257
1818, Apr. 10	FAVER,	WILLIAM	Married Frances Atishir	Book 1,	234
1826, Apr. 17	FEN,	CLARA	Married James Allen	Book 1,	242
1873, Jan. 3	FENTON,	ANN	Married Norman McKennon	Book 1,	34
1718,	FENWICK	THOMAS	Married Sarah, daughter of Ralph Rouzie	W 3,	94
1820, Sep. 18	FER,	GUSTAVE	Married Clary Davis	Book 1,	237
1812, Nov. 11	FERGUSON,	JOHN	Married Catharine New	Book 1,	228
1830, May 18	FERGUSON,	NATHANIEL	Married Lucy Johnson	Book 1,	247
1842, Aug. 15	FERNEYHOUGH	ROBERT W.	Married Frances C. Cauthorn	Book 1,	256
1809, Aug. 21	FERRELL,	EDMUND	Married Molly Davis	Book 1,	225
1826, Apr. 21	FERRIL,	EDMUND	Married Judith Fisher	Book 1,	243
1840, Mar. 24	FERRILL,	JANE	Married Joseph H. Fiddler	Book 1,	254
1836, Jan. 19	FERRILL,	UPSHAW	Married Kitty Clarke	Book 1,	252
1859, May 15	FERRILL,	UPSHAW	Married Louisa Tune	Book 1,	7
1835, Jan. 12	FERRIS,	EUGENE	Married Lucy Ann Micou	Book 1,	251
1835,	FERRIS,	EUGENE	Married Lucy Ann, daughter of John Micou	D 44,	516
1894, Nov. 29	FERRY,	E. V.	Married F. H. Cashell	Book 1,	115
1870, Jun. 23	FERRY,	JOHN T.	Married Alice J. Wright	Book 1,	26
1837, Jan. 25	FIDDLER,	BENJAMIN	Married Roberta Rouse	Book 1,	252
1831, Oct. 10	FIDDLER,	CHURCHILL	Married Joanna Broach	Book 1,	248
1835, Dec. 30	FIDDLER,	HORACE	Married Mary Ann Fiddler	Book 1,	251

					Book	Page
1838, Aug. 15	FIDDLER,	HORACE	Married Elizabeth Graves		Book 1,	253
1840, Mar. 24	FIDDLER,	JOSEPH H.	Married Jane Ferrill		Book 1,	254
1879, Mar. 12	FIDDLER,	JULIA F.	Married William G. McKendrie		Book 1,	51
1835, Dec. 30	FIDDLER,	MARY ANN	Married Horace Fiddler		Book 1,	251
1869, Aug. 5	FIDDLER,	MARY J.	Married Austin Brizendine		Book 1,	23
1815, Feb. 27	FIDDLER,	POLLY	Married Thomas Cross		Book 1,	231
1864, Jun. 16	FIDDLER,	ROBERTA	Married Arthur I. Sale		Book 1,	12
1849, Dec. 20	FIDDLER,	WILLIAM A.	Married Mary A. Barton		Book 1,	261
1877, Apr. 22	FIELDS,	PETER	Caroline, Co. married Alice Samuel, Caroline, Co.		Book 1,	45
1720,	FIELD,	THOMAS	Married daughter of Roger Prichard		W 3,	252
1869, Nov. 18	FIELDS,	WILLIAM	Caroline, Co. married Rosetta Stokes		Book 1,	23
1837, May 22	FISHER,	ANN S.	Married Charles B. Moss		Book 1,	252
1765,	FISHER,	BENJAMIN	Married Sarah, daughter of Mary Gatewood		W 12,	255
1810, Nov. 15	FISHER,	BENJAMIN	Married Frances Andrews		Book 1,	226
1849, Mar. 27	FISHER,	BERTHA C.	Married Washington Brooks		Book 1,	261
1816, Jul. 23	FISHER,	CATY	Married John Tucker		Book 1,	232
1834, Jul. 7	FISHER,	DAVID	Married Eliza A. Brown		Book 1,	250
1835,	FISHER,	DAVID	Married Eliza Brown		D 45,	20
1884, Nov. 11	FISHER,	EDITH	Married William L. Smith		Book 1,	79
1850, Nov. 18	FISHER,	ELIZA	Married Thomas L. King		Book 1,	261
1869, Feb. 4	FISHER,	ELIZA E.	Married Carolinus B. Gray		Book 1,	22
1724,	FISHER,	ELIZABETH	Married James Adkins		D 17,	308
1727,	FISHER,	ELIZABETH	Only sister of Jonathan, married John Kenny		O 7,	195
1805, Dec. 10	FISHER,	ELIZABETH	Married Leroy Davis		Book 1,	222
1887, Sep. 22	FISHER,	EMMA O.	Married W. F. Gouldman, Orange, Co.		Book 1,	92
1815, Dec. 18	FISHER,	FRANCES	Married William Breedlove		Book 1,	231
1852, Nov. 1	FISHER,	HARRIET D.	Married Stafford H. Mason		Book 1,	263
1832,	FISHER,	ISAAC	Married Nancy, sister of Mary Mullins		D 44,	34
1747,	FISHER,	JAMES	Amelia Co. married Elizabeth, daughter of Joseph Brown		D 24,	165
1832, Nov. 2	FISHER,	JAMES W.	Married Elizabeth Hill		Book 1,	249
1816, Nov. 30	FISHER,	JANE	Married William Clarke		Book 1,	232

				Book	Page
1835, Mar. 7	FISHER,	JOHN W.	Married Ann Dishmon	Book 1,	251
1836, Sep. 4	FISHER,	JOHN J.	Married Ann C. Andrews	Book 1,	252
1852, Jul. 31	FISHER,	JON. W.	Married Martha L. Gray	Book 1,	263
1855, Nov. 25	FISHER,	JOHN W.	Married Martha Todd Smith	Book 1,	6
1826, Apr. 26	FISHER,	JUDITH	Married Edmund Ferrill	Book 1,	242
1818, Dec. 21	FISHER,	KITTY	Married Larkin Griggsby	Book 1,	234
1884, Mar. 20	FISHER,	LENIE	Married P. T. Parr, Caroline, Co.	Book 1,	76
1804, Nov. 7	FISHER,	LEWIS	Married Betsey Boulware	Book 1,	222
1817, Jan. 15	FISHER,	LUCY	Married Thomas Turner	Book 1,	233
1819, Dec. 20	FISHER,	LUCY	Married Francis Trigger	Book 1,	236
1853, Sep. 14	FISHER,	MARTHA A.	Married James R. Hearn	Book 1,	1
1851, Sep. 30	FISHER,	MARY T.	Married William Dix	Book 1,	262
1817, Jan. 7	FISHER,	POLLY	Married Amos Cauthorn	Book 1,	233
1822, Oct. 21	FISHER,	REBECCA	Married Benjamin Munday	Book 1,	239
1804, Feb. 21	FISHER,	RUTHY	Married Reuben Cauthorn	Book 1,	222
1799,	FISHER,	SALLY	Daughter of Benjamin, married John Jones	W 15,	453,4
1852, Sep. 20	FISHER,	SARAH ANN	Married John Barton	Book 1,	263
1830, Oct. 20	FISHER,	SIDNEY	Married Spilsby Sale	Book 1,	247
1799,	FISHER,	SUCA	Daughter of Benjamin, married Lemuel Crittenden	W 15,	453
1814, Mar. 5	FISHER,	SUCKEY	Married Richard Motley	Book 1,	230
1825,	FISHER,	SUSANNA	Daughter of Benjamin, married Lemuel Crittenden	D 41,	413
1805, Mar. 18	FISHER,	URIAH	Married Nancy Greenwood	Book 1,	223
1808,	FISHER,	WILLIAM	Married Elizabeth Conoly	O 39,	377
1815,	FISHER,	WILLIAM	Married Ann, daughter of Erasmus Jones	D 39,	207
1822, Oct. 17	FISHER,	WILLIAM J.	Married Ann L. Clements	Book 1,	239
1832,	FISHER,	WILLIAM	Married Ann, daughter of Ewen Clements	D 44,	15
1834,	FISHER,	WILLIAM	Married Mary Ann, only child of Ewen Clements	D 45,	346
1883, Mar. 8	FISHER,	DR. WILLIAM	Married Abby Deniston, Croton Falls, N. Y.	Book 1,	70
1783,	FITCHETT,	THOMAS	Married Ann, daughter of James Griffing	D 32,	170
1787,	FITZJEFFRIES, ELIZABETH		Daughter of Thomas, married ? Brizendine	D 33,	66
1884, Jul. 2	FLEET,	REV. ALEX.	Married Josephine C. Jeffries	Book 1,	78

				Book	Page
1806,	FLEET,	WILLIAM	Married Sarah, daughter of Bennett Brown	O 38,	481
1807,	FLEET,	WILLIAM	Married Sarah, daughter of Mary Brown	W 17,	99
1833, Jan. 21	FLEET.,	WILLIAM B.	Married Elizabeth Street	Book 1,	249
1853, Nov. 26	FLEET,	WILLIAM COX	Westmoreland, Co. married Sarah E. Muse	Book 1,	264
1659,	FLEMING,	ALEXANDER	Married Ursula, widow of John Brown, Accomac, Co.	D 2,	174
1666,	FLEMING,	ALEXANDER	Married Elizabeth, widow of William Clapham, widow of Epaphroditus Lawson	D 3,	63
1691,	FLEMING,	ALEXANDER	Married Sarah, daughter of John Kennedy	O 2,	17
1841, Jun. 9	FLETCHER,	ANDREW	Married Frances Moody	Book 1,	255
1830, Sep. 21	FLETCHER,	ARTHUR	Married Jamson Pruett	Book 1,	247
1819, Feb. 4	FLETCHER,	FANNY	Married Chaney Broach	Book 1,	235
1816, Mar. 27	FLETCHER,	NATHAN	Married Elizabeth D. Pruett	Book 1,	232
1774,	FLETCHER,	SALLY	Married Charles Breedlove	W 12,	605
1720,	FLETCHER,	WILLIAM	Married Mary, daughter of Roger Prichard	Box 105,	B
1822, May 20	FLORELLA,	FLORIEL	Married Dillard Gordon	Book 1,	239
1822,	FLORELLA,	FLOREAL	Married Dillard Gordon	D 40,	439
1730,	FLOWERS,	MARTHA	Daughter of Isaac, married Edward Murrough	D 19,	163
1773,	FOGG,	ANNA	Daughter of Nathaniel, married Cornelius Noell Jr.	D 31,	121
1803,	FOGG,	ANN	Daughter of Joseph, married Jesse Hill	W 16,	220
1747, Apr. 21	FOGG,	CATHARINE	Daughter of Nathaniel, married ? Motley	D 24,	105
1770, Nov. 19	FOGG,	CATHARINE	Daughter of Nathaniel, married Henry Motley	D 30,	391
1803,	FOGG,	CATHARINE	Daughter of Joseph, married Enoch Wharton	W 16,	221
1876, Apr. 5	FOGG,	CELESTINE	Married Charles R. Scott	Book 1,	40
1800,	FOGG,	?	Married Delphia, daughter of Thomas Noell	W 16,	39
1803,	FOGG,	ELIZABETH	Daughter of Thomas, married ? Greene	D 36,	323
1803,	FOGG,	ELIZABETH	Daughter of Joseph, married Levi Pitts	W 16,	220
1832, Dec. 22	FOGG,	ELZER	Married Eliza S. Haile	Book 1,	249
1880, Dec. 23	FOGG,	ELZER	Married Ora H. Mitchell	Book 1,	58
1891, Feb. 4	FOGG,	ELZER	Widower, married Ida E. Brooks	Book 1,	106
1899, Oct. 26	FOGG,	ELZA	Married M E. Harmon	Book 1,	134
1876, Dec. 21	FOGG,	GEORGE H.	King & Queen Co. married Bettie James, daughter of James Longest & Catharine Minor	Book 1,	43

				Book	Page
1822, Feb. 25	FOGG,	GRANVILLE W.	Married Lucinda Atkinson	Book 1,	239
1844, Dec. 11	FOGG,	JAMES E.	Married Lucy Ann Dunn	Book 1,	257
1869, Feb. 24	FOGG,	JAMES E.	Married Laura A. C. Atkins	Book 1,	23
1879, Jan. 30	FOGG,	JANE ALICE	Married Thomas L. Courtney	Book 1,	50
1806, Feb. 13	FOGG,	JOHN	Married Martha Beazley	Book 1,	223
1892, Nov. 10	FOGG,	LAURA	Married C. H. Lumpkin	Book 1,	110
1832, Sep. 19	FOGG,	LEWIS B.	Married Polly Hester	Book 1,	249
1860, Sep. 13	FOGG,	LITTLETON	Married Mary Ann Wilmore	Book 1,	9
1812, Jan. 7	FOGG,	LUCY	Married Major Fogg	Book 1,	228
1812, Jan. 7	FOGG,	MAJOR	Married Lucy Fogg	Book 1,	228
1803,	FOGG,	MARY	Daughter of Joseph, married John Kesee	W 16,	220
1808, Mar. 18	FOGG,	MARY ANN	Married Edmond Jones	Book 1,	224
1872, Oct. 29	FOGG,	MARY SUSAN	Married Joseph Scott	Book 1,	31
1873, Feb. 27	FOGG,	MARY A.	Widow, married John L. Cox	Book 1,	32
1835, Nov. 16	FOGG,	WILCEY	Married Lucy S. Sullivan	Book 1,	251
1799,	FOOKE,	ROGER	Married Susanna Hawes, widow	O 35,	131
1688,	FORBES,	ARTHUR	Married Mrs. Alice Gouldman	O 2,	502 67
1690,	FORD,	RICHARD	Married Mrs. Dorcas Turner	O 2,	295
1858, Feb. 27	FOREACRES, ABSALOM		Married Frances Durham	Book 1,	6
1877, Dec. 11	FOREACRES, AMERICA		Married Charles L. Tucker	Book 1,	46
1863, Mar. 16	FOREACRES, FRANCES I.		Married James Acres	Book 1,	11
1840, Aug. 17	FOREACRES, GEORGE		Married Susan A. Johnson	Book 1,	254
1877, Jun. 20	FOREAKERS, HENRIETTA D.		Married Robert P. Brooks	Book 1,	45
1837, Dec. 18	FOREACRES, JAMES		Married Louisa Covington	Book 1,	252
1779,	FOREACRES, JOHN		Married Elizabeth, daughter of Henry Cauthorn	W 13,	295
1827, Apr. 17	FOREACRES, JOHN		Married Fanny Davis	Book 1,	243
1832, Mar. 19	FOREACRES, JOHN		Married Patsey Johnson	Book 1,	249
1865, Dec. 21	FOREACRES, MARTHA C.		Married Richard V. Brizendine	Book 1,	98
1833, Jan. 21	FOREACRES, SARAH		Married John Dunn	Book 1,	249
1874, Dec. 24	FOREACRES, SUSAN A.		Married Robert C. Brizendine	Book 1,	38
1835, Dec. 8	FOREACRES, THOMAS		Married Louisa Ursery	Book 1,	251

Date	Surname	Given	Event	Book	Page
1849, Feb. 1	FOREACRES,	THOMAS	Married Sophronia Taylor	Book 1,	261
1869, Dec. 28	FOREACRES,	WILLIAM L.	Married America Crispin	Book 1,	24
1845, Feb. 10	FORTUNE,	HUMPHREY	Married Ellen Reaves	Book 1,	258
1813, Jan. 23	FORTUNE,	JOHN	Married Jane Stiff	Book 1,	233
1810, Feb. 20	FORTUNE,	PATSY	Married Daniel Johnson	Book 1,	226
1850, Apr. 30	FORTUNE,	RICHARD	Married Elizabeth Richards	Book 1,	262
1840, Jun. 3	FORTUNE,	ROBERT	Married Mary Bird	Book 1,	254
1813, Dec. 23	FORTUNE,	THOMAS	Married Judith Kay	Book 1,	229
1691,	FOSAKER,	JOHN	Married Elizabeth, daughter of George Mott	O 2,	312
1713,	FOSAKER,	JOHN	Married Elizabeth Mott	D&C 13,	320
1729,	FOSTER,	ANN	Daughter of John, married Samuel Barber	D 19,	59
1855, Sep. 19	FOSTER,	EDMUND J.	Married Emily A. Pitts	Book 1,	3
1716,	FOSTER,	ELIZABETH	Married Robert Charlesworth	O 5,	17
1709,	FOSTER,	JOHN	Married Susan, daughter of Margaret Cammack Richmond Co.	W 3,	234
1721,	FOSTER,	ROBERT	Married Ann, daughter of George Loyd	D 17,	25
				D 17,	262
1721,	FOSTER,	ROBERT	His widow, married George Pettit	D 17,	25
1812, Oct. 20	FOSTER,	WILLIAM S.	Married Elizabeth Clements	Book 1,	228
1887, Jan. 6	FOSTER,	WILLIAM	Matthews Co. married Mary E. Hughes	Book 1,	91
1823, Aug. 18	FOWLER,	ELIZABETH B.	Married Jonathan Lathom	Book 1,	240
1891, Jan. 1	FOX,	HUGH	Married Lena M. Broaddus	Book 1,	106
1813, Jun. 12	FOX,	JEREMIAH	Married Nancy Beazley	Book 1,	229
1842, Dec. 19	FOX,	THOMAS	Married Martha A. Cauthorn	Book 1,	256
1677,	FOXSON,	PETER	Married Mary, eldest daughter of John Barrow	D 6,	6
1873, Sep. 15	FRANCES,	SARAH	Married William Carter	Book 1,	34
1726,	FRANK,	ANN	Daughter of Thomas, married Thomas Moss	D 18,	326
1874, Feb. 22	FRANK,	JAMES E.	Married Georgia French	Book 1,	35
1693,	FRANK,	KATHERINE	Married George Proctor	O 1,	236
1860, Jul. 10	FRANK,	MILDRED H.	Married Ross A. Cauthorn	Book 1,	9
1836, May 26	FRANK,	WILLIAM H.	Married Maria I. G. Williamson	Book 1,	252
1848, May 4	FRANK,	WILLIAM W.	Married Fenton F. Ball	Book 1,	260
1876, Dec. 14	FRANKLIN,	MARTHA E.	Married Charles L Barefoot	Book 1,	43

				Book	Page
1847, May 3	FRANKLIN,	RICHARD W.	Married Martha A. Clark	Book 1,	259
1855, Apr. 18	FRANKLIN,	RICHARD W.	Married Mary Elizabeth Cook	Book 1,	3
1874, Feb. 22	FRENCH,	GEORGIA	Married James E. Frank	Book 1,	35
1686,	FRENCH,	HUGH	Married widow of Simon Miller	D 18,	326
1737,	FRENCH,	ROBERT	Married Mary, relict of Thomas Rennolds	O 10,	187
1672,	FRESHWATER, THOMAS		Married Joan, widow of Wm. Hamock	D 5,	127
1740,	FRY,	JOSHUA	Married Mary Micou	W 6,	287
1675,	FUGETT,	JAMES	Married Dorothy, daughter of Thomas & Katherine Pettis	D 5,	489
1790,	FULLER,	RICHARD	Married Rosanna, sister of Ambrose Greenhill	W 15,	188
1799,	FULLER,	ROSY	Married Leroy Davis	D 35,	173
1777,	FULLERTON, ELIZABETH		Daughter of James, married Richard Johnston	D 35,	89
1713,	FULLERTON, JAMES		Married Sarah Pickett	D&W 13,	245
1690,	FULLERTON, MARY		Daughter of James, married Samuel Griffin	D 8,	190
1742,	FULLERTON, SARAH		Widow of James married ? Webb	O 13,	116

				Book	Page
1847, Jan. 21	GAINES,	ANN	Married Richard A. Watkins	Book 1,	260
1808,	GAINES,	DANIEL	Married Roadie, daughter of James Cavanaugh	D 37,	7
1757,	GAINES,	ELINOR	Daughter of Daniel, married Thomas Boulware	W 10,	157
1898, Mar. 9	GAINES,	J. L.	Married S. L. Kay	Book 1,	129
1831, Oct. 3	GAINES,	JOHNSON	Married Elizabeth Croxton	Book 1,	248
1686,	GAINES,	MARGARET	Widow of Daniel, married John Dangerfield	O 1,	184
1888, Nov. 14	GAINES,	MAXWELL C.	Anderson Co. S. C. married Lula B. Roane	Book 1,	96
1849, Feb. 4	GAINES,	MILDRED	Married John C. Tucker	Book 1,	261
1866, Jul. 8	GAINES,	NANCY	Married Robert Ellett Muse	Book 1,	15
1837, Oct. 9	GAINES,	ROBERT H.	Married Sarah Munday	Book 1,	252
1841, Aug. 11	GAINES,	ROBERT H.	Married Mildred Mahon	Book 1,	255
1822, Dec. 7	GAINES,	SUSANNA	Married Joseph Clarkson	Book 1,	239
1834,	GAINES,	WILLIAM F.	Married Jane, daughter of Philip Spindle	D 44,	394
1804,	GAMBRELL,	HENRY	South Carolina, married Susanna, daughter of Isaac Jordan	D 36,	421
1811, Feb. 25	GAMES,	ANN	Married William Games	Book 1,	227
1814, May 16	GAMES,	BETSEY	Married Jessie Boughan	Book 1,	230
1820, Dec. 28	GAMES,	FANNY	Married Benjamin Clarkson	Book 1,	237
1834,	GAMES,	FANNY	Daughter of John, married Benjamin Clarkson	D 45,	321
1765,	GAMES,	GEORGE	Married Betty, widow of William Jones	O 26,	41
1816, Dec. 26	GAMES,	JAMES	Married Nancy Boughan	Book 1,	232
1823,	GAMES,	JAMES	Married Sally, widow of John Boughan	D 41,	48
1850,	GAMES,	JAMES M.	Married Louisiana Mountague, daughter of Philip Mountague	W 27,	168
1703,	GAMES,	JOHN	Married Sarah, sister of William Green	D 11,	154
1812,	GAMES,	JOHN	Married Matilda Johnston	O 41,	110
1822, Sep. 7	GAMES,	JOHN	Married Margaret Taylor	Book 1,	239
1834,	GAMES,	JOHN	Married Matilda, daughter of James Johnston	D 45,	322
1834,	GAMES,	SALLY	Daughter of John, married William Cauthorn	D 45,	321
1834,	GAMES,	SUSAN	Daughter of John, married Joseph Clarkson	D 45,	321
1675,	GAMES,	THOMAS	Married Katherine, relict of Thomas Pettis	D 5,	490
1811, Feb. 25	GAMES,	WILLIAM	Married Ann Games	Book 1,	227

				Book	Page
1816, Dec. 20	GAMES,	WILLIAM	Married Sally Jones	Book 1,	232
1836, Nov. 24	GAMES,	W.	Married Louisiana Montague	Book 1,	252
1709,	GANNOCKE,	MARY	Daughter of William, married Matthew Collins	D&C 13,	289
1710,	GANNOCKE,	WILLIAM	Married Mary, daughter of Henry Peters	D&C 13,	322
1835, May 7	GARBROUGH,	RICHARD	Married Maria Southworth	Book 1,	251
1842, Dec. 31	GARDNER,	ELLIOTT	Married Mary A. Hundley	Book 1,	256
1848, Nov. 20	GARDNER,	ELLETT	Married Ann Clondat	Book 1,	260
1850, Feb. 15	GARDNER,	MARY A.	Married James Watts	Book 1,	262
1885, Dec. 17	GARDNER,	MARY	Married John Jackson	Book 1,	84
1685,	GARDINER,	RICHARD	Married Elizabeth, daughter of Honoria Jones	D 6,	64
1844, Oct. 21	GARDNER,	TILLMAN	Married Elinor E. Hundley	Book 1,	257
1859, Apr. 4	GARDNER,	WILLIAM C.	Middlesex, Co. married Margaret M. Dyke	Book 1,	7
1817, Jan. 20	GARLAND,	ADELAIDE	Married Joseph Janey	Book 1,	233
1845, Sep. 27	GARLAND,	SARAH	Married Henry Graves	Book 1,	258
1819, May 25	GARLAND,	VIRGINIA	Married Thomas Collins	Book 1,	235
1833, Feb. 6	GARLAND,	WILLIAM	Married Sarah Atkinson	Book 1,	249
1869, May 15	GARLICK,	MILDRED	Married Edmund Micou	Book 1,	23
1867, Apr. 24	GARNETT,	ANNA	Married Alexander Jones	Book 1,	17
1860, Jun. 5	GARNETT,	ANN E.	Married James H. Young, King & Queen Co.	Book 1,	9
1873, Jul. 27	GARNETT,	ANN	Married Aleck Jones	Book 1,	34
1733,	GARNETT,	ANTHONY	Married Elizabeth, relict of John Bowler	D 20,	15
1735,	GARNETT,	ANTHONY	Married Elizabeth, daughter of Robert Jones	O 9,	128
1743,	GARNETT,	ANTHONY	Married Elizabeth, eldest daughter of Robert Jones	D 23,	11
1871, Nov. 16	GARNETT,	BOOKER	Married Maria L. Roane	Book 1,	29
1822, Dec. 10	GARNETT,	CYNTHIA ANN	Married Robert Croxton	Book 1,	239
1825,	GARNETT,	CYNTHIA ANN	Daughter of William, married Robert Croxton	W 20,	220
1880, Nov. 9	GARNETT,	EDITH G.	Married Charles F. Goss	Book 1,	57
1797,	GARNETT,	ELIZABETH	Daughter of Austin, married John Segar	W 16,	306
1852, Nov. 29	GARNETT,	ELLA	Married Zebulon S. Farland	Book 1,	263
1797,	GARNETT,	FANNY	Daughter of Austin, married Andrew Monroe	W 16,	306
1807,	GARNETT,	FANNY	Married Andrew Monroe	O 39,	1

				Book	Page
1813, Jun. 27	GARNETT,	GRACE F. JR.	Married Muscoe G. Hunter	Book 1,	229
1740,	GARNETT,	JAMES	Married Mary Jones, widow	D 22,	46
1756,	GARNETT,	JAMES	Married Sarah, daughter of William Taylor	W 12,	69
1757,	GARNETT,	JAMES	Married Margaret Scott (single woman)	D 27,	314
1759,	GARNETT,	JAMES	Married Betty, sister of John Jones	W 11,	178
1763,	GARNETT,	JAMES	Married Sarah Taylor	W 12,	69
1820, Feb. 22	GARNETT,	JAMES JR.	Married Maria Hunter	Book 1,	237
1847, May 17	GARNETT,	JAMES H.	Married Elizabeth Spindle	Book 1,	259
1848, Oct. 16	GARNETT,	JAMES T.	Married Sarah A. Atkinson	Book 1,	260
1885, Feb. 12	GARNETT,	JAMES A.	Married Martha E. Brown	Book 1,	81
1842, May 12	GARNETT,	DR. JOHN M.	Married Priscilla B. Brown	Book 1,	256
1834, Feb. 18	GARNETT,	LUCY	Married Augustus Roy	Book 1,	250
1818, Oct. 15	GARNETT,	MARIA	Married David Jameson Ayres	Book 1,	234
1820,	GARNETT,	MARIA	Daughter of Reuben, married Dr. David Ayres	W 19,	47
1826,	GARNETT,	MARIA	Married James Hunter	D 42,	141
1827, Oct. 2	GARNETT,	MARIA	Married John P. McGuire	Book 1,	244
1840,	GARNETT,	MARIA	Daughter of James & Elizabeth, married Rev. John P. McGuire	D 47,	58
1872, Dec. 23	GARNETT,	MARIA B.	Married John L. Brooke	Book 1,	32
1821, Apr. 28	GARNETT,	MARY E.	Married Robert P. Waring Jr.	Book 1,	238
1867, Jan. 24	GARNETT,	MARY E.	Married Henry F. Sanford	Book 1,	16
1787,	GARNETT,	MILLY	Daughter of Ann, married William Jackson	W 14,	36
1827, Mar. 24	GARNETT,	MUSCOE	Married Sarah Booker	Book 1,	243
1838,	GARNETT,	MUSCOE	Married Sarah Booker	W 26,	616
1838, Sep. 21	GARNETT,	MUSCOE	Married Sarah Gatewood	Book 1,	253
1870, Dec. 22	GARNETT,	MUSCOE	Married Vannangus A. Dobyns	Book 1,	26
1884, Dec. 23	GARNETT,	NANNIE D.	Married James C. Henley	Book 1,	79
1804, Dec. 11	GARNETT,	PHILADELPHIA	Married William Duling	Book 1,	222
1807,	GARNETT,	PHILADELPHIA G.	Married William Duling	O 39,	1
1859, May 4	GARNETT,	SARAH E.	Married John T. T. Hundley	Book 1,	7
1751,	GARNETT,	SARAH	Daughter of John, married Reuben Noell	D 25,	151
1787,	GARNETT,	SARAH	Daughter of Ann, married William Hunter	W 14,	135

1860, May 10	GARNETT,	SARAH	Married Thomas B. Andrews	Book 1,	9
1835, Nov. 16	GARNETT,	THOMAS	Married Virginia Spindle	Book 1,	251
1812, Nov. 11	GARNETT,	WILLIAM A.	Married Dorothy Booker	Book 1,	228
1825,	GARNETT,	WILLIAM A.	Married Dorothy, daughter of Lewis Booker	D 41,	469
1847, Nov. 23	GARNETT,	WILLIAM G.	Married Jane Andrews	Book 1,	259
1895, Apr. 11	GARRETT,	A. E.	Married A. B. Brizendine	Book 1,	118
1878, Feb. 19	GARRETT,	COLLIN P.	Married Lucie D. Clarkson	Book 1,	48
1815, Feb. 8	GARRETT	ELIZABETH	Married Smallwood Coghill	Book 1,	231
1898, Jan. 13	GARRETT,	EUGENE	Married Minnie Durham	Book 1,	128
1836, Sep. 19	GARRETT,	HARRIET	Married James Crouch	Book 1,	252
1838,	GARRETT,	HARRIET	Daughter of Banks, married James Crouch	D 45,	458
1844, Dec. 23	GARRETT,	JOHN G.	Married Mary Brizendine	Book 1,	257
1886, Feb. 10	GARRETT,	LAURA E.	Married Libbens H. Beazley	Book 1,	86
1825, May 2	GARRETT,	LUCY	Married Robert T. Shsckelford	Book 1,	242
1868, Feb. 27	GARRETT,	MARGARET	Married William Crafton	Book 1,	20
1846, May 26	GARRETT,	RACHEL	Married Thomas Durham	Book 1,	258
1813, Dec. 18	GARRETT,	REUBEN	Married Sarah Toombs	Book 1,	229
1808, Dec. 29	GARRETT,	STEPHEN	Married Judith Boughton	Book 1,	224
1820, Jul. 13	GARRETT,	THEODORICK	Married Catharine Callis	Book 1,	237
1891, Oct. 7	GARRETT,	THOMAS	Married Florence Winder	Book 1,	107
1810,	GARRETT,	WILLIAM	Married Clara, daughter of Thomas & Susanna Faver	D 37,	14
1816, Feb. 5	GARRETT,	WILLIAM W.	Married Lucy Montague	Book 1,	232
1841, Nov. 30	GARRETT,	WILLIAM P.	Married Frances Cauthorn	Book 1,	255
1890, Feb. 6	GARRETT,	WILLIAM F.	Married Sarah E. Durham	Book 1,	103
1887, Mar. 3	GARY,	ALICE S.	Married Richard Davis	Book 1,	91
1860, Oct. 30	GARY,	LUCY ANN	Married William W. Cridlin	Book 1,	9
1855, Feb. 15	GARY,	ROBERT F.	Married Lucy Ann Taylor	Book 1,	3
1890, May 22	GARY,	R. B.	King William Co. married F. A. Brizendine	Book 1,	104
1756,	GATEWOOD	AMY	Daughter of John, sister of Isaac, married Thomas Bowcock	W 10, W 12,	127 11
1827, Dec. 17	GATEWOOD,	ANN	Married Thomas Clarke	Book 1,	243
1847,	GATEWOOD,	ANN	Daughter of Sally, married Thomas Clarke	W 26,	202

				Book	Page
1764,	GATEWOOD,	CATHARINE	Married Thomas Wood	D 29,	303
1866, Jun. 26	GATEWOOD,	CHARLES M.	Middlesex, Co. married Ellen H. Micou	Book 1,	15
1896, Jan. 30	GATEWOOD,	CHARLES	King & Queen Co. married Sallie B. Holmes	Book 1,	120
1829, Jan. 19	GATEWOOD,	CORDELIA	Married George Smither	Book 1,	246
1829,	GATEWOOD,	CORDELIA	Daughter of Thomas, married George Smither	D 43,	98
1840, Jan. 20	GATEWOOD,	DRUSILLA	Married Jonas Stokes	Book 1,	254
1743,	GATEWOOD,	ELIZABETH	Daughter of William, married Henry Purkins	W 7,	85
1847, Dec. 22	GATEWOOD,	ELLEN ANN	Married Reuben B. Boughton	Book 1,	259
1761,	GATEWOOD,	FRANKY	Widow of Richard, married Robert Cole	D 29,	81
1816, Aug. 30	GATEWOOD	GABRIEL	Married Rhoda Cook	Book 1,	233
1716,	GATEWOOD,	HENRY	Married Dorothy, daughter of Richard Dudley	D&W 15,	79
1730,	GATEWOOD,	JAMES	Married Penelope, daughter of Sarah Webb	W 8,	108
1799,	GATEWOOD,	JANE	Married Thomas Dunn	W 15,	436
1804, Jul. 13	GATEWOOD,	JOHN H.	Married Catharine Dunn	Book 1,	222
1835, Jul. 31	GATEWOOD,	JOHN	Married Julia Ann Gouldman	Book 1,	251
1898, Jan. 12	GATEWOOD,	JOHN R.	Married E. J. Elliott	Book 1,	128
1800,	GATEWOOD,	JOSEPH	Married Sally Pitts	O 35,	403
1800,	GATEWOOD,	JOSEPH	Married Sally, widow of Reuben Pitts	O 35,	403
1807, Jul. 21	GATEWOOD,	LEWIS	Married Polly Crow	Book 1,	224
1843, Jul. 4	GATEWOOD,	LOUISIANA	Married Thomas Croxton	Book 1,	256
1847,	GATEWOOD,	LOUISIANA	Grandaughter of Sally Gatewood, married Thomas Croxton	W 26,	202
1807,	GATEWOOD,	LUCY	Great grandaughter of Richard Burke, married William Howard	D 37,	264
1861, Jan. 20	GATEWOOD,	LUCY A.	Married John T. Clarke	Book 1,	10
1811, Jan. 23	GATEWOOD,	MARY	Married John Clarkson	Book 1,	227
1840, Feb. 26	GATEWOOD,	MARY M.	Married Benedict Clarke	Book 1,	254
1841,	GATEWOOD,	MARY M.	Daughter of Travis, married Benedict Clarke	D 47,	97
1847,	GATEWOOD,	MARY	Daughter of Sally, married William I. Clarkson	W 26,	202
1886, Mar.	GATEWOOD,	MARY L.	Married Robert L. Logan	Book 1,	86
1809, Mar. 21	GATEWOOD,	MATILDA	Married Samuel Bradford	Book 1,	225
1810, Jan. 18	GATEWOOD,	NANCY	Married William Ball Jr.	Book 1,	226
1880, Feb. 15	GATEWOOD,	PATSEY	Married James H. Ellett	Book 1,	54

				Book	Page
1810, Jun. 26	GATEWOOD,	PHILIP	Married Nancy Moody	Book 1,	226
1846, Dec. 29	GATEWOOD,	ROBERT	Married Lucy A. Goudy, daughter of Edmond Goudy	Book 1,	259
1881, Jul. 7	GATEWOOD,	ROBERT W.	Married Robinette Mitchell	Book 1,	60
1885, Sep. 28	GATEWOOD,	ROBERT W.	Widower, married Alice Ingram	Book 1,	83
1765,	GATEWOOD,	SARAH	Daughter of Isaac & Mary, Married Benjamin Fisher	W 12,	225
1838, Sep. 21	GATEWOOD,	SARAH A.	Married Muscoe Garnett	Book 1,	253
1833, Jan. 14	GATEWOOD,	SULLIVAN	Married Lucy Stokes	Book 1,	249
1833, Oct. 14	GATEWOOD,	SUSAN E. M.	Married Oscar Crutchfield	Book 1,	249
1836,	GATEWOOD,	SUSAN E.	Daughter of Kemp, married Oscar Crutchfield, Spottsylvania, Co.	D 45,	297
1845, Nov. 3	GATEWOOD,	SUSAN P.	Married Madison T. Jones	Book 1,	258
1806, Mar. 18	GATEWOOD,	THOMAS	Married Letty Davis	Book 1,	223
1812, Mar. 9	GATEWOOD,	TRAVERS	Married Ann Newbill	Book 1,	228
1730,	GATEWOOD,	WILLIAM	Married Katherine, sister of Richard Carter	D 19,	123
1761,	GATEWOOD,	WINIFRED	Daughter of John, married Vincent Vass	O 23,	401
1699,	GAUNTLET,	ANN	Daughter of William, married John Cole	D&W 10,	4
1878, Dec. 12	GAYLE,	JOSIAH P.	Caroline, Co. married Lottie C. Leavell, Spottsylvania, Co.	Book 1,	49
1824, Jan. 5	GAYLE,	WILLIAM	Married Polly Samuel	Book 1,	241
1876, Jan. 6	GENTRY,	JOSEPH B.	Married Emeline E. Cauthorn	Book 1,	16
1688,	GEORGE,	EDWARD	Married Margaret, relict of Samuel Johnson	O 2,	112
1690,	GEORGE,	ELIZABETH	Relict of Thomas, married Edward Read	O 2,	220
1756,	GEORGE,	JOSEPH	Married Elener Phitsimons, eldest daughter of Mary	W 10,	95
1816, Jan. 16	GEST,	JOHN	Married Elizabeth Harper	Book 1,	232
1806, Nov. 13	GEST,	WILLIAM	Married Caty Marlow	Book 1,	223
1800,	GIBBONS,	THOMAS	Matthews, Co. married Ann, widow of William Roane	D 35,	290
1821, Jul. 14	GIBSON,	CATY	Married James Dunn	Book 1,	238
1818, Dec. 24	GIBSON,	FANNY	Married Reuben Campbell	Book 1,	234
1744,	GIBSON,	GEORGE	Caroline, Co. married Sarah, sister of Christopher Butcher	D 23,	244
1810, Jul. 12	GIBSON,	JOHN	Married Delphia Burnett	Book 1,	226
1844, Dec. 12	GIBSON,	LUCY A.	Married Oscar O. A. Newbill	Book 1,	257
1722,	GIBSON,	MARY	Daughter of William, married Thomas Powell	D 17,	159
1814, Nov. 21	GIBSON,	RACHEL	Married John Steward	Book 1,	230

				Book		Page
1810,	GIBSON,	ROBERT	Married Hayne Bohannon	O	40,	354
1726,	GILBY,	JANE	Daughter of John, married Thomas Haywarton	W	4,	195
1875, Apr. 10	GILES,	SARAH	Married Alfred Stokes	Book 1,		39
1688,	GILLETT,	ANN	Relict of Thomas, married Vincent Vass	O	2,	97
1666,	GILLETT,	JANE	Executrix of John, married Thomas Button	D	3,	59
				D	4,	341
1684,	GILLETT,	THOMAS	Married Ann, relict of Thomas Roberts	O	1,	56
1758,	GILSON,	BEHETHLEM	Married Nehemiah Stokes	D	28,	76
1687,	GLADMAN,	THOMAS	Married Katherine, relict of Thomas Broad	O	2,	15
1808,	GLANTON,	BURWELL	Married Polly, daughter of James Cavanaugh	D	37,	7
1808,	GLANTON,	JOHN	Married Pheby, daughter of James Cavanaugh	D	37,	7
1816, Jan. 16	GLASSCOCK,	ISRAEL	Married Frances Aldridge	Book 1,		232
1677,	GLASSCOCK,	THOMAS	Married Ann, daughter of George Nicholls	W	2,	2
1691,	GLASSCOCK,	THOMAS	Married Ann, daughter of Mr. George Nicholls	D	8,	294
1894, Jun. 13	GLASSELL,	R. T.	Married M. R. Williams	Book 1,		114
1713,	GLENDENNING, JOHN		Married Ann, daughter of George Mott	D&C 13,		320
1679,	GLEW,	WILLIAM	Married Constance, daughter of Richard Tayler	D	6,	110
1750,	GODFREY,	MARY	Daughter of Dr. Peter Godfrey, married Williamson Young	D	25,	92
1670,	GODSON,	SARAH	Widow, married Peter Hopgood	D	4,	312
1865, Sep. 6	GODWIN,	AUGUSTA E.	Married Francis D. Wheat	Book 1,		13
1818, Oct. 14	GOOCH,	CLAIBORNE W.	Married Maria B. B. Barnes	Book 1,		234
1687,	GOODALL,	?	Isle of Wight, Co. married Lidia, sister of Edward Keeling	Box 101,		K
1789,	GOODE,	CLARY	Daughter of John, married Joseph Tucker	W	15,	378
1829, May 25	GOODE,	DENNETT	Married Polly Rose	Book 1,		246
1860, Dec. 11	GOODE,	ELIZA	Married Isaac Cauthorn	Book 1,		10
1839, May 20	GOODE,	ELIZABETH	Married Thomas Jeffries	Book 1,		254
1854, Dec. 28	GOODE,	FANNY E.	Married John Thomas Clarke	Book 1,		2
1820, Jan. 4	GOODE,	HANNAH	Married John Griffin	Book 1,		237
1845, Apr. 21	GOODE,	HENRY	Married E. A. Cauthorn	Book 1,		258
1889, Mar. 7	GOOD,	JAMES H.	Married Emma Parron	Book 1,		99
1841, Jan. 18	GOOD,	JOHN	Married Julia Broach	Book 1,		250
1860, Jan. 4	GOODE,	JOHN	Married Peggy Brooks	Book 1,		8

				Book	Page
1863, Sep. 15	GOOD,	MARIA A.	Middlesex, Co. married John L. Perks	Book 1,	12
1725,	GOODE,	MARTHA	Daughter of Richard, married John Hodson	W 4,	123
1852, Nov. 24	GOOD,	MARTHA	Married Robert Broach	Book 1,	263
1848, Mar. 8	GOODE,	MARY	Married William Brooks	Book 1,	260
1889, Jan. 23	GOODE,	NINA L.	Married J. M. Didlake	Book 1,	99
1816, Dec. 24	GOODE,	PHILIP	Married Sally Johnson	Book 1,	232
1861, Jan. 10	GOODE,	RICHARD	Married Drusilla Welch	Book 1,	10
1748,	GOODE,	THOMAS	Married Mary Rennolds	Rose's Diary	
1829, Dec. 21	GOODE,	WILLIAM D.	Married Elizabeth Clarke	Book 1,	246
1831,	GOODE,	WILLIAM	Married Elizabeth, daughter of Robin Clarke	D 43,	415
1696,	GOODRICH,	ALICE	Exec. of Benjamin, married Edward Sorrell, James City, Co.	D 9,	85
1680,	GOODRICH,	ANN	Exec. of Col. Thomas Goodrich married Edward Hill, Charles City, Co.	D 6,	126
1696,	GOODRICH,	ANN	Daughter of Col. Thomas, married John Lightfoot	D 9,	50
				D 11,	128
1804,	GOODRICH,	FRANCELLIA	Exec. of Joseph Goodrich, married Thomas Parker	O 1,	190
1824, Jun. 14	GOODWYN,	BOSWELL	Married Catharine Purkins	Book 1,	241
1804,	GORDON,	ALEXANDER	Married Susanna, daughter of James Leaker, Charlotte, Co	D 36,	386
1834, Feb. 17	GORDON,	ALICE	Married George Cox	Book 1,	250
1799,	GORDON,	ANN	Married Edward Edwards	O 35,	327
1830, May 18	GORDON,	BOWLER C.	Married Kitty C. Davis	Book 1,	247
1822,	GORDON,	DILLARD	Married Floreal Florella	D 40,	439
1822, May 20	GORDON,	DILLARD	Married Floriel Florella	Book 1,	239
1811, Nov. 25	GORDON,	ELIZABETH	Married Hundley Moody	Book 1,	227
1819, May 6	GORDON,	ELIZABETH	Married Lewis Walden	Book 1,	236
1828,	GORDON,	ELIZABETH	Daughter of Alexander, married Hundley Moody	D 42,	382
1864, Aug. 4	GORDON,	ELLEN DOUGLAS	Married Zebulon S. Farland	Book 1,	12
1808,	GORDON,	GABRIEL	Married Elizabeth, daughter of Thomas Cox	W 17,	118
1828, Jan. 1	GORDON,	GEORGE	Married Frances Meador	Book 1,	245
1873, Nov. 19	GORDON,	JAMES R.	Married Evelyn C. Croxton	Book 1,	35
1854, Sep. 16	GORDON,	JANE P. B.	Married Zebulon S. Farland	Book 1,	2
1821, Dec. 11	GORDON,	JOHN	Married Ann Crow	Book 1,	238

				Book	Page
1823,	GORDON,	LUCY	Daughter of Alexander, married John Rogers	D 41,	83
1880, Oct. 20	GORDON,	MARIA G.	Married Joseph B. Hodgkin	Book 1,	56
1870, May 24	GORDON,	MARTHA HARVIE	Married Henry W. Latane	Book 1,	26
1813, Dec. 21	GORDON,	MARY	Married Purkins Armstrong	Book 1,	229
1822, Jan. 9	GORDON,	MATILDA	Married Thomas Boughan	Book 1,	239
1821, Dec. 20	GORDON,	PEGGY	Married Josiah Minter	Book 1,	238
1827,	GORDON,	PEGGY	Daughter of Gabriel, married Josiah Minter	D 42,	286
1805, Dec. 16	GORDON,	POLLY	Married Robert L. Dunn	Book 1,	222
1828,	GORDON,	POLLY	Daughter of Alexander, married Purkins Armstrong	D 42,	382
1819, Nov. 9	GORDON,	REBECCA	Married Gregory Dennett	Book 1,	235
1879, Apr. 28	GORDON,	RICHARD	Married Ellen E. Southard	Book 1,	52
1854, Jan. 31	GORDON,	SUSAN E.	Married Henry Webb	Book 1,	265
1674,	GORDON,	THOMAS	Married Jane, widow of Thomas Button	D 5,	363
1818, Dec. 14	GORDON,	THOMAS	Married Lucy Shackelford	Book 1,	234
1828, Jul. 31	GORDON,	THOMAS C.	Married Martha M. W. Jones	Book 1,	245
1853, Jun. 11	GORDON,	VINCENT	Married Virginia McTyre	Book 1,	264
1866, Jan. 25	GORDON,	VIRGINIA	Married Leroy R. Taylor	Book 1,	14
1857, Nov. 18	GORDON,	WILLIAM W.	Married Fannie B. Brockenbrough	Book 1,	15
1744,	GORE,	ELIZABETH	Widow of John, married Richard Johnson	D 23,	189
1744,	GORE,	LILY ANN	Only Child of John & Elizabeth, married John Webb	D 23,	189
1688,	GORING,	HENRY	Married Relict of James Bodington	O 2,	74
1880, Nov. 9	GOSS,	CHARLES F.	Married Edith G. Garnett	Book 1,	57
1705,	GOSS,	SUSANNA	Married Thomas Medoes	D&C 12,	95
1704,	GOSWELL,	HENRY	Married Sarah, relict of John Pierce	D&C 12,	26
1852, Feb. 25	GOUDY,	ALFRED	Married Martha Tinsbloom	Book 1,	263
1854, Dec. 13	GOUDY,	ALFRED	Married Julia A. Dunn	Book 1,	3
1817, Jan. 20	GOUDY,	EDMUND	Married Lucy Green	Book 1,	233
1858, Dec. 24	GOUDY,	LOUISA	Married Joseph E. Davis	Book 1,	9
1846, Dec. 29	GOUDY,	LUCY A.	Married Robert Gatewood	Book 1,	259
1876, Apr. 27	GOULDIN,	DR. J. MILTON	Married Susan Jones Wright	Book 1,	42
1882, Feb. 28	GOULDIN,	SUSAN J.	Married John H. Rosler	Book 1,	64

				Book	Page
1752,	GOULDING,	ELIZABETH	Daughter of William, married Aaron Sadler	D 26,	21
1820,	GOULDING,	SARAH	Her niece, Rachel Thomas, married Augustine Oliver	W 19,	169
1820,	GOULDING,	SARAH	Her niece, Esther Thomas, married Philip Hudson	W 19,	170
1835,	GOULDING,	SILAS	Married Susan, daughter of Alexander Parker	D 44,	473
1841, Sep. 20	GOULDMAN,	ABSALOM	Married Sidney F. Dishman	Book 1,	255
1848, Mar. 7	GOULDMAN,	ALBERT P.	Married Maria E. Munday	Book 1,	260
1688,	GOULDMAN,	ALICE	Widow, married Arthur Forbes	O 2,	67
1857, Dec. 17	GOULDMAN,	ANN	Married Joseph Samuel	Book 1,	6
1793,	GOULDMAN,	ANN	Daughter of Thomas, married Richard, son of James Key	W 15,	314
1832, Jan. 14	GOULDMAN,	ASA	Married Emily Dishman	Book 1,	249
1793,	GOULDMAN,	BETSEY	Daughter of Thomas Married Edward Davis	W 15,	315
1806, Feb. 25	GOULDMAN,	DANIEL	Married Sally Noel	Book 1,	223
1858, Jun. 30	GOULDMAN,	EDWARD	Married Margaret F. Samuel	Book 1,	6
1839, Dec. 27	GOULDMAN,	ELIZA	Married William G. Selba	Book 1,	254
1824, Feb. 23	GOULDMAN,	HARRIET	Married Anthony Samuel	Book 1,	241
1834, Jan. 7	GOULDMAN,	HIRAM	Married Selina Dishman	Book 1,	250
1840, May 8	GOULDMAN,	HIRAM	Married Sarah Ann Gray	Book 1,	254
1848, Feb. 21	GOULDMAN,	JAMES J.	Married Fannie Johnson	Book 1,	260
1818, Feb. 16	GOULDMAN,	JESSE	Married Happy Clarke	Book 1,	234
1841, Jan. 18	GOULDMAN,	JOHN	Married Martha Parker	Book 1,	255
1835, Jul. 31	GOULDMAN,	JULIA ANN	Married John Gatewood	Book 1,	251
1874, Sep. 23	GOULDMAN,	KATE W.	Married R. M. Neale	Book 1,	37
1858, Sep. 23	GOULDMAN,	LUCY A.	Married Bennett Tuck	Book 1,	6
1842, Mar. 19	GOULDMAN,	LOUISA	Married John Broaddus	Book 1,	256
1793,	GOULDMAN,	LUCY	Married Christopher Key	W 15,	315
1805, Jun. 10	GOULDMAN,	LUCY	Married Aaron Ball	Book 1,	222
1830, Mar. 15	GOULDMAN,	LUNSFORD	Married Katherine Allen	Book 1,	247
1829, Jan. 14	GOULDMAN,	MAKENZIE	Married Ann L. Parker	Book 1,	246
1867, Jan. 17	GOULDMAN,	MARGARET E.	Married Samuel W. Pilkington	Book 1,	16
1714,	GOULDMAN,	MARTHA	Married William Winston	O 4,	583
1868, Oct. 8	GOULDMAN,	MARY F.	Married Charles E. Brown	Book 1,	21

			Book	Page
1793,	GOULDMAN, MOLLY	Daughter of Thomas, married John Parker	W 15, D 35,	315 135
1873, Jul. 29	GOULDMAN, NANNIE J.	Married James H. D. Hundley	Book 1,	34
1812, Dec. 29	GOULDMAN, NEDDY	Married Elizabeth Wright	Book 1,	228
1869, Mar. 4	GOULDMAN, PATTY L.	Married Henry H. Robinson	Book 1,	23
1816, Dec. 30	GOULDMAN, PHOEBE	Married Burkett Clarke	Book 1,	232
1819, Dec. 9	GOULDMAN, POLLY	Married Robert T. Parker	Book 1,	236
1843, Feb. 6	GOULDMAN, REBECCA	Married H. W. Parker	Book 1,	254
1841, Nov. 2	GOULDMAN, RICHARD	Married Ann Kay	Book 1,	255
1793,	GOULDMAN, SALLY	Daughter of Thomas, married William Parker	W 15,	313
1816, May 16	GOULDMAN, SALLY	Married Lewis Noel	Book 1,	232
1827, Nov. 20	GOULDMAN, RILEY	Married Elizabeth Conoly	Book 1,	243
1831, Sep. 17	GOULDMAN, SILAS B.	Married Susan Parker	Book 1,	248
1697,	GOULDMAN, THOMAS	Married Dorothy, widow of Richard Awbrey	D 9,	134
1752,	GOULDMAN, THOMAS	Married Sally Wiles	D 28,	261
1760,	GOULDMAN, THOMAS	Married Sally Wiles	D 28,	261
1845, Jan. 4	GOULDMAN, V. A.	Married Pat H. Clarke	Book 1,	258
1887, Sep. 22	GOULDMAN, W. F.	Orange, Co. married Emma O. Fisher	Book 1,	92
1866, Dec. 13	GOULDMAN, W. T.	Married Mary S. Pilkington	Book 1,	15
1832, Apr. 21	GOWAN, NANCY	Married Thomas Collins	Book 1,	240
1683,	GOWER, FRANCIS	Married Ann, daughter of Joane Clark	D 6, D 7,	5 542
1855, Jan. 16	GOIN, ALBERT	Married Elizabeth Jackson	Book 1,	266
1855, Feb. 22	GOWIN, ELIZABETH	Married Alexander Henry	Book 1,	266
1877, Feb. 28	GOWIN, JOHN N.	King William, Co. married Nancy Clarke	Book 1,	44
1712,	GRAFFORT, PHILIP	Stafford, Co. married Pellatia, daughter of Henry Newton	D&W 14,	240
1893, Oct. 25	GRAHAM, A. E.	Married R. B. Rouzie	Book 1,	112
1827, Oct. 24	GRAVATT, WILLIAM	Married Frances Dickenson	Book 1,	243
1838, Aug. 15	GRAVES, ELIZABETH	Married Horace Fiddler	Book 1,	253
1678,	GRAVES, FRANCIS	Married Jane, widow of John Maguffey	D 6,	57
1845, Sep. 27	GRAVES, HENRY	Married Sarah Garland	Book 1,	258
1816, Sep. 26	GRAVES, THOMAS	Married Caty Satterwhite	Book 1, q	233
1844, Mar. 8	GRAY, ANN I.	Married Robert S. Motley	Book 1,	257

1869, Feb. 4	GRAY,	CAROLINUS B. Married Eliza E. Fisher	Book 1,	22
1829, Mar. 30	GREY,	CATHARINE Married John Waring	Book 1,	246
1876, Jul. 30	GRAY,	JOANNA, Married Buck Marks	Book 1,	42
1811, Dec. 9	GRAY,	JOHN Married Mary Pilkington	Book 1,	227
1838,	GRAY,	JOHN Married Polly, daughter of Parmenas Pilkington	D 46,	78
1811, Feb. 28	GRAY,	LUCY Married Arthur Brockenbrough	Book 1,	227
1811,	GRAY,	MARTHA Daughter of Ann, grandaughter of John Spindle, married James Rennolds	D 39,	9
1852, Jul. 31	GRAY,	MARTHA L. Married Jon. W. Fisher	Book 1,	263
1817,	GRAY,	MARY Grandaughter of John Spindle, married Thomas D. Pitts	D 39,	384
1832, Apr. 12	GRAY,	MARY C. Married William A. Brockenbrough	Book 1,	248
1879, Feb. 20	GRAY,	MARY SUSAN Married James Vawter	Book 1,	50
1855, Feb. 15	GRAY,	ROBERT F. Married Lucy Ann Taylor	Book 1,	4
1878, Dec. 26	GRAY,	ROBERT B. Married Etta F. Dyke	Book 1,	50
1811, Dec. 7	GRAY,	SARAH, Married Samuel Dishman	Book 1,	227
1840, May 8	GRAY,	SARAH ANN Married Hiram Gouldman	Book 1,	254
1847, Nov. 20	GRAY,	SELINA Married John W. Dishman	Book 1,	259
1678,	GRAY,	WILLIAM His daughter married James Bowler	W&D 1,	144
1818, Mar. 3	GRAY,	WILLIAM Married Susanna Hill	Book 1,	234
1706,	GREEN,	ELIZABETH Widow of George, married Richard West	D&C 12,	293
1834, Oct. 27	GREEN,	ELIZABETH Married Taylor Key	Book 1,	250
1742,	GREEN,	GEORGE Married Mary, daughter of John Miller	W 7,	55
1781,	GREEN,	GEORGE Prince Edward, Co. married Betty, daughter of Thomas Watts, King & Queen Co.	D 32,	56
1812,	GREEN,	HANNAH H. Daughter of George, married Dr. John Lewis	D 38,	301
1817, Jan. 20	GREEN,	LUCY Married Edmund Goudy	Book 1,	233
1827, Apr. 10	GREEN,	MARY ANN Married Joseph Alexander	Book 1,	243
1834, Oct. 27	GREEN,	POLLY Married Warner McDowney	Book 1,	250
1726,	GREENHILL,	MARTHA Daughter of William, married Benjamin Waggener	W 4,	159
1790,	GREENHILL,	MARTHA Sister of Ambrose, married Nicholas Faulconer	W 15,	188
1790,	GREENHILL,	ROSANNA Sister of Ambrose, married Richard Fuller	W 15,	188
1817, Dec.	GREENSTEAD,	POLLY Married Sthreshley Stokes	Book 1,	233

				Book	Page
1832, Dec. 22	GREENSTREET, GARNETT	Married Rocksey Tate		Book 1,	249
1873, Aug. 21	GREENSTREET, H. H.	Married Henrietta Watkins		Book 1,	34
1865, Nov. 19	GREENSTREET, JAMES F.	Married Mary R. Taylor		Book 1,	13
1811, May 23	GREENSTREET, JOHN	Married Nancy Meador		Book 1,	227
1868, Dec. 17	GREENSTREET, THOMAS	Caroline, Co. married Emily Coleman		Book 1,	21
1894, Dec. 26	GREENSTREET, W. M.	Married Rosa E. Prince		Book 1,	116
1896, Mar. 26	GREENSTREET, WILLIAM T.	Caroline, Co. married Sarah Bareford		Book 1,	120
1856, Dec. 30	GREENWOOD, ALFRED C.	Married Susan E. Greenwood		Book 1,	4
1866, Mar. 8	GREENWOOD, ALFRED C.	Married Martha Jane Davis		Book 1,	14
1841, Jan. 18	GREENWOOD, ANN A.	Married Major Brook		Book 1,	255
1822, Nov. 19	GREENWOOD, BENJAMIN	Married Delilah Brizendine		Book 1,	239
1811, Dec. 5	GREENWOOD, CATY	Married John Covington		Book 1,	227
1867, Dec. 26	GREENWOOD, CHARLES H.	Married Columbia Jane Taylor		Book 1,	19
1860, Dec. 6	GREENWOOD, CHURCHILL A.	Married Polly Davis		Book 1,	10
1868, Jan. 8	GREENWOOD, CHURCHILL A.	Married Emily Clarke		Book 1,	20
1881, Dec. 13	GREENWOOD, DOLLY LEE	Married James Faulkner		Book 1,	62
1828, Nov. 22	GREENWOOD, ELIZA	Married William D. Clark		Book 1,	245
1874, Jul. 16	GREENWOOD, ELIZA	Married William F. Dickinson		Book 1,	37
1804, Dec. 17	GREENWOOD, ELIZABETH	Married Elijah McKan		Book 1,	222
1890, Sep. 25	GREENWOOD, EMMA	Married William Carter		Book 1,	104
1837, Jul. 25	GREENWOOD, FRANCES	Married Major Hodges		Book 1,	252
1845, Dec. 31	GREENWOOD, FRANCES	Married R. F. T. Cauthorn		Book 1,	258
1817, Jun. 1	GREENWOOD, GEORGE T.	Married Catharine McKendry		Book 1,	233
1820, Dec. 22	GREENWOOD, HENRY	Married Lucy Brizendine		Book 1,	237
1816, Feb. 27	GREENWOOD, ISAAC	Married Patsy Crow		Book 1,	232
1840, Jun. 25	GREENWOOD, ISAAC	Married Ann Cauthorn		Book 1,	254
1805, Nov. 12	GREENWOOD, JAMES	Married Ann Chaney		Book 1,	223
1821, Sep. 5	GREENWOOD, JAMES H.	Married Nancy Alexander		Book 1,	238
1827,	GREENWOOD, JAMES H.	Married Nancy, daughter of Aris Alexander		D 42,	359
1828, Jun. 14	GREENWOOD, JAMES C.	Married Elizabeth Jeffries		Book 1,	245
1828, Dec. 28	GREENWOOD, JANE	Married Henry Brizendine		Book 1,	245

Date	Name	Details	Book	Page
1889, May 23	GREENWOOD, JESSEY C.	Married John Covington	Book 1,	100
1824, Feb. 2	GREENWOOD, JOHN	Married Sarah Sheppard	Book 1,	241
1860, Feb. 2	GREENWOOD, KETURAH	Married William Greenwood	Book 1,	8
1892, Dec. 15	GREENWOOD, LAURA A.	Married William G. Carlton	Book 1,	110
1835, Dec. 23	GREENWOOD, LUCY	Married William Covington	Book 1,	251
1840,	GREENWOOD, LUCY ANN	Daughter of James, married Thomas F. Taff	D 47,	131
1891, Apr. 16	GREENWOOD, L. A. M.	Married R. H. Hall	Book 1,	107
1899, Dec. 7	GREENWOOD, L. M.	Married Robert L. Davis	Book 1,	135
1846, Nov. 4	GREENWOOD, M. A.	Married Thomas Hodges	Book 1,	259
1863, Jun. 19	GREENWOOD, MARTHA JANE	Married Isaac Davis	Book 1,	12
1846, Jul. 15	GREENWOOD, MARY W.	Married James F. Harper	Book 1,	259
1869, Dec. 9	GREENWOOD, MARY C.	Married George M D. Taylor	Book 1,	24
1897, Feb. 17	GREENWOOD, MARY	Married R. F. Hodges	Book 1,	124
1805, Mar. 18	GREENWOOD, NANCY	Married Uriah Fisher	Book 1,	223
1806, Jul. 20	GREENWOOD, NANCY	Married William Collins	Book 1,	223
1845, Jan. 21	GREENWOOD, OBADIAH	Married Ann Doggins	Book 1,	258
1821, Jan. 17	GREENWOOD, PATSEY	Married Brooking Jeffries	Book 1,	238
1833, Jan. 5	GREENWOOD, PATSEY	Married Wesley Griggs	Book 1,	249
1849, Sep. 27	GREENWOOD, PHILIP	Married Mira Boughton	Book 1,	261
1839, Feb. 21	GREENWOOD, PHOEBE	Married Walker Stephens	Book 1,	254
1863, Jul. 16	GREENWOOD, ROBERT I.	Married Adeline Crow	Book 1,	12
1816, Nov. 18	GREENWOOD, RUTHY	Married John Cauthorn, Jr.	Book 1,	232
1783,	GREENWOOD, SAMUEL	Married Sebell, daughter of Henry Street	W 14,	46
1825, Dec. 19	GREENWOOD, SUCA	Married Warner Shackelford	Book 1,	242
1856, Dec. 30	GREENWOOD, SUSAN E.	Married Alfred C. Greenwood	Book 1,	4
1820, Dec. 2	GREENWOOD, THOMAS	Married Patsy Mullins	Book 1,	237
1832,	GREENWOOD, THOMAS	Married Patsy, daughter of Frances Mullins	D 44,	94
1835, Dec. 31	GREENWOOD, THOMAS	Married Nancy Shackelford	Book 1,	251
1811, Mar. 23	GREENWOOD, TWYMAN	Married Elizabeth Shackelford	Book 1,	227
1857, Jan. 28	GREENWOOD, VIRGINIA	Married William Greenwood	Book 1,	5
1823, Jan. 2	GREENWOOD, WILLIAM	Married Patsey Minter	Book 1,	240

1857, Jan. 28	GREENWOOD, WILLIAM	Married Virginia Greenwood	Book 1,	5
1857, Dec. 21	GREENWOOD, WILLIAM A.	Married Sarah A. Pitts	Book 1,	267
1860, Feb. 2	GREENWOOD, WILLIAM	Married Keturah Greenwood	Book 1,	8
1853, Nov. 7	GREER, CHARLES H.	Married Adaline Carter	Book 1,	3
1852, Feb. 21	GREGG, PETER I.	Married Martha A. Brent	Book 1,	263
1862, Feb. 20	GREGGS, WM. HENRY	Soldier, married Susan Barefoot, King & Queen Co.	Book 1,	11
1704,	GREGSON, RACHEL	Sister of Thomas, married George Arthur of Bristol, Eng.	D&C 13,	131
1733,	GREGSON, THOMAS	Married Ann, daughter of Thomas Cooper, Mariner of Bristol	D 20,	246
1858, Nov. 19	GRESHAM, ALBERT	King & Queen, Co. married Mrs. Julia C. Clarke	Book 1,	6
1881, Oct. 11	GRESHAM, ALICE	Married John M. Temple	Book 1,	61
1891, Dec. 9	GRESHAM, ALICE J.	Married R. L. Ellis	Book 1,	108
1720,	GRESHAM, CHARLES	Married Mary, widow of William Arvin	O 5,	435
1729,	GRESHAM, CHARLES	Married Frances, daughter of Robert Parker	D 19,	91
1857, Oct. 13	GRESHAM, HENRY	Married Laura M. Jones	Book 1,	5
1833, Sep. 30	GRESHAM, KAUFFMAN	Married Keturah Cauthorn	Book 1,	249
1726,	GRESHAM, MARY	Married William Carnell	O 9,	196
1853, Dec. 22	GRESHAM, MARY KAUFFMAN	Married Richard M. Smith	Book 1,	1
1825, Nov. 21	GRESHAM, NANCY	Widow, married Humphrey C. Watkins	Book 1,	242
1885, Apr. 4	GRESHAM, SARAH	Married George Dunn, Jr.	Book 1,	81
1845, Dec. 22	GRESHAM, SYLVANUS	Married Susan E. Cauthorn	Book 1,	258
1893, Jun. 28	GRESHAM, W. A.	Married H. L. Cammack	Book 1,	111
1849, Jan. 4	GRIFFIN, ALBERT	Married Clara H. Pitts	Book 1,	261
1888, Mar. 29	GRIFFIN, A. J.	Married C. A. Carneal	Book 1,	95
1860, May 2	GRIFFIN, ANGELINA	Married Thomas Allen, Jr.	Book 1,	9
1884, Sep. 18	GRIFFIN, BETTIE A.	Married William Schools	Book 1,	78
1820, Aug. 16	GRIFFIN, ELIZABETH	Married Francis Coleman	Book 1,	237
1823, Apr. 10	GRIFFIN, ISAM	Married Sally Griffin	Book 1,	240
1820, Jan. 4	GRIFFIN, JOHN	Married Hannah Goode	Book 1,	237
1822, Jan. 22	GRIFFIN, JOHN	Married Elizabeth Tune	Book 1,	239
1828, Dec. 23	GRIFFIN, JOHN	Married Caty Smither	Book 1,	245
1836, Aug. 3	GRIFFIN, JOHN	Married Polly Griffin	Book 1,	252

				Book	Page
1882, Nov. 20	GRIFFIN,	JULIET C.	Married William L. Mahon	Book 1,	66
1684,	GRIFFIN,	KATHERINE	Sister of Col. Leroy Griffin, married William Fantleroy	D 7,	144
1874, Apr. 7	GRIFFIN,	MARY E.	Married Peleg S. Staples, Stockton, Mo.	Book 1,	36
1890, Feb. 14	GRIFFIN,	MARY F.	Married George Lewis	Book 1,	103
1885, Dec. 26	GRIFFIN,	MAUD	Married Robert H. Allen	Book 1,	85
1889, Dec. 29	GRIFFIN,	NANCY	Married Joan Passagaluppi	Book 1,	101
1836, Aug. 3	GRIFFIN,	POLLY	Married John Griffin	Book 1,	252
1823, Apr. 10	GRIFFIN,	SALLY	Married Isam Griffin	Book 1,	240
1690,	GRIFFIN,	SAMUEL	Married Mary, daughter of James Fullerton	D 8,	190
1881, May 5	GRIFFIN,	THOMAS W.	Married Mary A. Collier	Book 1,	60
1843, Dec. 18	GRIFFIN,	WILLIAM	Married Angelina Rouse	Book 1,	256
1884, Apr. 24	GRIFFIN,	WILLIAM T.	Married Catharine A. Collins	Book 1,	77
1783,	GRIFFING,	ANN	Daughter of James, married Thomas Fitchett	D 32,	170
1747,	GRIFFING,	MARGARET	Married John Holder	D 24,	127
1746,	GRIFFING,	SARAH	Married Thomas Ley	W 7,	475
1783,	GRIFFING,	SARAH	Daughter of James, married Charles Curtis	D 32,	170
1861, Aug. 20	GRIFFITH,	FRANCES E.	Married William E. Sheppard	Book 1,	11
1860, Jul. 4	GRIFFITH,	JOSEPH B.	Married Sarah Ann Dunn	Book 1,	9
1825, Oct. 17	GRIGGS,	ANDERTON	Married Caty Davis	Book 1,	241
1897, Mar. 3	GRIGGS,	CHASTINE	Married Laura Boughan	Book 1,	125
1842, Apr. 8	GRIGGS,	ELIZA	Married Thomas Hodges	Book 1,	256
1821, Dec. 12	GRIGGS,	FANNY	Married Lewis D. Brooks	Book 1,	238
1809, Feb. 20	GRIGGS,	JESSE	Married Mary Dunn	Book 1,	225
1822, Jun. 12	GRIGGS,	LUCY	Married Thomas Marlow	Book 1,	239
1827, Jan. 20	GRIGGS,	LUCY	Married Gregory Davis	Book 1,	243
1835, Jan. 23	GRIGGS,	MARY	Married William Harper	Book 1,	251
1808, Oct. 3	GRIGGS,	PHILIP	Married Catharine Broocke	Book 1,	224
1689,	GRIGGS,	RUTH	Daughter of Robert of Gloucester, Co. married Mattrum Wright	D 8,	154
1829, Dec. 9	GRIGGS,	SALLY	Married Chaney Broach	Book 1,	246
1859, Dec. 26	GRIGGS,	SUSAN E.	Married John Coleman	Book 1,	8
1812, Dec. 14	GRIGGS,	THOMAS	Married Lucy Dennett	Book 1,	228

				Book	Page
1833, Jan. 5	GRIGGS,	WESLEY	Married Patsey Greenwood	Book 1,	249
1818, Dec. 21	GRIGGSBY,	LARKIN	Married Kitty Fisher	Book 1,	234
1677,	GRIGORY,	ELIZABETH	Sister of John, married Thomas Wheeler	D 6,	11
1745,	GRIGORY,	ELIZABETH	Daughter of Richard, married Thomas Moore	D 23,	317
1726,	GRIGORY,	JOHN	Married Jane Kidd	O 7,	110
1702,	GRIGORY,	KATHERINE	Widow of Richard, married Thomas Snead	D&W 11,	41,42
1745,	GRIGORY,	SARAH	Daughter of Richard, married John Meador	D 23,	317
1834, Dec. 19	GRIMSTEAD,	NANCY	Married Robert Wilson	Book 1,	250
1681,	GRIMSTEAD,	RICHARD	Married Elizabeth, daughter of Anthony Jackman	D 6,	129
1865, Aug. 17	GRISTOL,	DENNIS	New York, married Margaret Clarke	Book 1,	13
1833, Dec. 2	GRISWOLD,	C. G.	Married Julia E. Newhall	Book 1,	249
1847, Nov. 20	GROOM,	WILLIAM	Married Lucie S. Montague	Book 1,	259
1890, Dec. 5	GRUEBEL,	JAMES L.	Germany, married Flora A. McKendrie	Book 1,	105
1836, Dec. 24	GRYMES,	LUCINDA	Married John Richards	Book 1,	252
1845, Dec. 29	GRIMES,	RICHARD	Married Roberta Brooks	Book 1,	258
1875, Dec. 25	GRYMES,	SALLIE	Married Thomas Jackson	Book 1,	40
1849, Sep. 27	GUESS,	HOWARD	Married Matilda N. Davis	Book 1,	261
1883, Apr. 19	GUESS,	ROBERT	Married Sophronia Davis	Book 1,	71
1687,	GULLOCKE,	JANE	Only daughter of Robert, married Isaac Jackson	D 9,	110
1703,	GULLOCKE,	JANE	Daughter of Robert, married John Butler	D&W 11,	72
1709,	GULLOCKE,	JANE	Daughter of Robert, married Garrett Neale	D&C 13,	206
1886, Apr. 12	GUTHRIE,	CHARLES W.	Married Louisa Durham	Book 1,	87
1784,	GWATHMEY	RICHARD	Married Betty, daughter of James Jones	W 13,	457
1829, Jul. 23	GWATHMEY,	ROBERT T.	Married Sarah Brown	Book 1,	246
1830,	GWATHMEY,	ROBERT T.	Married Sarah, daughter of Charles Brown	D 43,	133
1832,	GWATHMEY,	ROBERT T.	Married Sarah, daughter of Charles Brown	D 43,	504
1863, Nov. 3	GWATHMEY,	R. TEMPLE	Married Henrietta I. Cauthorn	Book 1,	12
1733,	GWYNNE,	ELIZABETH	Widow of George, married Edward Coleman	D 20,	246
1733,	GWYNNE,	GEORGE	Married Elizabeth, daughter of James New	D 20,	246

H

1773,	HADDON,	THOMAS	Married Mary, widow of Nicholas Pamplin	D 30, D 31,	370 139
1878, Dec. 18	HAGAN,	CHARLES H.	Richmond, City, married Mary L. Anderson	Book 1,	49
1856,	HAIG,	JAMES M.	Baltimore, married Sallie E. Noel, widow of James E. Noel	D 51,	42
1705,	HAILE,	ANN	Daughter of John, married Thomas Cox	O 3,	198
1715,	HAILE,	ANN	Daughter of John, married Thomas Cox	D& W 14,	497
1852, Jun. 5	HAILE,	ANN MADISON	Married Dr. Thomas Latane	Book 1,	263
1769,	HAILE,	BENJAMIN	Married Katherine, daughter of John Farguson	W 12,	382
1882, Dec. 7	HAILE,	BETTIE B.	Married Manly Broaddus	Book 1,	67
1830, Feb. 18	HAILE,	CATHARINE	Married Samuel L. Dawson	Book 1,	247
1882, Dec. 21	HAILE,	CHARLES L.	Married Ellen Thomas	Book 1,	67
1832, Dec. 22	HAILE,	ELIZA S.	Married Elzer Fogg	Book 1,	249
1828, Aug. 28	HAILE,	ELIZABETH V.	Married Dudley Tucker	Book 1,	245
1844, Dec. 16	HAILE,	ELIZABETH B.	Married John D. Hutchinson	Book 1,	257
1879, Feb. 4	HAILE,	ELLA	Married Richard H. Barefoot	Book 1,	50
1835, Oct. 7	HAILE,	EMILY A.	Married N. I. B. Whitlock	Book 1,	251
1837,	HAILE,	EMILY A.	Married Nathaniel Izard Bacon Whitlock	D 45,	470
1872, Sep. 26	HAILE,	EMILY	Married James P. Clarke	Book 1,	31
1698,	HAILE,	JOHN	Married Ann, Admrx. of John Clarke	D 9,	308
1784,	HAILE,	JOHN	Married Mary, eldest daughter of Thomas Dix	W 14,	38
1811, May 30	HAILE,	JOHN	Married Sarah Aldridge	Book 1,	227
1824,	HAILE,	JOHN	Married Mary, daughter of Adam Aldridge	W 20,	298
1846, Feb. 5	HAILE,	JOHN A.	Married Mary Ellen Ball	Book 1,	259
1849, Dec. 21	HAILE,	JOHN L.	Married Elizabeth Rouse	Book 1,	261
1872, Jun. 5	HAILE,	JOHN	Married Matilda R. Wright	Book 1,	30
1895, Aug. 21	HAILE,	JOHN R.	Married Eliza C. Wright	Book 1,	118
1885, Sep. 15	HAILE,	LIZZIE M.	Married Duncan L. McRae	Book 1,	83
1883, Dec. 11	HAILE,	LUCY EMMA	Married Richard C. McDonald	Book 1,	74
1884, Jun. 25	HAILE,	LUCY E.	Married James G. Cannon	Book 1,	77
1828, Jun. 16	HAILE,	MARY C.	Married Arthur Barnes	Book 1,	245
1871, Jun. 6	HAILE,	MARY ARCHER	Married Luther Hall, Louisa, Co.	Book 1,	28

				Book	Page
1897, Dec. 2	HAILE,	O. D.	Richmond, Co. married Mary D. Bray	Book 1,	126
1816, Dec. 17	HAILE,	RICHARD L.	Married Mahaley Alexander	Book 1,	232
1827,	HAILE,	RICHARD L.	Married Mahala Alexander, daughter of Aris	D 42,	359
1856, Jun. 12	HAILE,	ROBERT G.	Married Mary Susan Burke	Book 1,	4
1892, Nov. 9	HAILE,	ROBERT G.	Married Emma C. Hoskins	Book 1,	110
1844, Oct. 1	HAILE,	ROBERT S.	Married Mary C. Coghill	Book 1,	257
1859, Apr. 19	HAILE,	SALLIE	Married Alexander W. Broaddus	Book 1,	7
1759,	HAILE,	SARAH	Late Sarah Smith, relict of Benjamin, married James Blayse	O 23,	75
1829, May 12	HAILE,	SUSANNA A.	Married Joseph N. Armstrong	Book 1,	246
1880, Nov. 23	HAILE,	SUSAN B.	Married James T. McDonald	Book 1,	57
1870, Oct. 26	HAILE,	VIRGIE	Married James G. Cannon	Book 1,	26
1828, Apr. 4	HAILE,	WILLIAM G.	Married Clara Meadows	Book 1,	245
1857, Mar. 28	HAILE,	WILLIAM J.	Married Mary Catherine Jones	Book 1,	4
1793,	HALBERT,	JAMES	Married Sarah, daughter of James Shaddock	W 15,	140
1816, Dec. 20	HALBERT,	JAMES	Married Nancy Rennolds	Book 1,	232
1823, Feb. 24	HALBERT,	JAMES JR.	Married Lucy Pitts	Book 1,	240
1750,	HALBERT,	JOEL	Married Mary Cook	D 27,	71
1836, Dec. 5	HALBERT	JOEL	Married Elizabeth Carneale	Book 1,	252
1807, Jan. 8	HALBERT,	JOHN	Married Martha Ross	Book 1,	224
1843, Jan. 4	HALBERT,	MARGARET	Married Leonard Clarke	Book 1,	256
1842, Jan. 10	HALBERT,	MARY A.	Married Joseph Minter	Book 1,	256
1892, Oct. 2	HALBERT,	R. H.	King George, Co. married Maria Clarke	Book 1,	110
1883, Dec. 27	HALBERT,	SARAH A.	Married James W. Carter	Book 1,	74
1816, Apr. 27	HALBERT,	THOMAS	Married Susanna Lee	Book 1,	232
1709,	HALBERT,	WILLIAM	Married Mary Wood	D&C 13,	296
1789,	HALBERT,	WILLIAM	Married Mary, daughter of Nicholas Faulconer	W 14,	149
1806,	HALBERT,	WILLIAM	Married Rosy, daughter of William Ingram	O 38,	426
1881, Jun. 9	HALL,	BLADON	Richmond, Co. married Mrs. Fannie Vickers	Book 1,	60
1875, Oct. 27	HALL,	CHARLES	Married Jenette M. Powers	Book 1,	39
1889, Apr. 30	HALL,	JOHN LESLIE	Williamsburg, Va. married M. F. Farland	Book 1,	100
1892, Oct. 20	HALL,	LOUISA C.	Married William H. Noel	Book 1,	110

					Book	Page
1871, Jun. 6	HALL,	LUTHER	Louisa, Co. married Mary Archer Haile	Book 1,	28
1883, May 30	HALL,	RICHARD	Married Edmonia Hayes	Book 1,	72
1891, Apr. 16	HALL,	R. H.	Married L. A. M. Greenwood	Book 1,	107
1844, Feb. 3	HALL,	WILLIAM	Married Mary E. Collins	Book 1,	257
1763,	HAMMOND,	JOHN	Married Anne Tyler	D 22,	187
1723,	HANNAH,	ELIZABETH	Married John Zachre	D 17,	265
1739,	HARDEE,	ANDREW	Married Jane, sister-in-law of Richard Hutchins	D 22,	81
1866, Dec. 25	HARDY,	JOHN	Married Louisa A. Harper	Book 1,	16
1821, Jul. 18	HARDY,	NANCY	Married John Cooper	Book 1,	238
1723,	HARDY,	THOMAS	Married Grizell, relict of John Chamberlaine	O 7,	101
1876, Jan. 22	HARFORD,	MYRTLE	Married James E. Boughan	Book 1,	42
1874, Dec. 23	HARMON,	ALICE	Married William R. Allen	Book 1,	37
1832, Feb. 20	HARMON,	ELIZABETH	Married Allen Cauthorn	Book 1,	248
1894, Jul. 5	HARMON,	F. E.	Married Stapleton Brooks	Book 1,	114
1785,	HARMON,	ISHMAEL	Married Sarah, sister of William Thorp	D 32,	359
1867, Dec. 24	HARMON,	JAMES R.	Married Martha Jane Taylor	Book 1,	19
1861, Dec. 26	HARMON,	JOHN T.	Married Mary E. Dunn	Book 1,	11
1891, May 24	HARMON,	J. R.	Married Lucy A. Harmon	Book 1,	107
1857, Jan. 16	HARMON,	LOMARCUS	Married Jane E. Acres	Book 1,	4
1891, May 24	HARMON,	LUCY A.	Married J. R. Harmon	Book 1,	107
1809, Jan. 10	HARMON,	MARTHA	Married Moses Ball	Book 1,	225
1899, Oct. 26	HARMON,	M. E.	Married Elza Fogg	Book 1,	134
1834, Nov. 22	HARMON,	ROBERT	Married Nancy Evans	Book 1,	250
1838, Feb. 28	HARMON,	ROBERT	Married Lucy Ann Durham	Book 1,	253
1869, Sep. 15	HARMON,	ROBERT	Married Susan Williamson	Book 1,	23
1830, Dec. 20	HARMON,	SARAH	Married Ross A. Cauthorn	Book 1,	247
1868, Dec. 24	HARMON,	SARAH C.	Married Philip C. Brizendine	Book 1,	21
1866, Dec. 19	HARMON,	WILLIAM B.	Married Emma E. Brizendine	Book 1,	16
1890, Jul. 1	HARMON,	WILLIAM A.	Married Mary M. Bennett	Book 1,	104
1825,	HARNEY,	ROBERT B.	Tennessee, married Louisa, daughter of Major James Upshaw	D 41,	347
1896, Oct. 15	HARPER,	ADDIE E.	Married Thornton B. Treakle	Book 1,	121

				Book	Page
1885, Feb. 10	HARPER,	ALLIE	Married Milza Taylor	Book 1,	81
1854, Dec. 25	HARPER,	ANN E.	Married James A. Durham	Book 1,	3
1894, Dec. 6	HARPER,	A. S.	Married M. E. Burch	Book 1,	115
1821, Dec. 24	HARPER,	CATHARINE	Married Curtis Chamberlayne	Book 1,	238
1819, Feb. 10	HARPER,	DOROTHY	Married Alexander Elliott	Book 1,	235
1857, Jun. 25	HARPER,	DOWNING	Married Amanda F. Birch	Book 1,	5
1853, Apr. 22	HARPER,	ELIZA	Married James Brooke	Book 1,	264
1816, Jan. 16	HARPER,	ELIZABETH	Married John Gest	Book 1,	232
1841, Apr. 22	HARPER,	EMILY E.	Married Francis Smith	Book 1,	255
1804, Dec. 19	HARPER,	FRANCES	Married Cornelius Beazley	Book 1,	222
1819, Dec. 20	HARPER,	GEORGE	Married Laura H. Smith	Book 1,	235
1828, Aug. 14	HARPER,	GEORGE	Married Elizabeth Crouch	Book 1,	245
1804, Dec. 17	HARPER,	GRIFFIN	Married Patsy Davis	Book 1,	222
1812,	HARPER,	GRIFFIN	Married Patsy, daughter of Evan Davis	O 41,	57
1894, Apr. 4	HARPER,	HENRY J.	Married V. M. Hodges	Book 1,	114
1837, Dec. 18	HARPER,	JAMES	Married Ann Crow	Book 1,	252
1846, Jul. 15	HARPER,	JAMES F.	Married Mary W. Greenwood	Book 1,	259
1848, Jun. 19	HARPER,	JAMES	Married Susan C. Armstrong	Book 1,	260
1884, Jun. 5	HARPER,	JAMES T. JR.	Married Ida Blanche Seal	Book 1,	77
1845, Aug. 26	HARPER,	JOHN W.	Married Sarah F. Andrews	Book 1,	258
1812, Dec. 17	HARPER,	JUDITH	Married Abner Brizendine	Book 1,	228
1884, Jan. 15	HARPER,	KATE	Married William B. H. Taylor	Book 1,	75
1858, Dec. 30	HARPER,	LAWRENCE	Married Susan M. Dyke	Book 1,	9
1866, Dec. 25	HARPER,	LOUISA A.	Married John Hardy	Book 1,	16
1867, Feb. 23	HARPER,	LOUISA	Married John L. Johnson	Book 1,	17
1812, May 21	HARPER,	LUCY	Married William Dunn	Book 1,	228
1823, Jan. 8	HARPER,	LUCY	Married Rice Cauthorn	Book 1,	240
1825, Sep. 19	HARPER,	MAJOR	Married Peggy Broocks	Book 1,	241
1854, Dec. 21	HARPER,	MARTHA	Married Leonard Schools	Book 1,	3
1879, Feb. 5	HARPER,	MARY ELLEN	Married William H. Wake, Middlesex, Co.	Book 1,	50
1830, Dec. 20	HARPER,	MILLY	Married William Dunn	Book 1,	247

				Book	Page
1830, Feb. 15	HARPER,	NANCY	Married Joseph Minter	Book 1,	247
1822, Dec. 16	HARPER,	PATSY	Married Mourning Johnston	Book 1,	239
1827, Dec. 7	HARPER,	RICHARD	Married Frances Pruitt	Book 1,	243
1809, Aug. 21	HARPER,	ROBERT	Married Sally Allen	Book 1,	225
1813,	HARPER,	ROBERT	Married Lilly Allen	O 41,	188
1714,	HARPER,	SARAH	Only sister of William, married John Spiller, Richmond, Co.	D&W 14,	294
1868, Jan. 9	HARPER,	SARAH J.	Married Reuben Ball	Book 1,	20
1888, Dec. 27	HARPER,	SUSAN L.	Married Lewis M. Jeffries	Book 1,	97
1684,	HARPER,	THOMAS	His widow married William Lake	O 1,	159
1820, Dec. 22	HARPER,	THOMAS	Married Elizabeth Dunn	Book 1,	237
1844, Jun. 7	HARPER,	THOMAS	Married Lucy Cauthorn	Book 1,	257
1849, Dec. 26	HARPER,	THOMAS	Married Priscilla Davis	Book 1,	261
1838, Apr. 18	HARPER,	WATKINS	Married Martha Brizendine	Book 1,	253
1838,	HARPER,	WATKINS	Married Martha, daughter of Vincent Brizendine	D 46,	123
1850, Dec. 27	HARPER,	WATKINS	Married Martha J. Carter	Book 1,	262
1778,	HARPER,	WILLIAM	Married Margaret, daughter of Henry Crutcher	W 13,	300
1835, Jan. 23	HARPER,	WILLIAM	Married Mary Griggs	Book 1,	251
1887, Mar. 30	HARPER,	W. S.	King William Co. married Lucy A. Durham	Book 1,	91
1809, Dec. 18	HARRIS,	SALLY	Married Vincent Brizendine	Book 1,	225
1843,	HARRIS,	WILLIAM O.	Married Lucy, daughter of Ann S. Butler	W 24,	219
1712,	HARRISON,	JAEL	Daughter of James, married William Williams	O 4,	444
1690,	HARRISON,	JAMES	Married Relict of George Mott	O 2,	253
1817, Mar. 11	HARRISON,	JAMES	Married Margaret Farmer	Book 1,	233
1824,	HARRISON,	JAMES	Married Margaret Farmer	D 41,	357
1804, Dec. 17	HARRISON,	JOHN B.	Married Sally McCarty	Book 1,	224
1718,	HARRISON,	MARGARET	Daughter of Andrew, married Gabriel Long	W 3,	85
1806,	HARRISON,	SPENCER	Married Margaret, daughter of Thomas Pitts	W 16,	437
1818,	HARRISON,	SPENCER	Married Margaret, daughter of Thomas Pitts	W 18,	476
1754,	HARRISON,	WILLIAM	Married Martha, daughter of Mark Boulware	W 10,	2
1862, Nov. 20	HART,	DOROTHEA	Married Daniel Holland	Book 1,	11
1792,	HART,	JAMES	Married Peggy, daughter of John Muse	W 16,	190

				Book	Page
1831, Oct. 31	HART,	JONATHAN	Married Mary B. Allen	Book 1,	248
1852, Jul. 23	HART,	JONATHAN	Married Eliza M. Carter	Book 1,	263
1869, May 13	HART,	JOSEPH W.	Married Mary Columbia Derieux	Book 1,	23
1838, Jan. 15	HART,	MARY C.	Married Robert F. Longham	Book 1,	253
1808, Sep. 24	HART,	THOMAS	Married Catharine Dunn	Book 1,	224
1693,	HARVIE,	RICHARD	Married Mary, daughter of John Whitchurch	O 1,	161
1696,	HARWAR,	SAMUEL	Married Ann Killman	D 9,	54
1723,	HARWAY,	REBECCA	Sister of Henry, married Vincent Godfrey Pile	D 17,	173
1709,	HARWOOD,	MARY	Widow of Peter, married Owen Owens	D&C 13,	257
1869, Mar. 16	HARWOOD,	SAMUEL F.	Married Betty Brockenbrough	Book 1,	23
1809,	HARWOOD,	THOMAS	Married Elizabeth Jones Upshaw	O 39,	492
1686,	HASLE,	WILLIAM	Married Ann, widow of Thomas Short	O 1,	147
1749,	HASTIE,	THOMAS	Married Elizabeth, widow of Thomas Coleman	D 25,	1
1835,	HAWES,	PEGGY	Daughter of Elizabeth, married Sandy Bush	D 44,	449
1799,	HAWES,	SUSANNA	Married Roger Fowke	D 35,	123
1728,	HAWKINS,	GRACE	Widow of John, married John Morgan	O 8,	97
1689,	HAWKINS,	HANNAH	Daughter of Major Thomas Hawkins married Capt. William Moseley	O 2,	187
1721,	HAWKINS,	JOHN	Married Grace, relict of Samuel Stallard	O 5,	561
1807,	HAWKINS,	JOHN	Married Maria, daughter of James Upshaw	W 17,	8
1807,	HAWKINS,	JOHN	Married Maria Upshaw	O 39,	138
1757,	HAWKINS,	JOSEPH	Married Margaret, daughter of Martin Conner	D 27,	332
1763,	HAWKINS,	NICHOLAS	Married Mary, widow of William Miller	W 12,	71
1739,	HAWKINS,	THOMAS	Married Ann, sister of Richard Covington	W 6,	250
1807,	HAWKINS,	WILLIAM	Married Harriet Upshaw	O 39,	138
1762,	HAWKINS,	YOUNG	Married Margaret, widow of Simon Miller	O 24,	56
1867, Dec. 19	HAY,	JOHN	King William, Co. married India A. Dunn	Book 1,	19
1883, May 30	HAYES,	EDMONIA	Married Richard Hall	Book 1,	72
1894, May 2	HAYES,	E. J.	Married Elmore Dunn	Book 1,	114
1895, Dec. 31	HAYES,	H. H.	Married B. A. Atkins	Book 1,	119
1858, Oct. 7	HAYES,	JOHN	Married Mary C. Williamson	Book 1,	5
1886, Sep. 6	HAYES,	JOHN JR.	Married Sarah M. Collier	Book 1,	88

				Book	Page
1889, Mar. 20	HAYES,	J. M.	Married Martha W. Cox	Book 1,	99
1885, Aug. 20	HAYES,	LAURENCE E.	King George, Co. married Nannie R. James	Book 1,	83
1808, Nov. 21	HAYES,	MARY	Married John Dunn	Book 1,	224
1886, Nov. 11	HAYES,	MARY E. L.	Married John H. Brown	Book 1,	89
1863, Oct. 1	HAYES,	NANCY E.	Married Ruffin Clarke	Book 1,	12
1841, Jan. 12	HAYES,	ROSA	Married S. M. Brooks	Book 1,	255
1899, Jan. 19	HAYES,	WORTLEY	Married L. B. Collier	Book 1,	132
1798,	HAYNES,	ANTHONY	Married Fanny Throckmorton	D 35,	59
1820, Jan. 28	HAYNES,	DOROTHY	Married John M. Hoomes	Book 1,	237
1871, Apr. 25	HAYNES,	D. LENA	Married Sylvester H. Richardson, New Kent, Co.	Book 1,	28
1832, Jun. 18	HAYNES,	JAMES W.	Married Ann R. Young	Book 1,	249
1828, Nov. 4	HAYNES,	JUDITH B.	Married George N. Alderson	Book 1,	245
1831, Apr. 5	HAYNES,	MARTHA	Married William Smith, Jr.	Book 1,	248
1819, Oct. 23	HAYNES,	THOMAS	Married Elizabeth Brown	Book 1,	235
1883, Feb. 8	HAYNES,	THOMAS G.	Married Myrtine Taylor	Book 1,	69
1726,	HAYWARTON,	THOMAS	Married Jane, daughter of John Gilby	W 4,	195
1693,	HAZLEWOOD,	ANN	Relict of George, married William Tomlin	O 1,	152
1848, Jan. 24	HEALLY,	ENAS	Married Louisa C. Cauthorn	Book 1,	260
1853, Sep. 14	HEARN,	JAMES R.	Married Martha A. Fisher	Book 1,	1
1858, Dec. 23	HEARN,	MARTHA	Widow, married Samuel W. Mienly	Book 1,	7
1822, Jan. 10	HEATH,	ANN	Married James Cooper	Book 1,	239
1805, Jun. 10	HEATH,	JOHN	Married Ann Brizendine	Book 1,	223
1727,	HEELY,	THOMAS	Married Elizabeth, daughter of Thomas Wood	O 7,	168
1878, Mar. 7	HEFLIN,	ABSALOM	Fauquier, Co. married Caroline Taylor	Book 1,	48
1872, Feb. 8	HENLEY,	CHRISTIAN	Married Dr. John A. Boughan	Book 1,	30
1817, Apr. 2	HENLEY,	GEORGE M.	Married Mary E. Montague	Book 1,	233
1884, Dec. 23	HENLEY,	JAMES C.	Married Nannie D. Garnett Caroline, Co.	Book 1,	79
1833, Oct. 7	HENLEY,	LEONARD	Married Mary S. Purkins	Book 1,	249
1844, Oct. 21	HENLEY,	LEONARD	Married Martha Croxton	Book 1,	257
1853,	HENLEY,	LEONARD	Married Martha, daughter of James Croxton	W 27,	579
1888, Nov. 27	HENLEY,	J. L.	Married Nannie F. Jeffries	Book 1,	96

				Book	Page
1890, Jun. 26	HENLEY,	LOU	Married M. S. Sadler	Book 1,	104
1831, Sep. 24	HENLEY,	MARY T.	Married John Billups	Book 1,	248
1679,	HENLEY,	ROBERT	Married Elizabeth, widow of John English (Contract)	D 6,	86
1859, Dec. 22	HENLEY,	SARAH Y.	Married James M. Croxton	Book 1,	8
1860, Nov. 22	HENLEY,	THOMAS M. JR.	Married Martha A. Armstrong	Book 1,	10
1896, Jun. 24	HENLEY,	W. T.	Married H. E. Hoskins	Book 1,	121
1855, Feb. 22	HENRY,	ALEXANDER	Married Elizabeth Gowin	Book 1,	266
1706,	HENRY,	DANIEL	Married Dorothy North, widow, Gloucester, Co.	D&C 12,	369
1715,	HENSHAW,	SAMUEL	Married Keziah, daughter of Ealse Shipley	D&W 14,	475
1761,	HENSHAW,	SAMUEL	Married Martha, daughter of Samuel Noell	D 29,	58
1813, Feb. 8	HERBERT,	NATHANIEL	Married Clarissa Jones	Book 1,	229
1804, Jan. 26	HESTER,	JOSEPH	Married Phoeby Hill	Book 1,	222
1814, Jun. 9	HESTER,	JOSEPH	Married Patsy Thompson	Book 1,	230
1815, Nov. 22	HESTER,	JOSEPH	Married Ann Jarvis	Book 1,	231
1832, Sep. 19	HESTER,	POLLY B.	Married Lewis B. Fogg	Book 1,	249
1691,	HEWLETT,	JOHN	Northumberland, Co. married Mary, daughter of Mr. George Nichols	D 8,	294
1841, Feb. 2	HILL,	ALBERT	Married Adeline Micou	Book 1,	255
1817, Jun. 12	HILL,	ANN MARIA	Married Lemuel Pitts	Book 1,	233
1844, Sep. 17	HILL,	BETSEY F.	Married John R. Temple	Book 1,	257
1820, Nov. 6	HILL,	CATHARINE	Married Pascal Cooke	Book 1,	237
1822, Oct. 15,	HILL,	CATHARINE L.	Married William Coleman	Book 1,	239
1680,	HILL,	EDWARD	Charles City, Co. married Ann, Exec. of Thomas Goodrich	D 6,	126
1798,	HILL,	ELIZABETH	Daughter of Leonard, married James Dunlop	W 15,	467
1832, Nov. 2	HILL,	ELIZABETH	Married James W. Fisher	Book 1,	249
1844, Dec. 16	HILL,	EMILY C.	Married Washington Bayne	Book 1,	257
1803,	HILL,	JESSE	Married Ann, daughter of Joseph Fogg	W 16,	220
1687,	HILL,	JOHN	Married Elizabeth, relict of John Lincolne	O 2,	40 215
1748,	HILL,	JOHN	Married Barbary, daughter of John Watkins	W 8, W 13,	86 62
1838, Sep. 17	HILL,	JULIA ANN	Married John C. Sale	Book 1,	253
1804, Apr.	HILL,	LEWIS	Married Mary Dyke	Book 1,	222
1816, Dec. 14	HILL,	LOUISA	Married Gregory Robinson	Book 1,	232

				Book	Page
1874, Feb. 28	HILL,	MARTHA	Married Philip Johnson	Book 1,	36
1798,	HILL,	MARY	Daughter of Leonard, married Bennett Brown	W 15,	467
1798,	HILL,	MARY	Relict of Leonard, married ? Campbell	W 15,	467
1819, Dec. 20	HILL,	MARY B.	Married Robert S. Anderson	Book 1,	235
1873, Dec. 27	HILL,	MARY SUSAN	Married Erastus Jones	Book 1,	33
1804, Jan. 26	HILL,	PHOEBY	Married Joseph Hester	Book 1,	222
1811, Oct. 19	HILL,	POLLY	Married John Mahon	Book 1,	227
1825, Dec. 19	HILL,	POLLY	Married Benoni Broach	Book 1,	242
1835, Dec. 19	HILL,	RICHARD H.	Married Mary Dyke	Book 1,	251
1860, Aug. 16	HILL,	ROBERT	Married Sarah Frances Nelson	Book 1,	10
1818, Mar. 3	HILL,	SUSANNA	Married William Gray	Book 1,	234
1814, Sep. 25	HILL,	THOMAS	Married Harriet Montague	Book 1,	231
1813, Feb. 6	HILL,	WILLIAM JR.	Married Lucy G. Baylor	Book 1,	229
1821, Apr. 26	HILL,	WILLIAM H.	Married Nancy Croxton	Book 1,	238
1672,	HINDS,	RICHARD	Married Mary, relict of Hugh Daniel	D 4, W&D 1,	502 7
1764,	HIPKINS,	LEROY	Married Grisell, widow of Benjamin Smith	D 30, W 11,	194 407
1805, Mar. 21	HIPKINS,	LEROY	Married Sarah Bohannon	Book 1,	223
1762,	HIPKINS,	SAMUEL	Married Margaret, daughter of Hannah Upshaw	W 12,	52
1771,	HIPKINS,	SARAH	Daughter of Thomas, married John Carnal	W 12,	421
1813, Dec. 11	HIPKINS,	SARAH	Married James Evans	Book 1,	229
1818, Jun. 1	HICCOCK,	ELIZABETH	Married Jonas Stokes	Book 1,	234
1877, Jan. 14	HODGES,	ANNIE	Married William Lumpkin	Book 1,	44
1670,	HODGES,	ARTHUR	Married Mary, relict of Evan Davies	D 4,	252
1700,	HODGES,	ARTHUR	Married Ann, widow of William Jeffries	D&W 10,	82
1876, Dec. 28	HODGES,	CHARLES L.	Married Bettie Cox	Book 1,	44
1898, Dec. 29	HODGES,	E. M.	Married M. J. Carter	Book 1,	131
1861, Jan. 20	HODGES,	JAMES R.	Married Martha Ann Johnson	Book 1,	10
1819, Jul. 20	HODGES,	JOHN	Married Fanny Brizendine	Book 1,	235
1836, Mar. 22	HODGES,	JOHN	Married Mary Ann Taylor	Book 1,	252
1865, Dec. 28	HODGES,	JOHN L.	Married Eliza A. Davis	Book 1,	14
1876, Dec. 28	HODGES,	JOHN L.	Married Mollie Ball	Book 1,	44

				Book	Page
1894, Dec. 27	HODGES,	J. S.	Married D. E. Taylor	Book 1,	116
1832, Dec. 22	HODGES,	LUCY	Married Austin Clarke	Book 1,	248
1876, Jan. 18	HODGES,	LUCY C.	Married Albert Lumpkin	Book 1,	41
1872, Nov. 7	HODGES,	LUCY S.	Married Frances R. Shepherd	Book 1,	31
1837, Jul. 25	HODGES,	MAJOR	Married Frances Greenwood	Book 1,	252
1858, Dec. 23	HODGES,	MARY SUSAN	Married George W. Oglesby, King & Queen Co.	Book 1,	7
1887, Jan. 6	HODGES,	MARY E.	Married William Foster, Matthews, Co.	Book 1,	91
1833, Dec. 16	HODGES,	PHILIP T.	Married Mary A. Dyke	Book 1,	249
1784,	HODGES,	RACHEL	Married Reuben Davis	W 15, D 33,	103 303
1897, Feb. 17	HODGES,	R. F.	Married Mary Greenwood	Book 1,	124
1881, Mar. 24	HODGES,	RICHARD	Married Addie Mitchell	Book 1,	59
1815, Jan. 5	HODGES,	SUSAN	Married Lowry Brook	Book 1,	256
1811, Dec. 23	HODGES,	THOMAS	Married Polly Williamson	Book 1,	227
1842, Apr. 8	HODGES,	THOMAS	Married Eliza Griggs	Book 1,	256
1846, Nov. 4	HODGES,	THOMAS	Married M. A. Greenwood	Book 1,	259
1894, Apr. 4	HODGES,	V. M.	Married Henry J. Harper	Book 1,	114
1876, Dec. 14	HODGES,	WILLIAM	Married Virginia Mitchell	Book 1,	43
1880, Oct. 20	HODGKIN,	JOSEPH B.	Washington, D. C. married Maria G. Gordon	Book 1,	56
1674,	HODGKIN,	PHEBE	Widow of William, married William Slaughter	D 5,	440
1662,	HODGKIN,	WILLIAM	Married Phebe Smith	D 2, D 2,	35 274
1710,	HODGSON,	ELIZABETH	Daughter of John, married Josias Ship	D&W 14,	373
1725,	HODSON,	JOHN	Married Martha, daughter of Richard Goode	W 4,	123
1696,	HODGSON,	WINIFRED	Daughter of William, married Bartholomew Vawter	D 9,	54
1833,	HOFFMAN,	CHARLOTTE	Daughter of Daniel, Baltimore, Md. married Joseph Norris	D 44,	315
1887, Dec. 14	HOGGE,	JAMES H.	Gloucester, Co. married Hattie E. Hudgens, Gloucester, Co.	Book 1,	93
1815, Aug. 28	HOLBROOK,	SELAH	Married Frances Trible	Book 1,	231
1838,	HOLBROOK,	SELAH	Married Frances, daughter of John Trible	W 24,	310
1741,	HOLDER,	JOHN	Married Margaret, widow of James Griffing, (Contract)	D 24,	127
1839, Oct. 8	HOLDERBY,	MARTHA	Married Gordon Alexander	Book 1,	254
1821, Dec. 27	HOLDERBY,	TURNER	Married Martha Dunn	Book 1,	238
1858, Aug. 10	HOLLADAY,	WILLIAM	Married Mary E. Lawrence	Book 1,	6

					Book	Page
1862, Nov. 20	HOLLAND,	DANIEL	Tailor of Ireland, married Dorothea Hart		Book 1,	11
1855, Jul. 7	HOLLAND,	J.J.	Married Lucinda Burch		Book 1,	266
1861, Jun. 20	HOLLAND,	L. R.	Teacher of Bedford Co. married Mary Susan Bentley		Book 1,	11
1887, Dec. 25	HOLMES,	MARTHA	Married Peter Chamberlain		Book 1,	93
1896, Jan. 30	HOLMES,	SALLIE B.	Married Charles Gatewood, King & Queen Co.		Book 1,	120
1693,	HOLT,	ELIZABETH	Daughter of Richard, married John Brasier		O 1,	256
1760,	HOLT,	GRIZELL	Daughter of Mrs. Margaret Holt, Hanover Co. married Benjamin Smith		W 11,	407
1693,	HOLT,	MARGARET	Relict of Richard, married John Poole		O 1,	165
1791,	HOLT,	RICHARD	Married Peggy, daughter of Vincent Cauthorn		W 14,	282
1873, Dec. 23	HOOMES,	DAVID	Married Martha Willis		Book 1,	35
1835, Sep. 19	HOOMES,	DOROTHEA	Married A. M. Braxton		Book 1,	251
1835,	HOOMES,	DOROTHY	Married Augustine Braxton		D 45,	34
1870, Jan. 15	HOOMES,	HENRY	Married Katy Tunstall		Book 1,	25
1876, Jul. 27	HOOMES,	JENNY	Married James Jones		Book 1,	42
1820, Jan. 28	HOOMES,	JOHN M.	Married Dorothy Haynes		Book 1,	237
1810,	HOOMES,	MARTHA	Married Lawrence Muse		D 37,	553
1873, Jan. 16	HOOMES,	SUSAN	Married Arthur Mackerell		Book 1,	32
1670,	HOPGOOD,	PETER	Married Sarah Godson, widow		D 4,	312
1748,	HOPSON,	RICHARD	Married Margaret, daughter of Edward Martin		D 24,	254
1747,	HORD,	JANE	Married William Miller		W 8,	286
1727,	HORDE,	THOMAS	Married Jane Miller, cousin of Susanna Brice		O 7,	175
1800,	HORD,	WILLIAM	Married Catharine Hawkins		O 35,	504
1805,	HORTON,	ENOCH	Married Catharine, widow of Caleb Elliott		W 16,	438
1893, Apr. 26	HOSKINS,	A. T.	Married J A. White, King & Queen Co.		Book 1,	111
1675,	HOSKINS,	ELIZABETH	Daughter of Anthony, married Cornelius Wood		D 5,	15, 265
1892, Nov. 9	HOSKINS,	EMMA C.	Married Robert G. Haile		Book 1,	110
1818, Dec. 21	HOSKINS,	GEORGE	Married Catharine Montague		Book 1,	234
1896, Jun. 24	HOSKINS,	H. E.	Married W. T. Henley		Book 1,	121
1723,	HOSKINS,	JOHN	Married Martha, relict of George Coleman		D 17,	180
1782,	HOSKINS,	JOHN	King & Queen, Co. married Elizabeth, daughter of John Cheaney		D 33,	1
1846, Nov. 4	HOSKINS,	JOHN T.	Married Hannah E. Ware		Book 1,	259

					Book	Page
1895, Aug. 29	HOSKINS,	JOHN T.	Married L. V. Broaddus		Book 1,	118
1677,	HOSKINS,	KATHERINE	Relict of Robert, married Francis Downer		D 6,	31
1685,	HOSKINS,	KATHERINE	Relict of Robert, married Mr. Avery Nayler		D 7,	177
1882,	HOSKINS,	KATE W.	Married C. C. Warner		Book 1,	65
1874, Jun. 4	HOSKINS,	LOUISA W.	Married Robert Daniel		Book 1,	36
1884, Mar. 1	HOSKINS,	M. NETTIE	Married Junius M. Broaddus		Book 1,	76
1888, Dec. 26	HOSKINS,	M. S.	Married J. T. Baird, Columbia, Co. Florida		Book 1,	97
1878, Apr. 24	HOSKINS,	NANNIE BUCKNER	Married William Eubank		Book 1,	46
1806, Jan. 7	HOSKINS,	PATSY	Married Martin Coleman		Book 1,	223
1871, Dec. 21	HOSKINS,	RICHARD L.	King & Queen, Co. married Addie D. Waring		Book 1,	29
1857, Dec. 24	HOSKINS,	DR. WILLIAM	Married Jeannette C. Roy		Book 1,	264
1888, Oct. 3	HOSKINS,	W. D.	Married Ella G. Hundley		Book 1,	96
1877, Apr. 12	HOUSE,	ELLA T.	Married Thomas H. Armstrong		Book 1,	45
1858, Dec. 23	HOUSE,	FRANCES A.	Married William W. James		Book 1,	7
1865, Apr. 20	HOUSE,	MARY E.	Married Eri Jenkins		Book 1,	13
1870, May 19	HOUSE,	RICHARD E.	Married Mary L. Thomas		Book 1,	25
1838, Aug. 28	HOUSE,	SEYLOR F.	Married Frances Ann Faver		Book 1,	253
1816, Jan. 8	HOUSTON,	ALEXANDER	Married Polly Crow		Book 1,	232
1883, Dec. 23	HOUSTON,	ALLIEN T.	Married Benjamin G. Jeffries		Book 1,	74
1846, Feb. 11	HOUSTON,	JANE	Married Benjamin Boughton		Book 1,	258
1839, Jul. 15	HOUSTON,	POLLY	Married James H. Taylor		Book 1,	254
1810, Jul. 16	HOUSTON,	ROBERT	Married Elizabeth Crow		Book 1,	226
1820,	HOUSTON,	ROBERT	Married Mary, daughter of John Crow		W 19,	155
1894, Mar. 21	HOWARD,	BENJAMIN	Married Mary S. Stokes		Book 1,	113
1869, May 13	HOWARD,	RICHARD	Caroline, Co. married Mary Stokes.		Book 1,	23
1807,	HOWARD,	WILLIAM	Married Lucy Gatewood, great grandaughter of Richard Burke		D 37,	264
1838, Jan. 2	HOWE,	CATHARINE	Married Reuben Brooks		Book 1,	253
1821, Dec. 11	HOWERTON,	ANN	Married John Boughton		Book 1,	238
1824,	HOWERTON,	ANN	Daughter of Charles, married John Boughton		D 41,	272
1816, Apr. 27	HOWERTON,	CATHARINE	Married William Howerton		Book 1,	232
1805, May 20	HOWERTON,	CHARLES	Married Sarah Townley		Book 1,	223

				Book	Page
1827, Nov. 26	HOWERTON,	CHARLOTTE	Married Thomas Cole	Book 1,	243
1832,	HOWERTON,	CHARLOTTE,	Daughter of William, married Thomas Cole	D 43,	595
1836, Jul. 25	HOWERTON,	ELEANOR H.	Married Mortimer Smith	Book 1,	252
1757,	HOWERTON,	ELIZABETH	Daughter of Thomas, married ? Covington	W 11,	23
1818, Dec. 29	HOWERTON,	ELIZABETH	Married John St. John	Book 1,	234
1812, Nov. 16	HOWERTON,	FRANCES	Married John Baynham	Book 1,	228
1824,	HOWERTON,	FRANCES	Daughter of Charles, married John Boughan	D 41,	272
1778,	HOWERTON,	HERITAGE	Married Caty, daughter of Henry Crutcher	W 13,	300
1781,	HOWERTON,	JANE	Sister of John, married Henry Crutcher	W 13,	344
1801,	HOWERTON,	JANE	Daughter of Heritage, married Vincent Cauthorn	D 35,	465
1803,	HOWERTON,	JANE	Daughter of William, married Edmund Edmondson	D 36,	326
1757,	HOWERTON,	MARY	Daughter of Thomas, married Samuel Coates	W 11,	23
1792,	HOWERTON,	MARY	Widow of William, married Richard Jeffries (Divorced)	D 33,	387 429
1828, Jul. 21	HOWERTON,	MILDRED	Married Leonard Collins	Book 1,	245
1813, Dec. 7	HOWERTON,	NANCY	Married Washington Purkins	Book 1,	229
1798,	HOWERTON,	RACHEL	Daughter of Heritage, married Thomas Cheaney, Charlotte, Co.	D 35,	204
1806, Oct. 20	HOWERTON,	RACHEL	Married John Willis	Book 1,	223
1832, Feb. 20	HOWERTON,	THOMAS J.	Married Sophronia Covington	Book 1,	249
1834,	HOWERTON,	THOMAS	Halifax, Co. married Sophronia, daughter of Richard Covington	D 45,	343
1816, Jan. 15	HOWERTON,	WILLIAM	Married Catharine Howerton	Book 1,	232
1816, Oct. 29	HOWERTON,	WILLIAM	Married Ann Covington	Book 1,	232
1669,	HUBBERT,	KATHERINE	Widow of Richard, married Thomas Williamson	D 4,	190
1685,	HUBBERT,	DR. MOSES	Married Relict of John Barrow	O 1,	174
1701,	HUCKLESCOTT, MARY		Daughter of Thomas, married Salvator Muscoe	D&W 10,	112
1857, Nov. 26	HUCKSTEP,	JOHN H.	Married Sarah Parker	Book 1,	5
1887, Dec. 14	HUDGINS,	HATTIE	Married James H. Hogge	Book 1,	93
1810, Mar. 25	HUDGINS,	PHILIP	Married Polly Ayres	Book 1,	226
1883, Dec. 27	HUDGINS,	THOMAS F.	Married Mary A. Crafton	Book 1,	74
1711,	HUDSON,	HENRY	Married Katherine, sister of John Vass	D&C 13,	401
1818, Feb. 16	HUDSON,	MARY	Married Joseph Stokes	Book 1,	234
1820,	HUDSON,	PHILIP	Married Esther, niece of Sarah Goulding	W 19,	170

				Book	Page
1676,	HUESON,	DOROTHY	Daughter of Thomas, married Thomas Day	D 5,	514
1850, Sep. 16	HUGHES,	JEFFERSON	Married Martha Eubank	Book 1,	262
1841, Sep. 28	HUGHES,	WILLIAM C.	Married Lottie M. Smith	Book 1,	255
1687,	HULL,	MRS. ANN	Married William Colston	O 2,	29, 65
1684,	HULL,	REBECCA	Daughter of Henry Willoughby	D 6,	76
1707,	HUMPHREYS, ELIZABETH		Married Robert Armstrong	O 3,	388
1809,	HUNLEY,	AMBROSE	Married Elizabeth, daughter of John Haile	W 17,	210
1831, Jun. 20	HUNDLEY,	ANDREW	Married Ann S. Mann	Book 1,	248
1832,	HUNDLEY,	ANDREW	Married Ann Mann, widow of Philip Mann, Jr.	D 43,	533
1862, Jan. 8	HUNDLEY,	ANDREW	Married Martha E. Sizer, King William, Co.	Book 1,	11
1823, Mar. 17	HUNDLEY,	ANN	Married Robert Mackan	Book 1,	240
1819, Dec. 14	HUNLEY,	ANNA H.	Married Fountain Wood	Book 1,	236
1823,	HUNLEY,	ANNA	Daughter of Ambrose, married Fountain Wood	D 41,	37
1813, Nov. 29	HUNDLEY,	BETSEY	Married James Dyke	Book 1,	229
1823, Aug. 18	HUNDLEY,	DANIEL	Married Elizabeth Smith	Book 1,	240
1827, Jan. 18	HUNDLEY,	EDWIN	Married Virginia Montague	Book 1,	243
1831, Nov. 11	HUNDLEY,	ELIJAH	Married Lucy W. Dyke	Book 1,	248
1844, Oct. 21	HUNDLEY,	ELINOR	Married Tillman Gardner	Book 1,	257
1809, Jan. 6	HUNDLEY,	ELIZABETH	Married Mourning Smith	Book 1,	225
1816, Jan. 13	HUNDLEY,	ELIZABETH	Married Charles G. Layton	Book 1,	232
1872, Dec. 19	HUNDLEY,	ELIZABETH	Married Lewis P. Birch	Book 1,	32
1876, Apr. 20	HUNDLEY,	ELIZABETH B.	Married William H. Farinholt	Book 1,	40
1888, Oct. 3	HUNDLEY,	ELLA G.	Married W. D. Hoskins, King & Queen Co.	Book 1,	96
1850, Nov. 30	HUNDLEY,	DR. J. M.	Married Lucy Ann S. Layton	Book 1,	262
1853, Jan. 8	HUNDLEY,	JAMES H.	Married Sophronia Dyke	Book 1,	264
1854, Mar. 15	HUNDLEY,	JAMES B.	Married Hannah L. Dunn	Book 1,	265
1873, Jul. 29	HUNDLEY,	JAMES H. D.	Married Nannie J. Gouldman	Book 1,	34
1824, Jan. 14	HUNDLEY,	JOHN	Married Alice Dyke	Book 1,	241
1859, May 4	HUNDLEY,	JOHN T. T.	King & Queen Co. married Sarah E. Garnett, King & Queen, Co.	Book 1,	7
1819, Feb. 27	HUNDLEY,	LARKIN	Married Sophronia Evans	Book 1,	235
1830,	HUNDLEY,	LARKIN	Married Eliza Bush	D 43,	308

				Book	Page
1870, Apr. 21	HUNDLEY,	LUCIE ELLA	Married John A. Anderson, Fredericksburg	Book 1,	25
1886, Jan. 16	HUNDLEY,	LUCY B.	Married R. T. Shackelford	Book 1,	85
1899, Nov. 6	HUNDLEY,	L. T.	Married J. F. Anderson, Washington, D. C.	Book 1,	134
1816, Nov. 25	HUNDLEY,	MARIA	Married Miskel Dyke	Book 1,	232
1816, Dec. 7	HUNDLEY,	MARY	Married Peter Campbell	Book 1,	232
1835, Jan. 28	HUNDLEY,	MARY C.	Married A. G. Bohannon	Book 1,	251
1842, Dec. 31	HUNDLEY,	MARY A.	Married Elliott Gardner	Book 1,	256
1880, Oct. 7	HUNDLEY,	MAY	Married Louis Banley	Book 1,	56
1811, Dec. 16	HUNDLEY,	NANCY	Married William Dyke	Book 1,	227
1877, Sep. 13	HUNDLEY,	NANNIE	Widow, married George W. Rice	Book 1,	46
1810, Oct. 16	HUNDLEY,	SALLY	Married Beverley Carroll	Book 1,	226
1834, Apr. 7	HUNDLEY,	SARAH M.	Married Joseph H. Pendleton	Book 1,	250
1878, Nov. 10	HUNDLEY,	SOPHRONIA J.	Married Alfred Brooks	Book 1,	49
1821, Jun. 29	HUNDLEY,	SUSAN	Married Robert Mann	Book 1,	238
1832,	HUNLEY,	?	Married Alice, daughter of Bowler Dyke	D 43,	501
1771,	HUNLEY,	THOMAS	Married Elizabeth, dau. of James & Eleanor Medley	Box 1772,	D
1795,	HUNLEY,	THOMAS	Married Elizabeth, daughter of Josiah McTyre	W 15,	190
1814, Jul. 17	HUNDLEY,	THOMAS	Married Frances Phillips	Book 1,	231
1834, May 19	HUNDLEY,	THOMAS	Married Mary Ann Williams	Book 1,	250
1841, Dec. 20	HUNDLEY,	THOMAS I.	Married Maria E. Layton	Book 1,	255
1842, May 9	HUNDLEY,	VIRGINIA	Married James Dunn	Book 1,	256
1865, Dec. 28	HUNDLEY,	WILLIAM H.	Married Catharine Ann Mitchell	Book 1,	13
1721,	HUNT,	WILLIAM	Married Elizabeth Evans	O 5,	629
1876, Jun. 1	HUNTER,	BENJAMIN	Married Fenton Oakley	Book 1,	42
1819, Oct. 18	HUNTER,	JAMES	Married Apphia Rouzee	Book 1,	235
1826,	HUNTER,	JAMES	Married Maria Garnett	D 42,	141
1715,	HUNTER,	JOHN	Married Ann, relict of Robert Coleman	D&W 14	358
1820, Feb. 22	HUNTER,	MARIA	Married James Garnett, Jr.	Book 1,	237
1893, Dec. 21	HUNTER,	MARIA	Married Nelson Jordan	Book 1,	112
1813, Jun. 27	HUNTER,	MUSCOE G.	Married Grace Fenton Garnett, Jr.	Book 1,	229
1861, Nov. 8	HUNTER,	RICHARD	Married Eliza Powers	Book 1,	11

				Book	Page
1787,	HUNTER,	WILLIAM	Married Sarah, daughter of Ann Garnett	W 14,	135
1717,	HUSE,	RALPH	Married Alice, only daughter & heir of Garrett Evars	D 15,	134
1739,	HUTCHINS,	REBECCAH	Widow of Richard, married Thomas Smith	D 22,	81
1890, Dec. 23	HUTCHINSON, E. L.		Married Ida Motley	Book 1,	105
1844, Dec. 16	HUTCHINSON, JOHN D.		Married Elizabeth B. Haile	Book 1,	257
1720,	HUTCHINSON, JOSEPH		Married Mary, widow of John Jones	O 5,	543
1876, Dec. 14	HUTCHINSON, ROBERT		Married Mary E. Clarkson	Book 1,	43
1897, Jan. 27	HUTCHINSON, ROBERT		Married Alice W. Morris	Book 1,	124
1848, Feb. 16	HUTSON,	ELIZABETH	Married Henry Steavens	Book 1,	260

				Book		Page
1885, Sep. 28	INGRAM,	ALICE	Married Robert W. Gatewood	Book 1,		83
1867, Dec. 19	INGRAM,	ANN E.	Married James L. Brown	Book 1,		19
1838, Oct. 11	INGRAM,	ANNA	Married Samuel Turner	Book 1,		253
1689,	INGRAM,	DORCAS	Relict of Tobias, married John Sorrell	O	2,	202
1845, Jul. 7	INGRAM,	GEORGE	Married Nancy Ball	Book 1,		258
1850, Aug.	INGRAM,	GODFREY	Married Mary Coghill	Book 1,		262
1824, Dec. 20	INGRAM,	JAMES	Married Frances Schools	Book 1,		241
1833, Dec. 4	INGRAM,	JAMES	Married Matilda Taylor	Book 1,		249
1848, Jul. 21	INGRAM,	MARY E.	Married Mark S. Ashburn	Book 1,		260
1823, Dec. 24	INGRAM,	LUCY	Married Booker Taylor	Book 1,		240
1830, Apr. 19	INGRAM,	PATSY	Married Larkin Pitts	Book 1,		247
1806,	INGRAM,	ROSEY	Daughter of William, married William Halbert	O	38,	426
1806,	INGRAM,	SALLY	Daughter of William, married William Pitts	O	38,	426
1813, Dec. 22	INGRAM,	SPENCER	Married Elizabeth Short	Book 1,		229
1690,	INGRAM,	TOBIAS	Son of Magdalen Gibson, formerly wife of Tobias Ingram, married Dorcas, widow of Henry White	D O	6, 2,	78 202
1850, Dec. 12	INGRAM,	WILLIAM	Married Mary Saunders	Book 1,		262
1808, Nov. 21	INSER,	ANN	Married John Walker	Book 1,		225
1800,	IREDALE,	JOHN	Fauquier, Co. married Hannah, daughter of Griffing Boughan	D	35,	281
1677,	IVESON,	ABRAHAM	Married Jane or Jone, mother of James Kay	D	6,	26

				Book	Page

J

				Book	Page
1688,	JACOBS,	MARY	Relict of Rosamond, married Richard Wilton	O 2,	82
1688,	JACOBUS,	ANGELL	Married Elizabeth, daughter of Henry & Joan Clarke	D 8, D 7,	4 543
1681,	JACKMAN,	ELIZABETH	Daughter of Anthony, married Richard Grimstead	D 6,	129
1681,	JACKMAN,	MARY	Daughter of Anthony, married James Toone (Tune)	D 6,	129
1723,	JACKSON,	ELIZABETH	Married James Kelson, Bristol	D 17,	146
1855, Jan. 16	JACKSON,	ELIZABETH	Married Albert Goin	Book 1,	266
1839, May 11	JACKSON,	GANON	Married Alice C. Broocke	Book 1,	254
1697,	JACKSON,	ISAAC	Married Jane, only daughter of Robert Gullocke	D 9,	110
1700,	JACKSON,	JANE	Daughter of Robert Gullocke, married John Butler	D&W 11,	72
1787,	JACKSON,	?	Married Milly, daughter of Ann Garnett	W 14,	136
1723,	JACKSON,	RACHEL	Married Joseph End, Bristol	D 17,	146
1785,	JACKSON,	WILLIAM	Spottsylvania, Co. married Milly, daughter of Wm. Garnett	Land Trials,	156
1685,	JAMES,	FRANCIS	Married Mary, daughter of Philip Sherwood	O 1,	173
1885, Aug. 20	JAMES,	NANNIE R.	Laurence E. Hayes, King George Co.	Book 1,	83
1810, Feb. 5	JAMES,	SALLY I.	Married James Davis	Book 1,	226
1721,	JAMES,	SHERWOOD	Married Ann, daughter of Richard King	D 16,	264
1812, Dec. 21	JAMES,	SUSANNA	Married Abraham Brizendine	Book 1,	228
1725,	JAMES,	WILLIAM	Married Agnes, Admrx. of William Moss	O 6,	270
1858, Dec. 23	JAMES,	WILLIAM W.	Married Frances A. House	Book 1,	7
1817, Jan. 20	JANEY,	JOSEPH	Married Adelaide Garland	Book 1,	233
1827, Apr. 6	JANEY,	MARY A.	Married Edmund M. Ware	Book 1,	244
1835,	JANEY,	VIRGINIA	Daughter of Adelaide, married George Lorimer	D 44,	520
1815, Nov. 22	JARVIS,	ANN	Married Joseph Hester	Book 1,	231
1836, Nov. 23	JASPER,	ALICE	Married Charles Carr	Book 1,	252
1772,	JEATOR,	ELIJAH	Married Elizabeth, daughter of John Satterwhite	W 13,	258
1687,	JEDFORD,	ELIZABETH	Widow of Francis, married Ralph Whitton	D 7,	490
1869, Dec. 11	JEFFERSON,	ROBERT	Married Fanny Sale	Book 1,	24
1899, Feb. 2	JEFFRIES,	ADDIE B.	Married Magruder Dix	Book 1,	132
1802,	JEFFRIES,	ANDERSON	Married Elizabeth, daughter of John Shepard	D 36,	67
1700,	JEFFRIES,	ANN	Widow of William, married Arthur Hodges	D&W 10,	82

				Book	Page
1883, Dec. 23	JEFFRIES,	BENJAMIN G.	Married Allien T. Houston	Book 1,	74
1821, Jan. 17	JEFFRIES,	BROOKING	Married Patsey Greenwood	Book 1,	238
1882, Dec. 27	JEFFRIES,	BROOKING L.	Married Kate Jane Longest	Book 1,	68
1686,	JEFFRYS,	EDWARD	Married Elizabeth, daughter of Henry Wilson	Box 101,	K
1689,	JEFFRIES,	EDWARD	Married Mary, relict of John Diskin	O 2,	199
1698,	JEFFREYS,	EDWARD	Married Mary, daughter of Nicholas Putley	D 9,	314
1699,	JEFFREYS,	EDWARD	Richmond, Co. married Elizabeth relict of Nicholas Putley	D 9,	315
1816, Dec. 13	JEFFRIES,	ELIZABETH	Married Thomas Dunn	Book 1,	232
1828, Jun. 14	JEFFRIES,	ELIZABETH	Married James C. Greenwood	Book 1,	245
1857, Jul. 25	JEFFRIES,	ELLEN D.	Married William A. Oliver	Book 1,	5
1880, Apr. 7	JEFFRES,	HARRIET	Married William T. Seward	Book 1,	55
1884, Jul. 2	JEFFRIES,	JOSEPHINE C.	Married Rev. Alexander Fleet	Book 1,	78
1888, Dec. 27	JEFFRIES,	LEWIS M.	Married Susan L Harper	Book 1,	97
1838, Jan. 15	JEFFRIES,	LOUISA	Married Dabney Brooks	Book 1,	253
1855, Feb. 1	JEFFRES,	LUCY A.	Married John Williamson	Book 1,	3
1832, May 1	JEFFRIES,	MARTHA	Married Barnett Brown	Book 1,	248
1889, Sep. 25	JEFFRIES,	MELVILLE	Married N. Janey Bagby	Book 1,	101
1825, May 9	JEFFRIES,	MOSES	Married Juliet Jones	Book 1,	241
1851, Apr. 15	JEFFRIES,	NANCY	Married Washington Brooks	Book 1,	262
1888, Nov. 27	JEFFRIES,	NANNIE F.	Married J. L. Henley	Book 1,	96
1827, Jan. 23	JEFFRIES,	ORVAL	Married Mary Newbill	Book 1,	243
1790,	JEFFRIES,	RICHARD	Married Elizabeth, daughter of James Booker	W 15,	101
1792,	JEFFRIES,	RICHARD	Married Mary, widow of William Howerton (Divorced)	D 33,	386
1705,	JEFFERY,	ROBERT	Married Sarah Page	O 3,	198
1855, May 26	JEFFRIES,	ROBERT	Married Ann Brooks	Book 1,	3
1831, Jul. 6	JEFFRIES,	SARAH	Married William Tate	Book 1,	248
1830, Sep. 25	JEFFRIES,	SUSAN	Married Joseph Willmore	Book 1,	247
1804,	JEFFRIES,	THOMAS	Married Ann, daughter of William Smith	D 36,	380
1825, Jun. 10	JEFFRIES,	THOMAS	Married Maria Elliott	Book 1,	241
1839, May 20	JEFFRIES,	THOMAS	Married Elizabeth Goode	Book 1,	254
1849, Nov. 30	JEFFRIES,	THOMAS	Married Martha Cauthorn	Book 1,	261

				Book	Page
1852, Aug. 10	JEFFREY,	WILLIAM G.	Married Susan F. Croxton	Book 1,	263
1854, Oct. 28	JEFFRIES,	WILLIAM GEORGE	Married Ella Ann Lowry	Book 1,	2
1696,	JENKINS,	DAVID	Married Ann, relict of George Williams	D 9,	80
1865, Apr. 20	JENKINS,	ERI	Married Mary E. House	Book 1,	13
1761,	JENKINS,	ISAAC	Married Mary, widow of Nicholas Pamplin	W 11,	420
1890, Jul. 30	JENKINS,	MARY F.	Married W. W. Parks, Maryland	Book 1,	104
1872, May 9	JENKINS,	ROBERT A.	Married Sarah Coates	Book 1,	30
1873, Dec. 30	JENKINS,	WILLIAM B.	Married Mary E. Samuel	Book 1,	33
1879, Dec. 25	JESSE,	ELLVER A.	Married Lucinda Taylor	Book 1,	53
1868, Jul. 15	JESSE,	JAMES M.	Married Betty W. Burke	Book 1,	20
1837, Apr. 28	JESSE,	JOHN A.	Married Frances C. Montague	Book 1,	252
1843, Feb. 20	JESSE,	JOHN	Married Anna H. Crow	Book 1,	256
1886, Jul. 8	JESSEE,	LOGAN	Married Dora Taylor	Book 1,	88
1824, Dec. 28	JESSEE,	LUCINDA	Married Robert Daniel	Book 1,	241
1878, May 2	JESSE,	LUCY R.	Married Morton B. Evans	Book 1,	48
1877, Dec. 25	JESSE,	MARY E.	Married William T. Evans	Book 1,	46
1820, Mar. 11	JESSE,	NANCY K.	Married James E. Evans	Book 1,	237
1793,	JESSIE,	THOMAS	Middlesex County, married Ann, daughter of Richard Cauthorn, sister of Vincent Cauthorn	D 33,	498
1811, Dec. 9	JESSIE,	THOMAS M.	Married Ann B. Whiting	Book 1,	227
1814, May 19	JESSIE,	THOMAS M.	Married Amelia Montague	Book 1,	230
1659,	JESSON,	ELIZABETH	Daughter of Randall, married Hugh Wilson, Middlesex Co. (Mariner)	D 2,	287
1879, Mar. 20	JETER,	THEODORE F.	Married Alice Samuel	Book 1,	51
1745,	JETT,	PETER	King George Co., married Karen Happuk, daughter of Elizabeth Virgett, formerly Elizabeth Bendry	D 23,	296
1800,	JOHNSON,	ANDREW	Married Polly, daughter of John Patterson	D 35,	261
1762,	JOHNSON,	ANN	Daughter of Thomas & Ann, married Thomas Ward	W 12,	346
1800,	JOHNSON,	?	Married Anna, sister of John Vass	W 16,	46
1800,	JOHNSON,	BEN	Married Ann Cheyney, widow	W 16,	77
1877, Feb. 20	JOHNSON,	BENNETT	Married Vernangus Landrum	Book 1,	44
1825, Mar. 29	JOHNSON,	BETSEY	Married William Rollins	Book 1,	242
1876, Feb. 3	JOHNSON,	BETTIE	Married George W. Dunn	Book 1,	41

				Book	Page
1841, Dec. 24	JOHNSON,	CATHARINE	Married Zachariah Carter	Book 1,	255
1866, Dec. 29	JOHNSON,	CATHARINE	Married Matthew Kendall'	Book 1,	16
1871, May 10	JOHNSON,	CATHARINE	Married Moses Manokey	Book 1,	28
1828, Dec. 15	JOHNSON,	CURTIS	Married Mary Dunn	Book 1,	245
1810, Feb. 20	JOHNSON,	DANIEL	Married Patsy Fortune	Book 1,	226
1871, Oct. 17	JOHNSON,	EVELINE	Married James Evans	Book 1,	29
1832, Dec. 24	JOHNSON,	ELIZA	Married Leonard Johnson	Book 1,	249
1844, Oct. 17	JOHNSON,	ELIZABETH	Married John Corr	Book 1,	257
1848, Feb. 21	JOHNSON,	FANNIE	Married James J. Gouldman	Book 1,	260
1700,	JOHNSON,	HENRY	Married Elizabeth, daughter of Henry Bond's wife	D&W 10,	63
1703,	JOHNSON,	HENRY	Married Elizabeth, daughter of William Muffett of Stone's Island	D 11,	100
1822, Feb. 11	JOHNSON,	HENRY	Married Peggy Montague	Book 1,	239
1685,	JOHNSON,	ISRAEL	Married Daughter of Henry Reeves	O 1,	111
1828, Nov. 8	JOHNSON,	JOHN	Married Frances Bush	Book 1,	245
1829,	JOHNSON,	JOHN	Married Fanny Bush	D 43,	37
1867, Feb. 23	JOHNSON,	JOHN L.	Married Louisa Harper	Book 1,	17
1835,	JOHNSON,	JULY ANN	Married Alexander Rae	D 45,	68
1898, Feb. 20	JOHNSON,	K. L.	Married L. B. Riley	Book 1,	189
1832, Dec. 24	JOHNSON,	LEONARD	Married Eliza Johnson	Book 1,	249
1862, Jun. 19	JOHNSON,	LEONARD	Married Margaret Welch	Book 1,	11
1876, Feb. 3	JOHNSON,	LEVINIA	Married Thomas Coleman	Book 1,	41
1804, Dec. 17	JOHNSON,	LUCY	Married John Townsley	Book 1,	222
1830, May 18	JOHNSON,	LUCY	Married Nathaniel Ferguson	Book 1,	247
1688,	JOHNSON,	MARGARET	Relict of Samuel, married Edward George	O 2,	112
1852, Dec. 23	JOHNSON,	MARIA	Married Judson Davis	Book 1,	263
1843, Apr. 17	JOHNSON,	MARTHA M.	Married William Williamson	Book 1,	257
1861, Jan. 20	JOHNSON,	MARTHA ANN	Married James R. Hodges	Book 1,	10
1745,	JOHNSON,	MARY	Only daughter of James & Esther, married Charles Clarke	D 23,	325
1823,	JOHNSON,	MARY	Grandaughter of William Cole & niece of Nelson Cole, Mecklenburg County	D 41,	81
1875,	JOHNSON,	MARY	Married Ethelbert Williams	Book 1,	39

				Book	Page
1891, Mar. 19	JOHNSON,	MARY	Married William H. Coates	Book 1,	107
1834,	JOHNSON,	MATILDA	Daughter of James, married John Games	D 45,	322
1867, Jul. 21	JOHNSON,	MATILDA	Married William Jones	Book 1,	18
1832, Oct. 9	JOHNSON,	MIRANDA	Married Edmund Richards	Book 1,	249
1832, Mar. 19	JOHNSON,	PATSEY	Married John Foreacres	Book 1,	249
1810, May 7	JOHNSON,	PHILIP	Married Polly Yarrington	Book 1,	226
1867, Dec. 28	JOHNSON,	PHILIP	Married Judith Fauntleroy	Book 1,	19
1874, Feb. 28	JOHNSON,	PHILIP	Married Martha Hill	Book 1,	36
1825, Dec. 28	JOHNSON,	PITMAN	Married Polly Dunn	Book 1,	241
1832, Jan. 16	JOHNSON,	POLLY	Married Lewis Dunn	Book 1,	248
1727,	JOHNSON,	RICHARD	Married Elizabeth Goare	O 7,	159
1730,	JOHNSON,	RICHARD	Married Elizabeth Webb	W 8,	108
1744,	JOHNSON,	RICHARD	Married Elizabeth, relict of John Goare	D 23,	189
1829, Nov. 16	JOHNSON,	RICHARD	Married Frances Montague	Book 1,	246
1877, Sep. 20	JOHNSON,	RICHARD	Married Mary Anne Clarke	Book 1,	46
1693,	JOHNSON,	ROBERT	Married Christian Dison, grandaughter of Thomas Page	O 1,	260
1816, Dec. 24	JOHNSON,	SALLY	Married Philip Goode	Book 1,	232
1829,	JOHNSON,	SAMUEL	Married Catharine Dunn	D 43,	37
1840, Aug. 17	JOHNSON,	SUSAN A.	Married George Foreacres	Book 1,	254
1762,	JOHNSON,	SUSANNA	Married Christopher Smith	W 12,	436
1762,	JOHNSON,	THOMAS	Married Ann, sister of Matthew Yarrow	W 12,	436
1874, Mar. 24	JOHNSON,	THOMAS S.	Married Elizabeth Smith	Book 1,	45
1876, Dec. 25	JOHNSON,	THOMAS	Married Julia Kidd	Book 1,	43
1702,	JOHNSON,	WILLIAM	Married Elizabeth, widow of Henry Pickett	D&W 10,	127
1848, May 25	JOHNSON,	WILLIAM R.	Married Lucinda C. Beazley	Book 1,	260
1898, Jan. 13	JOHNSON,	W. R.	Married A. B. Bareford	Book 1,	128
1842, Dec. 6	JOHNSTON,	CATHARINE	Married Nathan Parker	Book 1,	256
1863, Feb. 4	JOHNSTON,	JOHN	Married Narcissa I. Davis	Book 1,	11
1827, Feb. 19	JOHNSTON,	LOUISA	Married Samuel Ursery	Book 1,	244
1822, Dec. 16	JOHNSTON,	MOURNING	Married Patsey Harper	Book 1,	239
1777,	JOHNSTON,	RICHARD	Married Elizabeth, daughter of James Fullerton	D 33,	89

				Book	Page
1873, Jul. 27	JONES,	ALECK	Married Ann Garnett	Book 1,	34
1867, Apr. 24	JONES,	ALEXANDER	Married Anna Garnett	Book 1,	17
1818, Dec. 29	JONES,	AMEY	Married Ephraim Beazley, Jr.	Book 1,	234
1765,	JONES,	ANN	Daughter of Francis, married John Dailie	W 12,	267
1784,	JONES,	ANN	Daughter of James, married Ambrose White	W 13,	456
1812, Sep. 10	JONES,	ANNE	Married Martin Lipscomb	Book 1,	228
1815,	JONES,	ANN	Daughter of Erasmus, married William Fisher	D 39,	207
1870, Apr. 2	JONES	BENJAMIN F.	Married Lala Lee	Book 1,	25
1759,	JONES,	BETTY	Sister of John, married James Garnett	W 11,	178
1784,	JONES,	BETTY	Daughter of James, married Richard Gwathmey	W 13,	457
1888, Dec. 5	JONES,	CARRIE C.	King William Co., married J. W. Faulconer	Book 1,	97
1879, Feb. 26	JONES,	CATHARINE	Married Charles Bray	Book 1,	51
1807,	JONES,	CLARA	Married Robert Stubblefield	O 39,	181
1813, Feb. 8	JONES,	CLARISSA	Married Nathaniel Herbert	Book 1,	229
1822, Dec. 16	JONES,	COLEMAN	Married Susanna Jones	Book 1,	239
1835, Dec. 28	JONES,	DOROTHY	Married Obadiah Alexander	Book 1,	251
1837,	JONES,	DOROTHY	Grandaughter of John Jones, married Joseph C. Courtney	Book 1,	252
1808, Mar. 18	JONES,	EDMUND	Married Mary Ann Fogg	Book 1,	224
1889, Jun. 6	JONES,	ELIZA E.	Married Jacob S. Durham	Book 1,	100
1685,	JONES,	ELIZABETH	Only heir of Thomas Jones, married Samuel Blomfield	D 7,	174
1687,	JONES,	ELIZABETH	Married Capt. Samuel Blomfield	O 2,	16
1735,	JONES,	ELIZABETH	Daughter of Robert, married Anthony Garnett	O 9,	128
1743,	JONES,	ELIZABETH	Eldest daughter of Robert of St. Ann's Parish, married Anthony Garnett	D 23,	11
1765,	JONES,	ELIZABETH	Widow of William, married George Games	O 26,	41
1808,	JONES,	ELIZABETH	Married James McFarlain	Book 1,	224
1812, Jul. 23	JONES,	ELIZABETH	Married Zachariah Carter	Book 1,	228
1828, Feb. 11	JONES,	ELIZABETH	Married Willis Brooks	Book 1,	245
1835,	JONES,	ELIZABETH	Daughter of Joseph & Nancy, married Willis Brooks	D 44,	441
1841, Apr. 9	JONES,	ELLEN H.	Married Joseph B. Smith	Book 1,	255
1833, Sep. 11	JONES,	EMANUEL M.	Married Mary E. Wright	Book 1,	249
1873, Dec. 27	JONES,	ERASTUS	Married Mary Susan Hill	Book 1,	33

				Book	Page
1806, Nov. 16	JONES,	FRANCES	Married John W. Belfield	Book 1,	224
1829, May 20	JONES,	FRANCES M.	Married Thomas A. Banks	Book 1,	246
1839,	JONES,	FRANCES M.	Married Thomas A. Banks	D 46,	227
1854, Mar. 3	JONES,	FRANCES ANN	Married Joseph Jesse Cammack	Book 1,	2
1868, Feb. 19	JONES,	FREDERICK	Married Maria Breedlove	Book 1,	20
1738,	JONES,	GABRIEL	Married Mary, widow of John Edmondson	O 11,	45
1747,	JONES,	GABRIEL	Orange Co., married Mary, Exec. of John Edmondson	D 24,	247
1684,	JONES,	GEORGE	Married Honoria, widow of John Weire	O 1,	66
1815, Sep. 26	JONES,	HARRIET	Married Robert Lumpkin	Book 1,	231
1874, Nov. 19	JONES,	HARRIET E.	Married Lewis H. Smoot, Rappahannock County	Book 1,	37
1877, Apr. 10	JONES,	HENRY C.	Married Julia Cauthorn	Book 1,	45
1685,	JONES,	HONORIA	Daughter of Elizabeth, married Richard Gardiner	D 6,	64
1700,	JONES,	JAMES	Married Katherine, daughter of Robert Armstrong	D 11,	249
1812, Mar. 9	JONES,	JAMES	Married Patsy Chilton	Book 1,	228
1827, Feb. 12	JONES,	JAMES W.	Married Mildred Sale	Book 1,	243
1831, Oct. 17	JONES,	JAMES W.	Married Sarah I. C. O'neale	Book 1,	248
1876, Jul. 27	JONES,	JAMES	Married Jenny Hoomes	Book 1,	42
1696,	JONES,	?	Married Jane, daughter of William & Elizabeth Lynch	D 9,	41
1720,	JONES,	JOHN	Married Mary, widow of Joseph Hutchinson	O 5,	503
1725,	JONES,	JOHN	Married Jane Collier	O 7,	8
1799,	JONES,	JOHN	Married Sally, daughter of Benjamin Fisher	W 15,	453, 454
1812, Sep. 21	JONES,	JOHN	Married Susan Wood	Book 1,	228
1809, Jan. 16	JONES,	JOSEPH	Married Nancy Alexander	Book 1,	225
1822,	JONES,	JULIA	Daughter of Erasmus, married Walter Bowie	O 44,	196
1825, Jun. 10	JONES,	JULIET	Married Moses Jeffries	Book 1,	241
1822, Nov. 13	JONES,	KETURAH	Married Reuben Pitts	Book 1,	239
1747,	JONES,	KEZIAH	Daughter of Richard, married ? Brown	W 8,	361
1857, Oct. 13	JONES,	LAURA	Married Henry Gresham	Book 1,	5
1892, Oct. 20	JONES,	LETITIA	Married John W. Nelson, Caroline Co.	Book 1,	110
1855, Oct. 29	JONES,	LEWIS	Married Lucinda E. Cauthorn	Book 1,	4
1805, Jul. 9	JONES,	LUCY	Married John Carter	Book 1,	222

				Book	Page
1845, Nov. 3	JONES,	MADISON T.	Married Susan P. Gatewood	Book 1,	258
1685,	JONES,	MARGARET	Daughter of Honoria, married Abraham Blagg	D 6,	64
1823, Jan. 13	JONES,	MARIA	Married Robert S. Noell	Book 1,	240
1743,	JONES,	MARTHA	Daughter of William, married Cornelius Sale	W 7,	95
1784,	JONES,	MARTHA	Daughter of James, married Thomas Broaddus, Jun.	W 13,	457
1828, Jul. 31	JONES,	MARTHA W.	Married Thomas C. Gordon	Book 1,	245
1676,	JONES,	MARY	Married Henry Creighton	W 2,	42
1677,	JONES,	MARY	Daughter of Rice, married John Broche	W 2,	74
1692,	JONES,	MARY	Sister of John, married John Broache	O 1,	156
1740,	JONES,	MARY	Widow, married James Garnett	D 22,	147
1747,	JONES,	MARY	Daughter of Richard, married ? Davis	W 8,	361
1816, Feb. 19	JONES,	MARY	Married Thomas Wright Jr.	Book 1,	238
1843, Sep. 28	JONES,	MARY ANN	Married Dr. Edward L. Wright	Book 1,	257
1847, Feb. 4	JONES,	MARY C.	Married William H. Moody	Book 1,	259
1857, Mar. 28	JONES,	MARY CATH.	Married William Jones Haile	Book 1,	4
1857, Jan. 15	JONES,	MARY L.	Married Edgar J. Saunders	Book 1,	4
1694,	JONES,	MILLICENT	Executrix of John, married James Blaise	O 1,	209
1811, Jun. 25	JONES,	OWEN	Married Sally Wayde	Book 1,	227
1834, Sep. 15	JONES,	PATSEY	Married John H. Smither	Book 1,	250
1835,	JONES,	PATSY	Daughter of Joseph & Nancy, married John H. Smither	D 44,	441
1822, Aug. 19	JONES,	PEGGY	Married Richard Dunn	Book 1,	239
1750,	JONES,	PHILIP E.	Married Sarah, daughter of Salvator Muscoe	D 25,	33
1867, Jan. 13	JONES,	PHILIP	Married Hannah Ross	Book 1,	16
1828, Sep. 29	JONES,	POLLY	Married George Durham	Book 1,	245
1836,	JONES,	POLLY	Daughter of Capt. John Jones, married Thomas Wright Jr.	D 45,	261
1807,	JONES,	REBECCA	Daughter of Erasmus, married ? Spindle	W 17,	314
1822,	JONES,	REBECCA	Daughter of Erasmus, married Barbee Spindle	O 44,	196
1806, Apr. 21	JONES,	RICHARD	Married Nancy Clarke	Book 1,	228
1807, Dec. 31	JONES,	RICHARD	Married Caty Brown	Book 1,	224
1817, Aug. 11	JONES,	RICHARD	Married Susanna Saunders	Book 1,	223
1866, Dec. 30	JONES,	ROBERT	Married Mary Banks	Book 1,	11

					Book		Page
1879, Nov. 30	JONES,	ROBERTA	Caroline County, married James D. Atkins		Book 1,		53
1684,	JONES,	ROBERICK	Married Grace Bedford, devisee of John Morrah		O	1,	70
1816, Dec. 20	JONES,	SALLY	Married William Games		Book 1,		232
1869, Jan. 28	JONES,	SALLY ANN	Married William H. H. Crittenden		Book 1,		22
1728,	JONES,	SAMUEL	His sister married William Brooke		D	19,	7
1742,	JONES,	SARAH	Daughter of Robert, married John Elliott, Westmoreland Co.		D	22,	419
1889, Nov. 7	JONES,	SARAH A.	Married Philip H. Brooks		Book 1,		101
1828, Mar. 31	JONES,	SARAH ANN	Married Lawrence Roane		Book 1,		245
1849, May 31	JONES,	SARAH I.	Married H. M. Dobins		Book 1,		261
1828, Jan. 10	JONES,	SARAH W.	Married Landelin Streigle		Book 1,		245
1830,	JONES,	SARAH	Married Landelin Streigle		D	43,	411
1834, Dec. 4	JONES,	SOPHRONIA	Married William McFarland		Book 1,		250
1759,	JONES,	SUCA	Married James Upshaw		W	11,	178
1816, Jan. 11	JONES,	SUSAN F.	Married George Wright		Book 1,		232
1819,	JONES,	SUSAN	Daughter of John, married George Wright		W	19,	53
1836,	JONES,	SUSAN F.	Daughter of Capt. John Jones, married George Wright		D	45,	261
1839, Jan. 16	JONES,	SUSAN A.	Married Theophilus Faver		Book 1,		254
1843, Feb. 1	JONES,	SUSAN	Married Henry W. S. Temple		Book 1,		257
1822, Dec. 16	JONES,	SUSANNA	Married Coleman Jones		Book 1,		239
1823, Aug. 13	JONES,	THOMAS	Married Julia Burnett		Book 1,		240
1835, May 18	JONES,	THOMAS C.	Married Margaret Ann Mercer		Book 1,		251
1878, Sep. 19	JONES,	THOMAS	Married Catharine Temple		Book 1,		49
1828, Dec. 20	JONES,	VIRGINIA F.	Married Jefferson Minor		Book 1,		245
1841,	JONES,	VIRGINIA	Daughter of John, married Jefferson Minor		D	47,	229
1798,	JONES,	WILLIAM S.	Married Sarah, heir of Oswald Davis		W	16,	267
1799,	JONES,	WILLIAM	Married Grace Colgin		O	35,	164
1854, Dec. 11	JORDAN,	EDWIN C.	Married Juliet Belle Eubank		Book 1,		2
1870, Sep. 29	JORDAN,	EMMA E.	Married Baylor Martin, Caroline County		Book 1,		26
1897, Dec. 28	JORDAN,	J. S.	Married Nannie Bareford		Book 1,		127
1869, Jan. 7	JORDAN,	KITTY A.	Married Baynham Martin		Book 1,		22
1855, Dec. 29	JORDAN,	LARRY B.	Married Elizabeth Frances Munday		Book 1,		266

					Book	Page
1868, Dec. 25	JORDAN,	LUCY E.	Married Larkin Dickenson		Book 1,	21
1842, Apr. 25	JORDAN,	SOPHRONIA	Married James Cropfield		Book 1,	256
1889, Dec. 11	JORDAN,	SOPHRONIA	Married J. B. Baldwin		Book 1,	93
1804,	JORDAN,	SUSANNA	Daughter of Isaac, married Henry Gambrell, Abbevile District, S. C.		D 36,	421
1853, Nov. 12	JORDAN,	WALKER	Married Matilda Williamson		Book 1,	264
1876, Dec. 25	JORDAN,	WILLIE W.	Married Georgia Broach		Book 1,	43

Date	Surname	Name	Details	Book	Page
1841, Nov. 2	KAY,	ANN	Married Richard Gouldman	Book 1,	255
1809, Feb. 22	KAY,	BETSEY	Married Robert Thomas	Book 1,	225
1846, Dec. 29	KAY,	EDWARD	Married Sarah A., Clarke	Book 1,	259
1691,	KAY,	JAMES	His Executrix married Thomas Arrowsmith	O 2,	313
1696,	KAY,	JAMES	Married Mary, daughter of Thomas & Katherine Pannell	D 9,	32
1850, Dec. 26	KAY,	JOHN C.	Married Nancy Dunn	Book 1,	262
1813, Dec. 23	KAY,	JUDITH	Married Thomas Fortune	Book 1,	229
1846, Nov. 12	KAY,	LUCY ANN	Married Edmund Taylor	Book 1,	259
1874, Dec. 27	KAY,	MACELLUS G.	Married George W. Samuel	Book 1,	37
1778,	KAY,	MARGARET	Daughter of James, married Andrew Gatewood	D 31,	417
1856, Oct. 8	KAY,	MARTHA E.	Married William Kay	Book 1,	4
1833, Nov. 11	KAY,	MARY	Married Edward G. Davis	Book 1,	249
1808,	KAY,	POLLY	Married William Bates	O 39,	350
1839,	KAY,	RICHARD	His sister-in-law, Sarah, married James Blake	D 46,	243
1690,	KAY,	ROBERT	Married Mary, daughter of John Waight	O 1,	379
1698,	KAY,	ROBERT	Married Mary, sister of Robert Waight	D 9,	226
1804, Mar. 10	KAY,	ROBERT	Married Elizabeth Dew	Book 1,	222
1811, May 11	KAY,	SALLY	Married William Thomas	Book 1,	227
1898, Mar. 9	KAY,	S. L.	Married J. L. Gaines	Book 1,	129
1856, Oct. 8	KAY,	WILLIAM	Married Martha E. Kay	Book 1,	4
1865, Nov. 28	KAY,	WILLIAM W.	Married Margaret Pilkington	Book 1,	13
1894, Apr. 4	KAY,	WILLIAM B.	Married Bettie F. Brown	Book 1,	114
1834, Oct. 7	KEY,	TAYLOR	Married Elizabeth Green	Book 1,	250
1873, Aug. 26	KEEBLE,	REV. JAMES W.	Married Lucy A. Robinson	Book 1,	34
1688,	KEELING,	EDWARD	Married Mary, daughter of Ralph Warriner	O 2,	62
1687,	KEELING,	LYDIA	Sister of Edward, married ? Goodall, Isle of Wight County	Box 101,	K
1803,	KEESE E.	JOHN	Married Mary, daughter of Joseph Fogg	W 16,	220
1689,	KELLY,	PENELOPE	Admrx. of Mathew, married Lawrence Barker	O 2,	176
1723,	KELSON,	JAMES	Bristol, married Elizabeth Jackson, sister of Arthur Jackson of Stafford County	D 17,	146

Date	Surname	Given Name	Description	Book	Page
1723,	KEMP,	ANN	Eldest Daughter of Richard, married Edward Evans, St. Mary's Parish	D 17,	195
1716,	KEMP,	ELINOR	Married Philip Stockdale	O 5,	17
1722,	KEMP,	RICHARD	Married Elinor Allen, widow	D 17,	108
1829, Jul. 20	KEMP,	SARAH	Married Hansford Anderson	Book 1,	246
1869, Jun. 17	KEMP,	THOMAS F.	Married Eliza J. Brooke	Book 1,	23
1833, Aug. 19	KENDALL,	CATHARINE	Married William R. Shackelford	Book 1,	249
1867, Feb. 16	KENDALL,	GEORGE	Married Angels Whiting	Book 1,	17
1833,	KENDALL,	JUDY	Daughter of Samuel, married ? Stewart	D 44,	230
1866, Dec. 29	KENDALL,	MATTHEW	Married Catharine Johnson	Book 1,	16
1822, May 20	KENDALL,	SAMUEL	Married Henrietta Day	Book 1,	239
1828, Dec. 12	KENDALL,	WILLIAM	Married Catharine Beazley	Book 1,	245
1727,	KENNY,	JOHN	Married Elizabeth, only sister of Jonathan Fisher	O 9,	195
1691,	KENNEDY,	SARAH	Daughter of John, married Alexander Fleming	O 2,	317
1832, May 16	KENNEDY,	WILLIAM	Married Laura Toombs	Book 1,	249
1895, Dec. 20	KENT,	W. J.	Married Anna Robinson	Book 1,	119
1811, Jul. 29	KERCHEVAL,	ANN	Married Richard Covington	Book 1,	227
1756,	KIDD,	ISAAC	Married Sarah, daughter of William Bohannon	W 10,	110
1761,	KIDD,	ISAAC	Married Lucy, daughter of John Minter	D 29,	72
1727,	KIDD,	JANE	Married John Grigory	O 9,	109
1896,	KIDD,	JOHN R.	Married Meda M. Andrews	Book 1,	122
1876, Dec. 25	KIDD,	JULIA	Married Thomas Johnson	Book 1,	43
1785,	KIDD,	MARY	Daughter of Henry, married John Brown	W 15,	23
1696,	KILLMAN,	ANN	Sister of George, daughter of John, married Samuel Harwar	D 9,	74
1690, Mar. 4	KILMAN,	SARAH	Orphan of John, married Patrick Cammell	O 2, / D 9,	289 / 264
1721,	KING,	ANN	Daughter of Richard, married Sherwood James	D 16,	264
1899, Jun. 7	KING,	CHARLES H.	Married Emma L. Reamy	Book 1,	133
1819, Jul. 29	KING,	GEORGE	Married Elizabeth Cox	Book 1,	236
1667,	KING,	JANE	Daughter of Richard, married John Peck	D 3,	443
1687,	KING,	RICHARD	Married widow of John Kennedy	O 2,	51
1850, Nov.18	KING,	THOMAS L.	Married Eliza Fisher	Book 1,	261
1899, Sep. 19	KING,	WILLIAM G.	Married Annie M. Wilkerson	Book 1,	134

				Book	Page
1711,	KIRK,	MARY	Married William Willis	D&W 14,	23
1871, Nov. 22	KIRK,	WILLIAM K.	Married Josephine Lewis	Book 1,	29
1884, Nov. 25	KRIETE,	ALICE	Married Edward Macon Ware	Book 1,	79
1897, Oct. 7	KRIETE,	GEORGE B.	Married Mae Phillips	Book 1,	126
1881, Oct. 25	KRIETE,	SADIE A.	Married George R. Scott	Book 1,	61

				Book	Page
1728,	LACY,	JOHN	Married Martha, widow of William Fletcher	O 7,	242
1765,	LAFON,	ELIZABETH	Widow of Nicholas, married John Rennolds	O 26,	40
1773,	LAFON,	ELIZABETH	Daughter of Nicholas, married Joseph Bohannon	D 31,	88
1825,	LAFON,	ELIZABETH	Married John Bohannon of Kentucky	D 42,	101
1762,	LAFON,	HANNAH	Married Robert Seayres	D 29,	67
1781,	LAFON,	MAJOR	His widow married ? McCombs	D 32,	12
1781,	LAFON,	MARY	Sister of Major, married John Upshaw	D 32,	12
1826,	LAFON,	NICHOLAS	Married Maria, daughter of John Upshaw, of Frankfort, Kentucky	D 42,	97
1826,	LAFON,	NICHOLAS	Married Elizabeth Streshley	D 42,	98
1684,	LAKE,	WILLIAM	Married widow of Thomas Harper	O 1,	159
1830,	LAMBETH,	BERNARD	Married Mildred Richardson	D 43,	320
1823, Dec. 29	LAMBETH,	ELIZABETH	Married Travis Brizendine	Book 1,	240
1813, Feb. 14	LAMBETH,	FRANCES	Married Thomas H. Pitts	Book 1,	229
1745,	LANDRUM,	DORCAS	Daughter of James, married Thomas Swelliphen	D 28,	83
1872, Dec. 28	LANDRUM,	GEORGE	Married Georgiana Lewis	Book 1,	32
1696,	LANDRUM,	JAMES	Married Mary, daughter of William & Elizabeth Browne	D 9,	52
1753,	LANDRUM,	JAMES	Married Mary, Daughter-in-law of Edmund Carroll	W 10,	10
1883, Dec. 27	LANDRUM,	THOMAS	Married Lucy Fauntleroy	Book 1,	74
1877, Feb. 20	LANDRUM,	VERNANGUS	Married Bennett Johnson	Book 1,	44
1889, Jan. 3	LANDRUM,	WILLIAM	Married Lucy Carter	Book 1,	99
1881, Feb. 3	LANE,	EDMUND	Married Bettie Carter	Book 1,	58
1809, Mar. 1	LANGHAM,	PATSY	Married John Martin	Book 1,	225
1838, Jan. 15	LANGHAM,	ROBERT F.	Married Mary C. Hart	Book 1,	253
1825, Aug. 31	LANKFORD,	POLLY	Married Philip Parker	Book 1,	242
1872, Nov. 23	LATANE,	ADAM	Married Mary Monroe	Book 1,	31
1810, Mar. 19	LATANE,	ANN S.	Married Warner Lewis	Book 1,	226
1814, Dec. 20	LATANE,	ANN C. R.	Married Moore G. Fauntleroy	Book 1,	230
1842, Aug. 9	LATANE,	ANN W.	Married Thomas W. Lewis	Book 1,	256
1848, Jun. 7	LATANE,	ANN W.	Married Edward A. G. Clopton	Book 1,	260
1860, Nov. 21	LATANE,	ANN E. B.	Married Robert L. Ware	Book 1,	10

				Book	Page
1810, Dec. 17	LATANE,	ELIZABETH	Married John Waring	Book 1,	226
1812,	LATANE,	ELIZABETH	Married John Waring	O 41,	152
1819, Oct. 16	LATANE,	HENRY W.	Married Susanna Allen	Book 1,	236
1826,	LATANE,	HENRY W.	Married Susanna, daughter of James Allen	W 21,	1
1870, May 24	LATANE,	HENRY W.	Married Martha Harvie Gordon	Book 1,	26
1841, Nov. 2	LATANE,	DR. JAMES H.	Married Janett Rouzee	Book 1,	255
1867, Dec. 3	LATANE,	JANNETT R. R.	Married William Campbell	Book 1,	18
1808,	LATANE,	LUCY	Daughter of William married Robert Payne Waring	W 17,	312
1812,	LATANE,	LUCY	Married Robert P. Waring	O 41,	109
1804, Jan. 7	LATANE,	MARY	Married John Temple	Book 1,	222
1812,	LATANE,	MARY	Married John Temple	O 41,	109
1745,	LATANE,	MARY ANN	Daughter of Mary, married John Clements, Physician	D 23,	281
1871, Dec. 5	LATANE,	MARY SUSAN	Married Charles J. Sale	Book 1,	29
1848, Nov. 7	LATANE,	LUCY R.	Married Joseph H. Lewis	Book 1,	260
1808,	LATANE,	POLLY	Daughter of William, married John Temple	W 17,	312
1847, Sep. 23	LATANE,	SUSAN E.	Married Thomas Latane	Book 1,	249
1812,	LATANE,	SUSANNA	Married Warner Lewis	O 41,	109
1847, Sep. 23	LATANE,	THOMAS	Married Susan E. Latane	Book 1,	249
1852, Jun. 5	LATANE,	DR. THOMAS	Married Ann Madison Haile	Book 1,	263
1872, Dec. 15	LATANE,	THOMAS	Married Fanny Ritchie	Book 1,	32
1816, Dec. 7	LATANE,	WILLIAM C.	Married Ann Elizabeth Burwell	Book 1,	232
1850, Feb. 14	LATHAM,	AMANDA J.	Married George H. Miskell	Book 1,	262
1817, Dec. 24	LATHOM,	CHARLES	Married Lucy Phillips	Book 1,	233
1824, Jun. 7	LATHOM,	HENRY	Married Lucinda Beazley	Book 1,	241
1832, Aug. 18	LATHOM,	JONATHAN	Married Elizabeth B. Fowler	Book 1,	240
1823, Jul. 7	LATHOM,	POLLY	Married John Schools	Book 1,	240
1824, Jun. 9	LATHOM,	ROBERT	Married Sarah Moody	Book 1,	241
1823, Nov. 5	LATHOM,	SUSAN	Married Thomas Mahoon	Book 1,	240
1832,	LATHOM,	SUSAN	Daughter of Susanna, married Thomas Mahoon	D 44,	14
1859, Oct. 20	LATHOM,	WILLIAM T.	Married Adaline W. Shelton	Book 1,	7
1723,	LATON,	JACOB	Married Frances Lee, widow	O 6,	57

				Book	Page
1858, Aug. 10	LAWRENCE,	MARY E.	Married William Holladay	Book 1,	6
1668,	LAWSON,	ELIZABETH	Daughter of Epaphroditus, married Robert Payne	D 3,	407
1807, Feb. 5	LAYALL,	ELIZABETH	Daughter of James, married James Anton	Book 1,	224
1816, Jan. 13	LAYTON,	CHARLES G.	Married Elizabeth Hundley	Book 1,	232
1835, Jan. 15	LAYTON,	EDMONIA E.	Married Joseph C. Eubank	Book 1,	251
1856,	LAYTON,	EDMONIA	Daughter of Charles married ? Eubank	W 27,	659
1852, Nov. 30	LAYTON,	LUCY ANN	Married Dr. J. M. Hundley	Book 1,	262
1841, Dec. 20	LAYTON,	MARIA E.	Married Thomas I. Hundley	Book 1,	255
1758,	LAYTON,	MARY	Daughter of Jacob, married John Yancey	O 22,	255
1759,	LAYTON,	MARY	Daughter of Jacob, married John Yancey, Culpeper County	D 28,	139
1804,	LEAKER,	CATHARINE	Daughter of James, Charlotte Co., married Peachy Dunn	D 36,	386
1805, Jun. 17	LEAKER,	MARY	Married Burnett Williamson	Book 1,	223
1804,	LEAKER,	SUSANNA	Daughter of James, Charlotte Co. married Alex. Gordon	D 36,	386
1838, Nov. 28	LEAVELL,	BYRD C.	Married Mary C. Barnes	Book 1,	253
1878, Dec. 12	LEAVELL,	LOTTIE C.	Spottsylvania Co., married Josiah P. Gayle, Caroline	Book 1,	49
1818, Dec. 21	LEE,	BROOKING	Married Polly Loving	Book 1,	234
1852, Jun. 18	LEE,	BROOKING	Married Lavinia Noel	Book 1,	263
1846, Jan. 15	LEE,	CLEMENZIE	Married David Clarke	Book 1,	258
1853,	LEE,	CLEMENZIE	Daughter of Fielding Lee, married David Clarke	W 27,	409
1816, May 22	LEE,	ELIZA	Married William F. Micou	Book 1,	232
1762,	LEE,	FRANCES	Daughter of Thomas, married John Seyars	W 12,	25
1819, Dec. 20	LEE,	FIELDING	Married Lucy Noel	Book 1,	236
1835,	LEE,	FIELDING	Married Lucy, daughter of Reuben Noel	D 45,	56
1798,	LEE,	GEORGE	Loudon Co., married Evelyn Byrd Beverley, daughter of Robert Beverley	D 35,	41
1842,	LEE,	GEORGE	Married Lucy A. Parker	Book 1,	256
1848, May 11	LEE,	HARRY H.	Married Vestilla M. Armstrong	Book 1,	260
1810,	LEE,	?	Married Ann, daughter of Elizabeth Montague	W 17,	40
1820, Dec. 14	LEE,	JAMES	Married Nancy Loven	Book 1,	237
1884, Jan. 17	LEE,	JAMES	Married Lucy Noel	Book 1,	75
1841, Apr. 16	LEE,	JANE	Married John Ball	Book 1,	255

				Book	Page
1803,	LEE,	JOHN	Father of John P. Lee, married Daughter of Philip Smith, Wicomico Parish, Northumberland Co.	D 36,	300
1846, Oct. 9	LEE,	JOHN	Married Martha Clarke	Book 1,	259
1870, Apr. 2	LEE,	LALA	Married Benjamin F. Jones	Book 1,	25
1786,	LEE,	LETTICE	Daughter of John, married Capt. Whiting	W 13,	430
1786,	LEE,	MARY	Daughter of John, married Paul Micou	W 13,	430
1825,	LEE,	MARY S.	Daughter of Philip, married James C. Anthony	D 41,	337
1817, Jan. 1	LEE,	PHILIP	Married Lucy Morton	Book 1,	233
1824, Oct. 21	LEE,	PHOEBE	Married Austin Oliver	Book 1,	241
1877, Apr. 12	LEE,	PATSEY	Daughter of Baldwin, married Harrison Beazley, Caroline Co.	Book 1,	45
1890, Nov. 19	LEE,	ROSETTA	Married John B. Potter	Book 1,	104
1816, Apr. 27	LEE,	SUSANNA	Married Thomas Halbert	Book 1,	232
1825, Jul. 28	LEE,	THOMAS	Married Sarah Parker	Book 1,	242
1888, Dec. 20	LEE,	THOMAS B.	Married Martha A. Loving	Book 1,	97
1829, Feb. 20	LEE,	WILLIAM	Married Olivia Courtney	Book 1,	246
1878, Jan. 6	LEE,	WILLIAM R.	Married Sally Patterson	Book 1,	47
1757,	LEY,	SARAH	Widow of Thomas, married Isaac Scandrett	O 22,	82
1773,	LEY,	SARAH	Widow of Thomas, married Isaac Scandrett	D 31,	119
1746,	LEY,	THOMAS	Married Sarah Griffing	W 7,	475
1713,	LEMON,	JOSEPH	Married Margaret, daughter of John Williams	D&W 14,	252
1673,	LENTON,	HENRY	Married Sarah, daughter of Dennis Swellivant	W&D 1,	184
1710,	LEPLEY,	?	Married Sarah, daughter of John Smith	D&C 13,	378
1708,	LEVERETT,	ROBERT	Richmond Co., married Elizabeth, daughter of Thomas Coggin	O 4,	92
1847, Aug. 16	LEWIS,	ANN L.	Married Robert A. Munday	Book 1,	259
1872, Sep. 19	LEWIS,	CATESBY E.	Married Lucy E. Temple	Book 1,	31
1866, Dec. 24	LEWIS,	CATHARINE	Married Henry Banks	Book 1,	16
1749,	LEWIS,	EDWARD	Married Esther Evans, sister of Macajah & Greensbee Evans	W 8,	312
1890, Feb. 14	LEWIS,	GEORGE	Lancaster Co., married Mary F. Griffin	Book 1,	103
1872, Dec. 28	LEWIS,	GEORGIANA	Married George Landrum	Book 1,	32
1864, Dec. 28	LEWIS	HARRIET S.	Married Robert M. Anderson, Richmond City	Book 1,	12

				Book	Page
1721,	LEWIS,	JAMES	Married Elizabeth, daughter of Richard Long	D 16,	262
1809, Jan. 17	LEWIS,	JOHN	Married Polly McGuy	Book 1,	225
1812,	LEWIS,	DR. JOHN	Married Hannah Hipkins Green, daughter of George Green	D 38,	301
1848, Nov. 7	LEWIS,	JOSEPH H.	Married Lucy R. Latane	Book 1,	260
1890, Oct. 29	LEWIS,	JOSEPH	Married Annie W. Temple	Book 1,	104
1871, Nov. 22	LEWIS,	JOSEPHINE	Married William K. Kirk	Book 1,	29
1867, Jan. 27	LEWIS,	JUDITH	Married Elijah Browne	Book 1,	16
1794,	LEWIS,	LAWRENCE	Married Susanna, daughter of John Edmondson	D 34,	64
1812,	LEWIS,	LUCY	Married John Thom	O 41,	109
1890, Sep. 17	LEWIS,	KATE	Married William N. Morris	Book 1,	104
1854, Sep. 14	LEWIS,	KITTY W.	Married Archibald R. Rouzie	Book 1,	2
1855, Sep. 5	LEWIS,	LUCINDA	Married William Rich	Book 1,	266
1878, May 2	LEWIS,	MARY L.	Married Philip W. Lewis, Dakota	Book 1,	48
1816, May 16	LEWIS,	NOEL	Married Sally Gouldman	Book 1,	232
1878, May 2	LEWIS,	PHILIP W.	Dakota, married Mary L. Lewis	Book 1,	48
1888, Apr. 18	LEWIS,	S. A.	Married C. M Smoot	Book 1,	95
1842, Aug. 9	LEWIS,	THOMAS W.	Married Ann W. Latane	Book 1,	256
1865, Dec. 12	LEWIS,	WARING	Married Louisa H. Noel	Book 1,	13
1880, Feb. 25	LEWIS,	WARING	Married Susan M. Noel	Book 1,	55
1810, Mar. 19	LEWIS,	WARNER	Married Ann S. Latane	Book 1,	226
1812,	LEWIS,	WARNER	Married Susanna Latane	O 41,	109
1823, Dec. 2	LEWIS,	WARNER	Married Catharine Butler	Book 1,	240
1872, Sep. 19	LEWIS,	WARNER	Married Mary Temple	Book 1,	31
1811, Jun. 1	LEWIS,	WILLIAM	Married Malinda McGuy	Book 1,	227
1696,	LIGHTFOOT,	JOHN	Married Ann, daughter of Thomas Goodrich	D 9,	50
1696,	LINCOLN,	ELIZABETH	Relict of John, married John Hill	O 2,	213
1861, Feb. 7	LINN,	MARTHA C.	Daughter of Josiah Minter, married Richard Atkins	Book 1,	10
1885, Nov. 17	LIPSCOMB,	GEORGE B.	Married Etta Southworth	Book 1,	84
1812, Sep. 10	LIPSCOMB,	MARTIN	Married Anne Jones	Book 1,	228
1875, Nov. 23	LITCHFIELD,	VICTOR	Mathews County, married Belle W. Spindle	Book 1,	40
1704,	LITTLE,	ABRAHAM	Married Jane, daughter of Thomas Tomlin	D 11,	252

				Book	Page
1781.	LIVINGSTON, JOHN	Married Susanna, daughter of Samuel Walker		W 13,	336
1741.	LIVINGSTON, JOHN	Married Frances, daughter of Salvator Muscoe		Land Trials,	97
1710.	LOCKHART, JAMES	Married Elizabeth Craske		W 3, Richmond, Co.	34
1886, Mar.	LOGAN,	ROBERT L.	Married Mary L. Gatewood	Book 1,	86
1848, Sep. 16	LOMAX,	HYACINTH	Married Henry Cousins	Book 1,	260
1704.	LOMAX,	JOHN	Married Elizabeth, daughter of Ralph Wormley	D&C 12,	4
1721.	LONG,	ANN	Daughter of Richard, married James Sherwood	D 16,	264
1721.	LONG,	ELIZABETH	Daughter of Richard, married James Lewis	D 16,	262
1718.	LONG,	GABRIEL	Married Margaret, daughter of Andrew Harrison	W 3,	85
1708.	LONG,	HENRY	Married Christian, daughter of Valentine Allen	D&C 13,	146
1712.	LONG,	KATHERINE	Married Capt. Richard Wyatt	D&W 14,	44
1897, Feb. 17	LONG,	VIRGINIA	Married John Carter	Book 1,	124
1895, Jan. 17	LONGEST,	ANNIE L.	Married A. B. Lumpkin	Book 1,	117
1876, Dec. 21	LONGEST,	BETTIE JAMES	Married George F. Fogg	Book 1,	43
1898, May 18	LONGEST,	B.	Married Mary J. Saunders	Book 1,	129
1813, Dec. 27	LONGEST,	DAVIS	Married Fanny Clarke	Book 1,	229
1859, Jan. 27	LONGEST,	ELTON	Married Richard T. Douglass	Book 1,	7
1814, Dec. 12	LONGEST,	FANNY	Married James Bastin	Book 1,	230
1870, Feb. 18	LONGEST,	FANNY A.	Widow, married Gordon F. Shackelford	Book 1,	25
1846, Mar. 11	LONGEST,	JANE	Married Lewis Carlton	Book 1,	258
1846, Jan. 28	LONGEST,	JOHN	Married Susanna Crittenden	Book 1,	259
1882, Dec. 27	LONGEST,	KATE JANE	Married Brooking L. Jeffries	Book 1,	68
1894, Dec. 27	LONGEST,	M. E.	Married Lally Brooks	Book 1,	116
1825, May 3	LONGEST,	REBECCA	Married Thomas Allen	Book 1,	242
1835, Feb. 6	LONGEST,	ROBERT D.	Married Deliah Ball	Book 1,	252
1899, Mar. 8	LONGEST,	ROBERT C.	Married N. E. Minter, King & Queen Co.	Book 1,	132
1833, Mar. 2	LORIMER,	GEORGE T.	Married Virginia Collins	Book 1,	249
1835.	LORIMER,	GEORGE	Married Virginia, daughter of Adelaide Janey	D 44,	520
1818, Dec. 21	LOVING,	JOSIAH	Married Lucy Loving	Book 1,	234
1818, Dec. 21	LOVING,	LUCY	Married Josiah Loving	Book 1,	234
1888, Dec. 20	LOVING,	MARTHA A.	Married Thomas B. Lee	Book 1,	97

1820, Dec. 14	LOVEN,	NANCY	Married James Lee	Book 1,	237
1818, Dec. 21	LOVING,	POLLY	Married Brooking Lee	Book 1,	234
1691,	LOWICK,	MARY	Relict of George, married John Butcher	O 2,	321
1854, Oct. 8	LOWRY,	ELLA ANN	Married William George Jeffries	Book 1,	2
1758,	LOWRY,	SARAH	Daughter of John, married Ischarner DeGraffenreidt	W 12,	49
1721,	LOYD,	ANN	Daughter of George, widow of Robert Foster, married George Pettit	D 17, D 17,	25 262
1752,	LOYD,	ANN	Daughter of Samuel, married ? Wren, King George Co.	D 26,	6
1717,	LOYD,	STEPHEN	His widow married John Taylor	D&W 14,	400
1684,	LOYD,	COL. WILLIAM	Married Relict of Col. John Hull	O 1,	177
1840, Nov. 17	LOYD,	WILLIAM	Married Susanna Taylor	Book 1,	254
1695,	LOYSON,	CLANDY	Married Elizabeth Williamson	D&W 10,	91
1668,	LUCAS,	THOMAS	Married Margaret, widow of John Upton	D 2,	326
1820, Jan. 24	LUDLOW,	RICHARD J.	Married Elizabeth G. Brooke	Book 1,	237
1828, Jun. 16	LUMPKIN,	ACHILLES	Married Ann Dix	Book 1,	245
1878, Jan. 18	LUMPKIN,	ALBERT	Married Lucy C. Hodges	Book 1,	41
1886, Jun. 8	LUMPKIN,	ANNIE F.	Married Richard H. Atkins	Book 1,	87
1895, Jan. 17	LUMPKIN,	A. B.	Married Annie L. Longest	Book 1,	117
1859, May 12	LUMPKIN,	BENJAMIN	Married Jane H. Atkins	Book 1,	7
1826,	LUMPKIN,	CARTER	Married Frances Clarke	Book 1,	242
1893, Feb. 22	LUMPKIN,	C. A.	Married Hugh G. Billups Jr.	Book 1,	111
1892, Nov. 10	LUMPKIN;	C. H.	Married Laura Fogg	Book 1,	110
1871, Jun. 4	LUMPKIN,	CHRISTOPHER	Married Adelaide G. Atkins	Book 1,	28
1830, Jul. 5	LUMPKIN,	EDWIN	Married Mary Purkins	Book 1,	247
1819, Sep. 13	LUMPKIN,	ELIZA	Married James Smither	Book 1,	236
1832,	LUMPKIN,	ELIZA	Daughter of John, married James Smither	D 44,	46
1885, Apr. 8	LUMPKIN,	FANNIE E.	Married Eugene L. Crow	Book 1,	81
1833, Oct. 30	LUMPKIN,	FRANCES	Widow, married Zebulon Carter	Book 1,	253
1854, Jan. 5	LUMPKIN,	JOHN	Married Susan Schools	Book 1,	1
1859, Dec. 24	LUMPKIN,	MARY C.	Married William H. Reed	Book 1,	8
1808, Dec. 19	LUMPKIN,	POLLY	Married Fielding Crow	Book 1,	224

				Book	Page
1826,	LUMPKIN,	POLLY	Daughter of John, married Fielding Crow	W 22,	305
1820, Dec. 9	LUMPKIN,	RICHARD	Married Susanna Purkins	Book 1,	237
1871, Dec. 21	LUMPKIN,	RICHARD T.	Married Alice Belle Valentine	Book 1,	30
1854, Aug. 26	LUMPKIN,	ROBERT	Married Catharine Brizendine	Book 1,	2
1894, Feb. 20	LUMPKIN,	R. C.	Married Laura B. Atkins	Book 1,	113
1899, Nov. 9	LUMPKIN,	R. E.	Married E. M. Carlton	Book 1,	134
1815, Sep. 26	LUMPKIN,	ROBERT	Married Harriet Jones	Book 1,	231
1874, Dec. 31	LUMPKIN,	ROBERT	Married Mary Ellen Dunn	Book 1,	38
1853, Oct. 20	LUMPKIN,	SUSAN A.	Married Thornton A. Crow	Book 1,	2
1878, Dec. 25	LUMPKIN,	SUSAN	Married Edgar Brizendine	Book 1,	50
1877, Jan. 14	LUMPKIN,	WILLIAM	Married Annie Hodges	Book 1,	44
1880, Jun. 16	LUMPKIN,	WILLIAM H.	Married Sarah F. Munday	Book 1,	56
1895, Jan. 16	LUMPKIN,	W. R.	Married Mary M. Winder	Book 1,	117
1848, Nov. 6	LUMPKIN,	WINTER B.	Married Eliza Boughton	Book 1,	260
1859, Feb. 13	LYALL,	JAMES M.	Married Bettie F. Munday	Book 1,	9
1884, May 1	LYELL,	BETTIE A.	Married William T. Marshall, Gloucester Co.	Book 1,	77
1885, Aug. 6	LYELL,	NANNIE	Married John Marshall	Book 1,	82
1696,	LYNCH,	JANE	Daughter of William & Elizabeth, married ? Jones	D 9,	41
1693,	LYON,	CALEB	Former husband of Daniel Diskin's wife, Mary	O 1,	115

1823, Mar. 17	MACKAN,	ROBERT	Married Ann Hundley	Book 1,	240
1873, Jan. 16	MACKERELL,	ARTHUR	Married Susan Hoomes	Book 1,	29
1678,	MAGUFFEY,	JANE	Widow of John, married Francis Graves	D 6,	57
1835, Dec. 21	MAHON,	E. F.	Married Lewis Dunn	Book 1,	251
1811, Oct. 9	MAHON,	JOHN	Married Polly Hill	Book 1,	227
1813, Nov. 25	MAHON,	MARGERY	Married Edmond P. Smither	Book 1,	229
1841, Aug. 11	MAHON,	MILDRED	Married Robert H. Gaines	Book 1,	255
1852, Jan. 21	MAHON,	POLLY	Married James Collier	Book 1,	263
1850, Jul. 2	MAHON,	RICHARD J.	Married Catharine S. Peters	Book 1,	262
1877, May 1	MAHON,	RICHARD	Married Betty Blanch Cox	Book 1,	45
1823, Nov. 5	MAHON,	THOMAS	Married Susan Lathom	Book 1,	240
1832,	MAHON,	THOMAS	Married Susan Lathom, daughter of Susanna Lathom	D 44,	14
1882, Nov. 2	MAHON,	WILLIAM L.	Married Juliet C. Griffin	Book 1,	66
1780,	MALLET,	ZACHARIAH	Married Mary Noell, now of Mecklenburg County	D 32,	41
1867, Nov. 5	MALLORY,	CHARLES O.	Elizabeth City Co., married Ann B. Baylor	Book 1,	18
1831, Jun. 20	MANN,	ANN S.	Married Andrew Hundley	Book 1,	248
1832,	MANN,	ANN	Widow of Philip Mann, Jr., married Andrew Hundley	D 43,	533
1852, Dec. 10	MANN,	BETTY B.	Widow, married Joseph Eubank, widower	Book 1,	263
1774,	MANN,	JOHN	Married sister of Thomas Edmondson	Box 1772-76,	
1805, Mar. 18	MANN,	JOSEPH JR.	Married Sarah Townley	Book 1,	223
1827, Mar. 20	MANN,	JUDITH	Married James Wright	Book 1,	244
1845, Sep. 2	MANN,	JULIA	Married William B. Davis	Book 1,	258
1807,	MANN,	?	Married Sally, sister of William Townley	W 17,	64
1826, Mar. 20	MANN,	MARTHA G.	Married Richard H. Mitchell	Book 1,	242
1849, Dec. 28	MANN,	OBED	Married N. J. M. Downey	Book 1,	261
1805, Feb. 26	MANN,	PEGGY	Married Peter B. Davis	Book 1,	222
1823, Jul. 30	MANN,	PHILIP	Married Ann Trible	Book 1,	240
1815, Nov. 26	MANN,	RICHARD	Married Margaret Sewell	Book 1,	231
1821, Jun. 29	MANN,	ROBERT	Married Susan Hundley	Book 1,	238
1871, May 10	MANOKEY,	MOSES	Maryland, married Catharine Johnson	Book 1,	28

					Book	Page
1836, Nov. 19	MARINER,	WILLIAM H.	Married Elizabeth Wilcox		Book 1,	254
1876, Jul. 30	MARKS,	BUCK	Richmond Co. married Joanna Gray		Book 1,	42
1810, Mar. 2	MARLOW,	AMEY	Married Lindsay Davis		Book 1,	226
1822, Oct. 15	MARLOW,	BETSEY	Married William Webb		Book 1,	239
1806, Nov. 13	MARLOW,	CATY	Married William Gest		Book 1,	223
1822, Feb. 14	MARLOW,	LUCY	Married John Williamson Jr.		Book 1,	239
1871, Aug. 18	MARLOW,	MAJOR	Married Matilda Davis		Book 1,	29
1822, Jun. 12	MARLOW,	THOMAS	Married Lucy Griggs		Book 1,	23
1825, Jan. 28	MARLOW,	THOMAS	Married Frances Shackelford		Book 1,	241
1825,	MARLOW,	THOMAS	Married Frances, daughter of Richard Shackelford		D 41,	438
1809, May 15	MARSHALL,	ANN B.	Married Nelson Dozer		Book 1,	225
1804, Aug. 20	MARSHALL,	CATY	Married Vincent Williamson		Book 1,	222
1888, Dec. 6	MARSHALL,	FANNIE B.	Married John R. Ellis		Book 1,	97
1865, Mar. 16	MARSHALL,	HENRY M.	Married Sidney C. Samuel		Book 1,	13
1885, Aug. 6	MARSHALL,	JOHN	Gloucester Co., married Nannie Lyell		Book 1,	82
1829, Dec. 21	MARSHALL,	RICHARD	Married Emily Pitts		Book 1,	246
1819, Dec. 13	MARSHALL,	TABITHA	Married Robert Sewell		Book 1,	236
1685,	MARSHALL,	THOMAS	Married Sarah, daughter of Philip Sherwood		O 1,	173
1884, May 1	MARSHALL,	WILLIAM T.	Gloucester Co., married Bettie A. Lyell		Book 1,	77
1899, Dec. 21	MARSHALL,	WILLIAM	King & Queen Co., married Judy Collier		Book 1,	135
1890, Nov. 23	MARTIN,	ANNIE B.	Married Charles T. Allen		Book 1,	105
1874, Jan. 29	MARTIN,	AZARILLA	Married Joseph Clarke		Book 1,	35
1869, Jan. 7	MARTIN,	BAYNHAM	Caroline Co., married Kitty Alice Jordan		Book 1,	22
1870, Sep. 29	MARTIN,	BAYLOR	Caroline Co., married Emma Ella Jordan		Book 1,	26
1891, Jan. 21	MARTIN,	BAYLOR	Caroline Co., married Willie J. Mundie		Book 1,	106
1889, Dec. 31	MARTIN,	BETTIE J.	Married Milton F. Chinault		Book 1,	102
1848, Sep. 13	MARTIN,	EMILY	Married Robert Schools		Book 1,	260
1829,	MARTIN,	GEORGE	Married Joanna Dunn		D 43,	53
1762,	MARTIN,	JAMES	Chesterfield Co., married Hannah, widow of Robert Seayres		D 29,	67
1722,	MARTIN,	JOAN	Married Richard Ballard		W, B&I 17,	109
1722,	MARTIN,	JOAN	Daughter of Edward, married Richard Ballard		Box 105 Folder E.	

				Book	Page
1740,	MARTIN,	JOHN	Married Mary, daughter of James Samuel	W 6,	312
1809, Mar. 1	MARTIN,	JOHN	Married Patsy Langham	Book 1,	225
1748,	MARTIN,	MARGARET	Daughter of Edward, married Richard Hopson	D 24,	254
1819, Jun. 8	MARTIN,	MARGARET W.	Married William Banks	Book 1,	235
1781,	MARTIN,	MARY	Niece of Major Lafon, married John Upshaw	D 32,	12
1809, Jun. 29	MARTIN,	NANCY	Married Ritchie Clarke	Book 1,	225
1889, Sep. 7	MARTIN,	VALVIN	Married A. L. Faulkner	Book 1,	134
1835, Dec. 21	MARTIN,	WILLIAM	Married Patsey Shearwood	Book 1,	252
1881, Mar. 17	MARTIN,	WILLIAM H.	Married Rebecca Cooper, King & Queen County	Book 1,	59
1876, Apr. 26	MASON,	BETTY	Married Reuben Potter, of Alabama	Book 1,	41
1765,	MASON,	JAMES	Married Betty, daughter of Thomas & Ann Barber	D 30,	13
1852, Apr. 7	MASON,	DON	Married Isabella A. Blackley	Book 1,	263
1861, Dec. 17	MASON,	MILES F.	Married Ida Taff	Book 1,	11
1844, Apr. 12	MASON,	RICHARD	Married Nancy Clarke	Book 1,	257
1852, Nov. 1	MASON,	STAFFORD H.	Married Harriet D. Fisher	Book 1,	263
1726,	MASON,	THOMAS	Married Ann, daughter of Thomas Franck	D 18,	236
1684,	MATHEWS,	ALICE	Daughter of William, married William Thacker, Lancaster Co.	D 7, D 8,	325 91
1787,	MATHEWS,	EDWARD	Married Judith, relict of James Garnett	D 33,	84
1672,	MATHEWS,	ELIZABETH	Daughter of Joanna, married Nicholas Catlett	D 5,	48
1815, Aug. 23	MATTHEWS,	FRANCES	Married Mordecai Shaddock	Book 1,	231
1830, Sep. 1	MATTHEWS,	FRANCES	Married James H. Temple	Book 1,	247
1678,	MATHEWS,	GILES	Married Ann, widow of Thomas Erwin	D 6,	56
1802,	MATHEWS,	JOHN	Married Mary, daughter of Thaddeus McCarty, Lancaster Co.	D 35,	523
1820, Oct. 25	MATTHEWS,	JOHN R.	Married Frances Ann Temple	Book 1,	237
1707,	MATHEWS,	MARGARET	Daughter of James, married Richard Tankersley	Wills 3, Richmond Co.	
1690,	MATHEWS,	RICHARD	Married Elizabeth, daughter of William Spicer	D 8,	193
1810, Apr. 28	MATTHEWS,	VIRGINIA	Married W. M. Baynham	Book 1,	226
1816, Jun. 19	MATTHEWS,	WILLIAM B.	Married Maria I. G. Wood	Book 1,	232
1822,	MATTHEWS,	WILLIAM B.	Married Maria, daughter of Carter Wood	D 40,	488
1874, May 6	MAUPIN,	CALVIN F.	Louisa Co., married Mrs. Mary S. Montague	Book 1,	36
1814, May 25	MAY,	LUCY	Married George Donahoe	Book 1,	230

Date	Surname	Given Name	Description	Book	Page
1733,	MAYFIELD,	ANN	Married Thomas Connaly	D&W 14,	21
1703,	MEAD,	ELIZABETH	Daughter of Hugh Mead of Piscataway, married Robert Deputy, Middlesex, Co.	D 11,	48
1758,	MEADOR,	ELIZABETH	Daughter of Thomas, married Benjamin Allen	W 11,	129
1758,	MEADOR,	FRANCES	Married ? Bell	W 11,	129
1828, Jan. 1	MEADOR,	FRANCES	Married George Gordon	Book 1,	245
1677,	MEADOR,	JOHN	Married Elizabeth, daughter of Richard White	D 6,	27
1811, May 23	MEADOR,	NANCY	Married John Greenstreet	Book 1,	227
1758,	MEADOR,	RACHEL	Daughter of Thomas, married Ambrose Armstrong	W 11,	129
1807,	MEADOR,	RICHARD	Married Mary, daughter of Richard Burke	D 37,	264
1758,	MEADOR,	WILLIAM	Married Frances, daughter of Mary Phitzsimmons	W 10,	95
1717,	MEADOES,	ANN	Relict of Thomas, married Thomas Ayres	O 5,	400
1825, Jan. 17	MEADOWS,	CATHARINE	Married Alexander Dunn	Book 1,	241
1828, Apr. 4	MEADOWS,	CLARA	Married William G. Haile	Book 1,	245
1723,	MEADOWS,	ELIZABETH	Married James Bradberry	O 6,	33
1705,	MEADOES,	THOMAS	Married Susanna, mother of John Goss	D&C 12,	95
1814, Nov. 30	MECKLEBROUGH, EDWARD		Married Hetty Evans	Book 1,	230
1771,	MEDLEY,	ELIZABETH	Daughter of James & Elinor, married Thomas Hundley	Box 1772-76, D	
1755,	MEDLEY,	JAMES	Married Susanna, daughter of Nicholas Smith	W 11,	19
1835, May 18	MERCER,	MARGARET ANN	Married Thomas C. Jones	Book 1,	251
1835, Jan. 19	MERCER,	ZEZORAH	Married Joseph Owen	Book 1,	251
1771,	MEREDITH,	JOHN	Married Mary, daughter of Augustine Boughan	W 12,	415
1765,	MEREDITH,	WILLIAM	Married Ann, daughter of William Dangerfield	D 30,	35
1819, Apr. 20	MEREDITH,	WILLIAM	Married Martha Simmons	Book 1,	236
1762,	MERIWETHER, ELIZABETH		Married Drury Bowling	Land Trials,	185
1708,	MERIWETHER, JANE		Sister of Thomas married William Browne	D&C 13,	185
1762,	MERIWETHER, JANE		Married James Skelton	Land Trials,	185-6
1762,	MERIWETHER, LUCY		Married Francis Smith	Land Trials,	186
1715,	MERIWETHER, MARY		Daughter of Francis, married William Cofton	O 4,	550
1723,	MERIWETHER, MARY		Married Reuben Welch	D 17,	327
1743,	MERIWETHER, MARY		Relict of Francis, married John Robinson	D 23,	169

				Book	Page
1762,	MERIWETHER, MARY		Daughter of Francis, married Thomas Wright Belfield	Land Trials,	185,194
1715,	MERIWETHER, THOMAS		Married Elizabeth, daughter of Henry Williamson	D	455
1693,	MERRIOTT,	WILLIAM	Married Elizabeth Norton	O 1,	236
1865, Jan. 31	MICKLEBORO, ALGERNON		Married Mary S. Armstrong	Book 1,	13
1841, Feb. 2	MICOU,	ADELINE	Married Albert Hill	Book 1,	255
1825, Jul. 18	MICOU,	ALBERT	Married Elizabeth M. Micou	Book 1,	241
1872, Oct. 10	MICOU,	ALBERT ROY	Married Sarah A. Tupman	Book 1,	31
1835, Jan. 12	MICOU,	ANN	Daughter of John, married Eugene Ferris	D 44,	516
1830, Apr. 1	MICOU,	CLARA A. F.	Married Alfred Terrell	Book 1,	247
1858, Jul. 15	MICOU,	CHRISTIAN G.	Married Robert L. Pendleton	Book 1,	6
1869, May 15	MICOU,	EDMUND	Married Mildred Garlick	Book 1,	23
1822, Aug. 22	MICOU,	ELIZABETH	Married Henry Samuel, Jr.	Book 1,	242
1825, Jul. 18	MICOU,	ELIZABETH	Married Albert Micou	Book 1,	241
1866, Jun. 26	MICOU,	ELLEN H.	Married Charles M. Gatewood	Book 1,	15
1857, Dec. 15	MICOU,	FANNIE B.	Married Thomas Seddon Roy	Book 1,	5
1816, Nov. 14	MICOU,	FRANCES M.	Married Paul Micou, Jr.	Book 1,	232
1803,	MICOU,	JAMES	Married Sally, daughter of Mary Brooke	W 17,	451
1835, Aug. 7	MICOU,	JAMES ROY JR.	Married Ellen H. Jones	Book 1,	251
1813, Jun. 14	MICOU,	JEAN MARIA	Married John Micou, Jr.	Book 1,	229
1819, Oct. 18	MICOU,	JEAN	Married Walker Roy	Book 1,	236
1820,	MICOU,	JANE	Married Walker Roy	D 40,	40
1806, Jan. 2	MICOU,	JOHN B.	Married Elizabeth Blackburn	Book 1,	223
1813, Jun. 14	MICOU,	JOHN JR.	Married Jean Maria Micou	Book 1,	229
1815, Oct. 12	MICOU,	JOHN	Married Catharine C. Wood	Book 1,	231
1822,	MICOU,	JOHN	Married Catharine, daughter of Carter Wood	D 40,	488
1835, Jan. 12	MICOU,	LUCY ANN	Married Eugene Ferris	Book 1,	251
1841, Jan. 13	MICOU,	MARTHA ELLEN	Married James Boughan	Book 1,	255
1740,	MICOU,	MARY	Daughter of Margaret, married Joshua Fry	W 6,	287
1824, Mar. 15	MICOU,	MARY F.	Married Thomas Coghill	Book 1,	241
1842,	MICOU,	MARY E.	Married William M. Farrar	D 47,	416
1849, Feb. 28	MICOU,	MARY F.	Married George W. Starke	Book 1,	26

Date	Surname	Given Name	Description	Book	Page
1709,	MICOU,	PAUL	Married Margaret, daughter of Margaret Cammack	W 3, Richmond Co.	234
1786,	MICOU,	PAUL	Married Mary, daughter of John Lee	W 13,	430
1816, Nov. 14	MICOU,	PAUL JR.	Married Frances M. Micou	Book 1,	232
1825, Aug. 25	MICOU,	PHILECIA L.	Married John L. Tupman	Book 1,	242
1830,	MICOU,	PHILECIA	Daughter of Paul, married John Tupman	D 43,	141
1875, Nov. 16	MICOU,	ROSALIND G.	Married George D. Nicholson, Middlesex Co.	Book 1,	39
1816, May 22	MICOU,	WILLIAM F.	Married Eliza Lee	Book 1,	232
1858, Dec. 23	MIENLY,	SAMUEL W.	Married Mrs. Martha Hearne	Book 1,	7
1706,	MILBURN,	MARY	Married Emanuel Stone	O 3,	224
1805, Mar. 18	MILES,	DOLLY	Married Philip Coleman	Book 1,	222
1727,	MILLER,	JANE	Cousin of Susanna Brice, married Thomas Horde	O 7,	175
1796,	MILLER,	JOHN	Married Lily Grant Baker, Executrix of John Baker,	D 33,	198
1762,	MILLER,	MARGARET	Widow of Simon, married Young Hawkins	O 24,	56
1742,	MILLER,	MARY	Daughter of John, married George Green	W 7,	55
1763,	MILLER,	MARY	Widow of William, married Nicholas Hawkins	W 12,	71
1833, Dec. 13	MILLER,	NANCY	Married Charles Carter	Book 1,	249
1686,	MILLER,	SIMON	His relict married Hugh French	O 1,	248
1724,	MILLER,	SUSANNA	Sister of John, married Henry Brice	W 4,	74 86
1747,	MILLER,	WILLIAM	Married Jane Hord	W 8,	286
1679,	MILLS,	ANN	Married John Burkett	D 6,	79
1679,	MILLS,	ELIZABETH	Married David Sterne	D 6,	79
1702,	MILLS,	FRANCES	Married Henry Byrom	D&W 11,	42
1709,	MILLS,	FRANCES,	Daughter of Robert, married Henry Byrom	D&C 13,	290
1706,	MILLS,	JOHN JR.	Married Mary, Executrix of William North	D&C 12,	330 365
1720,	MILLS,	MARY	Relict of John, married Pierce Griffin	O 5,	497
1851, Apr. 13	MINOR,	ANN ELIZABETH	Married Dr. Thomas L. Scott	Book 1,	262
1897,	MINER,	C.	Married Helen A. Rennolds	D 58,	355
1865, Dec. 28	MINOR,	EPHRAIM R.	Married Sarah E. Shearwood	Book 1,	14
1867, Jan. 1	MINOR,	GEORGE C.	Married Lucy A. Smith	Book 1,	16
1817, Dec. 7	MINOR,	HUBBARD T.	Married Jane Blake	Book 1,	233
1828, Dec. 20	MINOR,	JEFFERSON	Married Virginia F. Jones	Book 1,	245

1841,	MINOR,	JEFFERSON	Married Virginia, daughter of John Jones	D 47,	229
1837, Feb. 20	MINOR,	JOSEPH	Married Ann Moody	Book 1,	252
1899, Dec. 27	MINOR,	JOSEPH A.	Married R. E. Patterson	Book 1,	135
1894, Jan. 11	MINOR,	W. C.	Married V. H. Rennolds	Book 1,	113
1804, Jul. 16	MINTER,	BARKER	Married Sallie Croxton	Book 1,	222
1810, Dec. 15	MINTER,	CHARLES	Married Nancy Cox	Book 1,	226
1810, Jan. 15	MINTER,	ELIZABETH	Married James Durham	Book 1,	226
1830, Dec. 20	MINTER,	HARRIET	Married James Durham	Book 1,	247
1871, Dec. 24	MINTER,	JOHN	Married Betty Barefoot	Book 1,	29
1827,	MINTER,	JOSEPH	Married Peggy, daughter of Gabriel Gordon	D 42,	286
1830, Feb. 15	MINTER,	JOSEPH	Married Nancy Harper	Book 1,	247
1842, Jan. 10	MINTER,	JOSEPH	Married Mary A. Halbert	Book 1,	256
1818, Dec. 24	MINTER,	JOSIAH	Married Catharine Boughan	Book 1,	234
1820,	MINTER,	JOSIAH	Married Catharine Boughan	D 40,	145
1821, Dec. 20	MINTER,	JOSIAH	Married Peggy Gordon	Book 1,	238
1761,	MINTER,	LUCY	Married Isaac Kidd	D 29,	72
1840, Nov. 17	MINTER,	MARGARET	Married Caleb A. Noel	Book 1,	254
1807, Jul. 20	MINTER,	MARY	Married Richard Shearwood	Book 1,	224
1847, Feb. 16	MINTER,	MARY	Married Arthur Temple Acrey	Book 1,	259
1806, Mar. 17	MINTER,	NANCY	Married Bartlett Brizendine	Book 1,	223
1899, Mar. 8	MINTER,	N. E.	Married Robert C. Longest	Book 1,	231
1823, Jan. 2	MINTER,	PATSEY	Married William Greenwood	Book 1,	240
1845, Dec. 4	MINTER,	ROBERT	Married Elizabeth Atkins	Book 1,	258
1806, Dec. 24	MINTER,	THOMAS	Married Susannah Dishman	Book 1,	223
1807, May 18	MINTER,	THOMAS	Married Elizabeth Boyce	Book 1,	224
1857, Sep. 28	MISKELL,	AMANDA	Married Ephraim Beazley	Book 1,	267
1850, Feb. 14	MISKELL,	GEORGE H.	Married Amanda J. Lathom	Book 1,	262
1881, Mar. 24	MITCHELL,	ADDIE	Married Richard Hodges	Book 1,	59
1834, Dec. 18	MITCHELL,	ALEXANDER	Married Julia C. Brown	Book 1,	250
1835,	MITCHELL,	ALEXANDER	Married Julia, daughter of Daniel Brown	D 45,	19
1854, Nov. 11	MITCHELL,	AMANDA F.	Married Joseph S. Dorsey	Book 1,	265

Date	Surname	Given	Description	Book	Page
1893, Jul. 30	MITCHELL,	B. V.	Married F. W. Beatty	Book 1,	112
1865, Dec. 28	MITCHELL,	CATHARINE ANN	Married William H. Hundley, Baltimore, Md.	Book 1,	13
1852, May 3	MITCHELL,	CHARLES B.	Married Agness S. Munday	Book 1,	263
1865, Sep. 17	MITCHELL,	CHARLES R.	Married Mary Agnes Stokes	Book 1,	13
1812, Jan. 15	MITCHELL,	ELIZABETH	Married Richard Phillips	Book 1,	228
1876, Dec. 28	MITCHELL,	GEORGE W.	Married Molly Taylor	Book 1,	44
1710,	MITCHELL,	JANE	Relict of John, married Robert Webb	O 4,	276
1781,	MITCHELL,	JOHN	Married Mary, daughter of Thomas Watts, King & Queen Co.	D 32,	56
1841,	MITCHELL,	JOANNA	Widow, married George Pollard	D 47,	126
1886, Aug. 26	MITCHELL,	JULIA A.	Married Thomas B. Croxton	Book 1,	88
1897, Feb. 10	MITCHELL,	J. R.	Married Celia Davis	Book 1,	124
1857, Oct. 15	MITCHELL,	MARTHA E.	Married Lawrence B. Elliott	Book 1,	5
1877, Dec. 6	MITCHELL,	NETTIE B.	Married William H. Cook	Book 1,	46
1887, Dec. 26	MITCHELL,	NETTIE S.	Married A. C. Davis	Book 1,	93
1880, Dec. 23	MITCHELL,	ORA H.	Married Elzer Fogg	Book 1,	58
1828, Dec. 9	MITCHELL,	PITMAN	Married Ophelia Dunn	Book 1,	245
1826, Mar. 20	MITCHELL,	RICHARD	Married Martha G. Mann	Book 1,	242
1881, Jul. 7	MITCHELL,	ROBINETTE	Married Robert Gatewood	Book 1,	60
1885, Sep. 4	MITCHELL,	R. B.	Married Atlee Durham	Book 1,	83
1898, Sep. 15	MITCHELL,	R. B.	Married Mary J. Thurston	Book 1,	129
1875, Sep. 30	MITCHELL,	STEPHEN W.	Married Bettie A. Wright	Book 1,	39
1876, Dec. 14	MITCHELL,	VIRGINIA	Married William Hodges	Book 1,	43
1805, Nov. 28	MOCOMACK,	ANN	Married Samuel Perks	Book 1,	223
1685,	MONCASTER,	MARY	Relict of Henry, married Robert Reading	O 1,	150
1797,	MONROE,	ANDREW	Married Frances, daughter of Elizabeth Garnett	W 16,	306
1872, Nov. 23	MONROE,	MARY	Married Adam Latane	Book 1,	31
1871, May 17	MONROE,	NANNY B.	Married John Jackson	Book 1,	28
1814, May 19	MONTAGUE,	AMELIA	Married Thomas Jessee	Book 1,	230
1820, Sep. 8	MONTAGUE,	AMELIA	Married James Allen, Jr.	Book 1,	237
1810,	MONTAGUE,	ANN	Daughter of Elizabeth, married ? Lee	W 17,	40
1818, Dec. 21	MONTAGUE,	CATHARINE	Married George Hoskins	Book 1,	234

				Book	Page
1871, Oct. 5	MONTAGUE,	CATHARIEN E.	Married Warner Sisson, Richmond County	Book 1,	29
1837, Jul. 10	MONTAGUE,	ELIZA	Married Edwin Broaddus	Book 1,	252
1827, Dec. 10	MONTAGUE,	ERASTUS	Married Amelia Allen	Book 1,	244
1865, Dec. 14	MONTAGUE,	EVELYN	Married Xanthus Chartters, Spottsylvania Co.	Book 1,	14
1811, Dec. 30	MONTAGUE,	FRANCES	Married James Trice	Book 1,	227
1829, Nov. 16	MONTAGUE,	FRANCES	Married Richard Johnson	Book 1,	246
1837, Apr. 28	MONTAGUE,	FRANCES C.	Married John A. Jesse	Book 1,	253
1814, Sep. 25	MONTAGUE,	HARRIET	Married Thomas Hill	Book 1,	231
1838, Oct. 22	MONTAGUE,	HOWARD	Married Columbia Broaddus	Book 1,	253
1759,	MOUNTAGUE,	JANE	Married Vincent Vass	O 23,	131
1724,	MOUNTAGUE,	KATHERINE	Married Richard Tyler	D 17,	359
1819, Dec. 20	MONTAGUE,	LAURA L.	Married John Beazley, Jr.	Book 1,	235
1836, Nov. 24	MONTAGUE,	LOUISIANA	Married W. Games	Book 1,	252
1847, Nov. 20	MONTAGUE,	LUCIE S.	Married William Groom	Book 1,	259
1816, Feb. 5	MONTAGUE,	LUCY	Married William Garrett	Book 1,	232
1820, Apr. 28	MONTAGUE,	LUCY B.	Married Thornton L. Clarke	Book 1,	237
1817, Apr. 2	MONTAGUE,	MARY E.	Married George M. Henley	Book 1,	233
1858, Jul. 13	MONTAGUE,	MARY	Married James McClanahan	Book 1,	6
1874, May 6	MONTAGUE,	MARY S.	Widow, married Calvin F. Maupin	Book 1,	36
1822, Feb. 11	MONTAGUE,	PEGGY	Married Henry Johnson	Book 1,	239
1812, May 18	MONTAGUE,	SOPHRONIA	Married William Beale Evans	Book 1,	228
1712,	MOUNTAGUE,	THOMAS	Married Katherine Collins	O 4,	442
1810,	MONTAGUE,	VICTORIA	Daughter of John, married Bob Dobbins	W 17,	170
1827, Jan. 18	MONTAGUE,	VIRGINIA	Married Edwin Hundley	Book 1,	243
1811, Oct. 21	MONTAGUE,	VIRTURIA	Married Amos Newball	Book 1,	227
1831,	MONTAGUE,	VETURIA	Sister of Eneas, married ? Newball	D 43,	337
1845, Nov. 17	MONTAGUE,	W. E.	Married Richard Cooper	Book 1,	258
1845, Nov. 6	MONTAGUE,	WILLIAM S.	Married Susan M. Wood	Book 1,	258
1857, Oct. 22	MONTAGUE,	THOMAS	Married Matilda Powers	Book 1,	5
1872, Mar. 29	MONTGOMERY, THOMAS		Married Willie A. Powers	Book 1,	30
1837, Feb. 20	MOODY,	ANN	Married Joseph Minor	Book 1,	252

				Book	Page
1837, Nov. 21	MOODY,	ANN	Married Sthreshley Dunn	Book 1,	252
1815, Dec. 10	MOODY,	APHRY	Married Sthreshley Taylor	Book 1,	231
1814,	MOODY,	BETSEY	Daughter of Lewis, married Samuel Woodson	O 41,	429
1841, May 17	MOODY,	DANIEL I.	Married Delila Frances Dunn	Book 1,	255
1843, Jun. 28	MOODY,	DOROTHEA	Married George Taylor	Book 1,	257
1841, Jun. 9	MOODY,	FRANCES	Married Andrew Fletcher	Book 1,	255
1870, May 10	MOODY,	F.	Married William B. Smither	Book 1,	25
1804, May 8	MOODY,	HUNDLEY	Married Catharine Boughan	Book 1,	222
1811, Nov. 25	MOODY,	HUNLEY	Married Elizabeth Gordon	Book 1,	227
1823,	MOODY,	HUNDLEY	Married daughter of John Boughan	D 41,	49
1828,	MOODY,	HUNDLEY	Married Elizabeth, daughter of Alexander Gordon	D 42,	382
1878, Apr. 9	MOODY,	JAMES E.	Fredericksburg, married Mollie P. Baylis	Book 1,	48
1810, Jun. 26	MOODY,	NANCY	Married Philip Gatewood	Book 1,	266
1867, Jan. 13	MOODY,	REBECCA	Married Zachariah St. John	Book 1,	17
1822, Dec. 23	MOODY,	RICHARD	Married Lucy Shipp	Book 1,	239
1839, Jan. 8	MOODY,	ROBERT	Married Isabella Rouse	Book 1,	254
1856, Oct. 23	MOODY,	ROBERT J.	Married Mary Susan Powers	Book 1,	4
1895, Feb. 21	MOODY,	R. L.	Married J. F. McKendrie	Book 1,	117
1824, Jun. 9	MOODY,	SARAH	Married Robert Lathom	Book 1,	241
1827, Dec. 24	MOODY,	THOMAS	Married Frances Dyke	Book 1,	244
1799,	MOODY,	WILLIAM	Married Mary, daughter of Jonathan Sherwood	W 15,	508
1847, Feb. 4	MOODY,	WILLIAM H.	Married Mary Caroline Jones	Book 1,	259
1892, May 18	MOODY,	WILLIAM B.	Married Lucy B. Davis	Book 1,	109
1823, Sep. 22	MOOKLAR,	WILLIAM T.	Married Susan L. Tebbs	Book 1,	240
1882, Sep. 7	MOORE,	ALICE V.	Married Salathel G. W. Balderson	Book 1,	66
1876, Mar. 9	MOORE,	CHARLES H.	Married Robenette Schools	Book 1,	41
1812, Apr. 15	MOORE,	HABERN	Married Nancy Dunn	Book 1,	228
1884, Mar. 27	MOORE,	JOHN W.	Caroline Co., married Mary M. Pitts	Book 1,	76
1875, Jun. 14	MOORE,	MARTHA E.	Married George Allen	Book 1,	38
1870, Feb. 24	MOORE,	MARY FRANCES	Married William A. Schools	Book 1,	25
1871, Mar. 21	MOORE,	SARAH W.	Married Ira E. Clarke	Book 1,	28

				Book	Page
1743,	MOORE,	THOMAS	Married Elizabeth, daughter of Richard Grigory	D 23,	76 317
1703,	MORESS,	THOMAS	Married Dorcas Searle	O 3,	22
1690,	MORGAN,	ELIZABETH	Relict of Evan, married Capt. James Tayler	O 2,	220
1684,	MORGAN,	EVAN	Married Elizabeth, relict of William Brown	O 1,	53
1728,	MORGAN,	JOHN	Married Grace Hawkins	O 8,	97
1897, Jun. 27	MORRIS,	ALICE W.	Married Robert Hutchinson	Book 1,	124
1687,	MORRIS,	EDWARD	Married Elizabeth, relict of Peter Elder (North Farnham Parish)	O 2,	101
1689,	MORRIS,	ELINOR	Relict of Maj. George Morris, married Capt. John Story	O 2,	202
1709,	MORRIS,	JOHN	Married Dorcas, widow of John Sorrell	O 4,	146
1865, Feb. 12	MORRIS,	ROBERT L.	Louisa County, married Lucy C. Coleman	Book 1,	13
1890, Sep. 17	MORRIS,	WILLIAM N.	Married Kate Lewis	Book 1,	104
1867, Mar. 7	MORRISON,	MARY A.	Married William H. Faulconer	Book 1,	17
1863, Feb. 4	MORRISON,	SAMUEL J.	Married Lucy Latane Baylor	Book 1,	11
1817, Jan. 1	MORTON,	LUCY	Married Philip Lee	Book 1,	233
1709,	MOSELEY,	BENJAMIN	Married Elizabeth, relict of Nicholas Catlett	D&C 13,	261
1792,	MOSELEY,	ELIZABETH	Married Samuel Faulconer	D 33,	441
1689,	MOSELEY,	JOHN	Married Elizabeth, sister of William Williamson	D 8,	74
1684,	MOSELEY,	MARTHA	Married Capt. George Tayler	O 1,	52 61
1689,	MOSELEY,	WILLIAM CAPT.	Married Hannah, orphan of Thomas Hawkins	O 2,	187 107
1837, May 22	MOSS,	CHARLES B.	Married Ann S. Fisher	Book 1,	252
1839,	MOSS,	CHARLES B.	Married Ann L. Clements, daughter of Ewin Clements	D 46,	192
1685,	MOSS,	DOROTHY	Daughter of Robert, married Abraham Stapp	Box 101	M
1686,	MOSS,	ELIZABETH	Daughter of Thomas, married William Bendry	O 1,	197
1685,	MOSS,	FRANCES	Daughter of William, married William Brown	O 2,	115
1704,	MOSS,	ROBERT	Married Elizabeth, daughter of Richard West	O 3,	123
1711,	MOSS,	ROBERT	Married Martha Reeves	O 4,	427
1685,	MOSS,	THOMAS	His relict married Edmund Craske, Clerk of Court	O 1,	197
1820, Aug. 8	MOTHERSHEAD, NATHANIEL		Married Miranda Beazley	Book 1,	237
1889, Apr. 11	MOTLEY,	CLARENCE	Richmond Co., married Nannie G. Fauntleroy	Book 1,	100
1873, Sep. 22	MOTLEY,	ELLA	Married Henry L. Newbill	Book 1,	34

				Book	Page
1747,	MOTLEY,	HENRY ?	Married Catharine, daughter of Nathaniel Fogg	D 24,	105
1770,	MOTLEY,	HENRY ?	Married Catharine, daughter of Nathaniel Fogg	D 30,	391
1890, Dec. 23	MOTLEY,	IDA	Married E. L. Hutchinson	Book 1,	105
1814, Mar. 5	MOTLEY,	RICHARD	Married Suckey Fisher	Book 1,	230
1844, Mar. 8	MOTLEY,	ROBERT S.	Married Ann I. Gray	Book 1,	257
1806, Apr. 1	MOTLEY,	SALLIE	Married Robert L. Broaddus	Book 1,	223
1754,	MOTLEY,	WILLIAM	Married Hannah, daughter of John Cook	D 27,	71
1691,	MOTT,	ANN	Orphan of George, married John Glendenning	O 2,	312
1690,	MOTT,	?	Relict of George, married James Harrison	O 2,	253
1709,	MOTT,	ELEANOR	Married Richard Shippy	D&C 13,	320
1691,	MOTT,	ELIZABETH	Daughter of George, married John Fosaker	O 2,	312
1697,	MOTTRAM,	SPENCER	Married Sarah, daughter of William Young	D 9,	140
1703,	MUFFETT,	ELIZABETH	Daughter of William Muffett, of Stone's Island, married Henry Johnson	D 11,	100
1794,	MULLINS,	JANE	Daughter of Samuel, married Philip Brooks	D 34,	48
1832,	MULLINS,	MARY	Her sister Nancy, married Isaac Fisher	D 36,	466
				D 44,	34
1820, Dec. 2	MULLINS	PATSY	Married Thomas Greenwood	Book 1,	237
1832,	MULLINS,	PATSY	Daughter of Frances, married Thomas Greenwood	D 44,	94
1842, Nov. 21	MULLINS,	SUSAN	Married James Dunn	Book 1,	256
1846,	MULLINS,	SUSAN	Married James Dunn	W 26,	442
1852, May 3	MUNDAY,	AGNESS S.	Married Charles B. Mitchell	Book 1,	263
1887, Jul. 5	MUNDAY,	ALBERT R.	Married Virgie C. Carneale	Book 1,	92
1846, Dec. 14	MUNDAY,	ALFRED	Married Malinda Schools	Book 1,	259
1863, Jan. 7	MUNDAY,	ALICE	Married Robert H. Pratt	Book 1,	11
1877, Jan. 25	MUNDAY,	ANN E.	Married Howard B. Carneale	Book 1,	44
1822, Oct. 21	MUNDAY,	BENJAMIN	Married Rebecca Fisher	Book 1,	239
1824, Dec. 1	MUNDAY,	BENJAMIN	Married Sarah Munday	Book 1,	241
1869, Apr. 27	MUNDAY,	BENJAMIN KESEE	Married Mary Jane Munday	Book 1,	23
1859, Feb. 13	MUNDAY,	BETTIE F.	Married James M. Lyall	Book 1,	9
1831, Sep. 12	MUNDAY,	CATHARINE P.	Married Alexander Baker	Book 1,	248
1850, Aug. 22	MUNDAY,	CATHARINE	Married John Munday	Book 1,	259
1873, Feb. 13	MUNDAY,	CATHARINE	Married Robert H. Atkins	Book 1,	32

Date	Surname	Given Name	Description	Book	Page
1867, Dec. 10	MUNDAY,	CORNELIA E.	Married James L. Powers	Book 1,	18
1813, Nov. 12	MUNDAY,	EDMUND	Married Nancy Brown	Book 1,	229
1867, May 30	MUNDAY,	EDWARD D.	Married Vernangus A. Brown	Book 1,	18
1855, Oct. 29	MUNDAY,	ELIZA H.	Married Thomas H. Brooke	Book 1,	3
1741,	MUNDAY,	ELIZABETH	Executrix of John, married James Atkins	O 12,	141
1820, Dec. 19	MUNDAY,	ELIZABETH	Married Joseph B. Brown	Book 1,	237
1855, Dec. 29	MUNDAY,	ELIZABETH F.	Married Larry B. Jordan	Book 1,	266
1875, Mar. 11	MUNDAY,	ELLA J.	Married Thomas Coghill	Book 1,	38
1827, Feb. 7	MUNDAY,	FANNY	Married Benjamin Stokes	Book 1,	244
1835, Dec. 9	MUNDAY,	FRANCIS	Married Susan Clarkson	Book 1,	252
1835,	MUNDAY,	FRANCIS	Married Susan, daughter of Susan L Clarkson	D 45,	124
1888, Oct. 4	MUNDAY,	HAUSIE	Married John Carneale	Book 1,	96
1873, Feb. 20	MUNDAY,	HENRY	Married Ann Elizabeth Crutchfield, King William Co.	Book 1,	32
1828, Dec. 18	MUNDAY,	JAMES	Married Hannah S. Noel	Book 1,	245
1879, Dec. 18	MUNDAY,	JAMES ADDIE	Orphan, married John Allen	Book 1,	53
1850, Aug. 22	MUNDAY,	JOHN	Married Catharine Munday	Book 1,	262
1860, Nov. 15	MUNDAY,	JOHN	Married Susan Munday	Book 1,	10
1885, Sep. 21	MUNDAY,	JOHN	King & Queen Co. married Sophronia Crouch	Book 1,	83
1813, May 20	MUNDAY,	JOHNSON	Married Elizabeth G. Armstrong	Book 1,	229
1771,	MUNDAY,	KATHERINE	Married Thomas Shelton	D 30,	508
1857, Mar. 19	MUNDAY,	LEONARD	Married Lucy Ann Powers	Book 1,	5
1854, Nov. 30	MUNDAY,	LEWIS G.	Married Mary Catharine Parker	Book 1,	2
1868, Dec. 9	MUNDAY,	LIZZIE	Daughter of Robert, married H. W. Stampee, Jefferson Co., Ky.	Book 1,	21
1849, Nov. 28	MUNDAY,	LUCINDA	Married Augustus I. Allen	Book 1,	261
1858, Oct. 12	MUNDAY,	MARGARET A.	Married John Bayne	Book 1,	6
1848, Mar. 7	MUNDAY,	MARIA E.	Married Albert P. Gouldman	Book 1,	260
1771,	MUNDAY,	MARY	Married James Croxton	D 30,	508
1835, Dec. 9	MUNDAY,	MARY C.	Married Reuben Munday	Book 1,	251
1838, Oct. 4	MUNDAY,	MARY E.	Married Dandridge Sale	Book 1,	253
1855, Sep. 25	MUNDAY	MARY SUSAN	Married Bernard Eubank	Book 1,	3
1869, Apr. 27	MUNDAY,	MARY JANE	Married Benjamin Kesee Munday	Book 1,	23

				Book	Page
1869, Mar. 23	MUNDAY,	MARY L.	Married Archibald Thomas	Book 1,	23
1835, Dec. 9	MUNDAY,	REUBEN	Married Mary C. Munday	Book 1,	251
1855, Dec. 20	MUNDAY,	REUBEN	Married Virginia Munday	Book 1,	3
1831, Apr. 18	MUNDAY,	ROBERT	Married Sarah Younger	Book 1,	248
1847, Aug. 16	MUNDAY,	ROBERT A.	Married Ann L. Lewis	Book 1,	259
1873, May 15	MUNDAY,	ROBERT	Married Mary E. Waddell, Trigg County, Ky.	Book 1,	33
1868, Feb. 18	MUNDAY,	SALLIE E.	Married Simon Sykes Brown	Book 1,	20
1822, Dec. 23	MUNDAY,	SARAH	Married John Muscerelli	Book 1,	239
1824, Dec. 1	MUNDAY,	SARAH	Married Benjamin Munday	Book 1,	241
1837, Oct. 9	MUNDAY,	SARAH	Married Robert H. Gains	Book 1,	252
1873, Feb. 13	MUNDAY,	SARAH	Married James F. Atkins	Book 1,	32
1880, Jan. 16	MUNDAY,	SARAH F.	Married William Lumpkin	Book 1,	56
1860, Nov. 15	MUNDAY,	SUSAN	Married John Munday	Book 1,	10
1707,	MUNDAY,	THOMAS	Married Mary, relict of James Reeves	D&C 13,	35
1771,	MUNDAY,	URSULA	Daughter of James, married John Boughan	D 30,	508
1855, Sep. 20	MUNDAY,	VIRGINIA	Married Reuben Munday	Book 1,	3
1854, Dec. 26	MUNDAY,	WILLIAM S.	Married Sarah Ann Schools	Book 1,	3
1891, Feb. 11	MUNDIE,	C. C.	Married Pearl A. Andrews	Book 1,	106
1866, Dec. 3	MUNDIE,	EUGENIA A.	Married Ellwood M. Rennolds, King & Queen Co.	Book 1,	89
1879, Nov. 6	MUNDIE,	FRANCIS P.	Caroline Co., married Mary Susan Andrews	Book 1,	52
1892, Dec. 22	MUNDIE,	LELA	Married J. H. Allen	Book 1,	110
1893, Nov. 23	MUNDIE,	LUCY B.	Married L. H. Beazley	Book 1,	112
1886, Dec. 22	MUNDIE,	NANNIE C.	Married W. D. Allen	Book 1,	89
1891, Jan. 21	MUNDIE	WILLIE J.	Caroline Co., married Baylor Martin	Book 1,	106
1728,	MURRAY,	JAMES	Married Ann, Exec. of Benjamin Boulware	O 7,	275
1730,	MURROUGH,	EDWARD	Married Martha, daughter of Isaac Flowers	D 19,	163
1822, Dec. 23	MUSCERELLI, JOHN	Married Sarah Munday	Book 1,	239
1741,	MUSCOE,	FRANCES	Daughter of Salvator, married John Livingston Jun.	W 6,	352
1701,	MUSCOE,	SALVATOR	Married Mary, daughter of Thomas Hucklescott	Land Trials 97 D&W 10, 112	
1750,	MUSCOE,	SARAH	Daughter of Salvator, married Philip Edward Jones	D 25,	33
1857, Mar. 2	MUSE,	A. B.	Married James H. Muse	Book 1,	267

					Book	Page
1806, May 1	MUSE,	ALEXANDER	Married Polly Andrews		Book 1,	223
1869, Jan. 14	MUSE,	AMY	Married Henry Collier		Book 1,	22
1853, Aug. 16	MUSE,	ANNA B.	Married John B. Bigger		Book 1,	264
1850, Jul. 22	MUSE,	CATHARINE C.	Married Joseph T. Valentine		Book 1,	262
1812, Mar. 3	MUSE,	JAMES	Married Mary W. Coleman		Book 1,	228
1857, Mar. 2	MUSE,	JAMES H.	Married A. B. Muse		Book 1,	267
1869, Jul. 29	MUSE,	JAMES H.	Married Sarah Y. Croxton		Book 1,	23
1890, Dec. 29	MUSE,	JOHN R.	Married Annis G. Taylor		Book 1,	103
1870, Nov. 24	MUSE,	JULIA D.	Married F. E. Wright		Book 1,	26
1810,	MUSE,	LAWRENCE	Married Martha Hoomes		D 37,	553
1827, Aug. 27	MUSE,	LUCINDA	Married Muscoe Wood		Book 1,	244
1844, Dec. 16	MUSE,	LUCY A.	Married Peter S. Trible		Book 1,	257
1792,	MUSE,	PEGGY	Daughter of John, married James Hart		W 16,	190
1872, Dec. 24	MUSE,	RICHARD I.	Married Mary B. Trible		Book 1,	32
1866, Jul. 8	MUSE,	ROBERT E.	Married Nancy Gaines		Book 1,	15
1819,	MUSE,	SAMUEL	Married Elizabeth Banks		W 19,	31
1855, Dec. 25	MUSE,	SAMUEL W. Y.	Married Sarah F. J. Coates		Book 1,	3
1895, Dec. 26	MUSE,	S. Y.	Daughter of Samuel W. Y. Muse, married G. W. Taylor		Book 1,	119
1853, Nov. 29	MUSE,	SARAH E.	Married Fleet William Cox		Book 1,	1
1868, Feb. 13	MUSE,	SUSAN M.	Married Samuel T. Preston		Book 1,	20
1864, Oct. 3	MUSE,	WILLIAM S.	Westmoreland Co., married Sarah F. Andrews		Book 1,	12
1869, Dec. 28	MUSE,	WILLIAM	Married Flora C. Wright		Book 1,	24

1802,	McCARTY,	ELIZABETH	Daughter of Thaddeus of Lancaster Co., married James Craine	D	35,	522
1802,	McCARTY,	MARY	Daughter of Thaddeus, married John Mathews	D	35,	523
1802,	McCARTY,	NANCY	Daughter of Thaddeus, married William Cuthbert			
1804, Dec. 17	McCARTY,	SALLY	Married John B. Harrison	Book 1,		224
1875, Mar. 25	McCAULEY,	JOHN H.	Married Lucy Taff, Middlesex County	Book 1,		39
1845, Jun. 19	McCAWLEY,	SAMUEL	Married Sarah Evans	Book 1,		258
1858, Jul. 13	McCLANAHAN, JAMES		Married Mary Montague	Book 1,		6
1781,	McCOMBS,	?	Married Major Lafon's widow	D	32,	13
1841, Dec. 11	McCULLOCH,	CAROLINE A.	Married Leroy L. Payne	Book 1,		255
1867, Dec. 17	McDANIEL,	JOHN W.	Married Mary L. Croxton	Book 1,		19
1824, Aug. 30	McDANIEL,	REUBEN	Married Delilah Priddy	Book 1,		241
1834, Dec. 26	McDANIEL,	REUBEN E.	Married Delia Richeson	Book 1,		250
1882, Oct. 11	McDONALD,	BRON H.	Missouri, married Ada B. Banks	Book 1,		66
1835, Jul. 10	McDONALD,	JAMES	Married Mary A. Rouzie	Book 1,		251
1880, Nov. 23	McDONALD,	JAMES T.	Married Susan B. Haile	Book 1,		57
1854, Nov. 23	McDONALD,	JANE RITCHIE	Married Mortimer Evans	Book 1,		2
1883, Dec. 11	McDONALD,	RICHARD C.	Married Lucy Emma Haile	Book 1,		74
1834, Oct. 27	McDOWNEY,	WARNER	Married Polly Green	Book 1,		250
1811, Mar. 5	McENTREE,	JAMES	Married Catharine Sheperd	Book 1,		227
1808, Dec. 19	McFARLAIN,	JAMES	Married Elizabeth Jones	Book 1,		224
1838, Dec. 12	McFARLANE,	JAMES	Married Jane Dunn	Book 1,		253
1850, Feb. 18	McFARLAND,	ROBERT	Married Sarah E. Durham	Book 1,		262
1834, Dec. 4	McFARLANE,	WILLIAM	Married Sophronia Jones	Book 1,		250
1874, Nov. 5	McGEORGE,	BETTIE	Married George M. Clark	Book 1,		42
1868, May 5	McGEORGE,	THOMAS J.	Married Marietta Phillips	Book 1,		20
1868, Dec. 24	McGEORGE,	WALLACE R.	Married Mary F. Cauthorn	Book 1,		21
1883, Jan. 25	McGOWAN,	COLUMBIA F	Married Willis A. Pitts	Book 1,		69
1868, Jul. 28	McGUIRE,	GRACE FENTON	Married Kinloch Nelson	Book 1,		21
1827, Oct. 2	McGUIRE,	JOHN P.	Married Maria Garnett	Book 1,		224
1840,	McGUIRE,	JOHN P.	Married Maria, daughter of James & Elizabeth Garnett	D	47,	58

				Book	Page
1811, Jun. 1	McGUY,	MALINDA	Married William Lewis	Book 1,	227
1809, Jan. 17	McGUY,	POLLY	Married John Lewis	Book 1,	225
1804, Dec. 17	McKAN,	ELIJAH	Married Elizabeth Greenwood	Book 1,	222
1845, Jan. 15	McKAN,	HENRY	Married Ann Sadler	Book 1,	258
1862, Sep. 18	McKAN,	RICHARD M.	Married Virginia A. Dunn	Book 1,	11
1869, Dec. 22	McKANN,	VIRGINIA	Married John W. Street	Book 1,	24
1817, Jun. 1	McKENDRY,	CATHARINE	Married George T. Greenwood	Book 1,	233
1890, Dec. 5	McKENDRIE,	FLORA A.	Married Joseph L. Gruebel	Book 1,	105
1889, Apr. 21	McKENDRIE,	GEORGE P.	Married Mary A. Taylor	Book 1,	100
1895, Feb. 21	McKENDRIE,	J. F.	Richmond Co., married R. L. Moody	Book 1,	117
1828, Dec. 25	McKENDRIE,	JOHN	Married Polly Newbill	Book 1,	245
1872, Nov. 7	McKENDRIE,	LUCY A.	Married John L. Dunn	Book 1,	31
1837, Sep. 18	McKENDRIE,	SILAS	Married Sarah Covington	Book 1,	252
1871, Feb. 23	McKENDRIE,	TASKER	Married Emily Sheppard	Book 1,	28
1802,	McKENDRIE,	THOMAS	Married Mary, daughter of John Sheppard	D 36,	67
1860, Jan. 4	McKENDRIE,	WILLIAM F.	Married Lucy A. Dunn	Book 1,	8
1879, Mar. 12	McKENDRIE,	WILLIAM G.	Married Julia F. Fidler, Richmond Co.	Book 1,	51
1873, Jan. 3	McKENNON,	NORMAN J.	Married Ann Fenton	Book 1,	34
1849, Dec. 24	McKENNON,	RICHARD M.	Married Mary C. Croxton	Book 1,	261
1835, Jul. 13	McNORTON,	THOMAS	Married Judith Edwards	Book 1,	251
1885, Sep. 18	McRAE,	DUNCAN L.	Georgia, married Lizzie M. Haile	Book 1,	83
1885, Sep. 18	McTYRE,	ADOLPHUS	Middlesex Co., married Caroline Coleman	Book 1,	83
1839, Dec. 18	McTIRE,	ANN C.	Married Thomas Barefoot	Book 1,	254
1795,	McTYRE,	ELIZABETH	Daughter of Josiah, married Thomas Hundley	W 15,	190
1830, Oct. 19	McTYRE,	ELIZABETH	Married Samuel Dunn	Book 1,	247
1890, Dec. 26	McTYRE,	FANNIE	Married Warner L. Beazley	Book 1,	105
1827, Mar. 19	McTYRE,	FRANCES	Married Samuel Williamson	Book 1,	244
1858, Feb. 25	McTIRE,	MARY E.	Married Ennis Shackelford	Book 1,	6
1853, Jun. 11	McTYRE,	VIRGINIA	Married Vincent Gordon	Book 1,	264

N

				Book	Page
1722,	NALLE,	MARTIN	Married Mary Alleyn	D 17,	108
1722,	NANCE,	JOHN	Married Margaret, Exec. of Ralph Rouzie	O 5,	527
1685,	NAYLER,	AVERY	Married Katherine, widow of Robert Hoskins	D 7,	177
1791,	NEALE,	ELIZABETH	Married ? Callis	D 33,	345
1685,	NEALE,	GARRETT	Married Katherine, daughter of Robert Gullocke	D&C 13,	206
1791,	NEALE,	JUDITH	Daughter of Richard of Richmond Co., married Edward Mathews	D 33,	345
1791,	NEALE,	MARGARET	Daughter of Richard, Richmond Co., married Henry Garnett	D 33,	345
1874, Sep. 23	NEALE,	R. M.	Married Kate W. Gouldman	Book 1,	37
1897, Jun. 17	NEALE,	R. G.	Married P. C. Campbell	Book 1,	125
1758,	NEALE,	STEPHEN	Married widow of Bibby Bush	O 22,	255
1791,	NEALE,	SUSANNA	Married William Miller	D 33,	345
1835, May 13	NELSON,	BENJAMIN	Married Henrietta Brockenbrough	Book 1,	251
1875, Dec. 22	NELSON,	JOHN W.	Married Letitia Jones	Book 1,	40
1868, Jul. 28	NELSON,	KINLOCH	Fauquier County, married Grace Fenton McGuire	Book 1,	21
1860, Aug. 16	NELSON,	SARAH FRANCES	Married Robert Hill	Book 1,	10
1812, Nov. 11	NEW,	CATHARINE	Married John Ferguson	Book 1,	228
1733,	NEW,	ELIZABETH	Daughter of James, married George Gwynn	D 20,	246
1811, Oct. 21	NEWBALL,	AMOS	Married Virturia Montague	Book 1,	227
1812, Mar. 9	NEWBILL,	ANN	Married Traverse Gatewood	Book 1,	228
1886, Jan. 5	NEWBILL,	BETTIE F.	Widow of James City Co., married W. G. Farinholt, King & Queen Co.	Book 1,	87
1873, Sep. 22	NEWBILL,	HENRY	Married Ella Motley	Book 1,	34
1783,	NEWBILL,	KATHERINE	Married Richard Phillips	D 32,	190
1858, Oct. 24	NEWBILL,	LUCINDA	Married Russell A. Douglass	Book 1,	6
1827, Jan. 23	NEWBILL,	MARY	Married Orval Jeffries	Book 1,	243
1832, Feb. 6	NEWBILL,	MARY	Married John Street	Book 1,	249
1869, Mar. 24	NEWBILL,	MARY J.	Married William H. Street	Book 1,	23
1844, Dec. 12	NEWBILL,	OSCAR O.	Married Lucy A. Gibson	Book 1,	257
1828, Dec. 25	NEWBILL,	POLLY	Married John McKendrie	Book 1,	245
1846, Feb. 4	NEWBILL,	RACHEL	Married Thomas Brooks	Book 1,	258
1819, Jun. 3	NEWBILL,	RICHARD	Married Rebecca Shackelford	Book 1,	236

1829,	NEWBILL,	RICHARD	Married Rebecca, daughter of Roger Shackelford	W 22,	34
1825, Dec. 20	NEWBILL,	SALLY	Married William Cox	Book 1,	241
1831,	NEWBALL,	VETURIA	Sister of Eneas Montague	D 43,	337
1839, Dec. 16	NEWBILL,	WILLIAM G.	Married Frances C. Seward	Book 1,	254
1869, Aug. 3	NEWBILL,	WILLIAM J.	Married Ann Eliza Cauthorn	Book 1,	23
1826, Dec. 23	NEWCOMB,	JOHN	Married Lucy Brook	Book 1,	242
1828, Dec. 15	NEWCOMB,	JOSEPH	Married Eliza Davis	Book 1,	245
1833, Dec. 2	NEWHALL,	JULIA E.	Married C. G. Griswold	Book 1,	249
1747,	NEWMAN,	THOMAS	Married Elizabeth Vawter	Rose's Diary	
1708,	NEWTON,	DOROTHY	Executrix of Nicholas, married William Richardson	O 4,	135
1701,	NEWTON,	HENRY	Married Elizabeth, relict of John Stoakes	D&W 10,	88
1712,	NEWTON,	PELIATIA	Daughter of Henry, married Philip Graffort, Stafford Co.	D&W 14,	240
1758,	NEWTON,	THOMAS	Married Elizabeth, daughter of Nehemiah & Behethlem Stokes	D 28,	76
1677,	NICHOLLS,	ANN	Daughter of George, married Thomas Glascock	W 2,	2
1694,	NICHOLLS,	HENRY	Middlesex Co., married Alice, daughter of Griffin Roberts	O 1,	314
1691,	NICHOLLS,	MARY	Daughter of George, married John Hewlett, Northumberland County	D 8,	294
1875, Nov. 16	NICHOLSON,	GEORGE	Middlesex Co., married Rosalind G. Micou	Book 1,	39
1823, Feb. 19	NOEL,	ACHILLES	Married Harriet Andrews	Book 1,	240
1825, May 23	NOEL,	ACHILLES	Married Polly R. Parker	Bok	240
1807, Jul. 22	NOEL,	ALEXANDER	Married Susanna Clarke	Book 1,	224
1812, Nov. 16	NOEL,	ANDREW	Married Betsey Clarke	Book 1,	225
1827, May 12	NOEL,	ANN M.	Married Thomas Wright	Book 1,	244
1813, Oct. 18	NOEL,	ARMSTRONG	Married Elizabeth R. G. Noel	Book 1,	229
1750,	NOEL,	BERNARD	Married Sarah, daughter of William Scott	D 25,	147
1804,	NOEL,	BETSEY	Daughter of Edmund, married ? Priddy of Hanover Co.	W 17,	88
1840, Nov. 17	NOEL,	CALEB	Married Margaret Minter	Book 1,	254
1844, Feb. 19	NOEL,	CAMERINE	Married Richard Noel	Book 1,	257
1773,	NOELL,	CORNELIUS II	Married Anna, daughter of Nathaniel Fogg	D 31,	121
	NOELL,	EASTER	Married William Smither, of Kentucky	D 33,	181
1812, May 18	NOEL,	EDMUND	Married Elizabeth Barton	Book 1,	228
1813, Oct. 18	NOEL,	ELIZABETH R.	Married Armstrong Noell	Book 1,	229

				Book	Page
1814, Oct. 19	NOEL,	ELIZABETH	Married Thomas Coghill	Book 1,	230
1842, Jul. 4	NOEL,	ELIZABETH J.	Married Dr. John J. Wright	Book 1,	256
1805, Dec. 18	NOEL,	EUNICE	Married John Richeson	Book 1,	223
1811,	NOEL,	FANNY	Daughter of Caleb, married Ellis Armstrong	W 18,	145
1831, May 19	NOEL,	FRANCES	Married Thomas Farmer	Book 1,	248
1828, Dec. 18	NOEL,	HANNAH S.	Married James Munday	Book 1,	245
1723,	NOEL,	JAMES	Married Elizabeth, sister of Edward Evans	W 4,	136
1763,	NOEL,	JAMES	Married Elizabeth Taylor	W 12,	69
1846, Dec. 1	NOEL,	JAMES H.	Married Sarah C. Covington	Book 1,	259
1844, Jun. 17	NOEL,	JOHN	Married Susan Elliott	Book 1,	257
1820, Mar. 19	NOEL,	LARKIN	Married Maria J. Brown	Book 1,	237
1835,	NOEL,	LARKIN	Married Maria Brown	D 45,	19
1852, Jun. 18	NOEL,	LAVINIA	Married Brooking Lee	Book 1,	263
1865, Dec. 12	NOEL,	LOUISA H.	Married Waring Lewis	Book 1,	13
1819, Dec. 20	NOEL,	LUCY	Married Fielding Lee	Book 1,	236
1835,	NOEL,	LUCY	Daughter of Reuben, married Fielding Lee	D 45,	56
1884, Jan. 17	NOEL,	LUCY	Married James Lee	Book 1,	75
1761,	NOELL,	MARTHA	Daughter of Samuel, married Samuel Henshaw	D 29,	56
1780,	NOEL,	MARY	Married Zachariah Mallet of Mecklenburg County	D 32,	41
1832, Dec. 19	NOEL,	MARY	Married James Carneale	Book 1,	248
1816, Dec. 16	NOEL,	MUSCOE	Married Maria Taylor	Book 1,	232
1804, Mar. 14	NOEL,	NANCY	Married Caleb Elliott	Book 1,	222
1806, Apr. 1	NOEL,	NANCY	Married George Turner	Book 1,	223
1808, Dec. 22	NOEL,	OSWALD	Married Nancy Barton	Book 1,	224
1751,	NOEL,	REUBEN	Married Sarah, daughter of John Garnett	D 25,	151
1844, Feb. 19	NOEL,	RICHARD	Married Camarine A. Noel	Book 1,	257
1823, Jan. 13	NOEL,	ROBERT S.	Married Maria Jones	Book 1,	240
1806, Feb. 25	NOEL,	SALLY	Married Daniel Gouldman	Book 1,	223
1808, Aug. 24	NOEL,	SALLY	Married Thomas Price	Book 1,	225
1815, Dec. 26	NOEL,	SALLY	Married Samuel C. Parker	Book 1,	231
1856,	NOEL,	SALLIE E.	Widow of James H. Noell married James M. Haig, Baltimore	D 51,	42

				Book	Page
1826,	NOEL,	SARAH	Daughter of Leonard, married Mordecai Spindle	D 42,	26
1842, Apr. 18	NOEL,	SELINA	Married Thomas Vaughan	Book 1,	256
1880, Feb. 25	NOEL,	SUSAN M.	Married Waring Lewis	Book 1,	55
1825,	NOEL,	SUSANNA	Daughter of William, married Benjamin Coghill	D 41,	369
1892, Oct. 20	NOEL,	WILLIAM H.	Married Louisa C. Hall	Book 1,	110
1781,	NORGATE,	PHILIP	Northumberland Co., married Elizabeth, relict of Hezekiah Turner	D 36,	131
1870, Dec. 27	NORMAN,	CALVIN	Married Bettie Upshaw	Book 1,	25
1870, Jan. 8	NORMAN,	MORTIMER	Married Leannah Washington	Book 1,	25
1807, Dec. 23	NORMENT,	JOSEPH	Married Catharine Rennolds	Book 1,	224
1883, Jan. 11	NORRIS,	ADOLPHUS	Married Alice B. Brizendine	Book 1,	69
1870, Dec. 15	NORRIS,	ATWAY P.	Married Samuel Trible	Book 1,	25
1833,	NORRIS,	JOSEPH	Married Charlotte, daughter of Daniel Hoffman, Baltimore	D 44,	315
1842, Jan. 8	NORRIS,	LOWRY	Married Mary A. Atkins	Book 1,	256
1845,	NORRIS,	LOWRY	Married Mary Ann, daughter of Clayton Atkins	W 24,	453
1692,	NORTH,	ABRAHAM	Married Sarah Rouzie	O 1,	140
1706,	NORTH,	DOROTHY	Widow of Gloucester Co. Married Daniel Henry	D&C 12,	369
1706,	NORTH,	MARY	Widow of William, married John Mills Jun.	D&C 12,	330
1726,	NORTH,	WINIFRED	Wife of Anthony North	O 7,	23
1693	NORTON,	ELIZABETH	Married William Merriott	O 1,	236
1888, Oct. 14	NUNN,	EVELYN J.	Married Rosser Brooks	Book 1,	96
1826, May 6	NUNN,	GEORGE C.	Married Lucinda C. Townley	Book 1,	242
1846, May 25	NUNN,	GEORGE C.	Married Nancy Oliver	Book 1,	259

O

1876, Jun. 1	OAKLEY,	FENTON	Married Benjamin Hunter	Book 1,	42
1858, Dec. 23	OGLESBY,	GEORGE W.	King & Queen Co., married Susan Hodges	Book 1,	7
1838, Oct. 23	OLIVER,	ADALINE	Married William Walden	Book 1,	253
1843,	OLIVER,	ADALINE	Daughter of William, married William Walden	W 24,	152
1808, Mar. 17	OLIVER,	AUGUSTINE	Married Rachel Thomas	Book 1,	224
1820,	OLIVER,	AUGUSTINE	Married Rachel, niece of Sarah Goulding	W 19,	169
1824, Oct. 21	OLIVER,	AUSTIN	Married Phoebe Lee	Book 1,	241
1843,	OLIVER,	ELIZABETH	Daughter of William, married Philemon Bird	W 24,	152
1847, Jun. 14	OLIVER,	LEAH A.	Married Ethelbert Cauthorn	Book 1,	259
1829, Apr. 6	OLIVER,	MIRA	Married Thomas Dillard	Book 1,	246
1831, Apr. 1	OLIVER,	MORDECAI	Married Susan Conoly	Book 1,	248
1846, May 25	OLIVER,	NANCY	Married George C. Nunn	Book 1,	259
1830, Dec. 30	OLIVER,	WILLIAM	Married Mrs. Nancy Didlake	Book 1,	247
1857, Jul. 25	OLIVER,	WILLIAM A.	Married Ellen D. Jeffries	Book 1,	5
1825, May 27	ONEALE,	MARY	Married Robert P. Andrews	Book 1,	242
1831, Oct. 17	ONEALE,	SARAH I. C.	Married James W. Jones	Book 1,	248
1770,	ONEALE,	THOMAS	Married Sarah, widow of Thomas Thorpe	O 28,	15
1678,	ORCHARD,	JAMES	Married Mary Weire	D 6,	45
1708,	OSMAN,	ELINOR	Relict of James, married William Reed	O 4,	30
1726,	OSWALD,	MARY	Executrix of Lodowick Rouzie	O 7,	60
1850, Jul. 1	OWEN,	ARTHUR	Married Cordelia Owen	Book 1,	262
1850, Jul. 1	OWEN,	CORDELIA	Married Arthur Owen	Book 1,	262
1849, Nov. 12	OWEN,	ELIZABETH	Married John C. Brizendine	Book 1,	261
1802,	OWEN,	FIELDING	King George Co., married Mary, widow of Benjamin Weeks	D 36,	37
1817, Oct. 24	OWEN,	JAMES	Married Mary Allen	Book 1,	233
1825,	OWEN,	JAMES	Married Mary, daughter of Thomas Allen	D 41,	419
1807, Dec. 21	OWEN,	JANE	Married William Clark	Book 1,	224
1866, Jan. 25	OWEN,	JOHN	Married Priscilla Dunn	Book 1,	14
1873, Apr. 3	OWEN,	JOHN M.	Married Mary E. Shearwood	Book 1,	33
1835, Jan. 19	OWEN,	JOSEPH	Married Zezorah Mercer	Book 1,	251

				Book	Page
1848, Nov. 13	OWEN,	MARY C.	Married Robert D. Edwards	Book 1,	260
1709,	OWENS,	OWEN	Married Mary, widow of Peter Harwood	D&C 13,	257
1888, Oct. 18	OWEN,	ZORA S.	Married W. E. Dillard	Book 1,	96

P

				Book	Page
1676,	PAGE,	MARY	Daughter of Thomas, married Valentine Allen	W&D 1,	194
1705,	PAGE,	SARAH	Daughter of Thomas & Elizabeth, married Robert Jeffery	O 3,	198
1720,	PAIN,	ROBERT	Married Moneca, daughter of Mary Shippy	W 3,	254
1878, May 15	PALMER,	CHARLES H.	Married Nannie Sadler	Book 1,	48
1761,	PAMPLIN,	MARY	Widow of Nicholas, married Isaac Jenkins	W 11,	420
1773,	PAMPLIN,	MARY	Daughter of Henry Reeves, & widow of Nicholas Pamplin, married Thomas Haddon	D 31,	139
1682,	PANNELL,	KATHERINE	Relict of Thomas, married Thomas Swinborn	D 7,	16
1696,	PANNELL,	MARY	Daughter of Thomas, married James Kay	D 9,	32
1707,	PANNELL,	MARY	(Widow Kay,) married Francis Stone	D&C 13,	18
1871, Jan. 26	PARKER,	ALBERT S.	Married Letitia J. Blackburn	Book 1,	28
1811, Apr. 15	PARKER,	ALEXANDER	Married Polly Sale	Book 1,	227
1866, Jan. 11	PARKER,	ALICE C.	Married William S. Andrews	Book 1,	14
1693,	PARKER,	ANNE	Daughter of Thomas, married John Cardin	O 1,	235
1707,	PARKER,	ANN	Daughter of Robert, married Thomas Winslow	D&C 13,	2
1829, Jan. 14	PARKER,	ANN L.	Married Makenzie Gouldman	Book 1,	246
1876, Jul. 19	PARKER,	ANN	Married Peyton Parker	Book 1,	42
1872, Sep. 10	PARKER,	ARTHUR	Married Sarah Jeannette Shaddock	Book 1,	31
1844, Aug. 19	PARKER,	ELIJAH	Married Sarah J. Parker	Book 1,	257
1707,	PARKER,	ELIZABETH	Daughter of Robert, married John Watkins	D&C 13,	2
1807, Jul. 28	PARKER,	ELIZABETH	Married Richard Sale, Jr.	Book 1,	224
1884, Mar. 26	PARKER,	EMMA S.	Married James T. Atkins, King & Queen Co.	Book 1,	76
1897, Feb. 3	PARKER,	E. A.	Married James L. Crouch	Book 1,	124
1729,	PARKER,	FRANCES	Daughter of Robert, married Charles Gresham	D 19,	91
1853, Oct. 14	PARKER,	FRANCES F.	Married William H. Parker	Book 1,	1
1843, Feb. 6	PARKER,	H. W.	Married Rebecca Gouldman	Book 1,	257
1876, Aug. 13	PARKER,	HARRIET B.	Married Benjamin F. Coghill	Book 1,	42
1804, Nov. 14	PARKER,	JAMES	Married Sally Boulware	Book 1,	222
1875, Jun. 9	PARKER,	JAMES	Married Martha E. Davis	Book 1,	39
1859, Feb. 4	PARKER,	JEANNETTE	Married William B. B. Samuel	Book 1,	7

				Book	Page
1703,	PARKER,	JOHN	Married Martha, sister of Henry Tandy	O 3,	16
1793,	PARKER,	JOHN	Married Molly, daughter of Thomas Gouldman	W 15,	313
1894, Jul. 17	PARKER,	LAVINIA	Married Samuel Acres	Book 1,	114
1838, Feb. 19	PARKER,	LUCY	Married Washington Elliott	Book 1,	223
1842, Feb. 13	PARKER,	LUCY A.	Married George Lee	Book 1,	256
1841, Jan. 18	PARKER,	MARTHA	Married John Gouldman	Book 1,	255
1854, Nov. 30	PARKER,	MARY C.	Married Lewis G. Munday	Book 1,	2
1880, Mar. 10	PARKER,	NANNIE F.	Married Oscar F. Bradley	Book 1,	54
1842, Dec. 6	PARKER,	NATHAN	Married Catharine Johnston, daughter of Mourning Johnston	Book 1,	256
1813, Nov. 16	PARKER,	PATSY	Married Allen Smith	Book 1,	229
1876, Jul. 19	PARKER,	PEYTON	Married Ann Parker	Book 1,	42
1825, Aug. 31	PARKER,	PHILIP	Married Polly Lankford	Book 1,	242
1809, Nov. 4	PARKER,	PHOEBY	Married Churchill Blackburn	Book 1,	225
1825, May 23	PARKER,	POLLY R.	Married Achilles Noel	Book 1,	242
1819, Dec. 9	PARKER,	ROBERT T.	Married Polly Gouldman	Book 1,	236
1876, Aug. 1	PARKER,	ROBERT L.	Married Mary S. Rennolds	Book 1,	42
1866, Jan. 13	PARKER,	ROBERTA	Married Eli Coghill	Book 1,	14
1815, Dec. 26	PARKER,	SAMUEL C.	Married Sally N. Noel	Book 1,	231
1870, Dec. 22	PARKER,	SAMUEL	Married Jane Carter	Book 1,	27
1825, Jul. 28	PARKER,	SARAH	Married Thomas Lee	Book 1,	242
1844, Aug. 19	PARKER,	SARAH J.	Married Elijah Parker	Book 1,	257
1857, Nov. 26	PARKER,	SARAH	Married John Henry Huckstep	Book 1,	5
1868, Dec. 16	PARKER,	SARAH E.	Married Edward Powers	Book 1,	21
1831, Sep. 17	PARKER,	SUSAN	Married Silas B. Gouldman	Book 1,	248
1835,	PARKER,	SUSAN	Daughter of Alexander, married Silas Goulding	D 44,	473
1866, Jun. 7	PARKER,	SUSAN E.	Married John R. Shearwood	Book 1,	15
1694,	PARKER,	THOMAS	Married Francelia, Exec. of Joseph Goodrich	O 1,	190
1807, Jun. 10	PARKER,	THOMAS	Married Ann Pilkington	Book 1,	224
1831, Apr. 19	PARKER,	THOMAS	Married Susan R. Rennolds	Book 1,	248
1853, Oct. 6	PARKER,	VIRGINIA	Married John Coghill, Jr.	Book 1,	1
1879, Nov. 26	PARKER,	VIRGINIA	Daughter of Nathan, married Bennett Tuck	Book 1,	53

				Book	Page
1881, Nov. 22	PARKER,	WALLER J.	Married Nannie T. Broaddus	Book 1,	61
1793,	PARKER,	WILLIAM	Married Sally, daughter of Thomas Gouldman	W 15,	313
1810, Jul. 19	PARKHILL,	JOHN	Married Eleanor W. Quarles	Book 1,	226
1810,	PARKHILL,	JOHN	Married Eleanor, daughter of Henry Quarles	W 17,	244
1890, Jul. 30	PARKS,	W. W.	Maryland, married Mary F. Jenkins	Book 1,	109
1887, Nov. 23	PARR,	ADDIE L.	Married William G. Davis	Book 1,	92
1886, Dec. 29	PARR,	GEORGE R.	Married Fanny Ida Brooks	Book 1,	90
1700,	PARR,	JUDITH	Relict of Philip, married James Edmondson	D&W 10,	70
1898, Jun. 8	PARR,	M. K.	Married J. H Dillard	Book 1,	129
1889, Jan. 18	PARR,	NANNIE B.	Married William M. Doggins	Book 1,	99
1884, Mar. 20	PARR,	P. T.	Married Linie Fisher	Book 1,	76
1889, Mar. 7	PARRON,	EMMA	Married James H. Good	Book 1,	99
1870, Dec. 22	PARRON,	HENRY T.	Middlesex Co., married Martha J. Saunders	Book 1,	26
1835, Jul. 30	PARRON,	JOHN H.	Married Virginia V. Cauthorn	Book 1,	251
1875, Jun. 9	PARRON,	JOSEPH C.	Middlesex Co., married Mrs. Emma Derieux Skipwith	Book 1,	39
1893, Sep. 12	PARRON,	S. C.	Married H. L. Carlton	Book 1,	112
1835, Dec. 8	PARRON,	THOMAS	Married Julia D. Dunn	Book 1,	251
1843,	PARRON,	THOMAS	Married Julia, daughter of James Dunn	W 24,	49
1826, Jan. 17	PARRY,	YTHEL	Married Catharine M. Cauthorn	Book 1,	246
1886, Jun. 29	PARSONS,	GRACE E.	Married W. T. Wills, Washington, D. C.	Book 1,	88
1890, Nov. 23	PARSONS,	M. E.	Married B. F. Atkins	Book 1,	104
1865, Feb. 21	PASSAGALUPPI, JOAN		Married Ann Crow	Book 1,	13
1889, Sep. 22	PASSAGALUPPI, JOAN		Married Nancy Griffin	Book 1,	101
1895, May 22	PASSAGALUPPI, W. R.		Married Sallie A. Atkins	Book 1,	118
1749,	PATTEN,	URSULA	Married John Evans	D 27,	403
1880, Dec. 30	PATTERSON, CHARLES		Married Mary Brooks	Book 1,	58
1808, May 16	PATTERSON, NANCY		Married Thomas Cauthorn	Book 1,	224
1799,	PATTERSON, POLLY		Daughter of John, married Andrew Johnson	D 35,	261
1898, Sep. 15	PATTERSON, R. E.		Married Joseph A. Minor	Book 1,	135
1878, Jan. 6	PATTERSON, SALLY		Married William R. Lee	Book 1,	47
1680,	PAVIE,	WALTER	Married Mary, daughter of Richard Webly	D 6,	169

				Book	Page
1841, Dec. 11	PAYNE,	LEROY L.	Married Caroline A. McCulloch	Book 1,	255
1668,	PAYNE,	ROBERT	Married Elizabeth, daughter of Epaphroditus Lawson	D 3,	407
1690,	PAYNE,	ROBERT	Married Elizabeth, daughter of Epaphroditus Lawson	O 2,	271
1808,	PAYTON,	JOHN	Married Mary Weeks	O 39,	337
1812,	PEACHEY,	CATHARINE	Married Josiah Ryland	O 41,	100
1803,	PEACHEY,	ELIZABETH	Married James Pendleton	W 16,	205
1803,	PEACHEY,	JANE	Sister of William, married Major Thomas Armistead	W 16,	205
1664,	PECK,	JOHN	Married Jane, daughter of Richard King	D 3,	443
1885, Nov. 3	PENDLETON,	AGNES ROY	Married Edward Christian	Book 1,	84
1834, Apr. 7	PENDLETON,	JOSEPH H.	Married Sarah M. Hundley	Book 1,	250
1742,	PENDLETON,	MARY	Widow of Henry, married Edward Watkins	D 22,	407
1742,	PENDLETON,	NATHANIEL	Married Elizabeth, Admrx. of Joseph Anderson	O 13,	254
1810, Oct. 16	PENDLETON,	P. BAYLOR	Married Polly Wood	Book 1,	226
1858, Jul. 15	PENDLETON,	ROBERT L.	Married Christian G. Micou	Book 1,	6
1830, Jul. 5	PERKINS,	MARY	Married Edwin Lumpkin	Book 1,	247
1863, Sep. 15	PERKS,	JOHN L.	Caroline Co., married Maria A. Good	Book 1,	12
1819, May 21	PERRY,	BENJAMIN	Married Ann Day	Book 1,	236
1857, Nov. 28	PERRY,	CORNELIA E.	Married Andrew Wright	Book 1,	5
1693,	PERRY,	ROGER	Married Judith, relict of David Faulkner	O 1,	250
1807, Jan. 19	PERRYMAN,	PHILIP	Married Patsy Purkins, widow	Book 1,	224
1850, Jul. 2	PETERS,	CATHARINE	Married Richard J. Mahon	Book 1,	262
1842, Jun. 30	PETERS,	CHRISTIAN	Married Catharine Faulconer	Book 1,	256
1707,	PETERS,	MARY	Married Mathew Collins	D&C 13,	82
1710,	PETERS,	MARY	Married William Gannocke	D&C 13,	322
1893, Jul. 23	PETERSON,	EFFIE	Married M. B. Byrd	Book 1,	11
1701,	PETERSON,	MARY	Daughter of Neale & Elinor Peterson, married Thomas Covington	D&W 10,	94
1675,	PETTIT,	DOROTHY	Daughter of Thomas, married James Fugett	D 5,	48
1711,	PETTIT,	DOROTHY	Daughter of Thomas, married Godfrey Stanton	Land Trials, 2	
1721,	PETTIT,	GEORGE	Married widow of Robert Foster	D 17,	2
1721,	PETTIT,	RACHEL	Married Thomas Dimack	O 5,	63

				Book	Page
1685,	PETTUS,	CATHARINE	Sister of Thomas, married Capt. John ? Long	D 7,	179
1834, Jan. 8	PHILLIPS,	ELIZABETH	Married James H. Powers	Book 1,	250
1814, Jul. 17	PHILLIPS,	FRANCES	Married Thomas Hundley	Book 1,	231
1842, Jan. 17	PHILLIPS,	GEORGE W.	Married Susan E. Clarkson	Book 1,	256
1827, May 30	PHILLIPS,	JAMES	Married Judith Brizendine	Book 1,	244
1877, Feb. 1	PHILLIPS,	JAMES L.	King & Queen Co., married Bettie Dyke	Book 1,	44
1817, Dec. 24	PHILLIPS,	LUCY	Married Charles Lathom	Book 1,	233
1897, Oct. 7	PHILLIPS,	MAE	Married George B. Kriete	Book 1,	126
1868, May 5	PHILLIPS,	MARIETTA	Married Thomas G. McGeorge	Book 1,	20
1783,	PHILLIPS,	RICHARD	Married Katherine Newbill (Contract)	D 32,	190
1812, Jan. 15	PHILLIPS,	RICHARD	Married Elizabeth Mitchell	Book 1,	228
1819, Jan. 18	PHILLIPS,	SARAH	Married Caleb Elliott	Book 1,	235
1703,	PHILLIPS,	THOMAS	Married Ann, relict of Charles Atkinson	D&W 11,	94
1712,	PHILLIPS,	THOMAS	Married Ann Copeland	W 3,	139
1756,	PHITZSIMMONS, ELEANOR		Daughter of Mary, married Joseph George	W 10,	95
1756,	PHITZSIMMONS, FRANCES		Daughter of Mary, married William Meader	W 10,	95
1756,	PHITZSIMMONS, MARY		Daughter of Mary, married ? Faulconer	W 10,	95
1721,	PICKETT,	BLESSING	Daughter of John, married Richard Sanders	Box 105,	B
1675,	PICKETT,	BRIDGETT	Mother of Thomas Pickett	D 7,	402
1702,	PICKETT,	ELIZABETH	Relict of Henry, married William Johnson	D&W 10,	127
1700,	PICKETT,	HANNAH	Married Thomas Spencer	D&W 10,	62
1713,	PICKETT,	SARAH	Married James Fullerton	D&C 13,	245
1881, Jun. 2	PIERCE,	JOHN O.	James City Co., married Octavia Pitts	Book 1,	60
1704,	PIERCE,	SARAH	Relict of John, married Henry Goswell	D&C 12,	26
1833, Mar. 2	PIGGOT,	FIELDING D.	Married Eliza Trible	Book 1,	249
1746,	PILES,	SAMUEL	Married Ann, relict of Richard Williams	D 24,	52
1723,	PILE,	VINCENT G.	Married Rebecca, sister of Henry Harway	D 17,	193
1843, Jun. 21	PILCHER,	S. A. L.	Married Henry E. Sizer	Book 1,	257
1812, Jan. 15	PILCHER,	THOMAS	Married Elizabeth Bray	Book 1,	228
1807, Jun. 10	PILKINGTON, ANN		Married Thomas Parker	Book 1,	224
1826, May 20	PILKINGTON, EDMUND		Married Arabella Dishman	Book 1,	242

Date	Name	Detail	Book	Page
1865, Nov. 28	PILKINGTON, MARGARET	Married William W. Kay	Book 1,	13
1811, Dec. 9	PILKINGTON, MARY	Married John Gray	Book 1,	227
1866, Dec. 13	PILKINGTON, MARY S.	Married William T. Gouldman	Book 1,	15
1838,	PILKINGTON, POLLY	Daughter of Parmenas, married John Gray	D 46,	78
1867, Jan. 17	PILKINGTON, SAMUEL W.	Married Margaret E. Gouldman	Book 1,	16
1888, Oct. 9	PILKINGTON, VIRGINIA B.	Married William A. Browne	Book 1,	96
1680,	PINKHORN, ANN	Only daughter & heir of John Pinkhorn of James City Co., married William Price	D 6,	128
1878, Feb. 14	PITTS, ANDREW	King & Queen Co., married Martha Ellen Taylor	Book 1,	48
1822, Feb. 12	PITTS, ANN	Married Stephen D. Pitts	Book 1,	239
1853, Dec. 27	PITTS, ANN M.	Married Leonard D. Thomas	Book 1,	1
1826, May 15	PITTS, AUGUSTA	Married William Trice	Book 1,	242
1825, Mar. 27	PITTS, BENJAMIN	Married Catharine Banks	Book 1,	242
1812, May 12	PITTS, CATHARINE	Married Lewis Brown	Book 1,	228
1849, Jan. 4	PITTS, CLARA H.	Married Albert Griffin	Book 1,	261
1820, Apr. 17	PITTS, DAVID	Married Laura Sale	Book 1,	237
1829, Dec. 21	PITTS, EMILY	Married Richard Marshall	Book 1,	246
1855, Sep. 19	PITTS, EMILY A.	Married Edmund J. Foster	Book 1,	3
1822, Feb. 7	PITTS, ELI	Married Harriet Pitts	Book 1,	239
1851, Sep. 18	PITTS, ELIZABETH	Married James A. Dunn	Book 1,	262
1822, Feb. 7	PITTS, HARRIET	Married Eli Pitts	Book 1,	239
1849, Feb. 21	PITTS, JOHN H.	Married Sarah A. Ellis	Book 1,	261
1830, Apr. 19	PITTS, LARKIN	Married Patty Ingram	Book 1,	247
1817, Jun. 12	PITTS, LEMUEL	Married Ann Maria Hill	Book 1,	233
1803,	PITTS, LEVI	Married Elizabeth, daughter of Joseph Fogg	W 16,	220
1838, Jun. 28	PITTS, LUCINDA A.	Married Thomas Shearwood	Book 1,	253
1823, Feb. 24	PITTS, LUCY	Married James Halbert Jr.	Book 1,	240
1806,	PITTS, MARGARET	Daughter of Thomas, married Spencer Harrison	W 16,	437
1818,	PITTS, MARGARET	Daughter of Thomas, married Spencer Harrison	W 18,	476
1859, Dec. 30	PITTS, MARIA L.	Married Bennett Tuck Jr.	Book 1,	8
1867, Mar. 24	PITTS, MARINDA	Married William Jones	Book 1,	17
1821, Dec. 14	PITTS, MARTHA	Married William Pitts	Book 1,	238

Date	Surname	Name	Description	Book	Page
1824, Aug. 2	PITTS,	MARY E.	Married David Wright	Book 1,	241
1884, Mar. 27	PITTS,	MARY M.	Married John W. Moore	Book 1,	76
1792,	PITTS,	MOLLY	Daughter of David, married Edward Wright	W 15,	61
1877, Feb. 1	PITTS,	NORBORNE JR.	Married Ida E. Coghill	Book 1,	44
1881, Jun. 2	PITTS,	OCTAVIA	Married John O. Pierce of James City Co.	Book 1,	66
1805, Sep. 16	PITTS,	PHILIP	Married Lucy Andrews	Book 1,	223
1816, Oct. 23	PITTS,	POLLY	Married John Coghill	Book 1,	233
1822, Nov. 13	PITTS,	REUBEN	Married Keturah Jones	Book 1,	239
1848, Jan. 19	PITTS,	REUBEN	Married Haword Smither	Book 1,	260
1865, Jul. 27	PITTS,	RICHARD	Married Alice Vawter	Book 1,	13
1806,	PITTS,	ROSE	Daughter of Thomas, married Thomas Coghill	W 16,	436
1814, Dec. 20	PITTS,	SARAH I.	Married George Ellis	Book 1,	230
1857, Dec. 21	PITTS,	SARA A.	Married William A. Greenwood	Book 1,	267
1882, Mar. 26	PITTS,	SARAH J.	Married William A. Sale	Book 1,	64
1800,	PITTS,	SALLY	Married Joseph Gatewood	O 35,	403
1800,	PITTS,	SALLY	Admrx. of Reuben, married Joseph Gatewood	W 16,	7
1801,	PITTS,	SALLY	Daughter of Daniel, married Stephen Johnson, of Spottsylvania Co.	D 35,	508
1884, Jan. 17	PITTS,	SEBINA	Married Thomas Allen	Book 1,	75
1822, Feb. 7	PITTS,	STEPHEN D.	Married Ann Pitts	Book 1,	239
1792,	PITTS,	THOMAS	Married Ann, daughter of John Richardson	D 33,	424
1817,	PITTS,	THOMAS D.	Married Mary Gray, granddaughter of John Spindle	D 39,	384
1813, Feb. 4	PITTS,	THOMAS H.	Married Frances Lambeth	Book 1,	229
1838, Jun. 18	PITTS,	VENELIA HELEN	Married Burkett G. Rennolds	Book 1,	253
1821, Dec. 14	PITTS,	WILLIAM	Married Martha Pitts	Book 1,	238
1756, May 20	PITTS,	WILLIAM	Married Ann, daughter of Mary Boulware	D 28,	106
1806,	PITTS,	WILLIAM	Married Sally, daughter of William Ingram	O 38,	426
1883, Jan. 25	PITTS,	WILLIS A.	Married Columbia McGowan, widow	Book 1,	69
1698,	PLEY,	ANN	Daughter of Elizabeth, married Thomas Winslow	D 9,	223
1792,	PLUMMER,	THOMAS	Married Polly, daughter of Lillian Webb	W 14,	321
1774,	PLUNKETT,	WILLIAM	Married daughter of Thomas Thorpe	W 12,	591
1828, Mar. 15	POLLARD,	ELIZABETH	Married Elliott A. Vawter	Book 1,	245

				Book	Page
1841,	POLLARD,	GEORGE	Married Joanna Mitchell, widow	D 47,	126
1874, Sep. 30	POLLARD,	GEORGE R.	Married Maria L. Spindle	Book 1,	37
1693,	POOLE,	JOHN	Married Margaret, relict of Richard Holt	O 1,	165
1759,	PORTER,	WILLIAM	Married Elizabeth, daughter of Henry Reeves deceased	O 23,	190
1770,	PORTER,	WILLIAM	Married Elizabeth, daughter of Henry Reeves	D 30,	371
1890, Nov. 19	POTTER,	JOHN B.	King & Queen Co. married Rosetta Lee	Book 1,	104
1876, Apr. 26	POTTER,	REUBEN	Alabama, married Mrs. Betty Mason	Book 1,	41
1886, Jun. 15	POTTS,	REGINALD H.	Minister of Lancaster Co. married Sarah H. Cammack	Book 1,	87
1700,	POWELL,	ANN	Daughter of Thomas, married Edward Coffey	D& W 10,	75
1699,	POWELL,	JANE	Exec. of John, married Thomas Burnett	D& W 10,	14
1689,	POWELL,	JOHN	Married Michall, daughter of Hezekiah Turner	O 2,	155
1690,	POWELL,	JOHN	Married Margaret, daughter of James Cogwell	O 2,	253
1694,	POWELL,	JOHN	Married Margaret, daughter of James Coghill	O 1,	242
1723,	POWELL,	THOMAS	Married Mary, daughter of William Gibson	D 17,	159
1847, Dec. 20	POWERS,	CATHARINE	Married George H. Van Ness	Book 1,	260
1834, Dec. 15	POWERS,	EDWARD	Married Susan M. Browne	Book 1,	250
1835,	POWERS,	EDWARD	Married Susan Brown	D 45,	19
1868, Dec. 16	POWERS,	EDWARD	Married Sarah E. Parker	Book 1,	21
1861, Nov. 8	POWERS,	ELIZA	Married Richard Hunter of Westmoreland Co.	Book 1,	11
1899, Jun. 7	POWERS,	IDA S.	Married P. C. Courtney	Book 1,	133
1825, May 21	POWERS,	JAMES	Married Matilda Browne	Book 1,	242
1834, Jan. 8	POWERS,	JAMES H.	Married Elizabeth Phillips	Book 1,	250
1834, Jun. 2	POWERS,	JAMES	Married Susan S. Rouzie	Book 1,	250
1867, Dec. 10	POWERS,	JAMES L.	Married Cornelia E. Munday	Book 1,	1
1875, Oct. 27	POWERS,	JENETTE M.	Married Charles Hall	Book 1,	3
1854, Jan. 10	POWERS,	JOANNA S.	Widow, married Thomas L. DeShazo	Book 1,	
1894, Jun. 27	POWERS,	KATE E.	Married W. D. Saunders	Book 1,	11
1857, Mar. 19	POWERS,	LUCY ANN	Married Leonard Munday	Book 1,	
1856, Oct. 23	POWERS,	MARY SUSAN	Married Robert J. Moody	Book 1,	
1857, Oct. 22	POWERS,	MATILDA	Married Thomas Montgomery	Book 1,	
1872, Mar. 29	POWERS,	WILLIE A.	Married Thomas Montgomery	Book 1,	3

				Book	Page
1899, Dec. 20	POWERS,	W. B.	Married A. B. Rouse	Book 1,	135
1863, Jan. 7	PRATT,	ROBERT H.	Dentist of King George Co. married Alice E. Munday	Book 1,	11
1868, Feb. 13	PRESTON,	SAMUEL T.	Richmond City, married Susan M. Muse	Book 1,	20
1853, Sep. 13	PRICE,	GEORGE W.	Married Eliza A. Carter	Book 1,	264
1711,	PRICE,	EDWARD	Married Catharine, widow of John Waters	D&W 14, O 4,	32 495
1690,	PRICE,	JOHN	Married Easter, daughter of Col. John Walker	D 8,	315
1771,	PRICE,	KATHARINE	Daughter of John, married Stark Boulware	W 12,	448
1726,	PRICE,	SUSANNA	Relict of Richard, married Joseph Reeves	O 7,	134
1808, Aug. 24	PRICE,	THOMAS	Married Sally Noel	Book 1,	225
1680,	PRICE,	WILLIAM	Married Ann Pinkhorn, only child of John of James City Co.	D 6,	128
1720,	PRICHARD,	ELIZABETH	Daughter of Roger, married Thomas Field	W 3,	252
1721,	PRICHARD,	MARY	Daughter of Roger, married William Fletcher	Box 105,	B
1824, Aug. 30	PRIDDY,	DELILAH	Married Reuben McDaniel	Book 1,	241
1804,	PRIDDY,	?	Hanover Co., married Betsey, daughter of Edmund Noel	W 17,	88
1685,	PRIDUM,	BRIDGETT	Widow of Christopher, married Lewis Richards	D 6,	48
1678,	PRIDUM,	CHRISTOPHER	Married Bridgett, daughter of Capt. George Bryer	D 6,	70
1883, Apr. 18	PRINCE,	FANNY C.	Married James R. Davis	Book 1,	71
1844, Dec. 23	PRINCE,	JANE	Married James H. Davis	Book 1,	257
1846, May 5	PRINCE,	JOHN C.	Married Larry Brizendine	Book 1,	259
1856, Sep. 10	PRINCE,	JOHN C.	King & Queen Co., married Lucy Cook, widow	Book 1,	4
1870, Dec. 29	PRINCE,	JOHN H.	Married Lucy C. Crafton	Book 1,	27
1855, Jun. 18	PRINCE,	MARGARET A.	Married Benjamin Tucker	Book 1,	266
1889, Dec. 31	PRINCE,	MARIA	Married James H. Davis	Book 1,	102
1843, Mar. 8	PRINCE,	MARTHA	Married James Clarke	Book 1,	256
1884, Feb. 19	PRINCE,	MARY J.	Married George H. Tate	Book 1,	75
1894, Dec. 26	PRINCE,	ROSA E.	Married W. M. Greenstreet	Book 1,	116
1870, Dec. 22	PRINCE	TRAVIS	Married Susan M. Brooks	Book 1,	27
1693,	PROCTOR,	GEORGE	Married Katherine Frank (License)	O 1,	236
1710,	PROSSER,	ROGER	Married Katherine Ross	O 4,	264
1816, Mar. 27	PRUETT,	ELIZABETH D.	Married Nathan Fletcher	Book 1,	232
1835, Jan. 20	PRUITT,	ELIZABETH	Married John Byrd	Book 1,	251

				Book	Page
1827, Dec. 7	PRUITT,	FRANCES	Married Richard Harper	Book 1,	243
1830, Sep. 21	PRUETT,	JAMSON	Married Arthur Fletcher	Book 1,	247
1827, Dec. 4	PRUETT,	JONAH	Married Eliza Croxton	Book 1,	244
1863, Dec. 30	PRUETT,	SARAH E.	Married James S. Doggins	Book 1,	41
1829,	PURKINS,	CARY	Daughter of Thomas, married Thomas L. Dunn	D 42,	594
1824, Jun. 14	PURKINS,	CATHARINE	Married Boswell Goodwyn	Book 1,	241
1764,	PURKINS,	ELIZABETH	Married John Read, Culpeper Co.	D 29,	348
1804, May 8	PURKINS,	ELIZABETH	Married Mace Clements	Book 1,	222
1816, Aug. 7	PURKINS,	ELIZABETH	Married William Emmerson	Book 1,	232
1720,	PURKINS,	HENRY	Married Cary Caston	D 29,	348
1805, Jul. 15	PURKINS,	JESSE	Married Maria Stevens	Book 1,	223
1827, Jan. 3	PURKINS,	JOHN T.	Married Alice Cauthorn	Book 1,	244
1828,	PURKINS,	JOHN T.	Married Alice, daughter of John Cauthorne	D 43,	255
1833, Oct. 7	PURKINS,	MARY S.	Married Leonard Henley	Book 1,	249
1807, Jan. 19	PURKINS,	PATSY	Married Philip Perryman	Book 1,	224
1820,	PURKINS,	SARAH	Married John Armstrong	D 40,	145
1827, Dec. 15	PURKINS,	SARAH	Married John H. Collins	Book 1,	243
1805, Feb. 8	PURKINS,	SUSAN	Married Ewin Clements	Book 1,	222
1820, Dec. 9	PURKINS,	SUSANNA	Married Richard Lumpkin	Book 1,	237
1813, Dec. 7	PURKINS,	WASHINGTON	Married Nancy Howerton	Book 1,	229
1859, Dec. 21	PURKINS,	WILLIAM G.	Stafford Co., married Cornelia, daughter of Carter Croxton	Book 1,	8
1833, Jan. 3	PURKS,	JOHN	Married Rebecca Taylor	Book 1,	249
1805, Nov. 28	PURKS,	SAMUEL	Married Ann Mocomack	Book 1,	223
1698,	PUTLEY,	MARY	Daughter of Nicholas, married Edward Jeffreys	D 9,	314
1848, Mar. 21	PYNE,	CATHARINE R.	Married Henry Jackson Dyke	Book 1,	260

1810,	QUARLES,	ANN	Daughter of Henry, married Foushee Tebbs	W 17,	243
1810, Jul. 19	QUARLES,	ELEANOR	Married John Parkhill	Book 1,	226
1810,	QUARLES,	ELEANOR	Daughter of Henry, married John Parkhill	W 17,	244
1802,	QUARLES,	FRANCIS	Married Lucy, daughter of Meriwether Smith	D 36,	271
1867, May 11	QUARLES,	SUSAN ANN	Married Addison Coles	Book 1,	17
1810,	QUARLES,	SUSANNA	Daughter of Henry, married George Dabney Esq.	W 17,	243
1833, Mar. 14	QUESENBERRY, JOHN		Married Lucy Ann Dickenson	Book 1,	249
1835,	QUESENBERRY, JOHN		Married Lucy A. Dickenson daughter of William	D 45,	130
1888, Dec. 13	QUESENBERRY, SAMUEL		Married Bettie G. Smither	Book 1,	97
1849, Sep. 20	QUESENBERRY, WILLIAM		Married Mary E. Southall	Book 1,	261

R

				Book	Page
1846, Feb. 4	RADFORD,	JAMES B.	Married Lucy Ann Atkinson	Book 1,	251
1835,	RAE,	ALEXANDER	Married July Ann Johnson	D 45,	68
1808,	RAMSEY,	HENRY	Married Tabitha Connoly	O 39,	377
1836, Jan. 30	RAMSEY,	LUCY A.	Married Thomas H. Simcoe	Book 1,	252
1737,	RAMSEY,	LADY SUSANNA	London, married John Rennolds	D 42,	97
1808, Jul. 18	RAMSEY,	VINCENT	Married Martha Boughton	Book 1,	224
1790,	RANDOLPH,	BRETT	Married Lucy, daughter of Robert Beverley of Blandfield	D 33,	270
1886, Nov. 17	RANSONE,	ARMISTEAD	Married Bessie C. Saunders	Book 1,	89
1699,	RANSONE,	PETER	Married Dorothy, widow of Richard Awbrey	D&W 10,	16
1714,	RANSONE,	ROBERT	Married Frances, relict of Robert Bird	O 4,	586
1820, Mar. 29	RAW,	THOMAS	Married Elizabeth Emerson	Book 1,	224
1804,	READ,	EDMUND	Middlesex Co., married Lucy Clondas	D 36,	407
1690,	READ,	EDWARD	Married relict of Thomas George	O 2,	220
1764,	READ,	JOHN	Culpeper Co., married Elizabeth coheir of Griffing Purkins	D 29,	348
1866, Dec. 18	READ,	LUCY	Married James Durham	Book 1,	16
1685,	READING,	ROBERT	Married Mary, relict of Henry Moncaster	O 1,	150
1735,	REDD,	THOMAS	Married Sarah Farguson	W 5,	386
1899, Jun. 7	REAMY,	EMMA L.	Married Charles H. King	Book 1,	133
1895, Jan. 9	REAMY,	F. J.	Married Rosa E. Rennolds	Book 1,	116
1845, Feb. 10	REAVES,	ELLEN	Married Humphrey Fortune	Book 1,	258
1832, May 21	REAVES,	VIRGINIA	Married Spencer Saunders	Book 1,	249
1868, Dec. 31	REED,	VIRGINIA	Married Joseph N. Wiltshire	Book 1,	21
1859, Dec. 24	REED,	WILLIAM H.	Married Mary C. Lumpkin	Book 1,	8
1851, Dec. 23	REESE,	STERLING	Married Mary L. Rodgers	Book 1,	253
1711,	REEVES,	ANN	Married Edward Coleman	O 4,	427
1738,	REEVES,	ELIZABETH	Daughter of Henry, married John Allen	O 11, O 12,	47 97
1759,	REEVES,	ELIZABETH	Daughter of Henry, married William Porter	O 23,	190
1770,	REEVES,	ELIZABETH	Daughter of Henry, married William Porter	D 30,	371
1685,	REEVES,	HENRY	Daughter married Israel Johnson	O 1,	111
1726,	REEVES,	JOSEPH	Married Susanna, relict of Richard Price	O 7,	134

Date	Surname	Given Name	Description	Book	Page
1711,	REEVES,	MARTHA	Married Robert Moss	O 4,	427
1707,	REEVES,	MARY	Relict of James, married Thomas Munday	D&C 13,	35
1830, May 21	REEVES,	NELLY	Married Carter Sanders	Book 1,	247
1889, Mar. 26	REEVES,	WILLIAM L.	Married Fannie C. Davis	Book 1,	100
1874, Apr. 15	REID,	EMMA F.	Married Fontaine W. Crouch	Book 1,	17
1876, Dec. 21	REID,	MATTIE B.	Married Charles W. Basket	Book 1,	43
1877, Nov. 15	REID,	NANNIE	Married Leroy Taylor	Book 1,	46
1870, Dec. 29	REID,	SARAH T.	Married James A. Cridlin	Book 1,	27
1855, Apr. 5	REINICKER,	CHARLES H.	Married Emeline F. Watts	Book 1,	3
1804, Dec. 17	RENNO,	JOHN	Married Barbary Crow	Book 1,	222
1867, Nov. 14	RENNOLDS,	ALBERT	Married Hannah C. Trible	Book 1,	18
1780,	RENNOLDS,	ANN	Daughter of Robert, married Reuben Chapman	W 13,	338
1838, Jun. 18	RENNOLDS,	BURKETT G.	Married Venelia Helen Pitts	Book 1,	253
1802,	RENNOLDS,	CATHARINE	Daughter of James, married Thomas Hawkins	O 37,	220
1807, Dec. 23	RENNOLDS,	CATHARINE	Married Joseph Norment	Book 1,	224
1818, Jun. 15	RENNOLDS,	DANIEL	Married Frances Spindle	Book 1,	234
1822,	RENNOLDS,	DANIEL	Married Frances, daughter of Barbee Spindle	O 44,	96
1753,	RENNOLDS,	ELIZABETH	Daughter of Martha, married Thomas Rucker	W 9,	246
1866, Apr. 10	RENNOLDS,	ELIZABETH	Married Henry S. Rouzie	Book 1,	14
1886, Dec. 3	RENNOLDS,	ELLWOOD	King & Queen Co., married Eugenia A. Mundie	Book 1,	89
1867, Dec. 23	RENNOLDS,	HELEN A.	Married William Rennolds	Book 1,	19
1897,	RENNOLDS,	HELEN A.	Married C. Miner of Westmoreland County	D 58,	355
1811,	RENNOLDS,	JAMES	St. Ann's Parish, married Martha, daughter of Ann Gray, Grandaughter of John Spindle	D 39,	9
1842, Nov. 21	RENNOLDS,	J. A.	Married James Spindle	Book 1,	256
1765,	RENNOLDS,	JOHN	Married Elizabeth, widow of Nicholas Lafon	O 26,	40
1821,	RENNOLDS,	JOHN	London, married Lady Susanna Ramsey	D 42,	97
1849, Aug. 4	RENNOLDS,	JOHN S.	Married Jane S. Falkner	Book 1,	261
1834, Nov. 26	RENNOLDS,	LOUISA	Married Robert G. Rouzie	Book 1,	250
1870, Dec. 27	RENNOLDS,	LUCY	Married Nelson Jordan	Book 1,	27
1806, Mar. 25	RENNOLDS,	MARGARET	Married David Dishman	Book 1,	223

				Book	Page
1737,	RENNOLDS,	MARY	Relict of Thomas, married Robert French	O 10,	187
1802,	RENNOLDS,	MARY	Daughter of John, married John Miller	O 37,	220
1876, Aug. 1	RENNOLDS,	MARY S.	Married Robert L. Parker	Book 1,	42
1816, Dec. 20	RENNOLDS,	NANCY	Married James Halbert	Book 1,	232
1838, Jun. 18	RENNOLDS,	OTWAY	Married Malvina Cason	Book 1,	253
1813, Jan. 12	RENNOLDS,	PHILIP	Married Sidney Rennolds	Book 1,	229
1802,	RENNOLDS,	RICHARD	Married Sally, daughter of John Rennolds	O 37,	220
1895, Jan. 9	RENNOLDS,	ROSA E.	Married F. J. Reamy	Book 1,	116
1802,	RENNOLDS,	SALLY	Daughter of John, married Richard Rennolds	O 37,	220
1824, Jun. 3	RENNOLDS,	SARAH A.	Married Samuel Coleman	Book 1,	241
1813, Jan. 12	RENNOLDS,	SIDNEY	Married Philip Rennolds	Book 1,	229
1817,	RENNOLDS,	STHRESHLEY	His niece Alice, married Newton Berryman, Westmoreland, Co.	D 39,	416
1831, Apr. 19	RENNOLDS,	SUSAN R.	Married Thomas Parker	Book 1,	248
1727,	RENNOLDS,	VIOLETTA	Daughter of James, married John Retterford Jr.	O 7,	219
1894, Jan. 11	RENNOLDS,	V. H.	Married W. C. Minor	Book 1,	113
1867, Dec. 23	RENNOLDS,	WILLIAM	Married Helen Adelaide Rennolds	Book 1,	19
1868, May 7	RENNOLDS,	WILLIAMINA	Married William H. Williams	Book 1,	20
1727,	RETTERFORD, JOHN JR.		Married Violetta, daughter of James Rennolds	O 7,	219
1873, Jul. 2	REVERE,	PETER	Middlesex Co., married Mary E. Atkins	Book 1,	34
1806, Nov. 17	RIAN,	SOLOMON	Married Elizabeth Daily	Book 1,	223
1824, Oct. 20	RIDDLE,	PATSEY	Married Sthreshley Taylor	Book 1,	24
1680,	RICE,	DOMINICK	Married Ann, relict of James Toone	O 1,	147
1821, Jun.	RICE,	EVAN	Married Polly Bray	Book 1,	238
1877, Sep. 13	RICE,	GEORGE W.	Married Nannie I. Hundley, widow	Book 1,	46
1884, Apr. 17	RICE,	GEORGE W.	Married Kate G. Fauntleroy	Book 1,	77
1688,	RICE,	JOHN	Married Executrix of Col. William Travers	O 2,	76
1879, Mar. 26	RICE,	SARAH A,	Married William T. Sadler	Book 1,	5
1855, Sep. 5	RICH,	WILLIAM	Married Lucinda Lewis	Book 1,	22
1814, Mar. 16	RICHARDS,	BETSEY	Married William Young	Book 1,	23
1852, Oct. 4	RICHARDS,	DR. BUCHANAN	Married Mildred C. Bray	Book 1,	26
1832, Oct. 9	RICHARDS,	EDMUND	Married Miranda Johnson	Book 1,	24

					Book	Page
1850, Apr. 30	RICHARDS,	ELIZABETH	Married Richard Fortune		Book 1,	262
1811, Nov. 5	RICHARDS,	FANNY	Married Amos Cauthorn		Book 1,	227
1858, Apr. 15	RICHARDS,	HENRY	Married Martha Ware		Book 1,	7
1836, Dec. 24	RICHARDS,	JOHN	Married Lucinda Grymes		Book 1,	252
1685,	RICHARDS,	LEWIS	Married Bridgett, widow of Christopher Pridum		D 6,	418
1806, Dec. 1	RICHARDS,	LUCY	Married George Bagby		Book 1,	223
1827, Nov. 19	RICHARDS,	PETER	Married Suckey Saunders		Book 1,	247
1815, Dec. 18	RICHARDS,	RICHARD H.	Married Elizabeth Young		Book 1,	231
1792,	RICHARDSON, ANN		Daughter of John, married Thomas Pitts		D 33,	424
1830,	RICHARDSON, MILDRED		Married Bernard Lambeth		D 43,	320
1856, Jan. 23	RICHARDSON, ROBERT G.		Married Frances Clarke		Book 1,	3
1871, Apr. 25	RICHARDSON, SYLVESTER		New Kent Co., married D. Lena Haynes		Book 1,	28
1708,	RICHARDSON, THOMAS		Married Mary, widow of William Clapham		O 3,	408
1858, Nov. 22	RICHARDSON, THOMAS H.		Married Virginia A. Sale		Book 1,	8
1866, Feb. 13	RICHARDSON, WILLIAM P.		Married Janet Durham		Book 1,	14
1834, Dec. 26	RICHESON,	DELIA	Married Reuben E. McDaniel		Book 1,	250
1805, Dec. 18	RICHERSON,	JOHN	Married Eunice, daughter of Edward Noel		Book 1,	223
1858, Nov. 25	RICHERSON,	THOMAS H.	Married Virginia Sale		Book 1,	8
1898, Feb. 20	RILEY,	L. B.	Maryland, married K. L. Johnson		Book 1,	189
1828, Jan. 7	RITCHIE,	ARCHIBALD	Married Sarah Spindle		Book 1,	245
1872, Dec. 15	RITCHIE,	FANNY	Married Thomas Latane		Book 1,	32
1816, Mar. 25	RITCHIE,	JANET R.	Married Richard Rouzie		Book 1,	232
1803,	RITCHIE,	MARGARET	Daughter of Mary, sister of Thomas & Archibald, married William Ruffin		W 16,	228
1827, May 23	RITCHIE,	MARY JULIET	Married Jones C. Clopton		Book 1,	243
1833,	RITCHIE,	MARY JULIET	Daughter of Archibald, married Jones C. Clopton		W 23,	245
1841, Nov. 3	RITCHIE,	SALLY JANE	Married John Bird		Book 1,	255
1688,	ROADS,	RICHARD	Married Elizabeth, daughter of John Bates		O 2,	115
1800,	ROANE,	ANN	Widow of William, married Thomas Gibbons, Mathews Co.		D 35,	290
1817, Mar. 24	ROANE,	CATHARINE	Married Archibald Ruffin		Book 1,	232
1813,	ROANE,	JOHN	Married Elizabeth, daughter of Newman Brockenbrough		W 18,	258
1828, Mar. 31	ROANE,	LAWRENCE	Married Sarah Ann Jones		Book 1,	245

1864, Dec. 13	ROANE,	LAWRENCE D.	Married Josephine R. Smith	Book 1,	12
1888, Nov. 14	ROANE,	LULA B.	Married Maxwell C. Gaines	Book 1,	96
1871, Nov. 16	ROANE,	MARIA L.	Married Booker Garnett	Book 1,	29
1876, Dec. 28	ROANE,	ROSALIE	Married Anderson Commodore	Book 1,	43
1782,	ROANE,	WILLIAM	Married Ann Cook, Gloucester County	D 32,	144
1825, Sep. 19	ROBB,	ELIZA S.	Married Robert P. Waring	Book 1,	242
1770,	ROBB,	JAMES	Married Lucy, daughter of Francis Waring	W 12,	432
1832, Nov. 5	ROBB,	MARGARET	Married John M. Baynham	Book 1,	248
1694,	ROBERTS,	ALICE	Daughter of Griffin, married Henry Nichols, Middlesex Co.	O 1,	314
1684,	ROBERTS,	ANN	Relict of Thomas, married Thomas Gillett	O 1,	56
1727,	ROBERTS,	ELINOR	Relict of John, married James Robinson	O 7,	207
1714,	ROBEY,	MARGARET	Middlesex Co., married William Boulter of Great Britain	D& W 14,	351
1710,	ROBINS,	ANN	Daughter of Alexander, married William Wakelin	D&C 13,	327
1895, Dec. 20	ROBINSON,	ANNA	Married William J. Kent	Book 1,	119
1842, Jan. 22	ROBINSON,	CATHARINE	Married Alexander Taylor	Book 1,	256
1870, Dec. 24	ROBINSON,	ETTA	Married Charles Jackson	Book 1,	27
1772,	ROBINSON,	FRANCIS	Married Sarah, daughter of John Satterwhite	W 13,	258
1816, Dec. 14	ROBINSON,	GREGORY	Married Louisa Hill	Book 1,	232
1894, Nov. 29	ROBINSON,	HARRIET	Married Joseph Coleman	Book 1,	115
1869, Mar. 4	ROBINSON,	HENRY H.	Married Patty L. Gouldman	Book 1,	23
1727,	ROBINSON,	JOHN	Married Elinor, relict of John Roberts	O 7,	207
1743,	ROBINSON,	JOHN	Married Mary, relict of Francis Meriwether	D 23,	169
1863, May 5	ROBINSON,	LOGAN H.	Married Louisa C. Brockenbrough	Book 1,	12
1873, Aug. 26	ROBINSON,	LUCY A.	Married Rev. James Waller Keeble	Book 1,	3
1870, Dec. 24	ROBINSON,	MARY JANE	Married James H. Smith	Book 1,	27
1745,	ROBINSON,	MAXMILIAN	King George Co., married Frances, daughter of Samuel Blomfield	D 23,	247
1853, Apr. 7	ROBINSON,	PHILEMON B.	Physician, married Virginia M. Spindle	Book 1,	264
1677,	ROBINSON,	THOMAS	Relict, married William Thornbury	D 6,	53
1887, Jun. 14	ROBINSON,	W. B.	Physician, married Bettie L. Smith	Book 1,	92
1890, May 22	ROBINSON,	WALLER	Married H. W. Dunn	Book 1,	106

				Book	Page
1704,	ROBINSON,	WILLIAM	Married Frances, only daughter of Samuel Blomfield	D&C 12,	59
1864, Oct. 18	ROBINSON,	W. P.	Married Sallie E. Smith	Book 1,	12
1832, Dec. 17	RODDIN,	BETSEY	Married Elijah Williamson	Book 1,	249
1828, Mar. 31	RODDIN,	ELIZABETH	Married Thomas Brizendine	Book 1,	245
1742,	RODDING,	JOHN	Married Susanna, daughter of John Williamson	W 7,	257
1851, Dec. 23	RODGERS,	MARY L.	Married Sterling Reese	Book 1,	263
1853, Dec. 26	ROGERS,	ELIZABETH	Married Alfred Shackelford	Book 1,	1
1821, Jul. 18	ROGERS,	JOHN	Married Lucy Gordon	Book 1,	238
1823,	ROGERS,	JOHN	Married Lucy, daughter of Alexander & Susanna Gordon	D 41,	83
1825, Mar. 29	ROLLINS,	WILLIAM	Married Betsey Johnson	Book 1,	242
1704,	RORY,	WILLIAM	Married Hannah, widow of John Spicer	O 3,	101
1827, Dec. 22	ROSE,	DICIE	Married Chaney Broach	Book 1,	243
1830, Dec. 21	ROSE,	GEORGE	Married Mira E. Broocke	Book 1,	247
1814, Oct. 19	ROSE,	JENNY	Married William Brooke	Book 1,	230
1721,	ROSE,	JOHN	Married Ann Coughland	O 5,	636
1871, May 18	ROSE,	NANCY	Married William F. Dickinson	Book 1,	28
1829, May 25	ROSE,	POLLY	Married Dennett Goode	Book 1,	246
1741,	ROSE,	ROBERT	Married Mary, daughter of Leonard Tarent	D 22,	317
1860, Jan. 8	ROSE	ROBERT	Married Isabella Brooks	Book 1,	8
1827, Nov. 5	ROSE,	SALLY	Married Lewis D. Broocks	Book 1,	243
1689,	ROSIER,	DAVID	Married Sara, daughter of Philip Sherwood	D 8,	35
1673,	ROSIER,	JOHN	Westmoreland Co., married Mary, daughter of James Williamson	D 5,	201 289
1882, Feb. 28	ROSLER,	JOHN H.	Married Susan J. Gouldin	Book 1,	64
1867, Jan. 13	ROSS,	HANNAH	Married Philip Jones	Book 1,	16
1710,	ROSS,	KATHERINE	Married Roger Prosser	O 4,	264
1807, Jan. 8	ROSS,	MARTHA	Married John Halbert	Book 1,	224
1847, Apr. 14	ROUSE,	AGNES	Married Rice Cauthorn	Book 1,	259
1843, Dec. 18	ROUSE,	ANGELINA	Married William Griffin	Book 1,	256
1899, Dec. 20	ROUSE,	A. B.	Married W. B. Powers	Book 1,	135
1843, Dec. 20	ROUSE,	CLAIBORNE	Married Elizabeth C. Thomas	Book 1,	257
1849, Dec. 21	ROUSE,	ELIZABETH	Married John L. Haile	Book 1,	261

				Book	Page
1839, Jan. 8	ROUSE,	ISABELLA	Married Robert Moody	Book 1,	254
1842, Dec. 9	ROUSE,	LAVINIA A.	Married G. Southworth	Book 1,	256
1813, Jul. 30	ROUSE,	LEWIS	Married Maria Dunn	Book 1,	229
1826,	ROUSE,	LEWIS	Married Maria, daughter of Thomas Dunn	D 42,	15
1708,	ROUSE,	MARGERY	Married John Carnell	O 4,	18
1897, Mar. 31	ROUSE,	NANNIE	Married James R. Clarke	Book 1,	125
1808, Jan. 5	ROUSE,	POLLY	Married William Coleman	Book 1,	224
1837, Jan. 25	ROUSE,	ROBERTA	Married Benjamin Fiddler	Book 1,	252
1835, Aug. 5	ROUSE,	SCHLENISSA	Married Southall Stokes	Book 1,	251
1807, May 5	ROUSE,	WILLIAM	Married Judith Clarke	Book 1,	224
1819, Oct. 18	ROUZIE,	APPHIA	Married James Hunter	Book 1,	235
1854, Sep. 14	ROUZIE,	ARCHIBALD R.	Married Kitty W. Lewis	Book 1,	2
1685,	ROUZIE,	EDWARD	Married Relict of Thomas Whitlock	D 7,	174
1742,	ROUZIE,	ELIZABETH	Widow of Benjamin, married George Denny	D 22,	250
1835, Dec. 14	ROUZIE,	ELIZABETH	Married William B. Westmore	Book 1,	251
1807, Feb. 5	ROUZIE,	HARRIET	Married John Rouzie	Book 1,	224
1866, Apr. 10	ROUZIE,	HENRY S.	Married Elizabeth C. Rennolds	Book 1,	14
1841, Nov. 2	ROUZIE,	JANET	Married Dr. James H. Latane	Book 1,	255
1876, Jan. 18	ROUZIE,	JANNETTE J.	Married John S. Williamson	Book 1,	41
1804, Dec.	ROUZIE,	JOHN	Married Matilda Sale	Book 1,	222
1806,	ROUZIE,	JOHN	Married Matilda, daughter of William Sale	O 38,	492
1807, Feb. 5	ROUZIE,	JOHN	Married Harriet Rouzie	Book 1,	224
1869, Mar. 4	ROUZIE,	JOHN S.	Married Virginia M. Andrews	Book 1,	23
1891, Nov. 5	ROUZIE,	KATE L.	Married William D. Rouzie	Book 1,	108
1720,	ROUZIE,	MARGARET	Exec. of Ralph, married John Nance	O 5,	527
1751,	ROUZIE,	MARY	Daughter of Benjamin, married Stephen Chenault, Orange Co.	D 25,	212
1835, Jul. 10	ROUZIE,	MARY A.	Married James McDonald	Book 1,	251
1688,	ROUZEY,	RALPH	Married Rebecca, daughter of Robert Tomlin	O 2,	143
1802,	ROUZEE,	RALPH	Married Sarah, daughter of William Boulware	D 36,	92
1893, Oct. 25	ROUZIE,	R. B.	Married A. E. Graham	Book 1,	112
1773,	ROUZEE,	REUBEN	Married Franky, daughter of William Thomas	W 12,	539

Date	Surname	Name	Description	Book	Page
1816, Mar. 25	ROUZIE,	RICHARD	Married Janet R. Ritchie	Book 1,	232
1833,	ROUZIE,	RICHARD	Married Janet R. Ritchie, daughter of Archibald Ritchie	W 23,	245
1848, Dec. 18	ROUZIE,	RICHARD F.	Married Maria A. Eubank	Book 1,	260
1834, Nov. 26	ROUZIE,	ROBERT G.	Married Louisa Rennolds	Book 1,	250
1692,	ROUZIE,	SARAH	Married Abraham North	O 1,	140
1718,	ROUZIE,	SARAH	Daughter of Ralph, married Thomas Fenwick	W 3,	94
1839, Dec. 18	ROUZIE,	SARAH F.	Married Benjamin F. Baird	Book 1,	254
1847,	ROUZIE,	SARAH	Daughter of Edward, married Benjamin Baird	W 26,	217
1834, Jun. 2	ROUZIE,	SUSAN S.	Married James Powers	Book 1,	250
1891, Nov. 5	ROUZIE,	WILLIAM D.	Married Kate L. Rouzie	Book 1,	108
1881, Nov. 3	ROUZIE,	WILLIAM E.	Married M. E. Derieux	Book 1,	61
1867, Jan. 15	ROWE,	AMANDA C.	Married Richard Taylor	Book 1,	16
1888, Nov. 15	ROWE,	MARGARET	Married Shields B. Tate	Book 1,	96
1857, Apr. 29	ROWE,	WILSON	Married Amanda Didlake	Book 1,	5
1831, Dec. 3	ROY,	ANN C.	Married John Dyke	Book 1,	248
1834, Feb. 18	ROY,	AUGUSTUS	Married Lucy C. Garnett	Book 1,	250
1854, Jul. 20	ROY,	BEVERLEY D.	King & Queen Co., married Mary Juliet Clopton.	Book 1,	2
1806, Dec. 21	ROY,	JAMES	Married Mary Ann Campbell	Book 1,	223
1806,	ROY,	JAMES	Widow, married Andrew Balmain	D 37,	32
1857, Dec. 24	ROY,	JEANNETT C.	Married Dr. William Hoskins	Book 1,	264
1719,	ROY,	JOHN	Married Dorothy, relict of Charles Smith	D 16,	77
1865, Jun. 28	ROY,	LUCY	Married Robert Saunders	Book 1,	13
1858, May 20	ROY,	ROSALIE B.	Married Robert Hunter Spencer, King & Queen Co.	Book 1,	6
1857, Dec. 15	ROY,	THOMAS S.	Married Fannie B. Micou	Book 1,	5
1866, Jun. 21	ROY,	VIRGINIA B.	Married Robert H. Spencer	Book 1,	15
1819, Oct. 18	ROY,	WALKER	Married Jean Micou	Book 1,	236
1820,	ROY,	WALKER	Married Jane Micou	D 40,	40
1807, Aug. 29	ROYSTER,	JAMES H.	Married Mary G. Bohannon	Book 1,	224
1753,	RUCKER,	THOMAS	Married Elizabeth, daughter of Martha Rennolds	W 9,	246
1817, Mar. 24	RUFFIN,	ARCHIBALD	Married Catharine Roane	Book 1,	223

				Book	Page
1803,	RUFFIN,	WILLIAM	Married Margaret, daughter of Mary Ritchie, sister of Thomas & Archibald Ritchie	W 16,	228
1672,	RUSSELL,	JOHN	Married Elitia, daughter of Luke Billington	W&D 1,	114
1713,	RUSSELL,	JOSEPH	Married Jane, daughter of George Bruce	W 3, Richmond Co.	239
1800,	RUST,	BENJAMIN	Married Lettice Lee Smith, daughter of Meriwether Smith	D 36,	271
1742,	RUTHERFORD, MARGARET		Daughter of John, married William Wortham	W 6,	426
1856, Dec. 30	RYAN,	JOHN R.	Married Susan Tucker	Book 1,	4
1823, Oct. 1	RYAN,	SOLOMON	Married Dicey Cooper	Book 1,	240
1841,	RYAN,	SOLOMON	Married Dicey, daughter of John Cooper dec'd	D 47,	142
1883, Sep. 26	RYLAND,	ALFRED H.	Married Susie S. Derieux	Book 1,	73
1827,	RYLAND,	JANE	Married Lewis Whittemore	D 42,	361
1769,	RYLAND,	JOSEPH	Married Elizabeth, daughter of John Farguson	W 12,	382
1812,	RYLAND,	JOSIAH	Married Catharine Peachey	O 41,	100
1769,	RYLAND,	MARY	Daughter of Joseph, married Ambrose Hunley	W 12,	382 487
1779,	RYLAND,	MARY	Married William Cheek	O 29,	452
1827,	RYLAND,	NANCY	Married Wyatt Whittemore	D 42,	361
1827,	RYLAND,	SALLY	Married Joseph Tillman	D 42,	361
1769,	RYLAND,	THOMAS	Married Jael, daughter of John Farguson	W 12,	382

				Book	Page
1752,	SADLER,	AARON	Married Elizabeth Goulding	W 7,	277
1752,	SADLER,	AARON	Married Elizabeth, daughter of William Goulding	D 26,	21
1846, Dec. 19	SADLER,	AMELIA H.	Married Napoleon B. Street	Book 1,	259
1845, Jan. 15	SADLER,	ANN	Married Henry McKan	Book 1,	258
1885, Jan. 20	SADLER,	CHARLES R.	Married Linda H. Billups	Book 1,	80
1866, May 3	SADLER,	CYRUS	Married Fannie Smith	Book 1,	14
1796,	SADLER,	FEABY	Daughter of John, married Robert Daniel	W 16,	221
1810, Jan. 15	SADLER,	JOHN	Married Nancy Street	Book 1,	226
1885, Dec. 21	SADLER,	JOHN E.	Middlesex Co., married Sue N. Sadler	Book 1,	85
1852, Dec. 23	SADLER,	JON.	Married Amanda F. Cauthorn	Book 1,	263
1854, Dec. 13	SADLER,	JON. F.	Married Sara M. Billups	Book 1,	265
1885, Jul. 20	SADLER,	MARY F.	Married William Alexander Street	Book 1,	82
1890, Jun. 26	SADLER,	M. S.	Married Lou Henley	Book 1,	104
1878, May 15	SADLER,	NANNIE	Married Charles H. Palmer	Book 1,	48
1803,	SADLER,	RACHEL	Daughter of John, married John Downing	W 16,	221
1884, Jun. 17	SADLER,	SARAH A.	Married John H. Boughan	Book 1,	77
1885, Dec. 21	SADLER,	SUE N.	Married John E. Sadler	Book 1,	85
1819, Feb. 27	SADLER,	WILLIAM	Married Victoria Dobbins	Book 1,	236
1879, Mar. 26	SADLER,	WILLIAM T.	Married Sarah Rice	Book 1,	51
1847, Dec. 18	SALE,	ARTHUR I.	Married Arena Carter	Book 1,	259
1864, Jun. 16	SALE,	ARTHUR I.	Married Roberta Fidler	Book 1,	12
1872, Dec. 24	SALE,	BENJAMIN	Married Mary S. Wright	Book 1,	32
1815, Dec. 20	SALE,	CATHARINE	Married James Andrews	Book 1,	231
1837,	SALE,	CATHARINE B.	Daughter of William B. Sale, married James Andrews	D 45,	454
1871, Dec. 5	SALE,	CHARLES J.	Married Mary Susan Latane	Book 1,	29
1743,	SALE,	CORNELIUS	Married Martha, daughter of William Jones	W 7,	95
1838, Oct. 4	SALE,	DANDRIDGE	Married Mary E. Munday	Book 1,	253
1804, Aug. 16	SALE,	ELIZABETH	Married Reuben Pitts	Book 1,	222
1869, Dec. 11	SALE,	FANNY	Married Robert Jefferson	Book 1,	24
1834, Dec. 4	SALE,	HENRY S.	Married Mary Beazley	Book 1,	250

				Book	Page
1834,	SALE,	HENRY	Married Polly Beazley	D 44,	510
1836,	SALE,	HENRY	Married Polly Beazley	D 45,	411
1827, Dec. 17	SALE,	HORTENSIA	Married Edwin G. Andrews	Book 1,	243
1837, Dec. 20	SALE,	JOHN	Married Louisa Dunn	Book 1,	252
1838, Sep. 17	SALE,	JOHN C.	Married Julia Ann Hill	Book 1,	253
1820, Apr. 17	SALE,	LAURA	Married David Pitts	Book 1,	237
1795,	SALE,	LEWIS	Married Susanna Faver	W 16,	120
1833, Nov. 13	SALE,	LOUISA	Married Brooking Stokes	Book 1,	249
1832, Apr. 5	SALE,	LUCY ANN	Married Robert Saunders	Book 1,	249
1733,	SALE,	MARY	Daughter of Cornelius, married John Cook	W 5,	159
1840, Nov. 11	SALE,	MARY LOUISA	Married William T. Samuel	Book 1,	254
1804, Dec. 1	SALE,	MATILDA	Married John Rouzie	Book 1,	222
1806,	SALE,	MATILDA	Daughter of William, married John Rouzie	O 38,	492
1827, Feb. 12	SALE,	MILDRED	Married James Jones	Book 1,	243
1812, Jan. 13	SALE,	NANCY	Married Robert Samuel	Book 1,	228
1832,	SALE,	NANCY	Daughter of Brooking & Nancy Sale, married Robert Samuel Caroline Co.	D 43,	587
1835,	SALE,	NANCY	Daughter of William Brooking Sale, married Robert Samuel, Caroline Co.	D 45,	110
1811, Apr. 15	SALE,	POLLY	Married Alexander Parker	Book 1,	227
1806,	SALE,	REUBEN	Married Catharine, daughter of Jackson Dyke	D 37,	165
1807, Jul. 28	SALE,	RICHARD JR.	Married Elizabeth Parker	Book 1,	224
1813, Feb. 15	SALE,	ROBERT	Married Sally Broaddus	Book 1,	229
1848, Feb. 29	SALE,	SARAH P.	Married Raleigh D. Carter	Book 1,	260
1830, Oct. 20	SALE,	SPILSBY	Married Sidney Fisher	Book 1,	247
1798,	SALE,	WILLIAM B.	Married Nancy, heir of Oswald Davis	W 16,	267
1804, Jan. 9	SALE,	WILLIAM I.	Married Nancy Brooke	Book 1,	222
1882, Mar. 26	SALE,	WILLIAM J.	Married Sarah J. Pitts	Book 1,	64
1858, Nov. 22	SALE,	VIRGINIA A.	Married Thomas H. Richardson	Book 1,	8
1722,	SALLIS,	SARAH	Married Alexander Donaphan	O 5,	756
1722,	SAMES,	JAMES	Married Katherine Alleyn	O 6, D 17,	9 108
1877, Apr. 22	SAMUEL,	ALICE	Caroline Co., married Peter Fields, Caroline Co.	Book 1,	45
1879, Mar. 20	SAMUEL,	ALICE	Married Theodore F. Jeter	Book 1,	51

Date	Surname	Given	Marriage/Note	Book	Page
1824, Feb. 23	SAMUEL,	ANTHONY	Married Harriet Gouldman	Book 1,	241
1752,	SAMUEL,	CATHARINE	Exec. of Henry, married James Davis	O 18,	275
1898, Dec. 7	SAMUEL,	E. B.	Married J. C₁ Carter	Book 1,	130
1874, Dec. 27	SAMUEL,	GEORGE W.	Married Marcellus G. Kay	Book 1,	37
1883, Apr. 3	SAMUEL,	GEORGE W.	Married Maggie L. Bradley	Book 1,	26
1826, Aug. 22	SAMUEL,	HENRY JR.	Married Elizabeth Micou	Book 1,	242
1849, Nov. 27	SAMUEL,	JAMES	Married Susan Thomas	Book 1,	261
1857, Dec. 17	SAMUEL,	JOSEPH	Married Ann Gouldman	Book 1,	6
1836, Jan. 28	SAMUEL,	LEROY W.	Married Vannangus A. Samuel	Book 1,	252
1858, Jun. 30	SAMUEL,	MARGARET F.	Married Edward Gouldman	Book 1,	6
1740,	SAMUEL,	MARY	Daughter of James, married John Martin	W 6,	312
1845, Apr. 21	SAMUEL,	MARY .	Married Edmond Saunders	Book 1,	258
1873, Dec. 30	SAMUEL,	MARY E.	Married William B. Jenkins	Book 1,	33
1837, Jan. 31	SAMUEL,	NANCY	Married John Smither	Book 1,	252
1824, Jan. 5	SAMUEL,	POLLY	Married William Gayle	Book 1,	241
1828, Dec. 8	SAMUEL,	REUBEN	Married Polly Smither	Book 1,	245
1812, Jan. 13	SAMUEL,	ROBERT	Married Nancy Sale	Book 1,	228
1816, Dec. 24	SAMUEL,	ROBERT	Married Sarah B. Taylor	Book 1,	232
1818,	SAMUEL,	ROBERT	Married Sally Taylor	D 41,	116
1832,	SAMUEL,	ROBERT	Caroline Co., married Nancy, daughter of Brooking & Nancy Sale	D 43,	587
1835,	SAMUEL,	ROBERT	Married Nancy, daughter of William Brooking Sale	D 45,	110
1865, Mar. 16	SAMUEL,	SIDNEY C.	Married Henry M. Marshall	Book 1,	13
1884, Nov. 17	SAMUEL,	THOMAS A.	Married Sadie A. Watts	Book 1,	79
1836, Jan. 28	SAMUEL,	VANNANGUS A.	Married Leroy W. Samuel	Book 1,	252
1840, Nov. 11	SAMUEL,	WILLIAM T.	Married Mary Louisa Sale	Book 1,	254
1859, Feb. 4	SAMUEL,	WILLIAM B.	Married Jeanett Parker	Book 1,	7
1822, Jan. 17	SAMUEL,	ZACHARIAH	Married Lucy Smither	Book 1,	239
1837, Apr. 10	SAMUEL,	ZACHARIAH	Married Julia Bastin	Book 1,	253
1830, May 21	SANDERS,	CARTER	Married Nelly Reeves	Book 1,	247
1721,	SANDERS,	RICHARD	Married Blessing, daughter of John Pickett	Box 105,	B
1869, Apr. 22	SANDFORD,	ETHELWALD C.	Married Rosalie V. Sandy	Book 1,	23

1867, Jan. 24	SANDFORD,	HENRY F.	Married Mary E. Garnett	Book 1,	16
1847, Sep. 11	SANDY,	EDWARD	Married Mary Ann Croxton	Book 1,	259
1855, Sep. 11	SANDY,	PHILIP A.	Married Louisa Carter Croxton	Book 1,	4
1870, Oct. 3	SANDY,	ROSALIE V.	Married Ethelwald C. Sandford	Book 1,	26
1772,	SATTERWHITE, ELIZABETH		Daughter of John, married Elijah Jeator	W 13,	258
1772,	SATTERWHITE, JANE		Daughter of John, married Samuel Higginbottom	W 13,	258
1812, Feb. 5	SATTERWHITE, NANCY		Married James Coleman	Book 1,	228
1772,	SATTERWHITE, SARAH		Daughter of John, married Francis Robinson	W 13,	258
1823,	SAUNDERS,	ANN	Daughter of Charles, married Edmond Covington	D 41,	42
1886, Nov. 17	SAUNDERS,	BESSIE C.	Married Armistead Ransone, Gloucester Co.	Book 1,	89
1811, Dec. 16	SAUNDERS,	CHARLES	Married Mary Dunn	Book 1,	227
1898, Dec. 29	SAUNDERS,	C. E.	Married C. W. Davis	Book 1,	131
1869, Dec. 29	SAUNDERS,	CLARA	Married Frank Jackson	Book 1,	24
1857, Jan. 15	SAUNDERS,	EDGAR J.	Married Mary L. Jones	Book 1,	4
1882, Jun. 27	SAUNDERS,	EDGAR D.	Middlesex Co., married Susan E. Dunn	Book 1,	66
1845, Apr. 21	SAUNDERS,	EDMOND	Married Mary Samuel	Book 1,	258
1898, Feb. 16	SAUNDERS,	E. A.	Married James Bruce	Book 1,	128
1880, Dec. 2	SAUNDERS,	GEORGE W.	Married Catharine E. Dyke	Book 1,	57
1809, Nov. 20	SAUNDERS,	HENRY	Married Mary Covington	Book 1,	225
1826, Jan. 16	SAUNDERS,	JOHN	Married Sophia Bentley	Book 1,	242
1867, Mar. 7	SAUNDERS,	JOHN R.	Married Annie E. Durham	Book 1,	17
1868, Dec. 18	SAUNDERS,	JOHN H.	Married Mary L. Faulconer, daughter of Nicholas	Book 1,	21
1846, Jun. 1	SAUNDERS,	JOSEPH	Married Martha A. Taylor	Book 1,	259
1852, Jan. 6	SAUNDERS,	JOSEPH	Married Maria Ann Armstrong	Book 1,	263
1877, Feb. 27	SAUNDERS,	JOSEPH A.	Married Louella Allen	Book 1,	44
1869, Jan. 14	SAUNDERS,	LUCY W.	Married John H. Smith	Book 1,	22
1813, Dec. 13	SAUNDERS,	MARGARET	Married John Walker	Book 1,	229
1870, Dec. 22	SAUNDERS,	MARTHA J.	Married Henry Patton of Middlesex Co.	Book 1,	26
1850, Dec. 12	SAUNDERS,	MARY	Married William Ingram	Book 1,	262
1873, Jan. 9	SAUNDERS,	MARY E.	Widow, married Thomas Boughan	Book 1,	32
1898, May 18	SAUNDERS,	MARY J.	Married B. Longest	Book 1,	129

				Book	Page
1808, Dec. 19	SAUNDERS,	NANCY	Married Edward Covington	Book 1,	224
1832, Apr. 5	SAUNDERS,	ROBERT	Married Lucy Ann Sale	Book 1,	249
1865, Jun. 28	SAUNDERS,	ROBERT	Married Lucy Roy	Book 1,	13
1869, Feb. 18	SAUNDERS,	ROSA A.	Married Leonard Barefoot	Book 1,	22
1832, May 21	SAUNDERS,	SPENCER	Married Virginia Reaves	Book 1,	249
1827, Nov. 19	SAUNDERS,	SUCKEY	Married Peter Richards	Book 1,	247
1817, Aug. 11	SAUNDERS,	SUSANNA	Married Richard Jones	Book 1,	233
1858, Dec. 21	SAUNDERS,	THOMAS J.	Married Molly M. Durham	Book 1,	6
1848, Jun. 17	SAUNDERS,	VIRGINIA G.	Married John F. Dickenson	Book 1,	260
1834, Jan. 1	SAUNDERS,	WILLIAM	Married Rachel Williams	Book 1,	250
1860, Oct. 23	SAUNDERS,	WILLIAM H.	Married Annis Street	Book 1,	10
1864, Jan. 1	SAUNDERS,	WILLIAM H.	Married Martha I. Street	Book 1,	12
1894, Jun. 27	SAUNDERS,	W. D.	Married Kate E. Powers	Book 1,	114
1678,	SAVAGE,	ALICE	Daughter of Anthony, married Francis Thornton	D 6,	64
1773,	SCANDRETT,	ISAAC	Married Sarah, widow of Thomas Ley	D 31,	119
1812,	SCHELLING,	DANIEL	Married Nancy, daughter of Evan Davis	O 41,	57
1863, Jan. 9	SCHOOLS,	ALBERT	Married Nancy Tucker	Book 1,	11
1870, Mar. 16	SCHOOLS,	ALBERT	Married Nancy Brizendine	Book 1,	25
1874, Feb. 27	SCHOOLS,	ANNIE	Married Thomas Carneale	Book 1,	36
1870, Feb. 18	SCHOOLS,	AUGUSTINE	Married Rebecca C. Schools	Book 1,	25
1859, Dec. 20	SCHOOLS,	CHARLES H.	Married Polly Brooks	Book 1,	8
1870, Mar. 22	SCHOOLS,	CHARLES H.	Married Eltha Ann Clarke	Book 1,	25
1831, Apr. 18	SCHOOLS,	DAWSON	Married Lucy Cross	Book 1,	248
1871, Mar. 1	SCHOOLS,	DAWSON	Married Olivia Durham	Book 1,	28
1818, Dec. 16	SCHOOLS,	ELIZABETH	Married Larkin Schools	Book 1,	234
1867, Oct. 17	SCHOOLS,	ELIZABETH	Married James Collier	Book 1,	18
1898, Dec. 28	SCHOOLS,	ETTA LEE	Married N. L. Falkner	Book 1,	131
1824, Dec. 20	SCHOOLS,	FRANCES	Married James Ingram	Book 1,	241
1842, Jan. 24	SCHOOLS,	G. W.	Married Dorothy Wilson	Book 1,	256
1843, Jul. 7	SCHOOLS,	JOHN	Married Polly Lathom	Book 1,	240
1857, Feb. 12	SCHOOLS,	JOSEPH	Married Lucinda Williams	Book 1,	5

1818, Dec. 16	SCHOOLS,	LARKIN	Married Elizabeth Schools	Book 1,	234
1825, Jan. 10	SCHOOLS,	LARKIN	Married Margaret Wilmore	Book 1,	242
1854, Dec. 21	SCHOOLS,	LEONARD	Married Martha Harper	Book 1,	3
1881, Jan. 13	SCHOOLS,	LEWIS E.	Married Mary S. Carneale	Book 1,	58
1837, Mar. 20	SCHOOLS,	LUCY	Married Lunsford Atkins	Book 1,	252
1894, Dec. 27	SCHOOLS,	L. T.	Married J. R. Carneale	Book 1,	116
1846, Dec. 14	SCHOOLS,	MALINDA	Married Alfred Munday	Book 1,	259
1848, Mar. 10	SCHOOLS,	MARTHA	Married Robert Allen	Book 1,	260
1845, Jan. 4	SCHOOLS,	N. P.	Married Sarah Schools	Book 1,	258
1872, Sep. 26	SCHOOLS,	OLIVIA	Married John Tune	Book 1,	31
1841, Dec. 29	SCHOOLS,	PHOEBE	Married Edward Willmore	Book 1,	255
1895, Dec. 19	SCHOOLS,	P. A.	Married G. A. Wilson	Book 1,	119
1870, Mar. 16	SCHOOLS,	REBECCA C.	Married Augustine Schools	Book 1,	25
1876, Mar. 9	SCHOOLS,	ROBENETTE	Married Charles H. Moore	Book 1,	41
1846, Mar. 16	SCHOOLS,	ROBERT	Married Sarah Allen	Book 1,	259
1848, Sep. 13	SCHOOLS,	ROBERT	Married Emily Martin	Book 1,	260
1845, Jan. 4	SCHOOLS,	SARAH A.	Married N. P. Schools	Book 1,	258
1854, Dec. 26	SCHOOLS,	SARAH ANN	Married William Straughan Munday	Book 1,	3
1854, Jan. 5	SCHOOLS,	SUSAN	Married John Lumpkin	Book 1,	1
1833,	SCHOOLS,	URIAH	Married Harriet, daughter of Philip Thomas	D 44,	197
1844, Mar. 4	SCHOOLS,	WALKER	Married Patty A. Clarke	Book 1,	257
1870, Feb. 24	SCHOOLS,	WILLIAM A.	Married Mary Frances Moore	Book 1,	25
1871, Dec. 12	SCHOOLS,	WILLIAM B.	Married Ann Stevens	Book 1,	30
1884, Sep. 18	SCHOOLS,	WILLIAM	Married Bettie A. Griffin	Book 1,	78
1883, Mar. 1	SCOTT,	A. F.	Minister Northampton Co., married Julia T. Waring	Book 1,	70
1876, Apr. 5	SCOTT,	CHARLES L.	Married Celestine Fogg	Book 1,	40
1881, Oct. 25	SCOTT,	GEORGE R.	Gloucester Co., married Sadie A. Kriete	Book 1,	61
1876, Apr. 25	SCOTT,	FANNY E.	Married Thomas P. Bagby	Book 1,	41
1882, Oct. 31	SCOTT,	FRANCIS H.	Gloucester Co., married Kate W. Ware	Book 1,	66
1841, Mar. 16	SCOTT,	HENRY B.	Married Elizabeth F. Cauthorn	Book 1,	255
1872, Oct. 29	SCOTT,	JOSEPH	Westmoreland Co., married Mary Susan Fogg	Book 1,	31

					Book	Page
1899, Dec. 27	SCOTT,	J. B.	Married Ida G. Bray		Book 1,	135
1757,	SCOTT,	MARGARET	Married James Garnett		D 27,	314
1750,	SCOTT,	MARY	Daughter of William, married Thomas Ayres		D 25,	147
1814, Feb. 21	SCOTT,	NANCY L.	Married Travis Taff		Book 1,	230
1838, Jun. 16	SCOTT,	ROBERT	Married Mary E. Boughton		Book 1,	253
1750,	SCOTT,	SARAH	Daughter of William, married Bernard Noell		D 25,	147
1851, Apr. 13	SCOTT,	THOMAS L.	Physician, married Ann Elizabeth Taylor		Book 1,	262
1724,	SCRIMSHAW,	ANDREW	Married Elizabeth Butcher		D 17,	365
1855, Nov. 8	SEAL,	FESTUS D.	Married Elizabeth Frances Faulconer		Book 1,	3
1875, Dec. 23	SEAL,	FLORENCE L.	Married Augustus G. Courtney		Book 1,	40
1884, Jun. 5	SEAL,	IDA BLANCHE	Married James T. Harper Jr.		Book 1,	77
1760,	SEARLES,	COVINGTON	Married Betty, daughter of Daniel Warner		W 11,	301
1703,	SEARLE,	DORCAS	Married Thomas Moress		O 3,	22
1763,	SEARS,	WILLIAM	Gloucester Co., married Sarah, daughter of Elizabeth Waggener		D 29,	239
1762,	SEAYRES,	HANNAH	Widow of Robert, married James Martin, Chesterfield Co.		D 29,	67
1762,	SEAYRES,	ROBERT	Married Hannah, daughter of Nicholas Lafon		D 29,	67
1839, Dec. 28	SEGAR,	D. M.	Married William R. Allen		Book 1,	254
1797,	SEGAR,	JOHN	Married Elizabeth, daughter of Elizabeth Garnett		W 16,	306
1829, Mar. 20	SEGAR,	RICHARD C.	Married Drusilla Dunn		Book 1,	246
1712,	SEGAR,	WINIFRED	Married Isaac Webb		O 4,	444
1839, Dec. 27	SELBA,	WILLIAM G.	Married Eliza Gouldman		Book 1,	254
1698,	SELLINGER,	PETER	Married Elizabeth, sister of Robert Waight		D 9,	227
1893, Feb. 22	SEWARD,	C. B.	Married G. W. Trible		Book 1,	111
1839, Dec. 16	SEWARD,	FRANCES C.	Married William G. Newbill		Book 1,	254
1840, May 27	SEWARD,	JOHN E.	Married Virginia Ann Dunn		Book 1,	254
1805, Jan. 17	SEWARD,	LEWIS	Married Frances Brooke		Book 1,	223
1842, Jan. 17	SEWARD,	LUCY S.	Married John S. Boughton		Book 1,	256
1854, Jan. 11	SEWARD,	PETER E	Married Dorothy Dyke		Book 1,	265
1837, Dec. 12	SEWARD,	WILLIAM B. B.	Married Mary E. Eubank		Book 1,	253
1880, Apr. 7	SEWARD,	WILLIAM T.	Married Harriet E. Jeffries		Book 1,	55
1815, Nov. 26	SEWELL,	MARGARET	Married Richard Mann		Book 1,	231

			Book	Page
1819, Dec. 13	SEWELL, ROBERT	Married Tabitha Marshall	Book 1,	236
1762,	SEYARS, JOHN	Married Frances, daughter of Thomas Lee	W 12,	25
1688,	SEYMOUR, JOHN	Married relict of John Bates	O 2,	115
1853, Dec. 26	SHACKELFORD, ALFRED	Married Elizabeth I. Rogers	Book 1,	1
1882, Jan. 16	SHACKELFORD, ANNETTA	Married James Acres	Book 1,	63
1898, Jul. 7	SHACKELFORD, ALICE	Married Sandy Clarke	Book 1,	129
1891, Dec. 24	SHACKELFORD, ALONZO	Married Ellen Tune	Book 1,	108
1837, Sep. 18	SHACKELFORD, CARTER	Married Elizabeth Dunn	Book 1,	253
1811, Mar. 23	SHACKELFORD, ELIZABETH	Married Twyman Greenwood	Book 1,	227
1846, Apr. 2	SHACKELFORD, ELIZABETH	Married B. C. Smith	Book 1,	259
1858, Feb. 25	SHACKELFORD, ENNIS	Married Mary E. McTire	Book 1,	6
1825, Jan. 28	SHACKELFORD, FRANCES	Married Thomas Marlow	Book 1,	241
1825,	SHACKELFORD, FRANCES	Daughter of Richard, married Thomas Marlow	D 41,	438
1868, Dec. 3	SHACKELFORD, GARDNER F.	Married Fanny A. Longest, widow	Book 1,	21
1821, Nov. 26	SHACKELFORD, JOHN P.	Married Ann D. Bohannon	Book 1,	238
1877, Mar. 13	SHACKELFORD, JOHN	Married Alice Tinsbloom	Book 1,	45
1818, Dec. 14	SHACKELFORD, LUCY	Married Thomas Gordon	Book 1,	234
1891, Dec. 31	SHACKELFORD, LUCY A.	Married Joseph A. Brooks	Book 1,	108
1832, Apr. 6	SHACKELFORD, MARTHA	Married John Crow Sr.	Book 1,	248
1846, Dec. 17	SHACKELFORD, MARTHA	Married Frank S. Taylor	Book 1,	258
1835, Dec. 31	SHACKELFORD, NANCY	Married Thomas Greenwood	Book 1,	251
1819, Jun. 3	SHACKELFORD, REBECCA	Married Richard Newbill	Book 1,	236
1829,	SHACKELFORD, REBECCA	Married Richard Newbill	W 22,	34
1825, May 2	SHACKELFORD, ROBERT T.	Married Lucy Garrett	Book 1,	242
1805,	SHACKELFORD, ROGER	Married Frances, daughter of James Townley	D 36,	447
1867, Mar. 5	SHACKELFORD, RYBURN A.	Married Sarah Brown	Book 1,	17
1886, Jan. 16	SHACKELFORD, R. T.	Married Lucy B. Hundley	Book 1,	85
1873, Feb. 13	SHACKELFORD, SUSAN P.	Married Richard H. Brizendine	Book 1,	32
1825, Dec. 19	SHACKELFORD, WARNER	Married Suca Greenwood	Book 1,	242
1831, Apr. 18	SHACKELFORD, WILLIAM R.	Married Catharine Kendall	Book 1,	249
1852, Oct. 4	SHACKELFORD, WILLIAM A.	Married Frances C. Crow	Book 1,	263

				Book	Page
1781,	SHADDOCK,	JAMES	Married Hannah, daughter of James Samuel	D 32,	93
1850, Sep. 22	SHADDOCK,	JOHN	Married Elizabeth Atkinson	Book 1,	262
1815, Aug. 23	SHADDOCK,	MORDECAI	Married Frances Mathews	Book 1,	231
1793,	SHADDOCK,	SARAH	Daughter of James, married James Halbert	W 15,	140
1872, Sep. 10	SHADDOCK,	SARAH J.	Married Arthur Parker	Book 1,	31
1879, Mar. 11	SHAFFER,	LEONARD	Philadelphia, married Mildred Tune, widow	Book 1,	51
1691,	SHARPE,	MARY	Sister of John, married John Dyke	D 8,	281
1859, Oct. 20	SHELTON,	ADALINE W.	Married William T. Lathom	Book 1,	7
1883, Jun. 20	SHELTON,	CHARLES	Spottsylvania Co., married Donnia Crow	Book 1,	72
1826, Dec. 19	SHELTON,	ELIZABETH	Married Nathaniel Trimyer	Book 1,	242
1770,	SHELTON,	JAMES	Married Catharine, daughter of James Munday	Box 1772-76 O	
1834, Jun. 5	SHELTON,	MARY E.	Married Willis Crouch	Book 1,	250
1809, Sep. 18	SHELTON,	REBECCA	Married Ephraim Shepherd	Book 1,	225
1771,	SHELTON,	THOMAS	Married Katherine Munday	D 30,	239
1822, Jun. 3	SHELTON,	THOMAS	Married Mary E. Simco	Book 1,	239
1849, Jan. 9	SHEPHERD,	UDORA A.	Married S. Robert Blackburn	Book 1,	261
1811, Mar. 5	SHEPHERD,	CATHARINE	Married James McEntree	Book 1,	227
1857, Apr. 28	SHEPHERD,	CHARLES R.	Married Alice A. Boughton	Book 1,	5
1824,	SHEPHERD,	FRANCES	Daughter of Reuben, married James Boughton	D 41,	389
1719,	SHEPARD,	ELIZABETH	Daughter of Elizabeth, granddaughter of William Richards, married John Williamson	D 16,	107
1871, Feb. 23	SHEPPARD,	EMILY	Married Tasker McKendrie	Book 1,	28
1806, May 10	SHEPPARD,	EPHRAIM	Married Betsey Davis	Book 1,	223
1809, Sep. 18	SHEPHERD,	EPHRAIM	Married Rebecca Shelton	Book 1,	225
1811, Jan. 21	SHEPHERD,	FRANCES	Married James Boughton	Book 1,	227
1842, Dec. 23	SHEPARD,	JAMES H.	Married Ann D. Collins	Book 1,	256
1867, Dec. 26	SHEPPARD,	JOHN E.	Married Fannie R. Croxton	Book 1,	19
1899, Dec. 13	SHEPPARD,	L. E.	Married John E. Durham	Book 1,	135
1802,	SHEPHERD,	MARY	Daughter of John, married Thomas MacKendrie	D 36,	67
1866, Aug. 11	SHEPPARD,	MARY ANN	Married Lewis Cobb	Book 1,	15
1820, Apr. 17	SHEPHERD,	PATSEY	Married William Dunn	Book 1,	237
1821, Dec. 24	SHEPHERD,	REBECCA	Married James C. Cole	Book 1,	238

					Book	Page
1884, Apr. 17	SHEPHERD,	RICHARD S.	Married Susan A. Covington		Book 1,	77
1824, Feb. 2	SHEPPERD,	SARAH	Married John Greenwood		Book 1,	241
1841, Apr. 22	SHEPHERD,	SMITH T.	Married Frances Brizendine		Book 1,	255
1861, Aug. 20	SHEPPARD,	WILLIAM E.	Married Frances E. Griffith		Book 1,	11
1720,	SHEPPY,	MONECA	Daughter of Mary, married Robert Payne		W 3,	254
1690,	SHERWOOD,	ANN	Married James Dabney		D 8,	278
1837, May 3	SHEARWOOD, ANN		Married Churchill Brizendine		Book 1,	252
1838, May 25	SHEARWOOD, CATHARINE ANN		Married Wilson Coleman		Book 1,	253
1814, Dec. 24	SHEARWOOD, FANNY		Married Harrison Ball		Book 1,	230
1872, Jan. 10	SHEARWOOD, FRANCES A.		Married George T. Brooks		Book 1,	30
1844, Nov. 27	SHEARWOOD, H.		Married Emily Tate		Book 1,	257
1747,	SHEARWOOD, JACOB		Married Elizabeth, sister of John Radford, Chesterfield Co.		WB&I 17,	129
1866, Nov. 15	SHEARWOOD, JAMES A.		Married Adeline Brizendine		Book 1,	15
1866, Jun. 7	SHEARWOOD, JOHN R.		Married Susan E. Parker		Book 1,	15
1872, Feb. 15	SHEARWOOD, JOHN R.		Married Amanda J. Dyke		Book 1,	30
1884, Dec. 25	SHEARWOOD, JOHN R.		Married Molly K. Brizendine		Book 1,	80
1899, Jan. 19	SHEARWOOD, L. E.		Married John T. Crow		Book 1,	132
1685,	SHERWOOD,	MARY	Daughter of Philip, married Francis James		O 1,	173
1799,	SHERWOOD,	MARY	Daughter of Jonathan, married William Moody		W 15,	508
1873, Apr. 3	SHEARWOOD, MARY E.		Married John M. Owen		Book 1,	33
1835, Dec. 21	SHEARWOOD, PATSEY		Married William Martin		Book 1,	252
1893, Dec. 20	SHEARWOOD, R. A.		Married M. E. Boughan		Book 1,	112
1807, Jul. 20	SHERWOOD,	RICHARD	Married Mary Minter		Book 1,	224
1834, Dec. 18	SHEARWOOD, RICHARD		Married Lucy M. Boughan		Book 1,	250
1685,	SHERWOOD,	SARAH	Daughter of Philip, married Thomas Marshall		O 1,	173
1689,	SHERWOOD,	SARAH	Married David Rosier		D 8,	35
1865, Dec. 28	SHEARWOOD, SARAH E.		Married Ephraim R. Minor		Book 1,	14
1878, Jul. 18	SHEARWOOD, THERESA M.		Married Wilton Brizendine		Book 1,	49
1808, Dec. 19	SHEARWOOD, THOMAS		Married Maria Starke		Book 1,	224
1818, Jan. 2	SHEARWOOD, THOMAS		Married Catharine Croxton		Book 1,	234
1838, Jun. 28	SHEARWOOD, THOMAS		Married Lucinda A. Pitts		Book 1,	253

				Book	Page
1715,	SHIPLEY,	ELIZABETH	Daughter of Ealse, married Job Virgett	D&W 14,	475
1715,	SHIPLEY,	MARY	Married Jasper Cofton	D&W 14,	475
1716,	SHIPLEY,	MARY	Sister of Sarah, heir of George Boyce, married Jasper Cofton	D&W 15,	1,2
1822, May 20	SHIPP,	HARRIET	Married Jonathan Dunn	Book 1,	239
1710,	SHIPP,	JOSIAS	Married Elizabeth, daughter of John Hodgson	D&W 14,	373
1822, Dec. 23	SHIPP,	LUCY	Married Richard Moody	Book 1,	239
1709,	SHIPPY,	RICHARD	Married Eleanor Mott	D&C 13,	320
1686,	SHORT,	ANN	Widow of Thomas, married William Hasle	O 1,	147
1813, Dec. 22	SHORT,	ELIZABETH	Married Spencer Ingram	Book 1,	229
1719,	SHORT,	SAMUEL	Married Sarah, widow of John Armstrong	O 5,	359
1694,	SHORT,	THOMAS	Married Abigail, widow of Christopher Blackburn	O 1,	189
1750,	SHORT,	WILLIAM	Married Elizabeth, daughter of Elizabeth Bendry	D 25,	129
1808, Aug. 30	SHOWARD,	JOHN	Married Susanna Coleman	Book 1,	225
1808, Aug. 25	SIMCO,	HENRY	Married Ann Boughton	Book 1,	225
1822, Jun. 3	SIMCO,	MARY E.	Married Thomas Shelton	Book 1,	239
1827, Feb. 19	SIMCO,	SUSAN T.	Married George Broach	Book 1,	243
1836, Jan. 30	SIMCOE,	THOMAS A.	Married Lucy A. Ramsey	Book 1,	252
1819, Apr. 20	SIMMONS,	MARTHA	Married William Meredith	Book 1,	236
1888, Mar. 15	SIRLES,	MARY J.	Married Newton Davis	Book 1,	95
1859, Feb. 4	SISSON,	RICHARD H.	Married Mary E. Brizendine	Book 1,	8
1892, May 5	SISSON,	RICHARD	Richmond Co., married Cora Winder	Book 1,	109
1871, Oct. 5	SISSON,	WARNER	Richmond Co., married Catharine E. Montague	Book 1,	29
1843, Jan. 21	SIZER,	HENRY E.	Married S. A. E. Pilcher	Book 1,	257
1862, Jan. 8	SIZER,	MARTHA E.	Married Andrew Hundley	Book 1,	11
1850, Dec. 23	SKELTON,	ELIZA	Married John N. Crow	Book 1,	262
1760,	SKELTON,	JAMES	Married Jane, daughter of Francis Meriwether	D 21,	41
1846, Jan. 6	SKELTON,	PEGGY	Married James F. Blackburn	Book 1,	258
1853, Aug. 25	SKELTON,	MARIA S.	Married John W. Beazley	Book 1,	6
1875, Jun. 9	SKELTON,	EMMA	Widow, Married Joseph C. Parron	Book 1,	39
663,		SLAUGHTER, ELIZABETH	Widow of Capt. Francis Slaughter, daughter of Margaret Lucas, formerly Upton, married John Catlett	D 2,	326

Date	Surname	Given Name	Description	Book	Page
1877, Jun. 29	SMALL,	CATHARINE	Married William T. Dyke	Book 1,	45
1818, Dec. 21	SMITH,	ALICE T.	Married James Cockburn	Book 1,	234
1827, Feb. 14	SMITH,	ALICE LEE	Married William Bates	Book 1,	243
1813, Nov. 16	SMITH,	ALLEN	Married Patsy Parker	Book 1,	229
1694,	SMITH,	ANN	Married William Ayres (License)	O 1,	285
1694,	SMITH,	ANN	Married John Webster	O 1,	323
1804,	SMITH,	ANN	Daughter of William, married Thomas Jeffries	D 36,	380
1847, Jan. 6	SMITH,	ANNA E.	Married Fauntleroy Dishman	Book 1,	259
1874, Dec. 17	SMITH,	ANNIE E.	Widow, married John W. Smith	Book 1,	37
1876, Jan. 20	SMITH,	ARIADNE	Married Constantine D. Courtney	Book 1,	41
1760,	SMITH,	BENJAMIN	Married Grizell, daughter of Mrs. Margaret Holt, Hanover Co.	W 11,	407
1846, Apr. 2	SMITH,	B. C.	Married Elizabeth Shackelford	D 29,	259
1887, Jun. 14	SMITH,	BETTIE L.	Married Dr. W. B. Robinson	Book 1,	92
1866, Sep. 15	SMITH,	CATHARINE	Married Richard Cooper	Book 1,	15
1841, Aug. 31	SMITH,	CHARLES C.	Married Emily C. Dunn	Book 1,	255
1843,	SMITH,	CHARLES	Married Emily, daughter of James Dunn	W 24,	49
1881, Nov. 17	SMITH,	CHARLES S.	Married Lalla R. Wright	Book 1,	61
1811, Dec. 9	SMITH,	CLARA B.	Married Robert Weir	Book 1,	227
1719,	SMITH,	DOROTHY	Relict of Charles, married John Roy	D 16,	77
1841,	SMITH,	DOROTHY	Daughter of William, married Robert B. Smith	W 24,	480
1846, May 18	SMITH,	EDWARD	Married Catharine Dix	Book 1,	259
1866, Oct. 18	SMITH,	EDWARD T.	Married Bettie V. L. Yerby	Book 1,	15
1880, Dec. 23	SMITH,	EDWIN E.	Married Amanda Brooks	Book 1,	57
1677,	SMITH,	ELIZABETH	Daughter of Phebe, sister of Henry, married Edward Adcock	D 6,	8
1688,	SMITH,	ELIZABETH	Married Daniel Dobyns	O 2,	111
1696,	SMITH,	ELIZABETH	Daughter of William, married William Corbin	D 9,	55
1760,	SMITH,	ELIZABETH	Daughter of Francis, married William Young	W 11,	415
1823, Aug. 18	SMITH,	ELIZABETH	Married Daniel Hundley	Book 1,	240
1844, Dec. 11	SMITH,	ELIZABETH	Married A. O. Yerby	Book 1,	257
1877, Mar. 24	SMITH,	ELIZABETH	Married Thomas S. Johnson	Book 1,	45
1866, May 3	SMITH,	FANNIE	Married Cyrus Sadler	Book 1,	14

					Book	Page
1841, Apr. 22	SMITH,	FRANCIS	Married Emily E. Harper		Book 1,	255
1764,	SMITH,	GRIZELL	Widow of Benjamin, married Leroy Hipkins	D 30, W 11,		194 407
1701,	SMITH,	HENRY	Married Mary, relict of Richard Carter	D&W 10,		95
1853, Dec. 1	SMITH,	JAMES WM.	King & Queen Co., married Lelia Olivia Ellis	Book 1,		1
1870, Dec. 24	SMITH,	JAMES H.	Married Mary Jane Robinson	Book 1,		27
1694,	SMITH,	JANE	Married Edward Danalane (License)	O 1,		325
1738,	SMITH,	JANE	Daughter of John, married Thomas Deane	W 7,		189
1692,	SMITH,	JOHN	Married Jane Dohody	O 1,		32
1695,	SMITH,	JOHN	Married Elizabeth, daughter of Henry Cox	D 9,		62
1726,	SMITH,	JOHN	Married Frances, daughter & coheir of Thomas Harwar	O 7,		113
1727,	SMITH,	JOHN	Married Sarah, sister of Richard Covington	D 18,		282
1802,	SMITH,	JOHN	Married Mary, daughter of John & Judith Dunn	D 36,		134
1832,	SMITH,	JOHN	Married Polly, daughter of Caty Dunn	D 43,		580
1869, Jan. 14	SMITH,	JOHN H.	Married Lucy W. Saunders	Book 1,		22
1874, Dec. 17	SMITH,	JOHN W.	Married Mrs. Annie E. Smith	Book 1,		37
1837, May 10	SMITH,	JOSEPH B.	Married D. A. E. Dillard	Book 1,		253
1841, Apr. 9	SMITH,	JOSEPH	Married Ellen H. Jones	Book 1,		255
1864, Dec. 13	SMITH,	JOSEPHINE R.	Married Lawrence D. Roane	Book 1,		12
1819, Dec. 20	SMITH,	LAURA H.	Married George Harper	Book 1,		235
1800,	SMITH,	LETTICE LEE	Daughter of Meriwether, married Benjamin Rust	Land Trials,		186
1841, Sep. 28	SMITH,	LOTTIE M.	Married William C. Hughes	Book 1,		255
1800,	SMITH,	LUCY	Daughter of Meriwether, married Francis Quarles	Land Trials,		186
1867, Jan. 1	SMITH,	LUCY A.	Married George C. Minor	Book 1,		16
1895, Nov. 20	SMITH,	LUCY W.	Married T. B. Evans	Book 1,		119
1710,	SMITH,	MARGARET	Daughter of John, married Edward Fagen	D&C 13,		378
1824, Aug. 12	SMITH,	MARIA B.	Married David C. Belfield	Book 1,		241
1827,	SMITH,	MARIA	Daughter of Francis of Laurel Grove, married David Currie Belfield	D 42,		175
1855, Nov. 25	SMITH,	MARTHA TODD	Married John W. Fisher	Book 1,		6
1880, Jun. 1	SMITH,	MARTHA C.	Married J. W. Dillard	Book 1,		56
1760,	SMITH,	MARY	Daughter of Francis, married James Webb Jr.	W 11,		415
1866, May 24	SMITH,	MARY E.	Married Robert Wright	Book 1,		15

				Book	Page
1869, Nov. 7	SMITH,	MARY H.	Married Thomas H. Durham	Book 1,	23
1876, Nov. 21	SMITH,	MARY FRANCES	Married James A. Jackson	Book 1,	43
1893, Jan. 12	SMITH,	MARY	Married Alphonzo Brooks	Book 1,	111
1764,	SMITH,	MERIWETHER	Married Alice Corbin	D 29,	330
1836, Jul. 25	SMITH,	MORTIMER	Married Eleanor H. Howerton	Book 1,	252
1809, Jan. 6	SMITH,	MOURNING	Married Elizabeth Hundley	Book 1,	225
1876, Feb. 24	SMITH,	OSCAR E.	King & Queen Co., married Ann Eliza Trible	Book 1,	41
1674,	SMITH,	PHEBE	Daughter of Col. Toby Smith married William Hodgkin	D ʼ.,	144
1747,	SMITH,	RACHEL	Daughter of Maurice, King & Queen Co., married Henry Young	W 8,	344
1816, Sep. 18	SMITH,	RICHARD	Married E. S. Crittenden	Book 1,	232
1825,	SMITH,	RICHARD	Married Eliza, daughter of Lemuel & Susanna Crittenden	D 41,	413
1853, Dec. 22	SMITH,	RICHARD M.	Married Mary Frances Gresham	Book 1,	1
1841,	SMITH,	ROBERT B.	Married Dorothy, daughter of William Smith	W 24,	480
1873, Feb. 5	SMITH,	ROBERT W.	Married Annie E. Dillard	Book 1,	32
1864, Oct. 18	SMITH,	SALLIE E.	Married William P. Robinson	Book 1,	12
1704,	SMITH,	SAMUEL	Married Ann Dawkins, relict of Thomas Dawkins	D&C 12,	6
1722,	SMITH,	SAMUEL	Married Elizabeth Thompson	O 5,	675
1770,	SMITH,	SAMUEL	Married Mary, daughter of James Webb	W 12,	411
1721,	SMITH,	SARAH	Daughter of John, married John Bush	D 17, W 7,	3 189
1823, Nov. 8	SMITH,	SARAH	Married Fauntleroy Brockenbrough	Book 1,	240
1829, Jan. 12	SMITH,	SOPHRONIA ANN	Married William S. Croxton	Book 1,	246
1870, Oct. 26	SMITH,	SUSAN E.	Married Joseph Cauthorn	Book 1,	26
1803,	SMITH,	SUSANNA	Daughter of Philip, Northumberland Co., married John Lee	D 36,	300
1739,	SMITH,	THOMAS	Married Rebecca, widow of Richard Hutchins	D 22,	81
1655,	SMITH,	TOBY	Married Phebe, sister of Moore Fauntleroy	D 2,	35
1689,	SMITH,	WILLIAM	Married Eve, relict of John Williams of Morattico Creek	D 6,	179
1717,	SMITH,	WILLIAM	Married Ann, grandaughter of James Fullerton	D 16,	25
1831, Apr. 5	SMITH,	WILLIAM JR.	Married Martha Haynes	Book 1,	248
1838,	SMITH,	WILLIAM	Married Ann E. Young, sister of Henry Young dec'd	O 49,	145
1846, Dec. 22	SMITH,	WILLIAM F.	Married Elizabeth A. Wright	Book 1,	259
1884, Nov. 11	SMITH,	WILLIAM L.	Married Edith Fisher	Book 1,	79

					Book		Page
1888, Dec. 13	SMITHER,	BETTIE G.	Married Samuel Quesenberry		Book 1,		97
1828, Dec. 23	SMITHER,	CATY	Married John Griffin		Book 1,		245
1813, Nov. 25	SMITHER,	EDMOND P.	Married Margery Mahon		Book 1,		229
1829, Jan. 19	SMITHER,	GEORGE	Married Cordelia Gatewood		Book 1,		246
1829,	SMITHER,	GEORGE	Married Cordelia, daughter of Thomas Gatewood		D	43,	98
1848, Jan. 9	SMITHER,	HAWORD	Married Reuben Pitts		Book 1,		260
1819, Sep. 13	SMITHER,	JAMES	Married Eliza Lumpkin		Book 1,		236
1832,	SMITHER,	JAMES	Married Eliza, daughter of John Lumpkin		D	44,	46
1832, Jul. 26	SMITHER,	JAMES M.	Married Hannah N. Calliss		Book 1,		249
1833,	SMITHER,	JAMES M.	Married Hannah Callis		D	44,	184
1788,	SMITHER,	JOHN	Married Ann, daughter of John Watkins		W	8,	89
1830, Dec. 21	SMITHER,	JOHN S.	Married Polly Allen		Book 1,		247
1834, Sep. 15	SMITHER,	JOHN H.	Married Patsey Jones		Book 1,		250
1835,	SMITHER,	JOHN H.	Married Patsey, daughter of Joseph & Nancy Jones		D	44,	441
1837, Jan. 31	SMITHER,	JOHN	Married Nancy Samuel		Book 1,		250
1868, May 17	SMITHER,	JOHN L.	Married Mary F. Southard		Book 1,		20
1870, May 10	SMITHER,	JOHN H.	King & Queen Co., married Catharine Brooks		Book 1,		25
1822, Jan. 17	SMITHER,	LUCY	Married Zachariah Samuel		Book 1,		239
1851, May 31	SMITHER,	MARGARET A.	Married William B. Dyke		Book 1,		262
1763,	SMITHER,	MARY	Daughter of William, married ? Noell		W	12,	37
1828, Dec. 8	SMITHER,	POLLY	Married Reuben Samuel		Book 1,		245
1796,	SMITHER,	WILLIAM	Married Sally Keesee, daughter of George & Rachel		W	15,	419
1870, May 10	SMITHER,	WILLIAM B.	Married Sarah F. Moody		Book 1,		25
1873, Dec. 24	SMOOT,	CESLA M.	Married Ann E. Boughton		Book 1,		35
1888, Apr. 18	SMOOT,	C. M.	Married S. A. Lewis		Book 1,		95
1874, Nov. 19	SMOOT,	LEWIS H.	Rappahannock Co., married Harriet E. Jones		Book 1,		37
1703,	SNEAD,	ELIZABETH	Daughter of Charles, married Francis Taylor		O	3,	15
1703,	SNEAD,	THOMAS	Married Katherine, widow of Richard Grigory		D&W	10,	79, 141
1717,	SOMERVILLE,	ALEXANDER	Married Frances, relict of Henry Byrom		W	3,	138
1709,	SORRELL,	DORCAS	Relict of John, married John Morris		O	4,	146
1696,	SORRELL,	EDWARD	James City Co., married Alice, Exec. of Joseph Goodrich		D	9,	85

				Book	Page
1689,	SORRELL,	JOHN	Married Dorcas, relict of Tobias Ingram	O 2,	202
1833, Nov. 29	SOUTHALL,	AGNES W.	Married Lorenzo D. Brown	Book 1,	249
1810, Jan. 29	SOUTHALL,	CHARLES T.	Married Courtney Andrews	Book 1,	226
1849, Sep. 20	SOUTHALL,	MARY E.	Married William Quesenberry	Book 1,	261
1840, Apr. 11	SOUTHALL,	PLEASANT S.	Married Lucinda Allen	Book 1,	254
1879, Apr. 28	SOUTHARD,	ELLEN E.	Married Richard Gordon	Book 1,	52
1891, Jan. 8	SOUTHARD,	J. R.	Married Cora E. Davis	Book 1,	106
1868, May 17	SOUTHARD,	MARY F.	Married John L. Smither	Book 1,	20
1891, Apr. 8	SOUTHARD,	M. L.	Married L. R. Walton, King & Queen Co.	Book 1,	107
1840, Feb. 17	SOUTHWORD,	SOPHIA	Married Leonard Clark	Book 1,	254
1885, Nov. 17	SOUTHWORTH, ETTA		Married George B. Lipscomb	Book 1,	84
1842, Dec. 9	SOUTHWORTH, G.		Married Lavinia A. Rouse	Book 1,	256
1885, Nov. 20	SOUTHWORTH, HARRISON		Married Mary W. Banks	Book 1,	84
1893, Feb. 1	SOUTHWORTH, L. E.		Married Thomas L. Durham	Book 1,	111
1835, May 7	SOUTHWORTH, MARIA		Married Richard Garbrough	Book 1,	251
1828, Nov. 26	SOUTHWORTH, MARTHA		Married Townsend Carter	Book 1,	245
1833, May 30	SOUTHWORTH, WOODFORD		Married Mary Clark	Book 1,	249
1690,	SPENCE,	ALEXANDER	Married Elizabeth Browne	O 2,	220
1891, Apr. 21	SPENCER,	J. M.	Married Mary E. Cosby	Book 1,	107
1858, May 20	SPENCER,	RO: HUNTER	Married Rosalie Brooke Roy	Book 1,	6
1866, Jun. 21	SPENCER,	ROBERT H.	Married Virginia B. Roy	Book 1,	15
1700,	SPENCER,	THOMAS	Married Hannah, daughter of Henry Pickett	D&W 10,	67
1690,	SPICER,	ELIZABETH	Daughter of William, married Richard Mathews	D 8,	198
1690	SPICER,	GEORGE	Married Mr. Elizabeth Wilkes	O 2,	253
1714,	SPILLER,	JOHN	Married Sarah, only sister of William Harper	D&W 14,	274
1822,	SPINDLE,	BARBEE	Married Rebecca, daughter of Erasmus Jones	O 44,	196
1875, Nov. 23	SPINDLE,	BELLE W.	Married Victor Litchfield, Mathews Co.	Book 1,	40
1890, Sep. 24	SPINDLE,	CLARENCE J.	Married Josie C. Anderson	Book 1,	104
1825, Sep. 5	SPINDLE,	ELIZA E. B.	Married Leonard Spindle	Book 1,	242
1847, May 17	SPINDLE,	ELIZABETH	Married James H. Garnett	Book 1,	259
1836, Nov. 21	SPINDLE,	FANNIE M.	Married Lovel P. Tod	Book 1,	252

				Book	Page
1889, Jan. 31	SPINDLE,	FANNIE B.	Married J. P. Blackburn, Norfolk, Va.	Book 1,	99
1818, Jun. 15	SPINDLE,	FRANCES	Married Daniel Rennolds	Book 1,	234
1822,	SPINDLE,	FRANCES	Daughter of Barbee, married Daniel Rennolds	O 44,	196
1842, Nov. 21	SPINDLE,	JAMES	Married J. A. Rennolds	Book 1,	256
1834,	SPINDLE,	JANE	Daughter of Philip, married William F. Gaines	D 44,	294
1814, Oct. 24	SPINDLE,	JULIET	Married Walter Bowie	Book 1,	230
1825, Sep. 5	SPINDLE,	LEONARD	Married Eliza E. B. Spindle	Book 1,	242
1874, Sep. 30	SPINDLE,	MARIA L.	Married George R. Pollard	Book 1,	37
1822, Nov. 18	SPINDLE,	MARTHA	Married Silas Spindle	Book 1,	239
1844, Jan. 25	SPINDLE,	MARY B.	Married George Wright	Book 1,	257
1881, Dec. 15	SPINDLE,	MOLLIE F.	Married Robert S. Collawn	Book 1,	622
1826,	SPINDLE,	MORDECAI	Married Sarah, daughter of Leonard Noel	D 42,	26
1835, Nov. 30	SPINDLE,	MORDECAI	Married Frances M. Dickenson	Book 1,	251
1828, Jan. 7	SPINDLE,	SARAH	Married Archibald Ritchie	Book 1,	245
1822, Nov. 18	SPINDLE,	SILAS	Married Martha Spindle	Book 1,	239
1835, Nov. 16	SPINDLE,	VIRGINIA	Married Thomas Garnett	Book 1,	251
1853, Apr. 7	SPINDLE,	VIRGINIA M.	Married Dr. Philemon B. Robinson	Book 1,	264
1704,	SPIRES,	HANNAH	Relict of John, married William Roy	O 3,	103
1721,	STALLARD,	GRACE	Relict of Samuel, married John Hawkins	O 5,	561
1868, Dec. 9	STAMPER,	H. W.	Jefferson Co., Ky. Attorney, married Lizzie Munday	Book 1,	21
1711,	STANTON,	GODFREY	Married Dorothy, daughter of Thomas Pettit	Land Trials,	20
1874, Apr. 7	STAPLES,	PELEG S.	Stockton, Mo. married Mary E. Griffin	Book 1,	36
1896, Dec. 31	STAPLES,	SUSAN H.	Married Daffan L. Brannan	Book 1,	123
1678,	STAPP,	ABRAHAM	Husband of Dorothy North	D 7,	168
1685,	STAPP,	ABRAHAM	Married Dorothy, daughter of Robert Moss	Box 101,	M
1849, Feb. 28	STARKE,	GEORGE W.	Married Mary F. Micou	Book 1,	261
1804, Dec. 17	STARKE,	HARRIET	Married Godfrey Cauthorn	Book 1,	222
1711,	STARKE,	JOHN	Married Frances, daughter of Major James Boughan	Land Trials,	115
1721,	STEPHENS,	ANN	Mother of Samuel, married Peter Brooks	Box 105,	B
1885, Apr. 8	STEPHENS,	JAMES	Married Louisa Taylor, widow	Book 1,	82
1839, Feb. 21	STEPHENS,	WALKER	Married Phoebe Greenwood	Book 1,	254

				Book	Page
1678,	STERNE,	DAVID	Married Elizabeth, daughter of Peter Mills	D 6,	79
1871, Dec. 12	STEVENS,	ANN	Married William B. Schools	Book 1,	30
1898, Dec. 25	STEVENS,	C. B.	Married J. C. Dyott	Book 1,	130
1848, Feb. 16	STEVENS,	HENRY	Married Elizabeth Hudson	Book 1,	260
1876, Oct. 22	STEVENS,	JOHN L.	Married Amanda Carneale	Book 1,	43
1805, Jul. 15	STEVENS,	MARIA	Married Jesse Purkins	Book 1,	223
1863, Aug. 14	STEVENS,	MARIA A.	Married George W. Dunn	Book 1,	12
1819,	STEVENS,	WILLIAM	Rockbridge Co., married Catharine, legatee of Henry Allen	D 41,	483
1817, Nov. 25	STEWART,	ELIZABETH	Married Major Taylor	Book 1,	233
1814, Nov. 21	STEWARD,	JOHN	Married Rachel Gibson	Book 1,	230
1831, Dec. 21	STEWART,	PATSY	Married John Dunn	Book 1,	248
1833,	STEWART,	?	Married Judy, daughter of Samuel Kendall	D 44,	230
1892, Jun. 15	STEWART,	THOMAS C.	Married Susie C. Billups	Book 1,	109
1868, Dec. 22	STEWART,	WALTER H.	Westmoreland Co., married Lucy A. Croxton	Book 1,	21
1841, Mar. 1	STEWART,	WILLIAM	Married Mary Ann Trimyer	Book 1,	255
1826,	STHRESHLEY, ELIZABETH		Married Nicholas Lafon	D 42,	98
1799,	STHRESHLEY, WILLIAM		Married Lucy Waring	O 35, D 37,	334 162
1748,	STHRESHLEY, WILLIAM		Married Lucy, widow of Thomas Waring	Land Trials,	24
1893, Feb. 9	STIFF,	FRANK W.	Richmond, Va. married Kate A. Street	Book 1,	111
1813, Jan. 23	STIFF,	JANE	Married John Fortune	Book 1,	233
1741,	ST. JOHN	AMEY	Widow of Richard, married William Covington, Jr.	O 12,	304
1803,	ST. JOHN	CATHARINE	Daughter of Thomas, married Dura Dobbins	D 36,	263
1824,	ST. JOHN	CATHARINE	Daughter of Richard, married Dura Dobbins	W 20,	32
1690,	ST. JOHN	ELIZABETH	Daughter of Thomas, married William Cooper	D 9,	225
1818, Dec. 29	ST. JOHN	JOHN	Married Elizabeth Howerton	Book 1,	234
1700,	ST. JOHN	MARY	Relict of Thomas, married John Billington	D&W 10,	37
1763,	ST. JOHN	MARY	Widow of William, married James Coughland	W 12,	187
1824,	ST. JOHN	NANCY	Daughter of Richard, married Isaac Brooks	W 20,	32
1812, Dec. 24	ST. JOHN,	THOMAS	Married Cary Caston Boughan	Book 1,	228
1867, Jan. 13	ST. JOHN	ZACHARIAH	Married Rebecca Moody	Book 1,	17
1688,	ST. LEGER,	PETER	Married Elizabeth, relict of John Vickers	O 2,	133

				Book		Page
1716,	STOCKDALE, PHILIP	Married Elinor Kemp		O	5,	17
1724,	STOCKDALE, PHILIP	Married Ann Cloutson		D	18,	167
1725,	STOCKDELL, PHILIP	Married Ann, sister of Cornelius Clowson		D	18,	167
1723,	STODGILL, JAMES	Married Ann, granddaughter of Robert Armstrong		D	17,	266
1875, Apr. 10	STOKES, ALFRED	Married Sarah Giles		Book 1,		39
1824, Apr. 16	STOKES, ANN	Married Thomas Coleman		Book 1,		241
1827, Feb. 7	STOKES, BENJAMIN	Married Fanny Munday		Book 1,		244
1836, Feb. 8	STOKES, BENJAMIN	Married Elizabeth Younger		Book 1,		252
1833, Nov. 13	STOKES, BROOKING	·Married Louisa Sale		Book 1,		249
1874, Mar. 12	STOKES, DELAWARE	Married Fanny Carneale		Book 1,		36
1871, Dec. 26	STOKES, DICEY T.	Married James T. Elliott		Book 1,		30
1830, Mar. 16	STOKES, EDWIN	Married Lottsey E. Coleman		Book 1,		247
1701,	STOKES, ELIZABETH	Relict of John married Henry Newton		D& W 10,		88
1758,	STOKES, ELIZABETH	Daughter of Nehemiah & Behethlem, married Thomas Newton		D	28,	76
1851, Dec. 8	STOKES, FRANCES	Married Robert Armstrong		Book 1,		262
1840, Feb. 11	STOKES, JOANNA	Married William Taylor		Book 1,		254
1818, Jun. 1	STOKES, JONAS	Married Elizabeth Hiccock		Book 1,		234
1836, Sep. 30	STOKES, JONAS	Married Elizabeth Allen		Book 1,		252
1840, Jan. 20	STOKES, JONAS	Married Drusilla Gatewood		Book 1,		254
1818, Feb. 16	STOKES, JOSEPH	Married Mary Hudson		Book 1,		234
1872, Jul. 4	STOKES, JULIA	Married James T. Elliott		Book 1,		31
1833, Jan. 14	STOKES, LUCY	Married Sullivan Gatewood		Book 1,		249
1865, Sep. 15	STOKES, MARY AGNES	Married Charles R. Mitchell		Book 1,		13
1869, May 13	STOKES, MARY	Married Richard Howard, Caroline Co.		Book 1,		23
1894, Mar. 21	STOKES, MARY S.	Married Benjamin Howard		Book 1,		113
1758,	STOKES, NEHEMIAH	Married Behethlem Gilson		D	28,	76
1869, Nov. 18	STOKES, ROSETTA	Married William Fields		Book 1,		23
1835, Aug. 5	STOKES, SOUTHALL	Married Schlenissa Rouse		Book 1,		251
1817, Dec. 16	STOKES, STHRESHLEY	Married Polly Greenstead		Book 1,		233
1830, Jan. 18	STOKES, WILLIAM	Married Martha Coleman		Book 1,		247
1869, Nov. 25	STOKES, WILLIAM F.	Married Martha E. Taylor		Book 1,		23

1888, May 23	STONE,	ANNIE B.	Married R. J. Duke	Book 1,	95
1706,	STONE,	EMANUEL	Married Mary Milburne	O 3,	224
1707,	STONE,	FRANCIS	Married Mary, daughter of Thomas Pannell	D&C 13,	18
1672,	STONE,	JOHN COL.	Married Sarah, relict of Col. John Walker	D 5,	98
1829, Jun. 19	STONE,	RICHARD	Married Cordelia Bush	Book 1,	246
1829,	STONE,	RICHARD	Married Cordelia, daughter of John Bush	D 43,	36
1691,	STOPFORD,	MARTHA	Widow of Thomas Troath	O 2,	303
1689,	STORY,	JOHN CAPT.	Married Elinor, relict of Major George Morris	O 2,	202
1860, Oct. 23	STREET,	ANNIS	Married William H. Saunders	Book 1,	10
1838, Jan. 21	STREET,	ELIZABETH	Married William B. Fleet	Book 1,	249
1863, Nov. 24	STREET,	FANNIE B.	Married John A. Street	Book 1,	12
1867, Nov. 21	STREET,	FANNIE	Married William S. Ware	Book 1,	18
1769,	STREET,	HENRY	Married Catharine, daughter of Sebell Carlton	W 12,	365
1832, Feb. 6	STREET,	JOHN	Married Mary M. Newbill	Book 1,	249
1863, Nov. 24	STREET,	JOHN A.	Married Fannie B. Street	Book 1,	12
1869, Dec. 22	STREET,	JOHN W.	Middlesex Co., married Virginia McKann	Book 1,	24
1893, Feb. 9	STREET,	KATE A.	Married Frank W. Stiff	Book 1,	111
1865, Dec. 25	STREET,	LUCY I.	Married Joseph C. Eubank	Book 1,	14
1864, Jun. 1	STREET,	MARTHA I.	Married William H. Saunders	Book 1,	12
1810, Jan. 15	STREET,	NANCY	Married John Sadler	Book 1,	226
1846, Dec. 19	STREET,	NAPOLEON B.	Married Amelia H. Sadler	Book 1,	259
1783,	STREET,	SEBELL	Daughter of Henry, married Samuel Greenwood	D . 32,	191
1869, Mar. 24	STREET,	WILLIAM H.	Married Mary J. Newbill	Book 1,	23
1885, Jul. 20	STREET,	WILLIAM A.	Married Mary F. Sadler	Book 1,	82
1828, Jan. 10	STREIGLE,	LANDELIN	Married Sarah W. Jones	Book 1,	245
1830,	STREIGLE,	LANDELIN	Married Sarah Jones	D 43,	411
1807,	STUBBLEFIELD, ROBERT		Married Clara Jones	O 39,	181
1683,	STUBBLESON, ANN		Daughter of Stubble Stubbleson, married John Farguson	D 7,	129
1897, Jun. 9	STUBBS,	ROBERT H.	Gloucester Co., married Ella M. Carlton	Book 1,	125
1783,	STURMAN,	ELLIOTT	Married Mary, daughter of William Young	W 13,	374
1695,	SUGGIT,	JOHN	Married Elizabeth Smith (License)	O 1,	369

				Book	Page
1699,	SULLENGER,	PETER	Married Elizabeth, relict of John Dixon	D&W 10,	12
1800,	SULLIVAN,	ELIZABETH	Daughter of James & Elizabeth, married ? Jones	W 16	11
1835, Nov. 16	SULLIVAN,	LUCY S.	Married Wilcey Fogg	Book 1,	251
1836,	SULLIVAN,	MARY B.	Married Izard B. Bush, Kentucky	D 45,	128
1824, Mar. 30	SULLIVAN,	NANCY	Married Riley Dollins	Book 1,	241
1823, Dec. 15	SULLIVAN,	PHOEBE	Married John Thomas	Book 1,	240
1800,	SULLIVAN,	SARAH	Daughter of James & Elizabeth, married ? Noell	W 16,	11
1835,	SULLIVAN,	SUSAN	Married Tazewell Elliott	Book 1,	251
1689,	SULLIVANT,	JEAN	Widow of Dennis, married James Clayton	D 8,	116
1690,	SURLES,	JOHN	Married Dorcas, Exec. of Tobias Ingram	O 2,	257
1746,	SUTTON,	JOHN	Married Elizabeth, relict of Robert Welch	W 7,	450
1673,	SWELLIVANT, SARAH		Daughter of Dennis, married Henry Lenton	W&D 1,	184
1745,	SWELLIPHEN, THOMAS		Married Dorcas, daughter of James Landrum	D 28,	83
1672,	SWINBURNE,	THOMAS	Married Katherine, relict of Thomas Pannell	D 6,	54

Date	Surname	Given Name	Details	Book	Page
1888, Apr. 22	TABB,	PETER	Married Hila Eubank	Book 1,	95
1882, Aug. 1	TAFF,	BETTIE A.	Married Henry N. Dyke	Book 1,	66
1888, May 16	TAFF,	COPELAND F.	Married McDonald Evans	Book 1,	95
1866, Dec. 25	TAFF,	ELIZA	Married John A. Carlton	Book 1,	16
1861, Dec. 17	TAFF,	IDA	Married Miles T. Mason	Book 1,	11
1875, Mar. 26	TAFF,	LUCY	Middlesex Co., married John S. McCauley	Book 1,	39
1799,	TAFF,	PETER	Married Mary Evans	O 35,	213
1840,	TAFF,	THOMAS F.	Married Lucy Ann, daughter of James & Roenna Greenwood, Middlesex Co.	D 27,	131
1814, Feb. 21	TAFF,	TRAVIS	Married Mary L. Scott	Book 1,	230
1687,	TALIAFERRO,	CATHARINE	Daughter of Robert married John Battaile	O 2,	35
1725,	TALIAFERRO,	ELIZABETH	Sister of Robert, married Thomas Triplett (Stripling)	W 4,	155
1848, Feb. 28	TALIAFERRO,	FANNY A.	Married Curtis Carter	Book 1,	260
1687,	TALIAFERRO,	ROBERT	Married Sarah, daughter of John & Elizabeth Catlett	O 2,	25
1689,	TALIAFERRO,	SARAH	Relict of Robert, married Samuel Sallis	O 2,	158
1821, Dec. 20	TALIAFERRO,	SCHOOLS	Married Lucy Taylor	Book 1,	238
1741,	TANDY,	ANN	Daughter of Henry, married Edward Waller	Box 109,	H
1685,	TANDY,	HENRY	Married relict of John Watson	O 1,	151
1703,	TANDY,	MARTHA	Married John Parker	O 3,	16
1689,	TAP,	MARY	Married Joseph Bragg	O 2,	177
1691,	TAPP,	MARY	Married John Butcher	O 2,	307
1718,	TARENT,	LEONARD	Married Mary, dau. of Robt. Brooke	W 3,	27, 28
1741,	TARENT,	MARY	Daughter of Leonard, married Robert Rose	Book 1,	263
1852, Dec. 30	TATE,	EDWARD	Married Mary Bush	Book 1,	263
1844, Nov. 27	TATE,	EMILY	Married H. Shearwood	Book 1,	257
1846, Jan. 5	TATE,	GEORGE	Married Anna Ball	Book 1,	259
1884, Feb. 19	TATE,	GEORGE H.	Married Mary J. Prince	Book 1,	75
1868, Sep. 2	TATE,	LUCY E.	Married Cornelius A. Edwards	Book 1,	21
1832, Dec. 22	TATE,	ROCKSEY	Married Garnett Greenstreet	Book 1,	249
1888, Nov. 15	TATE,	SHIELDS B.	Married Margaret Rowe	Book 1,	96
1831, Jul. 6	TATE,	WILLIAM	Married Sarah Jeffries	Book 1,	248

					Book	Page
1689,		TAVERNER,	JOHN	Married Elizabeth, relict of John Cole	D 6,	63
1842, Jan. 22		TAYLOR,	ALEXANDER	Married Catharine Robinson	Book 1,	256
1869, Jun. 10		TAYLOR,	AMANDA J.	Married Benjamin F. Dunn	Book 1,	23
1750,		TAYLER,	ANN	Daughter of James, King & Queen Co., married Edward Eastham	D 25,	180
1861, Mar. 28		TAYLOR,	ANNIE E.	Married George W. Durham	Book 1,	10
1848, Dec. 26		TAYLOR,	ARTHUR	Married Caroline V. Dunn	Book 1,	260
1859, Jan. 31		TAYLOR,	ARTHUR	Married Mildred A. Dunn	Book 1,	7
1823, Dec. 24		TAYLOR,	BOOKER	Married Lucy Ingram	Book 1,	240
1878, Mar. 7		TAYLOR,	CAROLINE	Married Absalom Heflin, Fauquier Co.	Book 1,	48
1818, Dec. 14		TAYLOR,	CARTER	Married Sally Cook	Book 1,	234
1830, Nov. 30		TAYLOR,	CATHARINE	Married Walker Davis	Book 1,	247
1843,		TAYLOR,	CATHARINE	Daughter of Nancy, married Walker Davis	W 24,	149
1867, Dec. 26		TAYLOR,	COLUMBIA JANE	Married Charles H. Greenwood	Book 1,	19
1679,		TAYLOR,	CONSTANCE	Daughter of Richard, married William Glew	D 6,	110
1884, Dec. 25		TAYLOR,	DIDEMIA	Married Harvey T. Walton	Book 1,	80
1894, Dec. 27		TAYLOR,	D. E.	Married J. S. Hodges	Book 1,	116
1886, Jul. 8		TAYLOR,	DORA	Married Logan Jessee	Book 1,	88
1869, Feb. 11		TAYLOR,	DRUSILLA	Married Franklin L. Taylor	Book 1,	22
1877, Apr. 3		TAYLOR,	EDNA R.	Married Charles Carter	Book 1,	45
1846, Nov. 12		TAYLOR,	EDMUND	Married Lucy Ann Kay	Book 1,	259
1742,		TAYLOR,	EDWARD	Married Catharine, daughter of John Williamson	W 7,	251
1763,		TAYLOR,	ELIZABETH	Married James Noell	W 12,	69
1891, Jul. 29		TAYLOR,	ELLA J.	Married A. R. Carneale	Book 1,	107
1857, May 2		TAYLOR,	EMILY	Married John Clarke	Book 1,	6
1838, May 24		TAYLOR	FRANCES JANE	Married Thomas Coates	Book 1,	253
1843,		TAYLOR,	FRANCES	Daughter of Nancy, married Thomas Coates	W 24,	149
1848, Jan. 4		TAYLOR,	FRANCES,	Married John R. Cauthorn	Book 1,	260
1861, Jan. 25		TAYLOR,	FRANCES A.	Married Charles H. Brooks	Book 1,	10
1703,		TAYLOR,	FRANCIS	Married Elizabeth, daughter of Charles Snead	O 3,	15
1846, Dec. 17		TAYLOR,	FRANK S.	Married Martha Shackelford	Book 1,	258
1869, Feb. 11		TAYLOR,	FRANKLIN L.	Married Drusilla Taylor	Book 1,	22

					Book		Page
1684,		TAYLOR,	GEORGE CAPT.	Married Martha Moseley		O	1,	52, 61
1820, Dec. 18	TAYLOR,	GEORGE		Married Margaret D. Dunn		Book 1,	237
1837, Sep. 18	TAYLOR,	GEORGE		Married Ann Dalley		Book 1,	253
1843, Jun. 28	TAYLOR,	GEORGE		Married Dorothea Moody		Book 1,	257
1850, Oct. 8	TAYLOR,	GEORGE JR.		Married Mary Davis		Book 1,	262
1853, Jun. 16	TAYLOR,	GEORGE H.		Married Mary Adeline Dyke		Book 1,	264
1869, Feb. 14	TAYLOR,	GEORGE M. D.		Married Mary C. Greenwood		Book 1,	22
1876, Dec. 15	TAYLOR,	GEORGIANA		Married John G. Boughan		Book 1,	44
1895, Dec. 26	TAYLOR,	G. W.		Married S. Y. Muse		Book 1,	119
1879, Dec. 23	TAYLOR,	HARVEY R.		Married Emma J. Brizendine		Book 1,	53
1685,		TAYLER,	JAMES		Married Relict of Evan Morgan		O	1,	124
1686,		TAYLER,	JAMES		Married Elizabeth, mother of William Browne		D	7,	323
1690,		TAYLER,	JAMES		Married Ann, relict of Evan Morgan		O	2,	220
1839, Jul. 15	TAYLOR,	JAMES H.		Married Polly Houston		Book 1,	254
1850, Dec. 24	TAYLOR,	JAMES H.		Married Frances A. Dunn		Book 1,	262
1870, Aug. 25	TAYLOR,	JAMES K. F.		Married Rosa L. Brooks		Book 1,	26
1871, May 21	TAYLOR,	JAMES H. JR.		Married Indiana Brooks		Book 1,	28
1810, Dec. 29	TAYLOR,	JANE		Married Ambrose Heath Cook		Book 1,	226
1717,		TAYLOR,	JOHN		Married widow of Stephen Loyd		D&W 14,	400
1860, Jan. 1	TAYLOR,	JOHN M.		Married Mary R. Thomas		Book 1,	8
1892, Sep. 6	TAYLOR,	JOHN P.		Married M. A. Armistead		Book 1,	110
1898, Jul. 20	TAYLOR,	J. H.		Married F. L. Brizendine		Book 1,	129
1861, Dec. 5	TAYLOR,	JOSEPH E.		Married Mildred S. Faulconer		Book 1,	11
1836, Jun. 20	TAYLOR,	JULIA ANN		Married Jabez Watkins		Book 1,	252
1842, Jan. 12	TAYLOR,	JULIA		Married William Dix		Book 1,	256
1869, Dec. 23	TAYLOR,	JULIA E.		Married Sthreshley A. Cox		Book 1,	24
1812, Dec. 14	TAYLOR,	LEROY		Married Nancy Williamson		Book 1,	228
1825, Nov. 28	TAYLOR,	LEROY		Married Polly Durham		Book 1,	242
1866, Jan. 25	TAYLOR,	LEROY R.		Married Virginia Gordon		Book 1,	14
1877, Nov. 15	TAYLOR,	LEROY		Married Nannie Reid		Book 1,	46
1866, Dec. 25	TAYLOR,	LEWIS		Married Martha I. Broach		Book 1,	16

					Book	Page
1879, Dec. 25	TAYLOR,	LUCINDA	Married Ellver A. Jesse		Book 1,	53
1816, Nov. 7	TAYLOR,	LUCY	Married Philip Davis		Book 1,	233
1821, Dec. 20	TAYLOR,	LUCY	Married Schools Taliaferro		Book 1,	238
1844, Dec. 9	TAYLOR,	LUCY ANN	Married Thomas Faver		Book 1,	257
1855, Feb. 15	TAYLOR,	LUCY ANN	Married Robert F. Gary		Book 1,	3
1894, Jul. 5	TAYLOR,	LUCY J.	Married Josiah Williams, Richmond, Va.		Book 1,	114
1839, Mar. 18	TAYLOR,	LUNSFORD	Married Lucy Ball		Book 1,	254
1817, Nov. 25	TAYLOR,	MAJOR	Married Elizabeth Stewart		Book 1,	233
1822, Sep. 7	TAYLOR,	MARGARET	Married John Games		Book 1,	239
1816, Dec. 16	TAYLOR,	MARIA	Married Muscoe Noel		Book 1,	232
1846, Jun. 1	TAYLOR,	MARTHA A.	Married Joseph Saunders		Book 1,	259
1867, Dec. 24	TAYLOR,	MARTHA JANE	Married James Robert Harmon	Book 1,	19
1869, Nov. 25	TAYLOR,	MARTHA E.	Married William F. Stokes		Book 1,	23
1876, Nov. 7	TAYLOR,	MARTHA J.	Widow, married John W. Andrews	Book 1,	43
1878, Feb. 14	TAYLOR,	MARTHA ELLEN	Married Andrew Pitts		Book 1,	48
1818, Mar. 16	TAYLOR,	MARY	Married Jack Dyke		Book 1,	234
1836, Mar. 22	TAYLOR,	MARY ANN	Married John Hodges		Book 1,	252
1858, Apr. 27	TAYLOR,	MARY	Married Jon. Clark		Book 1,	268
1865, Nov. 19	TAYLOR,	MARY R.	Married James F. Greenstreet		Book 1,	13
1869, Feb. 18	TAYLOR,	MARY E.	Married Thomas W. Boughan		Book 1,	22
1889, Apr. 21	TAYLOR,	MARY A.	Married George P. McKendrie		Book 1,	100
1833, Dec. 4	TAYLOR,	MATILDA	Married James Ingram		Book 1,	249
1868, Dec. 30	TAYLOR,	MILDRED A.	Married Benjamin F. Clarke		Book 1,	21
1885, Feb. 10	TAYLOR,	MILZA	Married Allie Harper		Book 1,	81
1833, Dec. 10	TAYLOR,	M. H.	Married Julia Covington		Book 1,	249
1876, Dec. 28	TAYLOR,	MOLLY	Married George W. Mitchell		Book 1,	44
1883, Feb. 8	TAYLOR,	MYRTINE	Married Thomas G. Haynes		Book 1,	69
1834, Feb. 26	TAYLOR,	NANCY	Married Vincent Williams		Book 1,	250
1879, Mar. 6	TAYLOR,	NANCY	Married Edward Taylor		Book 1,	51
1898, Jan. 26	TAYLOR,	NANNIE B.	Married George W. Brooks		Book 1,	128
1872, Dec. 24	TAYLOR,	N. B.	Married Drucilla E. Davis		Book 1,	32

					Book	Page
1805, Jan. 12	TAYLOR,	PHOEBE	Married Mourten Elliott		Book 1,	223
1818,	TAYLOR,	POLLY	Married Jackson Dyke		D 41,	116
1822, Dec. 24	TAYLOR,	POLLY	Married Zachariah Williamson		Book 1,	239
1880, Nov. 20	TAYLOR,	RAMY S.	Married Emma E. Davis		Book 1,	57
1833, Jan. 3	TAYLOR,	REBECCA	Married John Purks		Book 1,	249
1827, Jan. 3	TAYLOR,	REUBEN	Married Barbara Brooks		Book 1,	244
1867, Jan. 15	TAYLOR,	RICHARD C.	Married Amanda C. Rowe		Book 1,	16
1868, Jul. 25	TAYLOR,	ROBERT W.	Married Elizabeth Clarke		Book 1,	20
1884, Jun. 26	TAYLOR,	ROSA L.	Married James W. Brooks		Book 1,	77
1818,	TAYLOR,	SALLIE	Married Robert Samuel		D 41,	116
1756,	TAYLOR,	SARAH	Daughter of William, married James Garnett		W 12,	69
1816, Dec. 24	TAYLOR	SARAH B.	Married Robert Samuel		Book 1,	232
1849, Feb. 1	TAYLOR,	SOPHRONIA	Married Thomas Foreacres		Book 1,	261
1815, Dec. 16	TAYLOR,	STHRESHLEY	Married Aphry Moody		Book 1,	231
1824, Oct. 20	TAYLOR,	STHRESHLEY	Married Patsey Riddle		Book 1,	241
1846, Apr. 20	TAYLOR,	SUSAN A.	Married John Croxton		Book 1,	258
1852, Nov. 24	TAYLOR,	SUSAN	Married Joseph B. Allen		Book 1,	263
1840, Nov. 17	TAYLOR,	SUSANNA	Married William Loyd		Book 1,	254
1765,	TAYLOR,	TABATHY	Daughter of James, married William Wyld		D 30,	42
1816, Dec. 26	TAYLOR,	TAMZON U.	Married John Beazley		Book 1,	232
1840, Jan. 20	TAYLOR,	TAMZIN	Married Sale Davis		Book 1,	254
1879, Mar. 20	TAYLOR,	THEIZA F.	Married Ellis Brooks		Book 1,	51
1877, Dec. 20	TAYLOR,	THOMAS R.	Married Louisa Brooks		Book 1,	46
1867, Mar. 21	TAYLOR,	THORNTON	Married Betty Ellis		Book 1,	17
1811, Jan. 21	TAYLOR,	WILLIAM	Married Fanny Durham		Book 1,	227
1837,	TAYLOR,	WILLIAM H.	Married Julia, daughter of John Covington		D 45,	275
1840, Feb. 11	TAYLOR,	WILLIAM	Married Joanna Stokes		Book 1,	254
1841, Jun. 7	TAYLOR,	WILLIAM	Married Nancy Coghill		Book 1,	255
1858, Mar. 29	TAYLOR,	WILLIAM A.	Richmond Co., married Phelecia C. Faulconer		Book 1,	6
1884, Jan. 15	TAYLOR,	WILLIAM B. H.	Married Kate Harper		Book 1,	75
1892, Feb. 17	TAYLOR,	W. J.	Maryland, married M. J. Eubank	Book 1,	109

· 230 ·

Date	Surname	Given Name	Details	Book	Page
1876, Apr. 13	TAYLOR,	WILLIAM H.	Married Mrs. Olympia Allen	Book 1,	42
1824, Mar. 3	TEBBS,	EMILY FOUSHEE	Married William B. Cooke	Book 1,	241
1833,	TEBBS,	EMILY FOUSHEE	Daughter of Foushee, married William B. Cooke	D 44,	192
1810,	TEBBS,	FOUSHEE	Married Ann, daughter of Henry Quarles	W 17,	243
1824, Mar. 30	TEBBS,	MARTHA E.	Married George H Dabney	Book 1,	241
1823,	TEBBS,	SARAH	Daughter of Foushee, married Raleigh Downman, Lancaster Co.	D 41,	93
1890, Oct. 29	TEMPLE,	ANNIE W.	Married Joseph Lewis	Book 1,	104
1878, Sep. 19	TEMPLE,	CATHARINE	Married Thomas Jones	Book 1,	49
1820, Oct. 25	TEMPLE,	FRANCES ANN	Married John R. Matthews	Book 1,	237
1843, Feb. 1	TEMPLE,	HENRY W. S.	Married Susan Jones	Book 1,	257
1830, Sep. 1	TEMPLE,	JAMES H.	Married Frances Matthews	Book 1,	247
1804, Jan. 7	TEMPLE,	JOHN	Married Mary Latane	Book 1,	222
1808,	TEMPLE,	JOHN	Married Polly, daughter of William Latane	W 17,	312
1812,	TEMPLE,	JOHN	Married Mary Latane	O 41,	109
1844, Sep. 17	TEMPLE,	JOHN R.	Married Betsey F. Hill	Book 1,	257
1858, Nov. 30	TEMPLE,	JOHN	Married Matilda J. Wright	Book 1,	6
1881, Oct. 11	TEMPLE,	JOHN M.	Arkansas, married Alice M. Gresham, daughter of Henry	Book 1,	61
1858, Dec. 2	TEMPLE,	LUCY WARING	Married Watson Walker, King & Queen Co.	Book 1,	6
1872, Sep. 19	TEMPLE,	LUCY E.	Married Catesby E. Lewis	Book 1,	31
1830, Apr. 1	TERRELL,	ALFRED	Married Clara A. F. Micou	Book 1,	247
1814, Feb. 21	TERRELL,	EDMUND	Married Caty Davis	Book 1,	230
1818, Feb. 28	TERRELL,	FANNY	Married John Crow	Book 1,	234
1806, Mar. 7	TERRELL,	PHEBA	Married Major Davis	Book 1,	223
1823, Feb. 17	TERRELL,	POLLY	Married Henry Barton	Book 1,	240
1814, May 25	TERRELL,	THOMAS	Married Betsey Crow	Book 1,	230
1694,	THACKER,	EDWIN	Married Mrs. Frances Dangerfield	O 1,	306
1714,	THACKER,	MARY	Widow of Samuel, married John Bagge	D&W 14,	304
1698,	THACKER,	SAMUEL	Married Mary, daughter of Ralph Warriner	D 9,	220
1684,	THACKER,	WILLIAM	Lancaster Co., married Alice, daughter of William Mathews	D 7, / D 8,	325 / 91
1812,	THOM,	JOHN	Married Lucy Lewis	O 41,	109
1866, Feb. 25	THOMAS,	ANN ELIZA	Married Henry Jackson	Book 1,	14

				Book	Page
1868, Dec. 24	THOMAS,	ANN ELIZA	Married Archibald Coghill	Book 1,	21
1869, Mar. 23	THOMAS,	ARCHIBALD	Married Mary L. Munday	Book 1,	23
1828, Jan. 1	THOMAS,	CATHARINE	Married William F. Faulconer	Book 1,	245
1790,	THOMAS,	CATY	Daughter of William, married William White	W 14,	206
1814, Apr. 26	THOMAS,	ELIZABETH	Married Humphrey Thomas	Book 1,	230
1820, Nov. 25	THOMAS,	ELIZABETH	Married Bowler Vawter	Book 1,	242
1843, Dec. 20	THOMAS,	ELIZABETH C.	Married Claiborne Rouse	Book 1,	257
1882, Dec. 21	THOMAS,	ELLEN	Married Charles L. Haile	Book 1,	67
1810, Aug. 17	THOMAS,	FANNY	Married William Clarke	Book 1,	226
1829,	THOMAS,	FANNY	Daughter of Philip, married William F. Faulconer	D 43,	82
1773,	THOMAS,	FRANKY	Daughter of William, married Reuben Rouzee	W 12,	539
1833,	THOMAS,	HARRIET	Daughter of Philip, married Uriah Schools	D 44,	197
1814, Apr. 26	THOMAS,	HUMPHREY	Married Elizabeth Thomas	Book 1,	230
1756,	THOMAS,	JOHN	Married Keziah, daughter of Samuel Henshaw	D 28,	43
1823, Dec. 15	THOMAS,	JOHN	Married Phoebe Sullivan	Book 1,	240
1837,	THOMAS,	JOHN	Married Phoebe Sullivan	D 45,	391
1881, Mar. 22	THOMAS,	JULIUS F.	Married Adaline Carneale	Book 1,	59
1844, Jan. 4	THOMAS,	LAURA	Married William Dunn	Book 1,	257
1853, Dec. 27	THOMAS,	LEONARD D..	Married Ann M. Pitts	Book 1,	1
1817, Mar. 17	THOMAS,	LEWIS H.	Married Elizabeth Davis	Book 1,	233
1826,	THOMAS,	LEWIS	Married Elizabeth, daughter of Edward G. Davis	D 41,	529
1742,	THOMAS,	MARK	Married Ann, daughter of William Ayres	D 22,	428
1809, Nov. 21	THOMAS,	MARY	Married William Crittenden	Book 1,	225
1866, Jan. 1	THOMAS,	MARY R.	Married John M. Taylor	Book 1,	8
1870, May 19	THOMAS,	MARY L.	Married Richard House	Book 1,	25
1851, Jun. 11	THOMAS,	MATILDA ANN	Married William Alexander	Book 1,	262
1704,	THOMAS,	PHILIP	Married Ann Adkinson	O 3,	124
1871, Sep. 6	THOMAS,	PHILIP	Married Elizabeth Collier, widow	Book 1,	29
1808, Mar. 17	THOMAS,	RACHEL	Married Augustine Oliver	Book 1,	224
1809, Oct. 27	THOMAS,	RACHEL	Married John Crittenden	Book 1,	225
1809, Feb. 22	THOMAS,	ROBERT	Married Betsey Kay	Book 1,	225

				Book	Page
1773,	THOMAS,	ROSEY	Daughter of William, married John Cross	W 12	539
1849, Nov. 27	THOMAS,	SUSAN	Married James Samuel	Book 1,	261
1860, Jun. 24	THOMAS,	SUSAN	Married Alexander Coghill	Book 1,	9
1739,	THOMAS,	WILLIAM	Married Susanna, daughter of John Boulware	D 22,	126
1811, May 11	THOMAS,	WILLIAM	Married Sally Kay	Book 1,	227
1812, Aug. 17	THOMAS,	WILLIAM	Married Sally Conoley	Book 1,	228
1722,	THOMPSON,	ELIZABETH	Married Samuel Smith	O 5,	675
1898, May 18	THOMPSON,	M. A.	Married James A. Brooks	Book 1,	133
1814, Jun. 9	THOMPSON,	PATSY	Married Joseph Hester	Book 1,	230
1708,	THOMPSON,	WILLIAM	Married Martha, daughter of William Moseley	O 4,	48
1677,	THORNBURY,	WILLIAM	Married relict of Thomas Robinson	D 6,	53
1724,	THORNTON,	ALICE	Daughter of Francis, married Lawrence Catlett	Box 105,	H
1678,	THORNTON,	FRANCIS	Married Alice, daughter of Anthony Savage	D 6,	64
1706,	THORPE,	FLORINDA	Exec. of Thomas, married Thomas Ayres	O 3,	273
1769,	THORPE,	FRANCES	Widow of Thomas, Sr. married Jeremiah Bizwell	D 30,	370
1770,	THORPE,	SARAH	Widow of Thomas, married Thomas Oneale	O 28,	15
1785,	THORPE,	SARAH	Sister of William, married Ishmael Harmon	D 32,	359
1774,	THORPE,	THOMAS	His daughter married William Plunkett	W 12,	591
1814, Jan. 4	THROCKMORTON, ANN		Married James Booker	Book 1,	230
1789,	THROCKMORTON, FANNY		Married Anthony Haynes	D 35,	59
1761,	THROCKMORTON, GABRIEL		Married Judith, daughter of Thomas Edmondson	O 23,	406
1805, Jan. 20	THROCKMORTON, JUDITH		Married Robert E. Brooking	Book 1,	222
1804, May 21	THROCKMORTON, LUCY		Married Robert Brooking	Book 1,	222
1814, May 25	THURSTON,	JOHN	Married Betty Gaines	Book 1,	230
1804, Dec. 18	THURSTON,	WILLIAM D.	Married Elizabeth Clarke	Book 1,	222
1898, Sep. 15	THURSTON,	MARY J.	Married R. B. Mitchell	Book 1,	129
1823, Sep. 22	TIBBS,	SUSAN L.	Married William T. Mooklar	Book 1,	240
1750,	TILLER,	WILLIAM	Married Catharine, daughter of Charles Brown	D 25,	270
1827,	TILLMAN,	JOSEPH	Married Sally Ryland	D 42,	361
1876, Aug. 1	TILTON,	CHARLES H.	Philadelphia, Pa. married Catharine Davis	Book 1,	42
1886, Jan. 12	TILTON,	LILLIE R.	Married Thomas W. Davis	Book 1,	85

				Book	Page
1877, Mar. 13	TINSBLOOM,	ALICE	Married John Shackelford	Book 1,	45
1860, May 10	TINSBLOOM,	JOHN	Married Lucy Coghill	Book 1,	9
1852, Feb. 25	TINSBLOOM,	MARTHA	Married Alfred Goudy	Book 1,	263
1860, Feb. 28	TINSBLOOM,	WILLIAM JR.	Married Elizabeth Jane Clarke, widow	Book 1,	8
1836, Nov. 21	TOD,	LOVELL P.	Married Fannie M. Spindle	Book 1,	252
1761,	TODD,	WILLIAM	Married Katy, daughter of Thomas Waring	W 11,	302
1804, Nov. 19	TODD,	WILLIAM	Married Mary H. Brown	Book 1,	222
1690,	TOMLIN,	EASTER	Daughter of Col. John Walker	D 8,	258
1704,	TOMLIN,	JANE	Daughter of Thomas, married Abram Little	D 11,	252
1688,	TOMLIN,	REBECCA	Daughter of Robert, married Ralph Rouzey	O 2,	143
1690,	TOMLIN,	WILLIAM	Married Ann, relict of Charles Dacres	O 2,	295
1692,	TOMLIN,	WILLIAM	Married Ann, relict of George Haslewood	O 1,	169
1827, Aug. 21	TOOMBS,	ELIZABETH	Married William Barber	Book 1,	243
1827,	TOOMBS,	ELIZABETH	Married William L. Barber	D 42,	317
1832, May 16	TOOMBS,	LAURA	Married William Kennedy	Book 1,	249
1835, Oct. 14	TOOMBS,	MARGARET	Married Robert H. Callis	Book 1,	251
1857,	TOOMBS,	MARGARET	Daughter of Gabriel, married Robert Callis	W 27,	723
1819, Apr. 1	TOOMBS,	NANCY	Married Thomas Catlett	Book 1,	236
1856, Mar. 26	TOOMBS,	PETER	Married Ann E. Croxton	Book 1,	4
1813, Dec. 18	TOOMBS,	SARAH	Married Reuben Garrett	Book 1,	229
1681,	TOONE,	JAMES	Married Mary, daughter of Anthony Jackman	D 6,	129
1825, Jan. 17	TOONE,	MARY	Married William Davis	Book 1,	241
1841, Feb. 12	TORRENT,	LUCY	Married Christopher Collins	Book 1,	255
1805,	TOWNLEY,	FRANCES	Daughter of James, married Roger Shackelford	D 36,	448
1804, Dec. 17	TOWNLEY,	JOHN	Married Lucy Johnson	Book 1,	222
1826, May 6	TOWNLEY,	LUCINDA C.	Married George C. Nunn	Book 1,	242
1829, Feb. 18	TOWNLEY,	MARY ANN	Married Temple Bagby	Book 1,	246
1829,	TOWNLEY,	MARY ANN	Daughter of John, married Henry Bagby	D 43,	37
1805, Mar. 18	TOWNLEY,	SARAH	Married Joseph Mann Jr.	Book 1,	223
1805, May 20	TOWNLEY,	SARAH	Married Charles Howerton	Book 1,	223
1807,	TOWNLEY,	SALLY	Sister of William, married ? Mann	W 17,	64

				Book	Page
1686,	TRAVERS,	REBECCA	Married John Rice	D 6,	88
1896, Oct. 15	TREAKLE,	THORNTON B.	Married Addie E. Harper	Book 1,	121
1823, Jul. 30	TRIBLE,	ANN	Married Philip Mann	Book 1,	240
1876, Feb. 24	TRIBLE,	ANN ELIZA	Married Oscar E. Smith, King & Queen Co.	Book 1,	41
1845, Apr. 30	TRIBLE,	AUSTIN M.	Married Mary E. Wright	Book 1,	258
1834, Aug. 26	TRIBLE,	DRUSILLA	Married John Cowles	Book 1,	250
1833, Mar. 2	TRIBLE,	ELIZA	Married Fielding D. Piggot	Book 1,	249
1847, Jan. 2	TRIBLE,	EMILY C.	Married Richard L. Covington	Book 1,	243
1816, Jan. 9	TRIBLE,	FRANCES	Married Selah Holbrook	Book 1,	232
1838,	TRIBLE,	FRANCES	Daughter of John, married Selah Holbrook	W 24,	310
1893, Feb. 22	TRIBLE,	G. W.	Married C. B. Seward	Book 1,	111
1867, Nov. 14	TRIBLE,	HANNAH C.	Married Albert Rennolds	Book 1,	18
1860, Sep. 12	TRIBLE,	JOHN	Married Bettie Faulconer	Book 1,	10
1828, Oct. 3	TRIBLE,	MARGARET R.	Married Smith Young	Book 1,	245
1871, Nov. 28	TRIBLE,	MARY ELIZA	Married William Justin Waring	Book 1,	29
1827, Sep. 17	TRIBLE,	MATILDA	Married Fontaine Wood	Book 1,	244
1844, Dec. 16	TRIBLE,	PETER S.	Married Lucy A. Muse	Book 1,	257
1870, Dec. 15	TRIBLE,	SAMUEL	Married Atway P. Norris	Book 1,	26
1811, Dec. 30	TRICE,	JAMES	Married Frances Montague	Book 1,	227
1876, Jul. 5	TRICE,	JOHN	King & Queen Co., married Mrs. Maria E. Dunn	Book 1,	42
1826, May 15	TRICE,	WILLIAM	Married Augusta Pitts	Book 1,	242
1819, Dec. 20	TRIGGER,	FRANCIS	Married Lucy Fisher	Book 1,	236
1861, Mar. 6	TRIMBLE,	HENRY	Hanover, Germany, married Elizabeth Davis	Book 1,	10
1898, Dec. 19	TRIMBLE,	H. H.	Germany, married Rosa Tucker, widow	Book 1,	130
1880, Mar. 10	TRIMYER,	MARGARET L.	Married William L. Trimyer	Book 1,	53
1841, Mar. 1	TRIMYER,	MARY ANN	Married William Stewart	Book 1,	255
1861, Apr. 3	TRIMYER,	MARY E.	Married Thomas Wood	Book 1,	10
1826, Dec. 19	TRIMYER,	NATHANIEL	Married Elizabeth Shelton	Book 1,	242
1854, Aug. 23	TRIMYER,	SARAH J.	Married George W. Clavoe	Book 1,	265
1880, Mar. 10	TRIMYER,	WILLIAM L.	Married Margaret L Trimyer	Book 1,	53
1725,	TRIPLETT,	THOMAS	Married Elizabeth, sister of Robert Taliaferro	W 4,	155

				Book	Page
1691,	TROATH,	THOMAS	Deceased husband of Martha Stopford	O 2,	303
1858, Dec. 23	TUCK,	BENNETT	Married Lucy A. Gouldman	Book 1,	6
1859, Dec. 30	TUCK,	BENNETT JR.	Married Maria L. Pitts	Book 1,	8
1879, Nov. 26	TUCK,	BENNETT	Married Virginia Parker	Book 1,	53
1865, Dec. 28	TUCK,	FRANCES E.	Married William A. Cox	Book 1,	14
1897, Dec. 15	TUCK,	VIRGINIA	Married L. B. Andrews	Book 1,	126
1815, Jan. 15	TUCKER,	BENJAMIN	Married Sally Bristow	Book 1,	231
1855, Jun. 18	TUCKER,	BENJAMIN	Married Margaret Ann Prince	Book 1,	266
1859, Jan. 18	TUCKER,	BENJAMIN	Married Frances E. Cox	Book 1,	7
1850, Sep. 16	TUCKER,	BEVIN	Married Ann A. Cox	Book 1,	262
1877, Dec. 11	TUCKER,	CHARLES L.	Married America Foreacres, widow	Book 1,	46
1828, Aug. 28	TUCKER,	DUDLEY	Married Elizabeth V. Haile	Book 1,	257
1848, Sep. 18	TUCKER,	ELIZABETH	Married Thomas Brizendine	Book 1,	260
1852, Feb. 11	TUCKER,	ELIZABETH D	Married James H. Carter	Book 1,	263
1851, Sep. 15	TUCKER,	JANE	Widow, married Arthur Barefoot	Book 1,	262
1816, Jul. 23	TUCKER,	JOHN	Married Caty Fisher	Book 1,	232
1849, Feb. 4	TUCKER,	JOHN R.	Married Mildred Gaines	Book 1,	261
1789,	TUCKER,	JOSEPH	Married Clary, daughter of John Goode	W 15,	376
1853, Mar. 16	TUCKER,	JULIA	Married James Clarke	Book 1,	264
1822, Feb. 13	TUCKER,	MARGARET	Married Dunston Davis	Book 1,	239
1843, Dec. 18	TUCKER,	MARTHA JANE	Married Zachariah Carter	Book 1,	256
1815, Apr. 17	TUCKER,	NANCY	Married James Carter	Book 1,	231
1863, Jan. 9	TUCKER,	NANCY	Married Albert Schools	Book 1,	11
1898, Dec. 19	TUCKER,	ROSA	Widow, married H. H. Trimble Germany	Book 1,	130
1849, Mar. 22	TUCKER,	SUSAN	Married Alexander Cooke	Book 1,	261
1856, Dec. 30	TUCKER,	SUSAN	Married John R. Ryan	Book 1,	4
1852, Dec. 10	TUNE,	ANTHONY	Married Louisa Crow	Book 1,	263
1885, Mar. 11	TUNE,	BELLE M.	Married Waller R. Allen	Book 1,	81
1822, Jan. 22	TUNE,	ELIZABETH	Married John Griffin	Book 1,	239
1866, Dec. 9	TUNE,	HENRY C.	Married Mildred Brooks	Book 1,	15
1823, Dec. 23	TUNE,	JOHN	Married Elizabeth C. Davis	Book 1,	240

					Book	Page
1872, Sep. 26	TUNE,	JOHN	Married Olivia Schools		Book 1,	31
1854, Dec. 15	TUNE,	JULIA C.	Married Henry Clarke		Book 1,	2
1875, Aug. 26	TUNE,	JUNIUS E.	Married Arabella M. Allen		Book 1,	39
1859, May 15	TUNE,	LOUISA	Married Upshaw Ferrill		Bok	7
1879, Mar. 11	TUNE,	MILDRED	Married Leonard Shaffer, Philadelphia, Pa.		Book 1,	51
1895, Apr. 24	TUNE,	W. H.	Married M. L. Dunn		Book 1,	118
1810, Dec. 31	TUNSTALL,	ALEXANDER	Married Elizabeth Baylor		Book 1,	226
1870, Jan. 15	TUNSTALL,	KATY	Married Henry Hoomes		Book 1,	25
1825, Aug. 25	TUPMAN,	JOHN L.	Married Philecia L. Micou		Book 1,	242
1826,	TUPMAN,	JOHN	Married Phelecia Micou		D 42,	42
1830,	TUPMAN,	JOHN	Married Phelecia Micou, daughter of Paul of Port Micou		D 43,	141
1872, Oct. 10	TUPMAN,	SARAH	Married Albert Roy Micou, Editor of Tidewater Index		Book 1,	31
1809, Sep. 18	TUREMAN,	GILBE	Married Elizabeth Coates		Book 1,	225
1690,	TURNER,	DORCAS	Widow, married Richard Ford		O 2,	295
1681,	TURNER,	ELIZABETH	Relict of Hezekiah, married Philip Norgate, Northumberland County		D 6,	131
1820, Jun. 3	TURNER,	ELIZABETH	Married Robert Crow		Book 1,	237
1806, Apr. 1	TURNER,	GEORGE	Married Nancy Noell		Book 1,	223
1809, Sep. 18	TURNER,	JOHN B.	Married Molly Dunn		Book 1,	225
1810, Nov. 12	TURNER,	JOHN	Married Sally Downey		Book 1,	226
1893, Nov. 23	TURNER,	LUCY	Married D. A. Bennett		Book 1,	112
1880, Jul. 1	TURNER,	MARY E.	Married James Acres		Book 1,	56
1888, May 11	TURNER	M. E.	Married Robert Crow		Book 1,	95
1689,	TURNER,	MICHALL	Daughter of Hezekiah, married John Powell		O 2,	155
1860, Dec. 24	TURNER,	RICHARD	Married Martha J. Clarke		Book 1,	10
1838, Oct. 11	TURNER,	SAMUEL	Married Anna Ingram		Book 1,	253
1817, Jan. 15	TURNER,	THOMAS	Married Lucy Fisher		Book 1,	233
1763,	TYLER,	ANN	Married John Hammond		D 29,	187
1877, Oct. 17	TYLER,	EMMA A.	Married Joseph L. Willroy, King William Co.		Book 1,	46
1724,	TYLER,	RICHARD	Married Katherine Montague		D 17,	359
1726,	TYLER,	RICHARD	Married Katherine, relict of William Young		D 19,	36

				Book	Page
1863, Feb. 16	TYLER,	ROBERT	Prince William Co., married Sallie S. Chinn	Book 1,	11
1838, Oct. 11	TYLER,	WATT H.	Married Jane L. Blake	Book 1,	253
1847,	TYLER,	WATT H.	Married Louisa, daughter of Benjamin Blake	W 26,	343

				Book	Page
1674,	UNDERWOOD,	ELIZABETH	Widow of Col. William Underwood, married Archdall Combs	D 5,	412
1811, Jan.	UPSHAW,	ALICE	Married Lewis G. Upshaw	Book 1,	227
1860, Oct. 2	UPSHAW,	ELIZA C.	Married Henry W. Daingerfield	Book 1,	10
1809,	UPSHAW,	ELIZABETH J.	Married Thomas Harwood	O 39,	492
1807,	UPSHAW,	HARRIET	Married William Hawkins	O 39,	138
1759,	UPSHAW,	JAMES	Married Suca Jones	W 11,	178
1781,	UPSHAW,	JOHN	Married Mary Martin, sister of Major Lafon	D 32,	12
1811, Jan.	UPSHAW,	LEWIS G.	Married Alice Upshaw	Book 1,	227
1825,	UPSHAW,	LOUISA	Daughter of Major James Upshaw, married Robert S. Harney, Tenn.	D 41,	347
1762,	UPSHAW,	MARGARET	Daughter of Mary, married Samuel Hipkins	W 12,	52
1807,	UPSHAW,	MARIA	Married John Hawkins	O 39,	138
1807,	UPSHAW,	MARIA	Daughter of James, married John Hawkins	W 17,	8
1826,	UPSHAW,	MARIA	Daughter of John Upshaw, Frankfort, Ky. married Nicholas Lafon	D 42,	97
1807,	UPSHAW,	MARTHA	Married Francis Buckner	O 39,	138
1807,	UPSHAW,	POLLY	Married Churchill Anderson	O 39,	138
1663,	UPTON,	MARGARET	Widow of Capt. John Upton, married Thomas Lucas	D 2,	326
1827, Dec. 26	URSERY,	JOHN	Married Elizabeth Carlton	Book 1,	244
1835, Dec. 8	URSERY,	LOUISA	Married Thomas Foreacres	Book 1,	251
1826, Mar. 25	URSERY,	LUCY	Married Edmond Dunn	Book 1,	242
1841, Sep. 27	URSERY,	MARY	Married Edmund Dunn	Book 1,	250
1811, Dec. 23	URSERY,	NANCY	Married James Brizendine	Book 1,	235
1827, Feb. 19	URSERY,	SAMUEL	Married Louisa Johnson	Book 1,	244
1832,	URSERY,	THOMAS	His daughter married Edmund Dunn	D 44,	13

1871, Dec. 21	VALENTINE,	ALICE B.	Married Richard T. Lumpkin	Book 1,	30
1881, Apr. 15	VALENTINE,	EDWARD D.	Lancaster Co., married Sarah T. Dyke	Book 1,	59
1850, Jul. 22	VALENTINE,	JOSEPH V.	Married Catharine C. Muse	Book 1,	262
1847, Dec. 20	VAN NESS	GEORGE H.	Married Catharine Powers	Book 1,	260
1878, May 9	VAN WAGNER, BAILEY		Middlesex Co., married Sarah T. Dillard	Book 1,	48
1753,	VASS,	ANN	Daughter of John Vass, married ? Brooks	W 10,	49
1711,	VASS,	KATHERINE	Sister of John, married Henry Hudson	D&C 13,	401
1688,	VASS,	VINCENT	Married Ann, relict of Thomas Gillett	O 2,	97
1759,	VASS,	VINCENT	Married Jane Mountague	O 23,	135
1761,	VASS,	VINCENT	Married Winifred, daughter of John Gatewood	O 23,	401
1825, Mar. 1	VAUGHAN,	THOMAS	Married Lucy Clarke	Book 1,	242
1842, Apr. 18	VAUGHAN,	THOMAS	Married Selina Noel	Book 1,	256
1865, Jul. 27	VAWTER,	ALICE	Married Richard A. Pitts	Book 1,	13
1698,	VAWTER,	BARTHOLOMEW	Married Winifred, daughter of William Hodgson	D 9,	54
1823, Dec. 24	VAWTER,	BARTHOLOMEW	Married Catharine Clarke	Book 1,	240
1821, Oct. 2	VAWTER,	BENJAMIN	Married Betsey Boulware	Book 1,	238
1812, Apr. 27	VAWTER,	BOWLER	Married Sally Davis	Book 1,	228
1825, Nov. 25	VAWTER,	BOWLER	Married Elizabeth Thomas	Book 1,	242
1874, Feb. 26	VAWTER,	CAROLINE	Married John Coleman	Book 1,	36
1860, May 10	VAWTER,	ELIZABETH	Married Eli Coghill	Book 1,	9
1828, Mar. 15	VAWTER,	ELLIOTT	Married Elizabeth Pollard	Book 1,	245
1879, Feb. 20	VAWTER,	JAMES	Married Mary Susan Gray	Book 1,	50
1832, Dec. 12	VAWTER,	MILTON	Married Lucy Anthony	Book 1,	249
1835, Dec. 21	VAWTER,	PATSEY	Married Thomas Anton	Book 1,	251
1829, Dec. 24	VAWTER,	RICHARD	Married Elizabeth Davis	Book 1,	246
1810, Nov. 7	VAWTER,	SALLY	Married William Walden	Book 1,	226
1836, Jul. 4	VAWTER,	WILLIAM E.	Married Polly Anton	Book 1,	252
1869, Feb. 18	VERLANDER,	BETTY F.	Married William F. Boughan	Book 1,	22
1866, Nov. 18	VERLANDER,	GEORGE	Married Dorothea Brooks	Book 1,	15
1843, Dec. 18	VERLANDER,	JAMES	Married Elizabeth F. Beazley	Book 1,	257

				Book		Page
1828,	VESSELS,	SUSAN	Daughter of Anna, married Carter Edmondson	D	47,	347
1675,	VICCARS,	JOHN	Married Jane, daughter of Elias Webb	D	5,	438
1688,	VICKERS,	ELIZABETH	Relict of John, married Peter St. Leger	O	2,	133
1881, Jun. 9	VICKERS,	FANNIE	Widow, married Bladon Hall	Book 1,		60
1679,	VICKERS,	JOHN	Married Elizabeth, daughter of John Waight	D	6,	109
1873, Dec. 18	VICKERS,	THOMAS	Married Frances A. Atkins	Book 1,		35
1745,	VIRGETT,	ELIZABETH	Her daughter, Keren Kappuk, married Peter Jett, King George Co.	D	23,	216
1708,	VIRGETT,	JOB	Married Elizabeth, relict of William Bendry	O	4,	53
1741,	VIVION,	FRANCES	Daughter of Thomas Vivion of King George Co., married Robert Brooking, King & Queen Co.	D	22,	235

1873, May 15	WADDELL,	MARY E.	Married Robert Munday	Book 1,		33
1726,	WAGGENER,	BENJAMIN	Married Sarah, daughter of William Greenhill	W	4,	159
1743,	WAGGENER,	MARY	Daughter of Herbert, married John Evans	W	7,	36
1763,	WAGGENER,	SARAH	Daughter of Elizabeth, married William Sears, Gloucester Co.	D	29,	239
1792,	WAIDE,	WILLIAM	Married Sally, daughter of Lillian Webb	W	14,	231
1690,	WAIGHT,	MARY	Daughter of John, married Robert Kay	O	1,	379
1879, Feb. 5	WAKE,	WILLIAM H.	Married Mary Ellen Harper	Book 1,		50
1710,	WAKELIN,	WILLIAM	Married Ann, daughter of Alexander Robins	D&C 13,		327
1819, May 6	WALDEN,	LEWIS	Married Elizabeth Gordon	Book 1,		236
1805, Aug. 13	WALDEN,	ONEY	Married Thomas Clarke	Book 1,		222
1810, Nov. 7	WALDEN,	WILLIAM	Married Sally Vawter	Book 1,		226
1838, Oct. 23	WALDEN,	WILLIAM	Married Adeline Oliver	Book 1,		253
1843,	WALDEN,	WILLIAM	Married Adeline, daughter of William Oliver	W	24,	152
1799,	WALKER,	ALEXANDER	Married Penelope Beckwith	D	35,	175
1827,	WALKER,	ALEXANDER	Married Penelope, daughter of Sir Jonathan Beckwith	D	42,	241
1876, Oct. 24	WALKER,	DR. B. F.	Married Martha H. Wright	Book 1,		43
1690,	WALKER,	EASTER	Daughter of Col. John Walker, married John Price	D	8,	315
1684,	WALKER,	JOHN	Married Mary, daughter of William Denby	D	7,	136
1808, Nov. 21	WALKER,	JOHN	Married Ann Inser	Book 1,		225
1813, Dec. 13	WALKER,	JOHN	Married Margaret Saunders	Book 1,		229
1813, Dec. 20	WALKER,	NANCY	Married Lewis Coleman	Book 1,		229
1672,	WALKER,	SARAH	Relict of Col. John Walker, married John Stone	D	5,	98
1781,	WALKER,	SUSANNA	Daughter of Samuel, married John Livingston	W	13,	336
1847, Dec. 22	WALKER,	THOMAS C.	Married Susan F. Crittenden	Book 1,		260
1858, Dec. 2	WALKER,	WATSON	King & Queen Co., married Lucy Waring Temple	Book 1,		6
1740,	WALLER,	CHARLES	Married Elizabeth, sister of John Rouzie	D	22,	163
1741,	WALLER,	EDWARD	Married Ann, daughter of Henry Tandy	W	6,	344
1838, Jan. 2	WALSH,	JOHN W. T. R.	Married Eliza Ann Beazley	Book 1,		253
1884, Dec. 25	WALTON,	HARVEY T.	Gloucester Co., married Didemia Taylor	Book 1,		80
1891, Apr. 8	WALTON,	L. R.	King & Queen Co., married M. F. Southall	Book 1,		107

				Book	Page
1695,	WARD,	GEORGE	Married Mary, relict of John Wills	O 1,	380
1708,	WARD,	GEORGE	Married Mary, widow of Richard Barber	D&C 12,	258
1762,	WARD,	GEORGE	Married Ann, daughter of Thomas & Ann Johnson	W 12,	436
1827, Apr. 6	WARE,	EDMUND M.	Married Mary Adelaide Janey	Book 1,	244
1831, Mar. 21	WARE,	EDMUND M.	Married Catharine Waring	Book 1,	248
1804, Feb. 8	WARE,	EDWARD	Married Susanna Bray	Book 1,	222
1877, May 23	WARE,	EDWARD MACON	Married Susanna C. Croxton	Book 1,	45
1884, Nov. 25	WARE,	EDWARD MACON	Married Alice Kriete	Book 1,	79
1865, Nov. 22	WARE,	EMMA C.	Married Dr. Lawson Waring	Book 1,	13
1826, Mar. 15	WARE,	FRANCES G.	Married Richard Croxton	Book 1,	242
1853, Aug. 30	WARE,	HANNAH E.	Married John T. Hoskins	Book 1,	259
1882, Oct. 31	WARE,	KATE W.	Married Francis H. Scott Gloucester County	Book 1,	66
1858, Apr. 15	WARE,	MARTHA	Married Henry Richards	Book 1,	7
1860, Nov. 21	WARE,	ROBERT L.	Married Ann E. B. Latane	Book 1,	10
1892, Jun. 1	WARE,	ROBERT L. JR.	Married Mary E. Wright	Book 1,	109
1867, Nov. 21	WARE,	WILLIAM S.	Married Fannie B. Street	Book 1,	18
1871, Dec. 21	WARING,	ADDIE D.	Married Richard L. Hoskins, King & Queen County	Book 1,	29
1803,	WARING,	ANN	Daughter of Thomas, married William Latane	W 16,	250
1831, Mar. 21	WARING,	CATHARINE	Married Edmund M. Ware	Book 1,	248
1761,	WARING,	ELIZABETH	Daughter of Thomas, married John Fauntleroy	W 11,	302
1770,	WARING,	ELIZABETH	Daughter of Francis, married Spencer M. Ball	W 12,	432
1879, Apr. 15	WARING,	FANNY GRAY	Married Robert P. Dillard	Book 1,	52
1810, Dec. 17	WARING,	JOHN	Married Elizabeth Latane	Book 1,	226
1812,	WARING,	JOHN	Married Elizabeth Latane	O 41,	152
1829, Mar. 30	WARING,	JOHN	Married Catharine Grey	Book 1,	246
1883, Mar. 1	WARING,	JULIA T.	Daughter of Robert P. Waring, married Rev. A. F. Scott, Northumberland County	Book 1,	70
1761,	WARING,	KATY	Daughter of Thomas, married William Todd	W 11,	302
1865, Nov. 22	WARING,	LAWSON	Physician, married Emma C. Ware	Book 1,	13
1770	WARING,	LUCY	Daughter of Thomas, married James Robb	W 12,	432
1799,	WARING,	LUCY	Married William Sthreshley	O 35,	334

1834, May 24	WARING,	LUCY	Daughter of Robert P. Waring, married Richard Baylor	Book 1,	250
1844,	WARING,	LUCY	Daughter of Robert P. Waring, married Richard Baylor	W 24,	217
1828, Dec. 8	WARING,	MARTHA ANN	Married Robert Wright	Book 1,	245
1898, Nov. 23	WARING,	MARY S.	Married Robert Daniel Jr.	Book 1,	130
1865, Jun. 22	WARING,	MERTINE M.	Married William L. Waring	Book 1,	13
1808,	WARING,	ROBERT	Married Lucy, daughter of William Latane	W 17,	312
1812,	WARING,	ROBERT PAYNE	Married Lucy Latane	O 41,	109
1821, Apr. 28	WARING,	ROBERT P. JR.	Married Mary E. Garnett	Book 1,	238
1825, Sep. 19	WARING,	ROBERT P.	Married Eliza S. Robb	Book 1,	242
1885, Nov. 14	WARING,	ROSALIE A.	Widow, married William L. Waring	Book 1,	84
1799,	WARING,	SARAH	Widow of Robert Payne Waring, married Thomas Bridges	W 15,	502
1779,	WARING,	WILLIAM JR.	Married Sarah, daughter of George Green	W 13,	297
1814, Nov. 8	WARING,	WILLIAM L.	Married Mary Banks	Book 1,	230
1821,	WARING,	WILLIAM L.	Married Mary, daughter of Elizabeth Banks	W 19,	351
1842, Jun. 20	WARING,	W. L.	Married M. M. M. Derieux	Book 1,	256
1865, Jun. 22	WARING,	WILLIAM L.	Married Mertine M. Waring	Book 1,	13
1871, Nov. 28	WARING,	WILLIAM JUSTIN	Married Mary Eliza Trible	Book 1,	29
1885, Nov. 14	WARING,	WILLIAM L.	Married Rosalie A. Waring, widow	Book 1,	84
1760,	WARNER,	BETTY	Daughter of Daniel, married Covington Searles	W 11,	301
1882, Apr. 13	WARNER,	C. C.	Married Kate W. Hoskins	Book 1,	65
1688,	WARRINER,	MARY	Daughter of Ralph, married Edward Keeling	O 2,	62
1698,	WARRINER,	MARY	Daughter of Ralph, married Samuel Thacker	D 9, D&W 14,	220 325
1763,	WASHINGTON, AUGUSTINE		Married Ann, daughter of William Aylett	D 29,	186
1687,	WASHINGTON, LT. COL. JOHN		His daughter married Mr. Wright	D 7,	419
1712,	WATERS,	KATHERINE	Executrix of John, married Edward Price	O 4,	495
1808, Jan. 21	WATERS,	RICHARD	Married Ann Cridland	Book 1,	225
1748,	WATKINS,	BARBARY	Daughter of John, married John Hill	W 8, W 13,	86 62
1742,	WATKINS,	EDWARD	Married Mary, widow of Henry Pendleton	D 22,	407
1873, Aug. 21	WATKINS,	HENRIETTA	Married H. H. Greenstreet	Book 1,	34
1825, Nov. 21	WATKINS,	HUMPHREY C.	Married Mrs. Nancy Gresham	Book 1,	242
1836, Jun. 20	WATKINS,	JABEZ	Married Julia Ann Taylor	Book 1,	252

				Book	Page
1706,	WATKINS,	JOHN	Married Elizabeth Parker	D&C 13,	2
1710,	WATKINS,	JOHN	Married Ann, late wife of Adam Deming	O	299
1707,	WATKINS,	MARGARET	Married Samuel Coates	D&C 13,	31
1857, Oct. 1	WATKINS,	SUSAN E.	Married James R. Cox	Book 1,	5
1847, Jan. 21	WATSON,	RICHARD A.	Married Ann Gaines	Book 1,	260
1866, May 3	WATSON,	RUFUS A.	South Carolina, married Matilda C. Williams	Book 1,	14
1781,	WATTS,	BETTY	Daughter of Thomas, King & Queen Co., married George Gresham, Prince Edward County	D 32,	56
1855, Apr. 5	WATTS,	EMELINE F.	Married Charles Reinicker	Book 1,	3
1844, Mar. 18	WATTS,	HENRY	Married Frances Brown	Book 1,	257
1850, Feb. 15	WATTS,	JAMES	Married Mary A. Gardner	Book 1,	262
1671,	WATTS,	JOHN	Married Jane, daughter of Honoria Weire	D 4,	444
1781,	WATTS,	MARY	Daughter of Thomas, King & Queen Co., married John Mitchell	D 32,	56
1868, Feb. 12	WATTS,	MARY E.	Married William L Dishman	Book 1,	20
1898, Sep. 27	WATTS,	N. J.	Married C. M. Dishman	Book 1,	129
1848, Mar. 29	WATTS,	ROBERT C.	Married Jane Brown	Book 1,	260
1884, Nov. 17	WATTS,	SADIE A.	Married Thomas A. Samuel	Book 1,	79
1868, Jan. 28	WATTS,	SALLIE F.	Married William A. Williams	Book 1,	20
1811, Jun. 25	WAYDE,	SALLY	Married Owen Jones	Book 1,	227
1812, Apr. 20	WEBB,	CATY	Married Dabney Brooks	Book 1,	228
1860, Feb. 1	WEBB,	DORINDA	Married Horace Davis	Book 1,	8
1854, Jan. 31	WEBB,	HENRY	Married Susan E. Gordon	Book 1,	265
1712,	WEBB,	ISAAC	Married Winifred, sister of John Segar	O 4,	444
1760,	WEBB,	JAMES	Married Mary, daughter of Francis Smith	W 11,	415
1880, Feb. 24	WEBB,	JAMES	Married Mrs. Janette Wilson	Book 1,	55
1675,	WEBB,	JANE	Daughter of Elias, married John Viccars	D 5,	438
1744,	WEBB,	JOHN	Married Lily Ann, daughter of John & Elizabeth Gore	D 23,	189
1771,	WEBB,	MARY	Daughter of James, married Samuel Smith	W 11,	415
1825, Jan. 28	WEBB,	NANCY	Married James Acres	Book 1,	242
1730,	WEBB,	PENELOPE	Daughter of Sarah, married James Gatewood	W 8,	108
1792,	WEBB,	POLLY	Daughter of Lillian, married ? Plummer	W 14,	321

				Book		Page
1710,	WEBB,	ROBERT	Married Jane, relict of John Mitchell	O	4,	276
1792,	WEBB,	SALLY	Daughter of Lillian, married William Waide	W	14,	321
1684,	WEBB,	WILLIAM	Married Mary, relict of Hugh Williams	D	7,	207
1685,	WEBB,	WILLIAM	Married Administratrix of Hugh Williams	Box 101, O	1,	I 150
1822, Oct. 15	WEBB,	WILLIAM	Married Betsey Marlowe	Book 1,		239
1834, Mar. 17	WEBB,	WILLIAM	Married Edmonia C. Dunn	Book 1,		250
1694,	WEBSTER,	JOHN	Married Anne Smith (License)	O	1,	323
1686,	WEEKES,	ABRAHAM	His daughter married John Collins, Middlesex Co.	O	1,	232
1808,	WEEKS,	ELIZABETH	Married Vincent Barrock	O	39,	337
1802,	WEEKS,	JENNY	Daughter of Charles, married Robert Currin	W	14,	230
1808,	WEEKS,	MARGARET	Married Edward Davis	O	39,	337
1808,	WEEKS,	MARY	Married John Payton	O	39,	337
1684,	WEIRE,	HONORIA	Relict of John, married George Jones	O	1,	66
1781,	WEIRE,	JANE	Daughter of Honoria, married John Watts	D	4,	444
1687,	WEIRE,	MARY	Relict of Walter, married James Orchard	D	7,	517
1811, Dec. 9	WEIR,	ROBERT	Married Clara B. Smith	Book 1,		227
1861, Jan. 10	WELCH,	DRUSILLA	Married Richard Goode	Book 1,		10
1746,	WELCH,	ELIZABETH	Widow of Robert, married John Sutton	W	7,	450
1887, Dec. 15	WELCH,	EMMA F.	Married Robert T. Banks	Book 1,		93
1862, Jun. 19	WELCH,	MARGARET	Married Leonard Johnson	Book 1,		11
1731,	WELCH,	MARY	Widow, married Hon. John Robinson, Spottsylvania Co.	D	20,	232
1723,	WELCH,	REUBEN	Married Mary Meriwether	D	17,	327
1880, Dec. 7	WELCH,	WILLIAM B.	Maryland, married Lulie P. Banks	Book 1,		57
1695,	WELLS,	MARY	Relict of John, married George Ward	O	1,	380
1771,	WEST,	ARCHER	Chesterfield Co., married Ann, daughter of James Byrom	D	30,	481
1843, Sep. 18	WEST,	EDWARD W.	Married Cornelia E. Burt	Book 1,		257
1704,	WEST,	ELIZABETH	Daughter of Richard, married Robert Moss	O	3,	123
1834, Jan. 1	WEST,	JAMES	Married Polly Currie	Book 1,		250
1706,	WEST,	RICHARD	Married Elizabeth, relict of George Green	D&C 12,		293
1847, May 5	WESTMORE,	ANN M.	Married Roger B. Atkinson	Book 1,		259
1835, Dec. 14	WESTMORE,	WILLIAM B.	Married Elizabeth Rouzie	Book 1,		251

				Book	Page
1865, Sep. 6	WHEAT,	FRANCIS D.	Bath Co., married Augusta E. Godwin, Middlesex Co.	Book 1,	13
1875, Dec. 29	WHEELER,	ELLA	Married Alexander Dickenson	Book 1,	40
1677,	WHEELER,	THOMAS	Married Elizabeth, sister of John Grigory	D 6,	11
1896, Dec. 23	WHITAKER,	CHARLES J.	Married Columbia F. Clarke	Book 1,	123
1897, Dec. 9	WHITAKER,	O. L.	Married George W. Brooks	Book 1,	126
1693,	WHITCHURCH, MARY		Daughter of John, married Richard Harvie	O 1,	161
1896, Jun. 16	WHITE,	ALICE G.	Baltimore, Md., married George A. Macomber	Book 1,	121
1784,	WHITE,	AMBROSE	Married Ann, Daughter of James Jones	W 13,	456
1703,	WHITE,	ARABELLA	Only daughter of Henry, married Randall Bird	D&W 11,	160
1695,	WHITE,	DORCAS	Widow of Henry, married John Sorrell	O 1,	261
1677,	WHITE,	ELIZABETH	Daughter of Richard, married John Meador	D 6,	27
1893, Apr. 26	WHITE,	J. A.	King & Queen Co., married A. T. Hoskins	Book 1,	111
1720,	WHITE,	RICHARD	London, married Ann, sister of John Baker	W 3,	222
1790,	WHITE,	WILLIAM	Married Caty, daughter of William Thomas	W 14,	206
1867, Feb. 16	WHITING,	ANGELS	Married George Kendall	Book 1,	17
1811, Dec. 9	WHITING,	ANN B.	Married Thomas Jesse	Book 1,	227
1786,	WHITING,	CAPT.	Married Lettice, daughter of John Lee	W 13,	430
1790,	WHITING,	HARRIET	Married Edmund Brooke	D 33,	230
1828, Sep. 22	WHITING,	MIRA W.	Married Richard Dudley	Book 1,	245
1835, Oct. 7	WHITLOCK,	N. I. B.	Married Emily Adeline Haile, daughter of Robert G. Haile	Book 1,	251
1837,	WHITLOCK,	NATHANIEL I. B.	Married Emily Adeline Haile	D 45,	470
1685,	WHITLOCK,	THOMAS	His relict married Edward Rouzie	D 7,	174
1827,	WHITTEMORE, LEWIS		Married Jane Ryland	D 42,	61
1827,	WHITTEMORE, WYATT		Married Nancy Ryland	D 42,	361
1687,	WHITTON,	RALPH	Married Elizabeth, widow of Francis Jedford	D 7,	490
1803,	WHORTON,	ENOCH	Married Catharine, daughter of Joseph Fogg	W 16,	221
1747,	WIATT,	THOMAS	Married Suky, daughter of Thomas Edmondson	D 24,	247
1836, Nov. 19	WILCOX,	ELIZABETH	Married William H. Mariner	Book 1,	252
1752,	WILES,	SALLIE	Married Thomas Gouldman	D 28,	261
1899, Sep. 19	WILKERSON,	A. M.	Married William G. King	Book 1,	134
1690,	WILKS,	ELIZABETH	Married George Spicer	O 2,	253

1744,	WILLARD,	JAMES	Married Mary, daughter of William Beazley	W	7,	490
1861, Dec. 26	WILLIAMS,	ADELINE	Married Richard T. Covington	Book 1,		11
1696,	WILLIAMS,	ANN	Relict of George, married David Jenkins	D	9,	80
1834, Feb. 17	WILLIAMS,	BENJAMIN	Married Mary Conoly	Book 1,		250
1849,	WILLIAMS,	BENJAMIN	Married Mary, daughter of Catharine Conoly	W	27,	187
1870, Mar. 13	WILLIAMS,	BETTIE	Married Robert L. Williams	Book 1,		25
1898, Jan. 6	WILLIAMS,	B. L.	Married Zack Carter	Book 1,		128
1821, Feb. 13	WILLIAMS,	BRIZENDINE	Married Susan Davis	Book 1,		238
1845, Jan. 21	WILLIAMS,	CHURCHILL	Married Sarah Broocke	Book 1,		258
1842, Dec. 21	WILLIAMS,	ELIZABETH	Married Iverson Charles	Book 1,		256
1875, Apr. 1	WILLIAMS,	ETHELBERT	Married Mary Johnson	Book 1,		39
1681,	WILLIAMS,	EVE	Relict of John of Morattico Creek, married William Smith	D	6,	179
1899, Oct. 23	WILLIAMS,	H. B.	Married M. W. Brown	Book 1,		134
1685,	WILLIAMS,	HUGH	Married relict of William Wood	O	1,	150
1893, Mar. 22	WILLIAMS,	I. M.	Married J. R. Davis	Book 1,		111
1836, Dec. 15	WILLIAMS,	JAMES	Married Frances E. Broocke	Book 1,		252
1677,	WILLIAMS,	JEANE	Relict of Roger, married Samuel Wills	D	6,	35
1895, Dec. 26	WILLIAMS,	J. G.	Married J. H. Acie	Book 1,		119
1849, May 26	WILLIAMS,	JOHN H.	Married S. D. Drinkwater	Book 1,		261
1879, Aug. 21	WILLIAMS,	JOHN R.	Married Mary H. Brooke	Book 1,		52
1870, Dec. 22	WILLIAMS,	JOSHUA J.	Married Jennie E. Dobyns	Book 1,		26
1848, Aug. 11	WILLIAMS,	LUCINDA C.	Married Burch Claiborne	Book 1,		260
1857, Feb. 12	WILLIAMS,	LUCINDA	Married Joseph Schools	Book 1,		5
1880, Nov. 1	WILLIAMS,	LUCY	Married George W. Dunn, Jr.	Book 1,		57
1709,	WILLIAMS,	MARGARET	Married Joseph Leeman	O	4,	117
1713,	WILLIAMS,	MARGARET	Daughter of John, married Joseph Lemon	D&W 14,		252
1755,	WILLIAMS,	MARY	Married Isaac Brooks	W	10,	39
1834, May 19	WILLIAMS,	MARY ANN	Married Thomas Hundley	Book 1,		250
1866, May 3	WILLIAMS,	MATILDA C.	Married Rufus A. Watson	Book 1,		14
1894, Jun. 13	WILLIAMS,	M. R.	Married R. T. Glassell	Book 1,		114
1898, Jan. 6	WILLIAMS,	MYRTLE	Married J. H. Carter	Book 1,		128

				Book	Page
1849, Nov. 4	WILLIAMS,	NANCY	Married William S. Birch	Book 1,	261
1806, Oct. 20	WILLIAMS,	PHILIP	Married Lucy Boughton	Book 1,	223
1834, Jan. 1	WILLIAMS,	RACHEL	Married William Saunders	Book 1,	250
1870, Mar. 13	WILLIAMS,	R. L.	Married Bettie Williams	Book 1,	25
1883, Oct. 10	WILLIAMS,	SAMUEL	Married Olivia A. Duff	Book 1,	73
1874, Aug. 3	WILLIAMS,	SARAH A.	Married John H. Brooks	Book 1,	37
1713,	WILLIAMS,	SUSANNA	Daughter of John, married John Boulware	D&W 14,	252
1785,	WILLIAMS,	THADDEUS	Married Catharine, daughter of John Corrie	W 14,	76
1882, Jan. 24	WILLIAMS,	THEODORE	King & Queen Co., married Jennie Brooks	Book 1,	63
1811, Nov. 18	WILLIAMS,	THOMAS	Married Alice Bush	Book 1,	227
1829,	WILLIAMS,	THOMAS	Married Alice, daughter of John Bush	D 43,	36
1834, Feb. 26	WILLIAMS,	VINCENT	Married Nancy Taylor	Book 1,	250
1872, Mar. 21	WILLIAMS,	VIRGINIA	Married Henry L. Carlton	Book 1,	30
1712,	WILLIAMS,	WILLIAM	Married Jael, daughter of James Harrison	O 4,	444
1868, Jan. 28	WILLIAMS,	WILLIAM A.	Married Sallie F. Watts	Book 1,	20
1868, May 7	WILLIAMS,	WILLIAM	Married Williamina F. Rennolds	Book 1,	20
1830, Jul. 22	WILLIAMSON, BRIZENDINE		Married Nancy Brizendine	Book 1,	247
1805, Jun. 17	WILLIAMSON, BURNETT		Married Mary Leaker	Book 1,	223
1702,	WILLIAMSON, CATHARINE		Married William Young	D&W 10,	114
1804, Dec. 17	WILLIAMSON, DAISY		Married William Davis	Book 1,	222
1839, Jan. 7	WILLIAMSON, DICEY		Married Thomas Brizendine	Book 1,	254
1812, May 19	WILLIAMSON, DOLLY		Married Morton Armstrong	Book 1,	228
1832, Dec. 17	WILLIAMSON, ELIJAH		Married Betsey Roddin	Book 1,	249
1689,	WILLIAMSON, ELIZABETH		Sister of William, married John Moseley	D 8,	74
1695,	WILLIAMSON, ELIZABETH		Daughter of John, married Clandy Loyson	D&W 10,	91
1761,	WILLIAMSON, ELIZABETH		Daughter of Thomas, married ? Cauthorn	W 12,	196
1858, Apr. 30	WILLIAMSON, EMELINE		Married Baylor F. Crow	Book 1,	6
1832, Nov. 24	WILLIAMSON, FRANCES		Married Leonard Clarke	Book 1,	248
1839,	WILLIAMSON, FRANCES,		Widow of Samuel, married Arthur Barefoot	D 46,	252
1761,	WILLIAMSON, JOHN		Married Alice, daughter of William Brizendine	D 29,	55
1791,	WILLIAMSON, JOHN		Married Elizabeth Shepard, grand-daughter of William Richards	D 16,	107

1813, Sep. 20	WILLIAMSON, JOHN	Married Elizabeth Clark	Book 1,	229
1822, Feb. 14	WILLIAMSON, JOHN JR.	Married Lucy Marlow	Book 1,	239
1855, Feb. 1	WILLIAMSON, JOHN	Married Lucy A. Jeffries	Book 1,	3
1860, Feb. 3	WILLIAMSON, JOHN JR.	Married Lucy Clarke	Book 1,	8
1876, Jan. 18	WILLIAMSON, JOHN S.	Married Jannette R. Rouzie	Book 1,	41
1834, May 19	WILLIAMSON, LETTY	Married Zachariah Brizendine	Book 1,	250
1853, Dec. 19	WILLIAMSON, LOUISA F.	Married Benjamin Armstrong	Book 1,	264
1673,	WILLIAMSON, MARGARET	Daughter of James, married Capt. William Ball, Lancaster Co.	D 5,	201
1856, Feb. 25	WILLIAMSON, MARGARET	Married Feriol Brizendine	Book 1,	4
1836, May 26	WILLIAMSON, MARIA	Married William H. Frank	Book 1,	252
1853, Dec. 28	WILLIAMSON, MARTHA M.	Married Thomas H. Brizendine	Book 1,	264
1673,	WILLIAMSON, MARY	Daughter of James, married John Rosier, Westmoreland Co.	D 5,	289
1742,	WILLIAMSON, MARY	Daughter of Williams, married ? Webb	W 7,	25
1845, Dec. 18	WILLIAMSON, MARY	Married James Croxton	Book 1,	258
1858, Oct. 7	WILLIAMSON, MARY C.	Married John Hays	Book 1,	5
1853, Nov. 12	WILLIAMSON, MATILDA	Married Walker Jordan	Book 1,	264
1812, Dec. 14	WILLIAMSON, NANCY	Married Leroy Taylor	Book 1,	228
1832, Mar. 22	WILLIAMSON, NANCY	Married Spencer Clarke	Book 1,	248
1811, Dec. 23	WILLIAMSON, POLLY	Married Thomas Hodges	Book 1,	227
1846, Dec. 21	WILLIAMSON, ROBERT	Married Mary Brooks	Book 1,	259
1806, Jan. 25	WILLIAMSON, SAMUEL	Married Fanny Davis	Book 1,	223
1812,	WILLIAMSON, SAMUEL	Married Fanny, daughter of Evan Davis	O 41,	57
1827, Mar. 19	WILLIAMSON, SAMUEL	Married Frances McTyre	Book 1,	244
1848, Dec. 21	WILLIAMSON, SAMUEL	Married Polly Bush	Book 1,	260
1869, Sep. 15	WILLIAMSON, SUSAN	Married Robert Harmon	Book 1,	23
1742,	WILLIAMSON, SUSANNA	Daughter of John, married John Boding	W 7,	257
1669,	WILLIAMSON, THOMAS	Married Katherine, widow of Richard Hubbert	D 4,	190
1821, Nov. 29	WILLIAMSON, THOMAS	Married Polly Dunn	Book 1,	238
1804, Aug. 20	WILLIAMSON, VINCENT	Married Caty Marshall	Book 1,	222
1761,	WILLIAMSON, WILLIAM	Married Ann, daughter of William Brizendine	D 29,	55
1843, Apr. 17	WILLIAMSON, WILLIAM	Married Martha M. Johnson	Book 1,	257

				Book	Page
1878, Dec. 26	WILLIAMSON,	WILLIAM F.	Married Virginia C. Broocke	Book 1,	50
1822, Dec. 24	WILLIAMSON,	ZACHARIAH	Married Polly Taylor	Book 1,	239
1698,	WILLIS,	JOHN	Married Mary, daughter of James Coghill	D&W 10,	3
1715,	WILLIS,	JOHN	Married Mary Duckbary	D&W 14,	428
1806, Oct. 20	WILLIS,	JOHN	Married Rachel Howerton	Book 1,	223
1873, Dec. 23	WILLIS,	MARTHA	Married David Hoomes	Book 1,	35
1691,	WILLIS,	RICHARD	Married relict of Richard Bray	O 2,	307
1711,	WILLIS,	WILLIAM	Westmoreland Co., married Mary, daughter of Thomas Kirk	D&W 14,	23
1848, Jul. 17	WILLMORE,	CATHARINE	Married Tazewell Ball	Book 1,	260
1841, Dec. 29	WILLMORE,	EDWARD	Married Phoebe Schools	Book 1,	255
1830, Sep. 35	WILLMORE,	JOSEPH	Married Susan Jeffries	Book 1,	247
1825, Jan. 10	WILMORE,	MARGARET	Married Larkin Schools	Book 1,	242
1841, Mar. 1	WILMORE,	MARY	Married John Atkins	Book 1,	255
1860, Sep. 13	WILMORE,	MARY ANN	Married Littleton G. Fogg	Book 1,	9
1877, Oct. 17	WILLROY,	JOSEPH L.	King William Co., married Emma A. Tyler	Book 1,	46
1677,	WILLS,	SAMUEL	Married Joane, relict of Roger Williams	D 6,	35
1886, Jun. 29	WILLS,	W. T.	Washington, D. C., married Grace E. Parsons	Book 1,	88
1842, Jan. 24	WILSON,	DOROTHY	Married G. W. Schools	Book 1,	256
1686,	WILSON,	ELIZABETH	Daughter of Henry, married Edward Jeffreys	Box 101,	K
1895, Dec. 19	WILSON,	G. A.	Married P. A. Schools	Book 1,	119
1659,	WILSON,	HUGH	Middlesex Co., married Elizabeth daughter of Randall & Jean Jessom	D 2,	287
1704,	WILSON,	JANE	Relict of Capt. John Wilson, King & Queen Co., married Colo. Gawin Corbin	O 3,	111
1880, Feb. 24	WILSON,	JANETTE	Widow, married James Webb	Book 1,	55
1873, Nov. 26	WILSON,	JOHN	Married Jannetta Clarke	Book 1,	35
1876, Mar. 2	WILSON,	JOHN W.	Married Indiana Atkins	Book 1,	41
1893, Aug. 3	WILSON,	KATE	Married J. R. Clarke	Book 1,	112
1834, Dec. 19	WILSON,	ROBERT	Married Nancy Grinstead	Book 1,	250
1796,	WILSON,	THOMAS	Married Nancy, daughter of Thomas Henry Brooks	W 15,	275
1869, Dec. 30	WILSON,	THOMAS H.	Married Clementine Barefoot	Book 1,	24
1688,	WILTON,	RICHARD	Married Mary, relict of Rosamond Jacobs	O 2,	82

				Book	Page
1868, Dec. 31	WILTSHIRE,	JOSEPH N.	Married Virginia A. Reed	Book 1,	21
1728,	WIMPEE,	JOHN	Married Elinor, daughter of James Byrom	W 8,	240
1892, May 5	WINDER,	CORA	Married Richard Sisson	Book 1,	109
1891, Oct. 7	WINDER,	FLORENCE	Married Thomas C. Garrett	Book 1,	107
1895, Jan. 16	WINDER,	MARY M.	Married W. R. Lumpkin	Book 1,	117
1885, Dec. 16	WINDER,	NINA N.	Married Robert H. Davis	Book 1,	84
1694,	WINSLOW,	THOMAS	Married Ann, daughter of Robert Parker	O 1,	356
1714,	WINSTON,	WILLIAM	Married Martha, mother of Francis Gouldman	O 4,	583
1783,	WISE,	NANCY	Daughter of Thomas & Sarah, married John Coghill	D 32,	193
1704,	WOCLEY,	MARY	Middlesex Co., daughter of George Keesell, Essex County	D&C 12,	65
1815, Oct. 12	WOOD,	CATHARINE C.	Married John Micou	Book 1,	231
1822,	WOOD,	CATHARINE	Daughter of Carter, married John Micou	D 40,	488
1675,	WOOD,	CORNELIUS	Married Elizabeth, daughter of Anthony Hoskins	D 5,	15, 265
1727,	WOOD,	ELIZABETH	Daughter of Thomas married Thomas Heely	O 7, O 9,	168 58
1805, Oct. 21	WOOD,	ELIZABETH	Married Thomas Dix	Book 1,	222
1819, Dec. 14	WOOD,	FOUNTAIN	Married Anna H. Hunley	Book 1,	236
1823,	WOOD,	FONTAINE	Married Ann, daughter of Ambrose Hundley	D 41,	37
1827, Sep. 17	WOOD,	FONTAINE	Married Matilda Trible	Book 1,	244
1699,	WOOD,	FRANCES	Widow of John, married William Cox	D&W 10,	13
1808, Oct. 10	WOOD,	JULIA	Married Henry W. Boughan	Book 1,	224
1823,	WOOD,	JULIA	Daughter of Thomas, married Henry Boughan	D 41,	51
1816, Jun. 19	WOOD,	MARIA I. G.	Married William B. Matthews	Book 1,	232
1822,	WOOD,	MARIA	Daughter of Carter, married William B. Matthews	D 40,	488
1709,	WOOD,	MARY	Widow of Thomas, married William Halbert	D&C 13,	296
1843, Mar. 8	WOOD,	MARY F.	Married Thomas Boughan	Book 1,	256
1827, Aug. 27	WOOD,	MUSCOE	Married Lucinda Muse	Book 1,	244
1810, Oct. 16	WOOD,	POLLY	Married P. Baylor Pendleton	Book 1,	226
1812, Sep. 21	WOOD,	SUSAN	Married-John Jones	Book 1,	228
1845, Nov. 6	WOOD,	SUSAN M.	Married William S. Montague	Book 1,	258
1764,	WOOD,	THOMAS	Married Catharine, daughter of Catharine Gatewood	D 29,	303
1861, Apr. 3	WOOD,	THOMAS	Married Mary E. Trimyer	Book 1,	10

				Book	Page
1708,	WOODFORD,	WILLIAM,	Married Elizabeth, relict of John Battaile	O 4,	98
1883, Aug. 30	WOODLIN,	JAMES M.	Gloucester Co., married Virginia C. Carlton, widow, daughter of Samuel C. Dunn	Book 1,	72
1814,	WOODSON,	SAMUEL	Married Betsey, daughter of Lewis Moody	O 41,	429
1742,	WORTHAM,	WILLIAM	Married Margaret, daughter of John & Mary Rutherford	W 6,	426
1708,	WORMLEY,	ELIZABETH	Daughter of Ralph, married John Lomax	D&C 12,	4
1870, Jun. 23	WRIGHT,	ALICE J.	Married John T. Ferry	Book 1,	26
1772,	WRIGHT,	AMBROSE	Married Elizabeth, widow of Ambrose Bohannon	W 11,	412
1787,	WRIGHT,	AMBROSE	Former husband of Elizabeth Booker	W 16,	44
1857, Nov. 28	WRIGHT,	ANDREW	Richmond City, married Cornelia Elizabeth Perry	Book 1,	5
1844, Nov. 26	WRIGHT,	BENJAMIN E.	Married Sarah R. Spindle	Book 1,	257
1864, Feb. 18	WRIGHT,	BENJAMIN P.	Married Mary Jane Wright, daughter of Dr. Edward Wright	Book 1,	12
1875, Sep. 30	WRIGHT,	BETTIE A.	Married Stephen W. Mitchell, merchant	Book 1,	40
1887, Dec. 26	WRIGHT,	BETTIE	Married John Jenkins	Book 1,	93
1866, Jan. 11	WRIGHT,	CHARLOTTE M.	Married George Hutchinson Denny	Book 1,	14
1824, Aug. 2	WRIGHT,	DAVID	Married Mary E. Pitts	Book 1,	241
1871, Jan. 26	WRIGHT,	DORINDA	Married William Jones	Book 1,	28
1792,	WRIGHT,	EDWARD	Married Molly, daughter of David Pitts	W 15,	61
1843, Sep. 28	WRIGHT,	EDWARD L.	Physician, married Mary Ann Jones	Book 1,	257
1895, Aug. 21	WRIGHT,	ELIZA C.	Married John R. Haile	Book 1,	118
1774,	WRIGHT,	ELIZABETH	Widow, Marriage Agreement with James Booker	D 31,	270
1812, Dec. 9	WRIGHT,	ELIZABETH	Married Neddy Gouldman	Book 1,	228
1846, Dec. 22	WRIGHT,	ELIZABETH A.	Married William F. Smith	Book 1,	259
1870, Nov. 24	WRIGHT,	F. E.	Married Julia D. Muse	Book 1,	26
1869, Dec. 28	WRIGHT,	FLORA C.	Married William Muse	Book 1,	24
1816, Jan. 11	WRIGHT,	GEORGE	Married Susan F. Jones	Book 1,	232
1836,	WRIGHT,	GEORGE	Married Susan F. Jones, daughter of Capt. John Jones	D 45,	261
1844, Jan. 25	WRIGHT,	GEORGE	Married Mary B. Spindle	Book 1,	257
1832,	WRIGHT,	HENRY	Married Kitty Ball	D 44,	108
1827, Mar. 20	WRIGHT,	JAMES	Married Judith Mann	Book 1,	244
1842, Jul. 4	WRIGHT,	JOHN J.	Physician, married Elizabeth J. Noel	Book 1,	256
1853, Apr. 11	WRIGHT,	JOHN	Married Jane Welch	Book 1,	264

Date		Name	Notes	Book	Page
1881, Nov. 17	WRIGHT,	LALLA R.	Married Charles S. Smith	Book 1,	61
1880, Nov. 30	WRIGHT,	LIZZIE H.	Daughter of Wm. Denny Wright, married Warner L. Baylor	Book 1,	57
1876, Oct. 24	WRIGHT,	MARTHA H.	Married Dr. B. F. Walker	Book 1,	43
1896, Dec. 17	WRIGHT,	MARTHA W.	Married Thomas E. Blakey, Middlesex Co.	Book 1,	123
1832, Sep. 11	WRIGHT,	MARY E.	Married Emanuel M. Jones	Book 1,	249
1845, Apr. 30	WRIGHT,	MARY E.	Married Austin Trible	Book 1,	258
1866, Dec. 13	WRIGHT,	MARY E.	Married Peter P. Derieux	Bo٠k 1,	15
1864, Feb. 18	WRIGHT,	MARY JANE	Married Benjamin P. Wright	Book 1,	12
1853, Aug. 30	WRIGHT,	MARY L.	Married Thomas J. Dabney	Book 1,	1
1872, Dec. 24	WRIGHT,	MARY S.	Married Benjamin Sale	Book 1,	32
1892, Jun. 1	WRIGHT.	MARY	Married R. L. Ware, Jr.	Book 1,	109
1858, Nov. 30	WRIGHT,	MATILDA J.	Married John Temple	Book 1,	6
1872, Jun. 5	WRIGHT,	MATILDA R.	Married John Haile	Book 1,	30
1689,	WRIGHT,	MATRUM	Married Ruth, daughter of Robert Griggs, Gloucester Co.	D 8,	154
1687,	WRIGHT,	MR.	Married daughter of Lt. Col. John Washington	D 7,	419
1809,	WRIGHT,	ROBERT	Married Margaret Boutwell	W 16,	139
1828, Dec. 8	WRIGHT,	ROBERT	Married Martha Ann Waring	Book 1,	245
1866, May 24	WRIGHT,	ROBERT	Married Mary E. Smith	Book 1,	15
1876, Apr. 27	WRIGHT,	SUSAN J.	Married Dr. J. Milton Gouldin, Caroline Co.	Book 1,	42
1816, Feb. 19	WRIGHT,	THOMAS JR.	Marrrid Mary Jones	Book 1,	238
1818,	WRIGHT,	THOMAS	Married Molly, daughter of Thomas Pitts	W 18,	476
1827, May 12	WRIGHT,	THOMAS	Married Ann M. Noel	Book 1,	244
1836,	WRIGHT,	THOMAS JR.	Married Polly, daughter of Capt. John Jones	D 45,	261
1846, Mar. 28	WRIGHT,	V. L.	Married Gray Boulware	Book 1,	258
1827, Jan. 10	WRIGHT,	WILLIAM A.	Married Charlotte Barnes	Book 1,	244
1827,	WRIGHT,	WILLIAM A.	Married Charlotte, daughter of Richard & Rebecca Barnes	D 42,	361
1855, Dec. 22	WRIGHT,	WILLIAM D.	Married Ann E. R. Dobyns	Book 1,	3
1857, Nov. 21	WRIGHT,	WILLIAM G.	King & Queen Co., married Mary Lunsford Dabney, widow and daughter of Robert & Martha Wright	Book 1,	5
1886, Dec. 13	WRIGHT,	W. E.	Married Emma Campbell	Book 1,	89
1822, Apr. 17	WYATT,	GEORGE	Married Sarah Dunn	Book 1,	239
1824, Dec. 24	WYATT,	GEORGE	Married Columbia Dunn	Book 1,	241

				Book	Page
1834, May 1	WYATT,	GEORGE	Married Susan Clarke	Book 1,	250
1840,	WYATT,	GEORGE	Married Susan, daughter of Robert Clarke	D 47,	81
1806, Jan. 16	WYATT,	MAJOR	Married Alice Clondas	Book 1,	223
1712,	WYATT,	RICHARD CAPT.	Married Katherine Long	D&W 14,	44
1875, Mar. 18	WYATT,	WILLIAM E.	Married Mildred A. Davis	Book 1,	38
1765,	WYLD,	WILLIAM	Married Tabathy, daughter of James Taylor	D 30,	42

Y

1758,	YANCEY,	JOHN	Married Mary, daughter of Jacob Layton	O	22,	255
1759,	YANCEY,	JOHN	Culpeper Co., married Mary, daughter of Jacob Layton	D	28,	139
1833,	YARRINGTON,ELIZABETH		Married James Burton	D	44,	216
1791,	YARRINGTON,MARY		Daughter of John, married John Clarke	W	14,	291
1810, May 7	YARRINGTON,POLLY		Married Philip Johnson	Book 1,		226
1762,	YARROW,	ANN	Sister of Mathew, married Thomas Johnson	W	12,	436
1844, Dec. 11	YERBY,	A. O.	Married Elizabeth Smith	Book 1,		257
1866, Oct. 18	YERBY,	BETTIE V.	Married Edward T. Smith	Book 1,		15
1697,	YOUNG,	ANN	Daughter of William, married William Covington	D	9,	140
1783,	YOUNG,	ANN	Daughter of William, married Sydnor Belfield	W	13,	374
1832, Jun. 18	YOUNG,	ANN R.	Married James W. Haynes	Book 1,		249
1838,	YOUNG,	ANN E.	Sister of Henry, married William Smith	O	49,	145
1783,	YOUNG,	ELIZABETH	Daughter of William, married Elliott Sturman	W	13,	374
1815, Dec. 18	YOUNG,	ELIZABETH	Married Richard H. Richards	Book 1,		231
1838,	YOUNG,	ELIZABETH	Sister of Henry, married Richard Richards	O	49,	145
1742,	YOUNG,	HENRY	Married Rachel, daughter of Maurice Smith	W	8,	344
1860, Jun. 5	YOUNG,	JAMES H.	Married Ann Elizabeth Garnett	Book 1,		9
1726,	YOUNG,	KATHERINE	Exec. of William, married Richard Tyler	O	9,	142
1783,	YOUNG,	LUCY	Daughter of William, married Leroy Dangerfield	W	13,	374
1697,	YOUNG,	MARY	Daughter of William, married Peter Contanceau	D	9,	141
1697,	YOUNG,	SARAH	Daughter of William, married Spencer Mottram	D	9,	140
1828, Oct. 3	YOUNG,	SMITH	Married Margaret Rebecca Trible	Book 1,		245
1702,	YOUNG,	WILLIAM	Married Catharine, sister of Frances Williamson	D&W 10,		114
1705,	YOUNG,	WILLIAM	Married Catharine, daughter of Henry Williamson	O	3,	178
1814, Mar. 16	YOUNG,	WILLIAM	Married Betsey Richards	Book 1,		230
1750,	YOUNG,	WILLIAMSON	Married Mary, daughter of Dr. Peter Godfrey	D	25,	92
				W	8,	42
1836, Feb. 8	YOUNGER,	ELIZABETH	Married Benjamin Stokes	Book 1,		252
1824, Oct. 13	YOUNGER,	MARY	Married Lowry Elliott	Book 1,		241
1831, Apr. 18	YOUNGER,	SARAH	Married Robert Munday	Book 1,		248